W9-BVB-066

YOUTH CULTURE IN GLOBAL CINEMA

YOUTH CULTURE
IN GLOBAL CINEMA

EDITED BY TIMOTHY SHARY

AND ALEXANDRA SEIBEL

UNIVERSITY OF TEXAS PRESS, AUSTIN

Requests for permission to reproduce material from this work should be sent to Permissions, University of Texas Press, P.O. Box 7819, Austin, TX 78713-7819
www.utexas.edu/utpress/about/bpermission.html

⊗ The paper used in this book meets the minimum requirements of ANSI/NISO Z39.48-1992 (R1997) (Permanence of Paper).

LIBRARY OF CONGRESS CATALOGING-IN-PUBLICATION DATA
Youth culture in global cinema / edited by Timothy Shary and Alexandra Seibel. — 1st ed.
    p.   cm.
Includes bibliographical references and index.
ISBN-13: 978-0-292-70930-0 (cloth : alk. paper)
ISBN-10: 0-292-70930-7 (alk. paper)
ISBN-13: 978-0-292-71414-4 (pbk. : alk. paper)
ISBN-10: 0-292-71414-9 (alk. paper)
1. Youth in motion pictures.   I. Shary, Timothy, 1967–
II. Seibel, Alexandra.
PN1995.9.Y6Y68   2007
791.43′65235—dc22
                              2006022240

Dedicated to the generations before and after me:
my parents, Cecilia and Robert, and my daughter, Olivia.
TIM

Dedicated to Christian—
for all the support and patience.
ALEXANDRA

CONTENTS

PREFACE

As this book goes to press in the summer of 2005, the latest book in a series about an adolescent wizard, *Harry Potter and the Half-Blood Prince*, is being released to a voracious audience of readers both young and old. Harry Potter's creator, J. K. Rowling, has developed a franchise of stories and subsequent movies that have enchanted many cultural imaginations, and that have provoked some debates on the roles and responsibilities of young people, in fiction and reality. Yet neither Rowling nor her famous character purports to represent all youth.

In creating this anthology, we also knew that we could not represent youth in films from all parts of the world. Furthermore, we knew that the lengthy process of publishing an anthology would preclude us from examining many films that have appeared recently. In dealing with international cinema, especially in the past few years, we faced the dilemma of locating youth films that have not been given adequate exposure, regardless of their significance and their messages.

We hereby bring together scholars from all over the globe to gather in a discussion of cinema dealing with youth, in terms of their attitudes, styles, sexuality, race, families, cultures, class, psychology, and ideas. Consider that the serious discussion of a teenage hero involved in sorcery would have seemed childish back in the twentieth century, and now Harry Potter is the subject of very intense examination. There is much more to be gained from further consideration of how youth in the new millennium can and should be represented and studied.

Timothy Shary   Alexandra Seibel
Worcester, Massachusetts   Vienna, Austria

ACKNOWLEDGMENTS

We began planning this book in early 2003, knowing that the field needed an anthology on the cinematic image of youth beyond the U.S. context, and we were quite happy that we received so many great proposals. We must first thank those scholars who submitted ideas and essays, especially since we could not publish all of the great work we received. We'd also like to give a special thanks to Murray Pomerance, who not only agreed to contribute an essay to this volume, but who met with us early in the process and encouraged our efforts.

We have further thanks for the support of the University of Texas Press, especially our editor, Jim Burr, who gave us the confidence to pursue this endeavor; Leslie Doyle Tingle, who advised us on manuscript preparation; Sue Carter, who copyedited this tricky text; and Lynne Chapman, who further advised us on editing. In an era of increasing difficulty for academic publishing, we are particularly fortunate to have enjoyed the attention and approval of this press.

We received a generous grant to pay for the completion of the manuscript in early 2005 from the Hillery Charitable Trust, and we thus offer them our heartfelt thanks as well. The Hillery funds allowed us to obtain the many great images herein.

We must also recognize our respective schools for their support. Tim thanks his colleagues and students at Clark University in Worcester, Massachusetts; particular appreciation goes to Marcia Butzel and Beth Gale for their perspectives on international cinema, and to Greer Muldowney and Chris Miller for help with printing images. Alexandra thanks her colleagues at New York University, as well as those she's worked with in recent years in Vienna.

Many friends and colleagues also offered suggestions and encouragement as we built this collection, and we'd like to acknowledge them. Devin Griffiths provided computer aid; Lukas Maurer helped with research; and members of the Society for Cinema Studies and the University Film and Video Association, as well as the Screen-L Film and TV Studies Discussion List at the University of Alabama, helped to circulate our call for papers.

And for their endurance, we thank our devoted partners.

YOUTH CULTURE IN GLOBAL CINEMA

■ ■

YOUTH CULTURE SHOCK

TIMOTHY SHARY

One of the best youth films released in the United States in 2005 was an unassuming drama called *The Sisterhood of the Traveling Pants*, which follows four teenage girls from the U.S. as they explore different locales during a high school summer. In Greece, Lena (Alexis Bledel) encounters both fascination and frustration with her relatives, who oppose her romance with a local boy. In Mexico, Bridget (Blake Lively) shows off her great athletic skills at soccer camp, even though her interest in a coach takes up most of her attention. Carmen (America Ferrera) travels to North Carolina (although the actual location is in Canada), hoping to enjoy the summer with her estranged father, only to be disappointed by his preoccupation with getting married to a woman she does not know. And Tibby (Amber Tamblyn) stays in their hometown in Maryland, working a local job to fund her true passion, making documentary movies. Across these distances, the girls remain connected by sending a pair of pants through the mail that somehow, despite their different body sizes, fits them all.

Sisterhood is a Hollywood movie to be sure, and yet its ability to explore teenage life across different cultures and through different families is a refreshing step forward in the depiction of adolescent experience. When Hollywood has focused on characters between childhood and adulthood, the films tend to follow the dreams of success and popularity that many young people share, and youth culture is portrayed as primarily white, middle class, non-religious, suburban, and fun. At the same time, teenagers around the world are navigating their ways to adulthood through a much greater diversity of experiences, and the U.S. films that explore youth beyond the mainstream tend to be made within the American independent film market, outside the studio system.

The Sisterhood of the Traveling Pants (2005). Left to right: Carmen (America Ferrera), Tibby (Amber Tamblyn), Lena (Alexis Bledel), and Bridget (Blake Lively).

Hollywood has been predominantly ethnocentric, concerned about the stories of U.S. citizens and only occasionally looking out to "foreign" lands, even as the vast majority of the world's population lives outside the U.S. And Hollywood's appeal to youth is essentially for profit, since young people constitute such a high portion of the moviegoing audience. Yet the stories of youth after childhood are quite compelling, since the coming-of-age process is familiar to all cultures and classes of people. Films made in the global marketplace illustrate this abundantly: adolescence and puberty are common subjects in many movies.[1]

In fact, cultural concerns about youth in the international media have been amply evident for decades. From the infamous Payne Fund studies in the U.S. during the 1930s, which were misguided efforts to "protect" youth from movies, to the seizures suffered by Japanese children watching *Pokemon* on television in the late '90s, both scientists and scholars—and especially parents—have questioned and explored how young people are affected by media. Numerous studies and books have been written on the negative and positive effects of media on youth, who are so often considered vulnerable to media messages, both because media industries target them and because their minds are thought to be particularly impressionable.

Yet not nearly as much time or effort has been expended in examinations of how youth are *represented* by the media. A number of pop culture books have looked at the happy days of child stars in the '30s and '40s, as well as young television actors in recent years, but there have been strikingly few serious studies of how the pre-adult population is portrayed by the adults who control media the world over. In fact, serious studies of adolescence in U.S. cinema only began in the 1980s, with such books as *The Cinema of Adolescence* by David Considine (1985) and *Teenagers and Teenpics: The Juvenilization of American Movies in the 1950s* by Thomas Doherty (1988; revised 2002). Since then, a few more studies of teenagers in U.S. films have appeared, including *The Road to Romance and Ruin: Teen Films and Youth Culture,* by Jon Lewis (1992), and my own *Generation Multiplex: The Image of Youth in Contemporary American Cinema* (2002). Nonetheless, this growing scholarship on youth cinema is paltry compared to the multitude of studies of other film roles whose real-life equivalents are much less common, such as gangsters, cowboys, monsters, and soldiers. One could easily draw the conclusion that, despite the cultural concerns for how young people may *use* media, the image of youth on screen is of little interest to adults.

This anthology is intended to change that perspective, since all of the essays contained herein are written by established academics who take seriously the stakes of representing youth. This is also the first time that a collection on young adult roles in international cinema has been published in English.[2] Occasionally, some "classic" youth films have generated analysis in the past, primarily due to the surrounding oeuvre of their stars and/or directors; examples include *Los Olvidados* (Luis Buñuel, Mexico, 1950), *Rebel Without a Cause* (Nicholas Ray, U.S., 1955), *Aparajito/The Unvanquished* (Satyajit Ray, India, 1957), *Les Quatre cents coups/The 400 Blows* (François Truffaut, France, 1959), *Ivanovo detstvo/Ivan's Childhood* (Andrei Tarkovsky, Soviet Union, 1962), *Walkabout* (Nicholas Roeg, Australia, 1971), *Diabolo menthe/Peppermint Soda* (Diane Kurys, France, 1977), *Mitt liv som hund/My Life as a Dog* (Lasse Hallström, Sweden, 1985), *Au revoir les enfants/Goodbye Children* (Louis Malle, France, 1987), and *Europa Europa* (Agnieszka Holland, Poland, 1990). This anthology looks at other youth films that have primarily achieved significance through what they say about young people and the culture around them. We sought out essays that were not strictly representative studies of certain popular titles or national traditions, but rather, essays that would illuminate the many conditions under which youth live around the world and that would generate dialogue on how those youth are represented in movies.

To gain an appreciation for the sheer number and range of youth films made throughout the world, I worked with our contributors to compile a filmography of as many feature films that we could find which focused on one or more young characters in adolescence or puberty (see Appendix A). This resulted in a list of over 700 titles, which I then researched in an effort to determine the films' themes (see Appendix B). (Even though some U.S. films are examined and mentioned in certain essays, no U.S. titles are listed in the filmography; U.S. teen films from 1980 to 2001 are listed in my *Generation Multiplex* book.)

Despite its potential limitations—we have likely missed some examples, and I could not find ample descriptions of many films—the filmography reveals numerous interesting trends and themes in international youth cinema. As in U.S. teen films, the most common characterizations of youth globally are in terms of delinquency, and we thus begin the book with essays that examine themes of youth resistance and rebellion, wherein crimes and misdemeanors range from casual drug use and petty theft to rape and murder. Teenagers are not always the perpetrators of delinquent acts, however. In an alarming number of films, young people are abused by their peers and adults, and incest occurs at a rather high rate as well.

Unlike U.S. teen films, many international youth films deal with topics of politics and religion, and more often, with tensions around cultural and national identity. The next two sections of the book examine such issues, identifying a wide variety of desires and conflicts that young people face in their social and spiritual lives. Adults create laws, establish churches, and start wars; many films show us that children are often the most affected by these phenomena.

Of course, adolescence and puberty are times of intense sexual development for young people as well, and global cinema offers a wide range of experiences that youth encounter during that development. We thus take up topics related to gender in the next two sections, focusing first on issues of gender distinctions, and concluding the book with a section that specifically addresses queer youth. Many films celebrate, and often exploit, the youthful discovery of sex, and given its vast variety of motives and results, we see young people not only losing their virginity but also questioning their sexual orientation, dealing with pregnancy, and occasionally finding pleasure. Fortunately, most films in recent years have shown an improving maturity about the topic of youthful sexuality, offering sympathy and sensitivity.

The 17 essays herein are written by scholars from 11 different national backgrounds, and they discuss films from numerous global perspectives.[3] Such a diverse range of geographical coverage parallels the range of topics featured in these essays, for while they all discuss films featuring young characters, each has a unique focus. Thus we did not require our contributors to follow a common methodology of analysis. Some of the essays offer close readings of films, while others examine advertising and reception or explore psychological issues; some delve into historical documents, while others are more personal reflections.

We were not able to represent every important depiction of adolescent life in international cinema over the past century. We also anticipate that some readers will disagree with and challenge many of the ideas presented here. At the same time, we have endeavored to collect essays that are all cogent and stimulating in their arguments about youth in international cinema, and we hope that this anthology will only be the start of much more research on the roles of youth in global media. In time, we also hope that the culture shock many adults face in looking at young people, and that many young people face in looking at each other, will be alleviated through an authentic understanding of global youth culture at large. Such an understanding is the primary goal of this book.

NOTES

1. We employ the terms "youth" and "young adult" rather interchangeably, and conceive these populations to generally be between the ages of 12 and 20. There are instances where the young characters we study are slightly younger than 12 or older than 20, but are nonetheless dealing with issues related to leaving childhood and becoming an adult. We conceive of adolescence and puberty as covering this range of ages, even though the terms have a wide variety of applications in different contexts and cultures. "Teen" and "teenager" are terms that we use only when referring specifically to teenaged characters.

We conceive of "global cinema" as representing all moviemaking nations, and we thus include U.S. films within these essays, even though our emphasis is on the cultural experience of youth beyond dominant Hollywood.

2. We attempted to contact the few authors who have written books on youth in international cinema to join this project, but none were available. According to the Library of Congress, only 10 books on youth films have been published outside the U.S.:

Albero Spezzato: Cinema e Psicoanalisi su Infanzia e Adolescenza, by Maurizio Regosa (Italy, 2003)
Calaccitre Santrasa o Yuba Samaja: Gabeshana Pratibedana, no author listed (Bangladesh, 2002)
Cinema e Adolescenza: Saggi e Strumenti, by Flavio Vergerio (Italy, 2000)
Film w Zyciu i Wychowaniu Mlodziezy, by Henryk Depta (Poland, 1983)

Gioventù Perduta: Gli Anni Cinquanta Dei Giovani e del Cinema in Italia, by
   Enrica Capussotti (Italy, 2004)
Kultura Filmowa Mlodziezy, by Stanislaw Morawski (Poland, 1977)
Seishun eiga gurafiti, by Takayoshi Nada (Japan, 1980)
Seishun eiga no keifu, by Tadao Sato (Japan, 1976)
Sinama Ksetraya Udesa Antar Jatika Taruna Varsayedi Tarunaya ge Anugrahaya, by
   Piyasoma Medis ge vigr (Sri Lanka, 1985)
Zwischen Bluejeans und Blauhemden: Jugendfilm in Ost und West, by Ingelore
   König and Dieter Wiede (Germany, 1995)

3. We are aware that only Claudia Preckel's essay addresses youth in any African
countries, and only Arab cultures at that. We had hoped to include at least one essay
on youth in sub-Saharan African cinema, but at this time, we do not have contact with
any scholar who could provide such a study. We welcome suggestions for future edi-
tions of this book.

PART 1

REBELLION AND RESISTANCE

■ ■ ■ ■ ■ ■ ■ ■ ■ ■ ■ ■ ■ ■ ■ ■ ■ ■ ■ ■

CHAPTER 1

AMERICAN JUVENILE DELINQUENCY MOVIES AND THE EUROPEAN CENSORS

The Cross-Cultural Reception and Censorship of The Wild One, Blackboard Jungle, *and* Rebel Without a Cause

DANIEL BILTEREYST

In the mid-1950s, the gradual relaxation of the Hollywood Production Code and the growth of independent filmmaking brought to the forefront a whole series of American movies which openly explored taboo-breaking subjects around sexuality, crime, and the use of drugs. One strand of movies causing a heated public controversy dealt with the social problem of juvenile delinquency. Films like *The Wild One* (1953), *Blackboard Jungle* (1955), and *Rebel Without a Cause* (1955) directly confronted the issue of postwar youngsters' crime and gang life, initiating cycles of teenpic exploitation films often called juvenile delinquency movies (Gilbert, 178–195; Doherty, 1–18; Shary 2002, 82).

In the U.S., these successful film cycles about the "misbehavior" of rebellious "GI baby boomers" sparked a wider controversy about the increase in juvenile crime, the failing educational system, and the loss of family values in American society. The movies only increased, as Thomas Doherty (51) notes, the "anxious inquiries from concerned clergymen, baffled parents, tireless social scientists, and an alarmed Congress." What is so interesting about these 1950s juvenile delinquency movies is that they could stir up such a heated debate across various groups and organizations. Everyone from the average audience to the U.S. Senate—including leading journalists, intellectuals, politicians, and religious leaders—was moved to raise their voices about these movies' effects on "endangered" core social values. This situation, where various "moral guardians" express their concern over key values, often signals a societywide moral panic.

The controversy and moral panic were not restricted to the U.S. In the U.K. and other European countries, a wider public debate addressed juvenile delinquency and the influence of imported American movies. In the U.K., for instance, *The Wild One* was the only movie of the 1950s to be denied a censorship certificate. Many other juvenile delinquency pictures from the other side of the ocean had great difficulties with local European censors, while film critics often expressed their disbelief about the growing openness of the American censorship system.

However, looking more closely at the historical reception and censorship of these movies, we should acknowledge very different positions, including a growing respect for the refreshing audacity of these imported movies. Especially leftist intellectuals and film critics soon started to glorify the critical tone of these movies. In France, for instance, independent producers and filmmakers such as Richard Brooks, Stanley Kramer, and Nicholas Ray were increasingly praised by young film critics, who claimed that these new American auteurs were showing the right direction for contemporary cinema.

This article examines how these controversial movies were received outside the U.S., concentrating on the censorship and reception of *The Wild One*, *Blackboard Jungle*, and *Rebel Without a Cause* in various European countries, with a special focus upon the U.K. and France. I rely upon original film censorship files, censors' internal correspondence, and religious (Catholic) classification sources, supplemented with other contemporary sources such as reviews in journals and articles in the press.

JUVENILE DELINQUENCY MOVIES, MORAL PANIC, AND THE CENSORS

In 1954, when European censors, critics, and audiences first saw the motorcycle gang movie *The Wild One*, the issue of youth crime and the influence of cinema had been a hot item for a long time. The metaphor of cinema as a dangerous school of crime went back to the very beginning of motion pictures, but it was still vibrantly present in public debates after the war. In the immediate postwar years, many major European cities were confronted by poverty, a large number of orphans, and a spectacular increase in juvenile delinquency. Cinema attendance rose as never before, while film theater screens were almost completely filled with Hollywood's imagery. The issue of cinema and youth delinquency was a regular item, not only in the popular press, but also in social science, law, and criminology journals (Decharneux).

European politicians, like those in the U.S., put the issue high on the agenda. As early as 1948, for instance, a special committee on children and cinema was installed by the Home Office in the U.K., presenting its report in May 1950 to Parliament.[1] For critics the report was too tame, mainly because it concluded that the "criminogenic action" of motion pictures was not proven. The British inquiry reflected a more nuanced view of juvenile delinquency and film consumption. It followed sociopsychological research, which at the time considered personality traits and social context to be more relevant than movie content. Motion pictures, so the committee claimed, were only effective in some very particular cases, but mostly they were harmless. By the end of the 1940s, also, social welfare programs had succeeded in curbing youth crime in many parts of Europe, while the introduction of television slowly took attention away from the influence of motion pictures.

However, this didn't mean that the media's appetite for juvenile delinquency diminished. The continuing interest correlated with the new phenomenon of rebellious youth subcultures in the 1950s. Originating in the U.K. and the U.S., youth cultures such as the (working-class oriented) teddy boys, mods, and later rockers were increasingly associated with street crime and gang life. Not only in the U.K., but soon also in France, Germany, and other Western European countries, young people adopted these new subcultural ways of life. Music and movies were symbolic spearheads in spreading models for these subcultural codes of conduct.

The popular media devoted much space to these youth subcultures, mainly through stigmatization and by focusing upon criminal outbursts. Following critical sociological literature, this selective construction of youth cultures as dangerous and deviant is often associated with a conservative moral backlash in society or with a moral panic. The latter deals with a shared feeling held by a substantial number of people that society and moral order are threatened by the deviant behavior of particular groups in society (such as mods or rockers). It refers to a spiraling debate and a dramatic overreaction whereby the media function as a catalyst in whipping up the debate. This may ultimately lead to an overreaction by "moral guardians," or even to a restrictive action by police or other law or morality enforcers. From this perspective it is not difficult to see censorship boards as institutional moral guardians.

This context of overreaction to youth subcultural violence might help explain why some film censors and critics reacted so severely when *The Wild One* and other American juvenile delinquent movies appeared from 1954 onward. It wasn't that the topic of juvenile delinquency was new; the issue of juvenile crime had been picked up by European film directors before. Inspired by a critical social naturalism, directors such as de Sica (*Sciuscia*, 1946), Fellini (*I Vitelloni*, 1953), and Cayatte (*Avant le Déluge*, 1953) had already explored youth violence. But these movies did not spark controversy.

Marlon Brando (center) and his motorcycle gang in *The Wild One* (1953) seem to ooze menace.

In these movies, the young deviants were often portrayed as victims of a society reproducing class inequalities, and class conflicts seemed to motivate their mode of conduct.

American juvenile delinquency movies, though, were rather quickly perceived as part of a wider flow of highly confrontational, more violent, and openly antisocial movies that either reflected a dangerous social reality or were thought to stimulate the same. *The Wild One* is a landmark movie in this respect. The film showed Marlon Brando as the charismatic leader of the Black Rebels, a gang terrorizing a small, quiet California town. Brando's image as a biker in leather jacket and jeans became an icon for the age. *The Wild One*, which was inspired by real events, cultivated the image of young motorcyclists as outlaws, underlining the controversial character of drag racing. The movie was realistic in its portrayal of crime and gang life, while it contained lots of rough language.

When the movie had to face Hollywood's internal censorship system, it was clear that severe concessions would have to be made in order to get the Production Code Administration's approval. In a letter to the production team, the PCA director, Joseph Breen, wrote that the movie contained "very dangerous elements" suggesting that youngsters might "get away with hood-lumism, if they [would] only organize into bands" (Lewis 2000, 108). Breen and the PCA feared that the movie might lead to an imitation of crime. Besides some minor changes, the negotiation between the PCA, producer Kramer, and Columbia led to the inclusion of a public warning at the beginning and the end of *The Wild One*. The film opened with the announcement that "this is a shocking story," followed by, "it could never take place in most American towns—but it did in this one. It is a public challenge not to let it happen again." In his comment on the PCA's impact on the movie, Jon Lewis (2000, 110) underlines *The Wild One*'s ambiguity and irony: the moral lesson the PCA had in mind was completely counter to the audience's identification with and the implied sympathy for Brando's character in the movie.

The Wild One's success inspired a couple of teenpics such as *Motorcycle Gang* (1957), but it was mainly *Blackboard Jungle* and *Rebel Without a Cause* which set the model for juvenile delinquency movies (Doherty). Brooks' 1955 *Blackboard Jungle* was an MGM production, with Glenn Ford in the role of English literature teacher Richard Dadier, who's new to a difficult urban high school. Dadier is confronted by the students' disobedience, hostility, and rough physical violence. Brooks, who previously had been a screenwriter for movies such as John Huston's *Key Largo* (1948), did not hesitate to include some real tough scenes in his movie. In *Jungle* we see how a student tries to rape a female schoolteacher, followed by Dadier's heavy-handed intervention. Later in the movie, Dadier himself is nearly killed by some of his students in a back alley attack. The use of Bill Haley's song "Rock Around the Clock" only increased the movie's potential for controversy.

Blackboard Jungle was a shocking film for its time. This was also the analysis of the PCA and its new chief censor, Geoffrey Shurlock, who declared that with *Blackboard Jungle* he was "confronted with a situation that could make a joke of the censorship code sections on violence and brutality" (Schumach, 176). He asked Brooks and MGM to tone down the brutality in the movie, but Brooks practically refused. The movie was released in March 1955. The day before its premiere in New York, a Bronx high school teacher was stabbed to death by a student, an incident that only fueled the controversy around *Jungle*. The world press caught the dramatic coincidence between the movie's content and the killing, and in many countries the movie would have to undergo major changes before it could be screened.

On the domestic front, several cities, including Atlanta, banned the movie, while educational groups severely denounced it. The influential Catholic Legion of Decency decided to put the movie firmly into its B-classification code, reserved for "morally objectionable movies." The Legion ar-

This Mexican lobby card from *The Blackboard Jungle* (1955) illustrates the sensational marketing of the film's violence and sexuality.

gued that Brooks' movie was courageous in treating a "sociological problem of our times," but that "its treatment contains morally objectionable elements (brutality, violence, disrespect for lawful authority) and tends to negate any constructive conclusion."[2] The controversy around the movie's frankness only increased its success among young adolescents.

Intense negative reaction to the movie would explode once again at the Venice Film Festival in late October 1955. Mrs. Claire Booth-Luce, then ambassador to Italy, became so angered by *Jungle*'s portrayal of violent American adults that she forced the picture's withdrawal from the festival. The ambassador's action, which was fully covered by the world press, again increased the controversy surrounding *Jungle*. The movie was also mentioned during a Senate committee's work on delinquency and the motion pictures, which started in June 1955 and was presided over by Senator Estes Kefauver. In its 1956 report, the committee recognized the artistic value of the movie but concluded that "the film will have effects on youth other than the beneficial ones described by its producers" (in Doherty, 118).

MGM, quick to discern the value of controversies, started to use the international diplomatic incident in its publicity material. *Blackboard Jungle* quickly became the most widely publicized film on the worldwide market, soon inspiring exploitation movies on the theme. Movies with titles such as *Juvenile Jungle* (1958) and *High School Confidential* (1958) were clearly inspired by Brooks' success.

The third milestone movie, *Rebel Without a Cause*, was also released in 1955, by Warner Bros. More even than *The Wild One* and *Jungle*, Nicolas Ray's movie would soon grow into a generation's cult movie. *Rebel* tells the story of Jim Stark (James Dean), an upper-middle-class young man with a troubled past who comes to a new town and struggles as much with his new school environment and its youth gangs as with himself and his parents. With this movie, Ray succeeded in giving Dean's character a deeper structure, trying to "explain" youngsters' rebellion in a more psychological manner. While gang life and youth violence in *Wild One* and *Jungle* are mainly explained by arguments on the juveniles' social background, *Rebel* offers a more universally identifiable adolescent role model. Adolescents' rebellion was part of "identity politics," or the search for one's true nature. This search for autonomy and difference included a hybrid relation with parent culture. This (revolutionary) shift in dealing with adolescents and youth crime helps to explain why the controversy around *Rebel*, certainly in Europe, had less to do with youngsters' hooliganism and violence, and more to do with the rough portrayal of traditional parental culture values.

In its original script version, however, *Rebel* contained more potentially controversial material than the movie as Ray finally made it. In a series of meetings with Ray and the producers, Shurlock showed a great sensitivity toward the public debate in the U.S. around juvenile delinquency. This awareness strongly influenced the final changes in the script. PCA's concerns included vulgar language, a possible suggestion of the use of drugs, and some scenes of violence and rebelliousness. Shurlock's list of difficulties also dealt with the suggestion of sexual intimacy between Jim and his teenage neighbor, Judy, played by Natalie Wood (Simmons 1995).

The Hollywood censorship system ensured that *Rebel* would not run into problems with local censors; in fact, only one board, in Memphis, banned the movie. Even the Legion of Decency was rather mild in terms of its condemnation of violent scenes. Putting *Rebel* in the "acceptable" A category, though only for adults, the Legion still argued that "[this] study of juvenile delinquency from the viewpoint of typically maladjusted youth results in a film as depressing as it is disturbing." For the Legion's reviewer, the movie "indicts contributory causes such as divorce, disharmony and poor parental example, without a single whisper against lack of sound moral and religious training in school and home."[3]

Rebel was released soon after James Dean's dramatic and widely publicized death (September 30, 1955). Not only in the U.S., but also in Europe and elsewhere, the movie soon grew into one of the most successful and influential pictures of the 1950s. *Rebel* and Dean's angst-laden performance became a touchstone for a whole generation of teenagers, while for the film industry it worked as a catalyst for exploring younger audiences. This process of "progressive juvenilization" resulted in the production of an unprecedented wave of teenpics, especially juvenile delinquency and rock 'n' roll movies.

In the U.S. market, most of these exploitation movies encountered few difficulties. Referring to a certain timidity of teenpics, Thomas Doherty (186) claims that "despite a reputation for daring, taboo-breaking subject matter . . . exploitation moviemakers who specialized in teenpics were a conservative and timorous lot." Despite this timidity and the stringent internal censorship system, many of these American pictures ran into problems when they crossed the ocean. Especially in the U.K., by far the most important nondomestic market for Hollywood, imported juvenile delinquency movies caught the censors' eye.

THE BRITISH BOARD OF FILM CENSORSHIP'S BATTLE AGAINST UNBRIDLED, REVOLTING HOOLIGANISM

The British film censorship system has the reputation of being among the toughest in Europe. After the Second World War, the British Board of Film Censorship, which is an independent nonprofit body, continued its work under the main principles of protecting moral standards against the movies' harmful effects on reasonably minded audiences. At the beginning of the 1950s, the BBFC's leading figures, Secretary Arthur Watkins and President Sidney Harris, both originating from the Foreign Office, were confronted with new challenges. The arrival of more sexually explicit movies, mainly from the Continent, was one such challenge; the increasing number of movies containing antisocial and rebellious behavior was another.

In order to avoid the outright ban of these types of movies, the Board decided in 1951 to adopt the X certificate. This category excluded children and young adolescents, but made it possible that "good" adult entertainment would be allowed without many cuttings (Matthews, 125–126). However, in order to avoid the R (refusal) category and to place the difficult movies into the new X category, more frequent and extensive editing became a BBFC standard practice. A very special case in this respect was the swelling number of imported juvenile delinquency movies—starting with *The Wild One*, directed by Hungarian László Benedek. In the background of the public debate and moral panic on youngsters' hooliganism in the U.K., these American pictures grew into a symbolic battlefield for the BBFC standards.

In the U.K., Benedek's motorcycle picture was rejected several times. Referring to the "present widespread concern about the increase in juvenile crime," the Board claimed in January 1954 that they did not want to pass *The Wild One*, "even with an 'X' certificate," given its "unbridled hooliganism."[4] Columbia's London office offered a new, heavily recut version of the movie, but *The Wild One* was banned twice in 1955 and once more in 1959. Several teddy-boy incidents gave the BBFC reviewers the impression that their decision was justified. Only in November of 1967 did the BBFC finally agree to award an X certificate to the movie. The new BBFC secretary, the more liberal John Trevelyan, then argued that *The Wild One* had become a "period piece" (Matthews, 130). In the meantime, the juvenile delinquency movie cycle from the U.S. had increased with dozens of other titles, while in the U.K. violent incidents committed by adolescent gangs were receiving more publicity than ever.

The worldwide negative publicity about *Blackboard Jungle* in 1955 functioned as the backdrop for BBFC reception of Brooks' movie, and in March 1955, the BBFC rejected the film, claiming that this "spectacle of youth out of control" would "have the most damaging and harmful effect on such young people."[5] In the same letter to the London-based MGM subsidiary, BBFC secretary Watkins referred to "the widespread concern which is felt by responsible people throughout this country about the behavior of some of the younger elements in our population." He was sure that "*Blackboard Jungle*, filled as it is with scenes of unbridled, revolting hooliganism, would, if shown in this country, provoke the strongest criticism from parents and all citizens concerned with the welfare of our young people."

On MGM's request, new negotiations and viewing sessions were organized and cuttings made, but the BBFC continued to be extremely sensitive to the negative publicity around the movie. The British popular press closely followed public reactions against *Jungle* in the U.S. The *Daily Mail* characterized Senator Kefauver, who chaired the Senate committee on juvenile delinquency and movies, as a "crime-busting politician" who "opened a campaign to stem the recent spate of sex and sadism in Hollywood films, already sharply criticized by Britain's film censors."[6]

After additional cuttings proposed by the Board, the movie finally received an X certificate in August 1955. When *Jungle* was finally shown in British theaters, the press again highlighted stories about the euphoric and cynical reception of the picture by local teddy boys. Now that the BBFC had granted the movie a certificate, the censors had to defend their decision (and the movie). In several letters to the public, civic organizations, and local licensing committees, Watkins claimed that "the main theme of the film is the master's unwavering belief that the boys can be won over," and also that "the Company [MGM] made the cuts to our satisfaction."[7] John Trevelyan, who was one of the examiners at the time, wrote in his memoirs that "eventually we passed [Jungle], although we were nervous about it" (1973, 157).

This tumultuous censorship process explains why the British censors were on their guard in October 1955 when Warners presented *Rebel Without a Cause*. Watching Ray's movie for the first time, the BBFC wrote in an internal note that this "is another story involving delinquency in an American high school, this time with the accent on the sins of neglectful and quarrelling parents."[8] In the same note, examiner Audrey Field reported that she "did not like the film on censorship grounds and thought it would be no loss from the artistic point of view," but she also wrote that "it was not thought practicable to reject it in view of the action which we [finally took] on *Blackboard Jungle*—a better, but also more violent film."

The Board, however, decided to reject *Rebel* unless Warner Bros. agreed to heavily edit the movie. Referring again to the "widespread public anxiety about juvenile delinquency," Watkins argued that "the moral values [should be] sufficiently firmly presented to outweigh any harmful influence which the film might otherwise have on young and impressionable members of the cinema audience."[9] Watkins included a long list of cuts to be made, including the suggestion to remove the (now classic) knife fight outside the planetarium. Also, the historical cliff-top sequence was to be reduced to a minimum, since "the less we have of this unpleasant idea of young people [meeting] together to witness a contest which could end in the death of one of the participants, the better."[10]

In the following months, a series of negotiations and letters were organized between the BBFC and Warners representatives. The latter tried to please the censors by cutting deeply into several key scenes, including the car race, and by completely removing other scenes, such as the one where Jim tries to throttle his father. In November 1955, the BBFC agreed to issue an X certificate,[11] but now Warner Bros. asked the Board to reconsider the classification and to grant an A certificate so that *Rebel* could "be seen by people accompanied by their parents."[12] Clearly targeting the lucrative younger audience, Warners argued that it wanted to avoid "the morbid element of the population by branding [the movie] with an X." Defending an A certificate, Warners' managing director Arthur S. Abeles underlined that his company agreed not only to fulfill all requests, but even to put in something praiseworthy, which should lift the film out of the X category ("a line

The knife fight between Buzz (Corey Allen) and Jim (James Dean) in *Rebel Without a Cause* (1955) was problematic to European censors.

of dialogue in which the hero refuses to fight with knives"). In order to resolve the British problems with *Rebel*, Warners even asked Nicholas Ray to go to London and cut certain scenes to make his picture acceptable.[13]

The BBFC now reacted with feeling. Arguing that they were not impressed by Abeles' "naive arguments," the BBFC examiners noted, in an internal document,[14] that *Rebel* "is rubbish for adults but poisonous stuff for the teddy inclined adolescent." The BBFC examiners declared that they had the "rather uncomfortable feeling that an 'X' may be heavy weather for this film as cut." Now, the BBFC again proposed a long list of nearly 20 additional cuts (e.g., the removal of complete scenes such as Jim's drunkenness scene, and the kiss between Jim and Judy).[15] The British censors also claimed that the main "obstacle is the behavior of the parents" and that "children, even accompanied, should not be allowed to witness the spectacle of ridiculous and ineffectual parents."

For Warners' managing director, the weakness of the parents could not be removed from the movie because it was a key motivation for the unhappiness and loneliness of the adolescents. On December 1, 1955, *Rebel* officially received its X certificate, but it had been cut so drastically that it was at times incomprehensible.

In the months and years after censoring *Jungle* and *Rebel*, the BBFC continued to cut hard into other American teenage exploitation movies. *Motorcycle Gang* (1957), reviewed in January 1958, was restricted to an adult audience, with nearly 10 scenes being removed or cut. The cuttings again included violent actions, fight scenes, and vulgar speech. Also *Juvenile Jungle* (1958), *King Creole* (1958), and *Young and Wild* (1958) were severely mutilated and restricted to adult audiences. *The Beat Generation* (1959), about the "wild, weird, world of the Beatniks," received an X grade and had to be shortened by many cuttings. The censors' reception of Jack Arnold's *High School Confidential* (1958), with its tagline "A teacher's nightmare!" is comparable to *The Wild One*, *Jungle*, and *Rebel*. First rejected in June 1958, the movie finally received its X certificate after many cuttings in November 1958.[16]

In retrospect, the BBFC's attitude might easily be denounced as extremely reactionary and paternalist. But its reception of American delinquency movies in the 1950s must be understood as a reaction to a wider moral panic around a hot social issue. In the 1960s and 1970s, a more liberal attitude was adopted. In November 1967, *The Wild One* was finally granted a certificate. At the occasion of the rerelease of *Jungle* in 1996, the BBFC restricted the movie to 12-year-olds and up without any cuts. In April 1976, *Rebel* got a wide audience certificate and was rereleased without cuts. On this occasion, the BBFC examiners agreed that two decades previously the film had caused the censors "some anxiety because of its apparent challenge to parental authority and its possible effect on the increase of juvenile delinquency." They concluded that "re-viewing it all these years later, we felt that the story tells a moral tale."[17]

OFFICIAL CENSORSHIP, CATHOLIC CLASSIFICATION, AND CRITICAL DISCOURSES

Official censorship boards in other European countries, although not as extreme as the British censors in their rejection of American juvenile delinquency movies, also expressed their anxiety about the possible impact. In most countries children and young adolescents were not allowed to see the movies. In Belgium, Germany, Italy, and the Scandinavian countries, for instance, the censors prohibited youngsters under 16 or 18 years from seeing *The Wild One*, *Jungle*, and *Rebel*. In France, *Jungle* was not banned, but it was given the most extreme category of "forbidden for minors under 16." In 1956 and again in 1963 the movie was reexamined by the French censorship

Even though Jim (far right) makes the moral choice of going to the police in *Rebel*, the film was still controversial throughout Europe for decades.

board, the Commission de Classification, but the movie's initial category didn't change.[18]

Rebel also received verdicts that hindered its commercial career as family entertainment. In Germany, for instance, the film industry's self-imposed censorship board stated that neither the movie nor the trailer could be shown to children under 16. In 1972 and again in 1989 a similar decision was made; only in 1996 was the age limit lowered to 12 years.[19] In France, it would take nearly two decades before *Rebel* would be open to the general public. In January 1956, when the movie was first examined, it was immediately put into the 16 category, due to "some extremely violent scenes such as a knife-fight, murders committed by adolescents, and so on."[20] In March 1956, December 1962, and July 1973, the Commission repeatedly decided to preserve the original classification. The distributor lodged an appeal against the 1973 decision, and finally in October 1973 the movie was approved for a general audience without any cutting.[21]

In many European countries of the 1950s, cutting movies or, more elegantly, "suggesting" cuts was a standard practice among official censorship boards. In order to avoid them, producers and distributors often intervened with self-censorship and carried out "preventive" cuts. In Italy, for instance, the censors made four cuts, including editing the knife fight, Jim's fight with his father, and the kiss (Baldi, 40). The French commission granted a license for adolescents and adults (over 16 years) to *The Wild One* and *Jungle* after the distributor had removed some minor scenes himself. Even in Sweden the official censor decided to award a 16 certificate to *Rebel* only after cutting 5 meters, while in Finland 45 meters had to be removed.[22]

In the 1950s, official censorship boards were not the only forces hindering the free flow of movies. Another important barrier was related to religious initiatives to influence film culture. As with the influential Catholic Legion of Decency in the U.S., European Catholic film organizations succeeded in lobbying against "unhealthy" movies. These often-fanatic film movements were quite successful from the 1930s to the 1960s, particularly in Belgium, France, Italy, and Spain. They had no legal authority to censor films, but by controlling thousands of active believers, influencing a good deal of the daily press, and building a wide network of parochial cinemas, they had a great influence on the film audience, distributors, and cinema managers. A central key in the Catholic film action was classifying movies through a system of descriptions and moral codes. In their judgments of American movies, these national Catholic organizations often looked at the U.S. Legion's decisions.

In the U.S., the Legion had objected "to excessive brutality, lack of moral compensation and suggestiveness" in *The Wild One*, while it claimed that *Jungle* contained too many "objectionable elements" to let it pass for the normal audience (B++ and B code). *Rebel* received a milder classification (A++, meaning that it was open for a wider, adult audience).[23] Quite similar descriptions and classifications were found in Europe. In countries such as Belgium, France, Germany, Italy, and The Netherlands, the three movies were denounced with the adult "severe reservations" label.

However, this did not keep Catholics from looking at the juvenile delinquency movies in a more nuanced manner. In their moral and aesthetic comments, the Catholic film reviewers gradually came to appreciate the movies' audacity in treating a vivid social problem. In France, for instance, where the Centrale Catholique du Cinéma recognized that *Jungle* was "an exceptionally fine piece of cinema," the movie was considered to have an educational potential.[24] Catholic organizations showed and even distributed the movie to teachers and parents.

This gradual shift can, finally, also be recognized in press articles and film criticism. Space does not permit a detailed review of the press coverage of *The Wild One* and other U.S. juvenile delinquency movies, but the critics' ideological background is a key issue in understanding their reception of these movies. In general, more conservative, Catholic, or other religiously inspired newspapers continued to denounce the movies for their brutality, the absence of compensating moral values, and the unflattering portrayal of parents. More leftist critics soon recognized the critical undertones in the movies. In France, for instance, most mainstream critics decried *The Wild One*, with one journalist calling it the "most unpleasant American movie ever seen."[25]

However, the new left film magazine *Positif* somewhat provocatively called *The Wild One* a masterpiece and even the film of the year, while Benedek entered the pantheon of real "film auteurs."[26] Benedek's picture was seen as a courageous piece of anti-American or anticapitalist propaganda.[27]

The critical appreciation of *Jungle* and *Rebel* only increased, mainly among the younger and more left-leaning critics. *Jungle* was mostly regarded a hard but humanist and technically superb movie, while *Rebel* was soon seen as a film which gave a new impulse to the "genre" and added a new dimension to the understanding of juvenile delinquency. Although in conservative reviews *Rebel* continued to have problems (mainly on the issue of parental and family values), other film critics started to analyze Ray's movie as a classical tale with deeper psychoanalytical dimensions. In France, François Truffaut called Benedek a "sociologist," Brooks a "reformer," and Ray a "poet" of "moral solitude."[28] Eric Rohmer, then film critic at *Cahiers du Cinéma*, compared *Rebel Without a Cause* to a classic Greek tragedy.[29] In the U.K., Penelope Houston devoted a long essay to recent U.S. juvenile delinquency movies, calling *Rebel* a social document, touching society "in its most elementary aspect, the individual's own adjustment to the world he has to live in." For Houston, the movie's "basic sense of insecurity" and "malaise" call into question the American dream.[30]

This critical appreciation completely went against the grain of the censors' denouncing discourse. In a letter to the New Zealand censorship board, Watkins tried to defend the BBFC policy, ending his comments with the sober remark that "rather to our surprise, and also our relief, the film received universal praise from the critics in this country, and is enjoying a great success." In perfect bureaucratic style, he added: "We have received no complaints."[31]

CONCLUSION

A retrospective look at the historical reception and censorship of these milestone movies of the 1950s clearly indicates that these films were subjected to a wider public debate, including severe criticisms and attempts to soften or control their content. These attempts ranged from distributors giving the movies a more moralistic title and making preemptive cuts, to conservative actions by critics, religious organizations, and censorship boards. In some countries, such as the U.K., movies were severely cut, even to such a degree that the original version was nearly unrecognizable. In a classical sociological sense, it is easy to look back at these debates and actions as forming another moment of a moral or media panic, where moral guardians (censors, critics, religious leaders, etc.) try to control or diminish the critical edge of controversial media products.

It is also clear that the American origin of the juvenile delinquency movies influenced their historical reception. Some critics tried to diminish the movies' relevance to European social reality by characterizing their content as uniquely American. Other critics pessimistically speculated that these movies might portend the near future in European society. In both cases, American values were associated with ideas of cultural and social decline. In line with a wider stream of European cultural criticism on Americanization in the 1950s, some critics warned their (adult) readers about the possible negative influence of these movies on young people and on the disintegration of harmonious family life.

The arrival of American movies on juvenile delinquency and new youth subcultures had, without a doubt, a major influence upon young adolescents and younger filmmakers in Europe. Notwithstanding the censors' attempts to stop them, these pictures inspired young people with concrete scripts for how to talk, dress, and behave. Together with rock 'n' roll music and dance, the movies carried new tastes and literal codes of conduct. Movies such as *The Wild One* and *Rebel* helped give shape to a new model of youth autonomy and rebellion. Although many critics tried to convince their readers about their own "nausea" when watching the movies, they also recognized that this type of critical cinema about youth was nearly completely absent in Europe.

From this perspective it is not surprising that, in France, for instance, young critics such as Truffaut, Godard, Kast, or Rohmer, who would soon start as filmmakers, praised the teenpics. With these American juvenile crime movies in mind, the later New Wave directors argued that the French film industry had forgotten how to deal with contemporary problems and issues in relation to young people. The New Wave critics' admiration for younger American directors such as Brooks and Ray was part of a reevaluation of Hollywood as a creative site where genuine auteurs flourish. It also included a refutation of the older generation of French filmmakers, often called the "cinéma de papa," which specialized in "bourgeois" literary adaptations. The American juvenile delinquency movies, which were vibrantly contemporary and controversial, were then useful in fighting out what was basically a generational conflict within the French film scene. In some sense, Truffaut, Rohmer, and other euphoric critics must have recognized themselves in the young rebels in the movies, who impatiently challenged their parents, adults, and the whole established (film) order.

NOTES

I would like to thank the different censorship/classification boards, including those in Brussels, Copenhagen, Frankfurt, London, and Paris.

1. *Report of the Departmental Committee on Children and the Cinema*, Secretary of State, May 1950, London.

2. "Legion Approves Eight of 15 New Productions," *Motion Picture Herald*, March 12, 1955.

3. W. H. M. "*Rebel Without a Cause.*" *The Tidings*, Oct. 28, 1955.

4. BBFC file on *The Wild One*, Robertson (1989: 105).

5. Watkins (BBFC) to Ayres (MGM), March 24, 1955, BBFC file on *Blackboard Jungle (BJ)*.

6. "Hollywood Told: Reform Film Code." *The Daily Mail*, June 16, 1955.

7. Watkins to Derby Town Clerk, Nov. 1, 1955, BBFC file *BJ*.

8. Internal document, Oct. 14, 1955, BBFC file on *Rebel Without a Cause (RWaC)*.

9. Watkins to Abeles (Warners London), Oct. 17, 1955, BBFC file *RWaC*.

10. Ibid.

11. Ibid., Nov. 4, 1955.

12. Ibid., Nov. 8, 1955.

13. Ray to Watkins, Dec. 10, 1955; Watkins to Ray, Dec. 15, 1955, BBFC file *RWaC*. Also: "Cuts Ease Way in Britain for 'Rebel,'" *Variety*, Nov. 23, 1955.

14. Internal document AW/JT, Nov. 21, 1955, BBFC file *RWaC*.

15. Watkins to Abeles, Nov. 24, 1955, BBFC file *RWaC*.

16. *BBFC Minutes of Exceptions*, London, 1957, 1958, 1959.

17. Internal document, April 12, 1976, BBFC file *RWaC*.

18. CNC—Commission de Classification file on *Graine de Violence*, documents Aug. 4, 1955; Feb. 17, 1956; July 14, 1963.

19. See FSK (Freiwillige Selbstkontrolle) files 11405 (a, b, c, and d) and 11755 on . . . *denn sie wissen nicht, was sie tun*.

20. CNC—Commission de Classification file on *Fureur de Vivre*, internal document, Feb. 24, 1956.

21. Ibid., Oct. 4, 1973.

22. Statens Filmcensur file 61469 on *Vildt Blod*.

23. *The Tidings*, Jan. 8, 1954; March 11, 1955; Oct. 28, 1955.

24. CCRT (Centre catholique de radio et de television) Fiche *Graine de Violence*, Nov. 1955.

25. "La bêtise à l'état pur: L'Equipée Sauvage," *La Croix*, May 5, 1954.

26. Pierre Kast, "Sur Laszlo Benedek," *Positif* 3 (March–April 1955).

27. Jean De Baroncelli, "L'Equipée Sauvage," *Le Monde*, April 24, 1954.

28. François Truffaut, "La Fureur de vivre," *Arts*, April 4, 1956.

29. Eric Rohmer, "Ajax ou Le Cid?" *Cahiers du Cinéma* 59 (May 1956): 32–36.

30. Penelope Houston, "Rebels without Causes," *Sight and Sound* 25 (Spring 1956): 178–181.

31. Watkins to Mirams, Feb. 1956, BBFC file *RWaC*.

■ ■·■ ■

CHAPTER 2

THE IMPORTED REBELLION

Criminal Guys and Consumerist Girls in Postwar Germany and Austria

ALEXANDRA SEIBEL

In April of 1956, a West German film production company organized a discussion panel that set out to negotiate a fervent question. The question was directed toward Berlin's postwar youth, printed on red billboards throughout the city: "Are you really like this?" "This" meant deviant, delinquent, or dangerous.

The actual reason for posing the question at this particular time was the promotional campaign that had just started for Georg Tressler's teen movie *Die Halbstarken* (West Germany, 1956). Even before its completion, the film gained special attention with the public, not least because of the title "Halbstarke" and its pejorative association with rebellious youth, considered a social problem since public awareness for juvenile delinquency—not unlike the moral panics about juvenile delinquency in the U.S.—had been generated by media reports which exaggerated youth culture as deviant and dangerous.

Die Halbstarken, produced by the Austrian-born director Georg Tressler, became one of the biggest postwar box office successes in Germany. It was released in the U.S. that same year under the English title *Teenage Wolfpack* and was reviewed in *Variety* as follows:

> It is the first German pic on juvenile delinquency, one of postwar Germany's biggest problems. It makes an obvious attempt to cash in on the wide popularity of American pix of the same sort, such as *Blackboard Jungle* and *Rebel Without a Cause.* It's an obvious effort to give young Horst Buchholz, idol of local bobbysox set and winner of the 1955 Federal Film Award . . . the opportunity to come along. *Halbstarke* (which means "Half-Strong Ones") has the kids, the basic problem and also the realistic approach . . . , but all similarity with its American predecessors

stops here. Neither can it stand comparison with Hollywood pix on the same subject. It's little more than a mediocre documentary report concentrating on a corny thrill story. Nevertheless, the film will appeal to mass audiences here, particularly juveniles. (Nov. 14, 1956)

In this essay, I explore the influence of American youth culture on Germany and Austria in the '50s and investigate how films like *The Wild One* (1953), *Rebel Without a Cause* (1955), and *Blackboard Jungle* (1955) shaped the screen images of youth in German and Austrian films of the time. I will particularly focus on the representation of girls and discuss how their precarious relationship to consumer culture reveals the ambiguity of postwar society vis-à-vis a growing influence of American pop culture in central Europe.

As the sociologist Thomas Grotum has pointed out, the so-called Halbstarken-riots in West Germany reached their peak between 1956 and 1958 and were especially hyped by the yellow press and their journalists, who eagerly reported on local "Panthergangs," "packs of gangsters in Munich," and "criminal boys in Essen" (*Die Zeit*, April 26, 1956). The term "Halbstarke" itself dates back to the turn of the century, when supposedly rebellious urban male youth from lower classes were labeled "Halbstarke." In the mid-fifties, however, the public equated nonconformist young people with deviance and delinquency, in large part due to the unwillingness of the media to differentiate between "real" juvenile criminals and comparatively harmless groups of young people roaming the streets (Grotum, 224). In Austria, we find a similar situation: according to the sociologist Kurt Luger, less than 10 percent of young people were actually involved in criminal acts, but this criminalized minority was greatly exaggerated by the media (Luger, 112).

Interestingly, the representation of teenagers had changed significantly between the immediate years after World War II and the more prosperous years of the mid-fifties. As the film historian Jürgen Felix has argued, in films immediately released after the war (like *Irgendwo in Berlin/Somewhere in Berlin*, 1946; or *. . . und über uns der Himmel/The Sky Above Us*, 1947), youth represented the idea of hope, optimism, and the possibility of future, especially with regard to the "Wiederaufbau," the reconstruction of society after the devastation of the war. Due to the "re-empowering of the generation of fathers" in the course of the German economic miracle in the '50s, the images of youth changed again. Growing up in the midst of a prospering society, young people indulged in what was dubbed the "teenager revolution" that got imported from the U.S.: they danced to rock 'n' roll music, went to the movies, and drove motorcycles—in short, they resorted (in the perception of their parents' generation) to anomie, deviance, sexual regression, and conspicuous consumption. In other words, the danger for young people emanated not—as one might assume in the midst of the Cold War—from the East; instead, the bad influence stemmed supposedly from the West because the promise of easy living threatened to undermine German working morals. Thus, the generational conflict in the fifties in Germany (and the same can be said about Austria) took place within a republic already oscillating between moral restoration on the one hand and technological modernization on the other (Felix, 317).

In this respect, it is of utmost importance to consider the role of the U.S. in the reconstruction of Europe after the Second World War. Shortly after the war and, as the Austrian historian Reinhold Wagnleitner has pointed out, after European self-inflicted annihilation and cultural ruin, "it seemed that the United States alone had a corner on the codes of modernization. Especially the fascination that the myth 'America' had for young people must not be underestimated in this context" (Wagnleitner, 2). In Austria, for example, the impoverished and starving population was extremely grateful for the material support supplied especially by the U.S. in the course of the Marshall Plan. These relief measures had a tremendous impact on the image of America as a country of affluence, freedom, modernization, and consumer culture—in short, everything every young citizen in Austria and Germany was dreaming of. Also, in comparison to the British, French, and Russian occupation forces, the U.S. was much more effective in controlling the reorganization of the democratic process and of cultural life in Austria. Pax Americana was secured by the massive export of U.S. culture. Good connections to the population by the U.S. army and the ISB (Information Service Branch, of the cultural and propaganda department of the U.S. occupation force) prepared the culture for a positive attitude toward everything American. The ISB became particularly active within the realm of symbolic capital: press, radio, publications, information, film, theater, and music. It is also particularly informative that the cultural missionaries of the U.S. emphasized similarities within a European-American culture and attempted a conscious exclusion of African American culture and mixed cultural forms. In that vein, U.S. propaganda officers completely underestimated the impact of pop culture, and it was only through the tremendous success of jazz that they eventually engaged with these aspects of popular culture as well. Overall, as Wagnleitner concludes, the "activities of U.S. cultural officers had opened unimaginable possibilities for the U.S. culture industry . . . which allowed the path to modernization to seem on the whole, to be an 'American' one" (Wagnleitner, 295). And this appeared to be of special political relevance in the context of the Cold War.

In Germany and Austria, both parents and children were fascinated by the imported mass culture from the U.S. But whereas the adult generation desired affluence and prosperity associated with an American standard of modern living, they rejected the imported codes of youth culture and rebellion as propagated in films like *Rebel Without a Cause* and *Blackboard Jungle*. Whenever the yellow press reported on juvenile delinquency, they never forgot to blame mediated U.S. youth culture as the imported bad influence on young domestic people. This allegedly bad American influence was dubbed "Ami-Kultur" and referred to "low" cultural artifacts such as pulp fiction and comics, films and music, or in short, everything young people embraced to protest parental authority. The consumption of rock 'n' roll, together with films like *The Wild One* and *Rebel Without a Cause*, articulated a symbolic resistance of mostly working class (male) youth rebelling against cultural tastes of a bourgeois mainstream. U.S. commercial culture, then, signified both desirable affluence and prosperity on the one hand, and on the other hand, youth culture, "Halbstarken riots," and the decline of high cultural standards.

In the following, I read the youth films of Georg Tressler in relation to the imported "Ami-Kultur" with a particular focus on the representation of girls and their relation to consumer culture. As I demonstrate, the moral positioning of teenage girls is coded in terms of an increasingly affluent society gone wrong: their fate of either becoming a "good" girl or a "bad" girl is mostly played out in relation to their consumer habits.

Die Halbstarken opens within a frame similar to the opening of Laszlo Benedek's *The Wild One:* it designates itself, in a sensational mode, as a "true story of youth in between the longing for adventure and crime." At the same time, this self-designation is coded as a moral warning. Essentially, Tressler equates youth culture with criminality in his juvenile delinquency film. But before his teenage protagonists are punished for their obvious wrongdoings in the course of the narrative, the film focuses carefully on a variety of locations that are typically associated with youth and youth culture. These "spaces of transition," as Lesley Speed has dubbed them with regard to the works of Erik Erikson and Lawrence Grossberg (Speed, 26), are associated with youth and youth pics; they epitomize a certain state of being in between a young person and an adult, a transitory and fragmented rite of passage. Unlike the makers of American youth pics, where diners and cars play an important role in teenage culture and teenage rites of passage, Tressler spatialized the "cool places" of the young within the context of postwar Berlin: public pools, the Italian espresso bar, a basement, bombed out industrial wastelands, and an empty boathouse all signify places of subcultural prac-

Freddy (Horst Buchholz, center) casts an ominous stare with his buddies in *Die Halbstarken* (1956).

tices which are to be celebrated and exposed at the same time. The celebrated authenticity of the postwar reality with its bombed out houses was mostly generated through location shooting and the expressive cinematography of cameraman Heinz Pehlke (Grob, 217).

The ambivalent stance of the parent culture vis-à-vis the young generation is especially played out in a scene that takes place in an Italian espresso bar, where the teenagers gather and dance to rock 'n' roll. The Italian owner, himself a recently moved migrant and therefore still a foreigner within a very homogenous national framework, tries to navigate his rebellious customers with a mixture of contempt and humbleness: "Signore Spaghetti," as he is nicknamed, is economically dependent on his young customers as much as he is scared by them. The youth challenge the hegemonic culture of a reestablishing postwar society and its petit bourgeois values—at least on a symbolic level—by wearing jeans and black leather jackets, riding motorcycles, and so forth. At the same time, they already stand for the increasing purchasing power typical of a rising teenage consumer culture: after the decline of the Halbstarken riots in 1958, teenagers were primarily perceived as consumers. A critical twist in this shift was the possibility for girls and women to "conquer" public spaces. It is especially this relation of females to youth culture and consumerism that is a structuring moment in Georg Tressler's youth films.

The female protagonist Sissy (Karin Baal) in *Die Halbstarken*, a teenage girl of 15 from the lower classes in postwar Berlin, dreams the dream of material abundance, upward mobility, and transcendence of her working-class status. Her purchasing power, though, is dependent upon her boyfriend Freddy (teen star of the time Horst Buchholz), who is the leader of a small gang and commits petty crimes. But whereas he "only" wants money in order to lead an eventually decent life with wife and family, Sissy is coded as a teenage femme fatale straight out of an American film noir. Not only does she reject a projected position as potential wife and mother, but when Freddy invites his brother Jan to Sissy's house and asks him to "feel at home"—implying that Sissy is preparing for their dinner—the first conflict arises. We see her in a medium shot in front of the kitchen stove, her face distorted with disgust. Too obvious is the anticipated family scenario with her as the caring wife, and too close is the deterrent model of her working-class mother, who does the laundry in the backyard, with her face having aged too early because of too much work. Sissy desires purchasing power, not motherhood. But her appetite for luxury, diamonds, and fur coats exceeds by far the "healthy" and socially desired consumer attitude of an average teenage girl and future housewife. Eventually, she not only tries to seduce her boyfriend's brother to plot a new crime, but also cold-heartedly shoots an old man, then her own boyfriend Freddy.

Compared to her malicious noir character, Freddy appears as an admittedly confused but ultimately decent boy, a potentially responsible member of society who can be reunited with his father at the end of the narrative. Sissy, on the other hand, is comparable to the character of Sal Mineo in *Rebel*, who is too "pathological" (he is a potential homosexual and he has killed puppies) to be reintegrated into society (see Biskind, 197). Unlike Plato, though, Sissy is not killed at the end of the film, but taken to prison. One can easily imagine how Freddy's lawyer pleads for mitigation of the sentence because the boy seems relatively harmless in comparison to his evil girlfriend. Also, Freddy's father, who has so far been characterized as a violent but ultimately impotent patriarchal figure, takes on responsibility for his two children (and again, this is similar to the ending of *Rebel*, where the father of Jim Stark finally "takes control" by shutting up his wife and embracing his son "like a man"). Freddy's father, however, represents a failing generation of fathers who are to blame for being unable to introduce a system of moral values to their children (their sons, that is) that would keep them from falling prey to the lures of consumer culture. In the moment of Freddy's arrest, however, a biker gang passes by as if directly cast from *The Wild One*: this last shot signifies once again the ongoing dangers of an Americanized youth culture and its deviant tendencies.

As Jürgen Felix has argued, this equation of youth culture and juvenile delinquency in *Die Halbstarken* negotiates the reaction-formation of a re-established father-generation in West Germany vis-à-vis an emerging alternative youth culture on the one hand and a progressing "Americanization" of Germany on the other. At the same time, though, I would like to argue that for Tressler, this moral ending and the connotation of youth as materialist, hedonistic, and criminal doesn't come easy. It is true that at the end, the syntax of the gangster genre domesticates, so to speak, the semantic excesses of the youth pic. Nevertheless, in the course of his narrative, Tressler cannot help but celebrate the cool places of youth culture and the anarchic energies of teens dancing to rock 'n' roll: when suddenly in the espresso scene, a record of a marching song gets accidentally played, the teenagers mock and despise this piece of military memory. In all their "deviance," as they are perceived by the parent generation, they come out as far more sympathetic than the generation of their fathers, who have marched to military music on the actual battlefields of Europe in World War II.

Deviance, however, is coded differently when it comes to gender. Whereas rebellious boys can still be potentially useful citizens, deviant girls are in a much more endangered position. German reviewers of *Die Halbstarken* acknowledged the different trajectories of the teenagers with relation to gender: "A boy who can steal a car, can also repair it and become a mechanic," the German critic Helmuth de Haas pointedly remarked, "but I am worried about Sissy: what is to become of her? A gangster's moll or a mannequin?" (*Die Welt*, Sept. 29, 1956).

Although Tressler could not repeat his great success of *Die Halbstarken* with any of his following films, his next project, *Unter Achtzehn/Under 18* (1957), produced in Austria, once again negotiates the themes of youth and deviance. This time, the course of the narrative alters significantly from *Die Halbstarken*, not least because of a different gender perspective. Attention rests solely upon the female character, Elfie (Vera Tschechova, granddaughter of actress Olga Tschechova), a working-class girl like Sissy, who, again, wishes to transcend the lower status of her class. At the beginning of the film, she tries to reach this goal by capitalizing on her "half-strong" boyfriend; she then chooses not to become the gangster's moll (like Sissy), but rather a live store mannequin. In prudish postwar Vienna, where the story takes

This ad for *Unter Achtzehn* (1957) indicates the isolation of Elfie (Vera Tschechova) in contrast to boys in other films.

place, such a mannequin would have been immediately equated with prostitution. A female social worker—played by the famous Austrian actress Paula Wessely, who also produced the film—intervenes on behalf of the morally "endangered" girl Elfie. Through her character, a therapeutic/diagnostic discourse gets introduced into the narrative suggesting that society as a whole and the family in particular are pathological and in need of help. The fathers are still suffering from the war, the mothers are either weak or irresponsible, and living conditions are impoverished. Peter Biskind argued for *Rebel* that "the film attacks the family on behalf not of the kids but of the experts" (Biskind, 197), and this analysis holds true for *Unter Achtzehn* as well.

Another striking difference between *Die Halbstarken* and *Unter Achtzehn* concerns the representation of youth culture itself. Whereas in the former, youth practices its rebellion through spectacular outfits, music, and nonconformist behavior, in *Unter Achtzehn* these are hardly represented at all. The remaining handful of "half-strong ones" in the film pathetically approach the social worker for help in order to get their local hangout established, something completely unthinkable for "real" youngsters. Thereby, the therapeutic discourse of the social worker addresses youth via different gender perspectives: if the young ones are male, they are potential criminals, whereas if they are female, they are potential prostitutes. Elfie's attempt to become a mannequin in a noble boutique is coded as morally unacceptable and finally exposes the precarious intersection of consumerism, femininity, and public space.

Typical locations of youth cultural expression are to be found in public space, a sort of "hiding in the light" according to Dick Hebdige, that has traditionally precluded the participation of girls. As Angela McRobbie has famously argued: "Girls had to take care not to 'get into trouble' and excessive loitering on the street corners might be taken as a sexual invitation to the boys. The double standard was probably more rigidly maintained in the 1950s than in any other time since" (McRobbie, 117).

If there has historically existed an activity in the public sphere in which women were allowed to move around freely and without harassment, it was, of course, shopping. As argued by scholars like Mica Nava and others, the intersection of femininity and consumerism can be traced to the beginning of modernity and the rise of mass culture. Already by the late nineteenth century, the emerging commercial culture had an empowering impact on middle-class women, who were allowed to roam the semipublic space of department stores. Their newly acquired independence (and I cut a very complex argument very short at this point) challenged the authority of a concerned male-dominated public. In response, the argument that was put forth against the female shopper claimed that the wide variety of consumer goods on display in department stores were a moral threat to easily seduced females. Mindless women shoppers would be poisoned by consumer products, an unhealthy desire for glamour and romance would be incited, and their senses would become confused (Nava, 63).

In the context of postwar Austria (in *Unter Achtzehn*), Elfie's affinity for consumer culture and the sexually charged lures of the "economic miracle" are immediately coded as a morally inflicted position. The potentially empowering aspect of Elfie's desire to become a mannequin and to be looked at in a semipublic space (the store) is denied by the narrative, both in terms of her class and her gender position. The social worker wants her to go back to her laundry job because she cannot imagine that the young girl could be able to capitalize on her good looks *and* to control the male gaze by making money out of it at the same time. But Tressler lays bare the hypocrisy of postwar society by depicting her not as a fallen angel but as a potential businesswoman. For the American reviewer in *Variety*, these double moral standards put forward by the narrative are not comprehensible: "Scripters are to blame for such nonsense as not permitting an 18-year-old 'bad girl' with a million dollar figure to become a mannequin and ordering her to work in a laundry instead" (*Variety*, 1958). Elfie, for sure, almost ends up in a striptease club and becomes the mistress of a rich married man before she gets reunited (thanks to the social worker) with her former poor boyfriend. At the end, the discourse of the state institutions (the police, the social worker) contains the semantics of the exploitation genre (since Elfie's adventures in the striptease club are shown to full length), and her desire for upward mobility gone wrong ends in a morality play. Her attempts to make a career out of her good looks are replaced by the promise of a petit bourgeois family life. The happy ending is uneasy: it is surprising and unbelievable at the same time.

As I have tried to show with respect to Georg Tressler's youth films, and first and foremost his big box office success *Die Halbstarken* and other films following in its vein, the male characters are modeled after their American predecessors played by James Dean and Marlon Brando. They challenge the authority of their parents—notably their fathers—by participating in subcultural practices such as wearing leather pants, riding motorcycles, and listening to rock 'n' roll. The films oscillate between celebrating these practices as spectacular and subversive *and* condemning them as materialist and prone to criminality. Most interesting in this respect is the representation of American pop culture and its supposedly bad influence on German and Austrian teenagers. The dangers for the young generation emanate from the "West" (and, interestingly enough, in the context of the Cold War, not from the East). It is the West and its promise of high living standards, affluence, and fast cars that eventually spoil German working morals and decency. As I have tried to argue, these films can be read as a reaction-formation of a father-generation that not only tries to negotiate an emerging alternative youth, but also a progressing "Americanization" of German and Austrian culture. American jukeboxes and big limousines represent an excessive materialism of the "West"; its promises of "easy living" and exuberant consumerism threaten to undermine the moral codes of respectability and decency in the young generation. But it is especially the precarious positioning of girls and their affinity to consumer culture through which the true lesson of postwar ideology can be taught. If their appetite for "Western" luxury and purchasing power grows too strong, their integrity is immediately at stake. They either assume the role of the glamorous but ill-fated teenage femme fatale, and embrace consumption to the point of becoming commodities themselves, being put on display as prostitutes and strip dancers—or they have to confine themselves to the dull eagerness of becoming a German or Austrian housewife. Tough choice.

■ ■

CHAPTER 3

REBELS *WITH* A CAUSE

Children versus the Military Industrial Complex

MICK BRODERICK

The postwar period from 1945 has been labeled many things—the jet age, the television age, the space age—yet the most resilient nomenclature is that of the atomic age or nuclear era. Throughout the Cold War (1945–1991), American cinema produced a significant number of films that broached issues concerning the development, testing, and deployment of nuclear weapons, and their associated technologies.[1] This essay considers a small but important number of films that challenge assumptions about the depiction of children as naïve innocents or impotent victims of the atomic age.

Much of the scholarship on this body of film has recognized the importance of representations of children and adolescents in narratives concerning nuclear weapons and warfare. Most often the literature in relation to such films (Evans, Perrine, Henriksen, Newman, Shapiro) to varying degrees suggests that such fictional dramas engender a sense of fear, alienation, and/or resignation in these younger characters, who appear seemingly impotent in the face of national and global nuclear politics. However, drawing from close textual readings of key film sequences, I will demonstrate that a significant number of movies foreground active *resistance* to—if not *subversion* of—the Cold War consensus that seemingly inured postwar generations to expect nuclear war as imminent, predetermined, and survivable.[2]

I have argued elsewhere that the bulk of the nuclear film genre presents children as "innocents" and "victims" of the nuclear epoch.[3] However, not all Cold War films depict children and adolescents as passive and devoid of narrative or political agency in relation to atomic affairs. While most nuclear movies eschew direct action by children in challenging the military-industrial complex and/or the political establishment's complicity in a spiraling arms race, some Cold War films do provide alternative representations, such as *The Space Children* (1958), *Wild in the Sky* (1972), *WarGames* (1983), *Amazing Grace and Chuck* (1986), *The Manhattan Project: The Deadly Game* (1986), *Project X* (1987), and *Terminator 2: Judgment Day* (1991).

Wild in the Sky, *WarGames*, *Project X*, and *Terminator 2: Judgment Day* each portray radical acts by youth that lead to an undermining or usurping of the defense industries and strategic postures that are premised upon both nuclear deterrence and the infrastructure that supports mutual assured destruction (M.A.D.). Strongly influenced by *Dr. Strangelove* (1963), the hippie comedy *Wild in the Sky* depicts a trio of adolescent draft-dodgers commandeering a nuclear armed B52. In an early scene, an air force base commander (played by *Strangelove*'s Keenan Wynn) confirms rumors to his assembled staff "that the men of S.A.C. are to be phased-out in favor of a completely automated system." As in *WarGames* and *Terminator 2*, a repeated fear in such films is the removal of human choice from the nuclear decision-making "loop." This becomes a narrative trope that the "wisdom" of children and adolescents narratively seeks to redress. Produced at a time when the U.S. was still at war with North Vietnam and (secretly) bombing its Indo-Chinese neighbors, *Wild in the Sky* irreverently parodies U.S. military and political institutions. Facing imprisonment, and possibly death, the three juveniles decide to attack a major U.S. financial institution in order to halt the nation's war economy.[4] When the plane is reported as deviating from its assigned course, fighters are sent to intercept it, and the crew reluctantly arms its two H-bombs. The president intervenes, interrupting his dune-buggy vacation ("I take one day off—one *stinking* day—and the whole country collapses") and demands the teens return the B-52 to base. Recalling President Nixon's notorious invective and Vice President Agnew's assertion that antiwar protesters didn't get "spanked" enough as children, the president immediately begins a patronizing, insulting, and hostile rant: "You think we *like* violence and war? You people want simple solutions to complicated problems and there are none"; he then derides the trio as "adolescent twirps" and "punks."[5] Yet the solution *is* simple for one of hijackers, who suggests: "All I'm going to do is take this bomb and drop it on Fort Knox. . . . You said so yourself—you can't run wars on credit cards." The threat of economic sabotage is too much for the president, who is left to holler ineffectually down the line as the hijackers obliterate the nation's federal gold reserve and fly off, unrepentant and unchallenged.

A decade after these counterculture, antiwar protesters are portrayed irradiating the nation's gold reserves, *WarGames* also shows the folly of removing human choice from the nuclear command and control system. While playing "global thermonuclear war" over the Internet, David Lightman (Matthew Broderick), a teenage hacker in Seattle, accidentally activates a dormant military Artificial Intelligence (A.I.) program embedded within NORAD's defense system.[6] The high school student uses a "backdoor" to enter the system and accidentally "awakens" Joshua, the strategic A.I. game program that "mistakes" young David for his creator, the officially deceased strategic games theorist Dr. Stephen Falken. Presented with a menu of games, which include poker and chess, through to conflicts involving weapons of mass destruction, David and his classmate Jennifer (Ally Sheedy) excitedly select "global thermonuclear war," choosing to be the Russians in this two-player game, and joyfully deciding to "nuke" Las Vegas and Seattle, unaware that this "game" immediately launches the attack alert at NORAD's early warning and missile command. It raises the DEFCON status and initiates automated preparations for an American ICBM counterstrike. The alert is eventually recognized as a simulation, and the threat vanishes from the NORAD control screen the instant David unplugs his computer. But Joshua regains contact with David and continues the countdown to the thermonuclear war game's conclusion, which once again initiates a phantom attack on the U.S. and prepares for a counterstrike. To avoid war and the scientific nihilism and fatalistic responses that Falken and the military adhere to, David has to teach "Joshua" the futility of war, long after his elders have resigned themselves to oblivion by abrogating their responsibilities to an advanced computer program.

Three years later, as airman Jimmy Garrett in *Project X*, Matthew Broderick once again is portrayed clashing with the military-scientific establishment. A probationary air force flier demoted to animal handler on an air base in Florida, Garrett risks court martial for insubordination by undermining his superiors' secret nuclear project before a group of congressional visitors. After refusing to transport his chimp into a reactor room, the airman interrupts the scheduled demonstration and reveals a key methodological fallacy in conducting "human reliability" studies using chimps to assess whether pilots can complete their missions after exposure to lethal amounts of ionizing radiation in simulated nuclear attacks. Later, when removed from the base for his outburst and failure to comply with commands, he joins a young researcher who has previously trained one of the chimps (named Virgil) to communicate by sign language. Together the pair arrange for the simians to escape to the Everglades. Despite enormous personal risk (jail, accidental irradiation, threatened use of deadly force by military police), Garrett's principled actions in *Project X* demonstrate the passion of youth to countermand orders that are perceived as illogical and/or immoral, while adults unquestioningly, or grudgingly, obey. Garrett's public refusal to carry out direct orders, whether from the chief research scientist or base commander, is also portrayed as potentially seditious when at least one other air force animal handler is shown deliberately ignoring a command to transfer a chimp for irradiation. Just as teenage David Lightman in *WarGames* is depicted teaching his elders (scientists, politicians, and soldiers) and the Pentagon's A.I. program the folly of playing "global thermonuclear war," in *Project X* Jimmy Garrett consciously rejects the chain of command, military duty, national security, and personal safety to liberate a group of test subjects from spurious research conducted in the name of ensuring Mutual Assured Destruction.

These three film scenarios are predicated upon the threat of nuclear war as an instrument of the state somehow being usurped by youth who undermine the logics and/or apparatus of the military-industrial complex. As the final film of the Cold War period to depict children actively subverting the institutions complicit in weapons of mass destruction production, *Terminator 2: Judgment Day* is a nuanced and considered sequel to the original 1984 feature. The epistemology of the *Terminator* films is dependent upon a nuclear war having *already* occurred. Narratively, it is a fait accompli. Hence, *T2* opens with Sarah Connor's narration: "Three billion human lives ended on August 29, 1997. The survivors of the nuclear fire called the war Judgment Day . . ." Yet the dramatic conceit of the movie is one articulated by several characters: "The future is not set. There is no fate but what we make for ourselves." It is this potential for radical intervention that marks *T2* as prophetic eschatology, as opposed to a predetermined apocalyptic theology where the future is immutable and divinely ordained. Human agency, according to this narrative, *can* alter the trajectory of history (even retroactively). In the devastated ruins of Los Angeles in 2029, Sarah Connor's son John is a resistance leader fighting a guerilla war against the A.I. machines (Skynet) that control the postnuclear world. From the future, John Connor sends emissaries back in time to prevent "terminators" from killing his mother and himself. In (contemporary) 1991, we find 12-year-old John playing Missile Command at a video arcade, fighting off enemy ICBMs that MIRV and stream toward him. Trained by his mother to be self-sufficient as a future "great military leader," he's already an accomplished petty thief, using a portable credit card PIN reader to access automatic teller machines for cash. Together with his mother, a reprogrammed T-800 terminator (Arnold Schwarzenegger), and computer scientist Myles Dyson, John works to destroy the advanced secret technology at Cyberdyne Systems that will even-

This lobby card for *The Space Children* (1958) clearly shows the suspicion and contempt that many adults have for youth in nuclear-era movies.

tually be used to create the Pentagon A.I. that initiates the nuclear war.[7] Amid a firefight with local police SWAT teams, the quartet of saboteurs assemble all of the classified files and materials relevant to Dyson's research and destroy the building in a massive explosion, thereby preventing or forestalling Armageddon. Teenage John Connor is fundamental to these events, succeeding where his mother fails. He averts Dyson's assassination, reprograms the T-800 to learn (importantly, nonlethal violence), and gains entry into the secure lab through his computer dexterity. It is this adolescent's direct action and command of the T-800 that secures a future for humanity.

As these four brief examples demonstrate, some Cold War movie narratives entertain notions of children as catalysts of revolutionary change, challenging the role of the military-industrial complex. However, the origins of such themes and approaches can be found as early as 1958, with B-movie director Jack Arnold's subversive narrative template, *The Space Children*. This film sought not only to question the veracity of working Americans (and others internationally) participating in weapons of mass destruction development, testing, and deployment, but to depict children actively engaged in sabotage and subversion. It is a marked departure from much of the postwar, mass entertainment imagery of American youth as subservient to parental authority and/or national security interests.

The Space Children can be usefully approached from the perspective of Jack Arnold's oeuvre and auteurist predilections. Perhaps more than any other American filmmaker throughout the Cold War, Arnold was preoccupied with humanist considerations of atomic energy and society's capacity to effectively harness nuclear power or fall victim to its apocalyptic potential.[8] Generally in Arnold's science fiction oeuvre, children are conspicuously absent. *The Space Children* is the exception—and in its representation of the empowerment of this atomic age generation, it is an exception that sits outside classical Hollywood cinema of the time. As a key countertext to the representation of Cold War children, this critically neglected B-film deserves a close reading.

On their way to the Eagle Point launch facility between San Francisco and Los Angeles—presumably a reference to the U.S.A.F. missile range at Vandenberg—a family of four (the Brewsters) encounter car trouble on a deserted stretch of beachside road. The young boys (Bud and Ken Brewster) hear a weird and otherworldly hum, accompanied by an angular beam of light that diagonally crosses the sky before reaching the seashore. During this brief close encounter, the family station wagon engine stalls as all the electrical systems cut out. The children excitedly describe what they've just seen and heard, but as a fighter jet screeches overhead and the car's battery once again turns over, both parents patronizingly dismiss their story as fanciful.

Upon arrival at the Eagle Point security gate, it becomes evident that the father, Dave Brewster, is a contractor for the *Thunderer*—a six-stage ICBM which is to carry a "hydrogen warhead" into space and orbit indefinitely, capable of sending its destructive payload instantaneously anywhere on the planet. At the military base's trailer home for civilians, self-proclaimed "city girl" Anne Brewster, disgruntled at having to leave San Francisco, is unimpressed with her husband's new posting. Significant discursive time is given to the overt marital dissent over the nature of Dave's employment. Anne repeatedly questions her evasive husband about the project, challenging his feigned disavowals with the suggestion that he and his company must have detailed knowledge of the project since he has "worked on it for months." Dave's retort is telling: "I worked on *one* part out of thirty-five thousand parts. It's more than just an intercontinental missile." The response is evocative of President Eisenhower's famous 1960 televised farewell address to the nation, warning against the "grave consequences" of a "New American experience," namely the "conjunction of an immense military establishment and a large arms industry," one whose "total influence—economic, political, even spiritual—is felt in every city, every state, every house, every office of the Federal government":

> In the councils of government, we must guard against the acquisition of unwarranted influence, whether sought or unsought, by the military-industrial complex. The potential for the disastrous rise of misplaced power exists and will persist. We must never let the weight of this combination endanger our liberties or democratic processes. We should take nothing for granted. Only an alert and knowledgeable citizenry can compel the proper meshing of the huge industrial and military machinery of defense with our peaceful methods and goals, so that security and liberty may prosper together.[9]

After more expository sparring over the nature of the new ICBM, its accuracy, and what the enemy might possess, Anne ironically adds: "It's almost funny, isn't it, having the kids living here in the middle of all this?" Dave turns in protest, rhetorically challenging his wife: "Would you have wanted me to say 'no' after the company *insisted* I go?" Taken together, these statements depict not only an unresolved domestic tension, but articulate a commonplace personal defense designed to minimize, or excuse, Brewster's individual contribution to the arms race while reinforcing the enormous size of the civilian interdependency with the military-industrial complex. It demonstrates the massive fiscal resources and the tens of thousands of personnel directly employed in just *one* arms race program.

This conversation also recognizes the domestic, economic imperative to maintain such lucrative employment. As a later exchange between the Brewsters and another Eagle Point family demonstrates, being part of the daily production of weapons of mass destruction seemingly requires either the jingoistic certainty of an ideologue or a constant denial and disavowal of being actively complicit in manufacturing weapons systems designed to obliterate millions of families just like theirs. It is precisely this dualism that has been described as a "Faustian" bargain by Manhattan Project scientists Frank Barnaby and Freeman Dyson.[10] As anthropologist Hugh Gusterson has demonstrated in his groundbreaking study of life inside a nuclear weapons laboratory:

> We must partly understand laboratory practices of secrecy as a means of creating a disciplinary distance between weapons scientists and their families. Often working in concert with traditional American notions of appropriate roles in marriage, they open a space between the labo-

ratory and the domestic sphere that, to some extent at least, insulates weapons scientists from questions and challenges about their work and maintains a seal between the values of the public and domestic spheres.[11]

Cracks in the façade of routine life for the civilians on the base are reinforced in a scene soon after. While the children play offscreen, the adults of the trailer homes meet for an evening BBQ. The discourse immediately switches to the Cold War, nuclear weapons, and their children's concerns over atomic attack. Gathered around a table with the children out of earshot, the adults articulate distinct positions. Schoolteacher Anne Brewster expresses concern about the impact of her husband's work. Hank Johnson is cheerfully bellicose, advocating preemptive nuclear strikes, while his wife Frieda attempts to diffuse any potential conflict among the couples.

ANNE: At the parents and teachers meeting they put me on the spot. They kept asking me, "When is it going to end? We keep trying to find ourselves something bigger and better to blow ourselves off the planet." When they ask me these questions, what do I tell them?
HANK: Well, you just say that down there stands the *Thunderer*, and what are we waiting for?
FRIEDA: Hank, dear, let's not be serious tonight.
HANK: It's your first day here, Dave. What's your viewpoint?
DAVE: Same as my wife's. In all its history, our country's never *started* a war. The *Thunderer* is to prevent war.
HANK: I still say that when that satellite gets up there with the *Thunderer*, and it gets into its orbit, we should . . .
FRIEDA: . . . take a vacation! That's what we need Hank, a nice vacation.

Frieda is here both proud wife and domestic peacemaker underplaying her husband's belligerence, an ambiguity that women married to nuclear weapons scientists have demonstrated from the Manhattan Project's Laura Fermi to contemporary, post–Cold War weapons lab wives.[12] Similar parental concerns are voiced by the Eagle Point commander, Colonel Manley, and chief weapons scientist, Dr. Wahrman, as the pair relax on the California coast in the late afternoon, while their respective teenage son and daughter return from a swim. The men reflect on their children's youthful affection: "Life's a wonderful thing, doctor." To which Wahrman adds sullenly: "Let's hope we can preserve it for them."

Not long after arriving at the coastal space base, the Brewster boys team up with five other children. All witness another beam of light at the beach, this time transporting a small object from the sky into a nearby cave. Once inside, they encounter an incandescent, pulsating extraterrestrial that communicates with the group telepathically. Arnold's mise-en-scène and editing carefully feature the children nodding knowingly, and Bud is shown smiling, seemingly in acquiescence. Convincing their parents that they have found something that fell out of the sky, the Brewster boys and other children take Dave to the cave. After more telepathic exchanges, the alien is secreted back to the Brewster trailer, to the horror of Anne. Dave Brewster realizes that the arrival of the alien and the launching of the *Thunderer* is not coincidental and tries to warn his superiors, but he is prevented by an unseen alien force. With the aid of the creature's inexplicable power, the children effortlessly slip by security guards and through locked gates. The children are shown to be complicit in the destruction of a supply truck bringing rocket fuel to the site, and cheerily eat ice creams while ensuring a failure in communications occurs between the security gate and the sabotaged tanker.

Later, when Wahrman realizes the children have conspired with the alien force to sabotage his ICBM project, the scientist pleads before the now enormous space organism:

Why have you taken our children and made them do your work? I've spent a lifetime in the search for truth and knowledge, trying to make this world a better place; a world where the very children you are controlling can live in peace instead of fear. I'm their friend. I beg you, tell me what you want of them, what you're making them do. . . . Is there no man on this Earth who has the wisdom and innocence of a child?[13]

His rhetoric betrays the military-industrial mind-set that perpetuates his work in weapons of mass destruction. Wahrman firmly believes in deterrence predicated upon mutual annihilation as a rational process. As Hugh Gusterson has argued, "No matter how intellectually exciting nuclear weapons work may be, it brings with it moral dilemmas that laboratory employees must either confront or ignore as they go about their work."[14] For Gusterson, these scientists develop a socioideological "central axiom" that legitimates their daily work: "the laboratory designs nuclear weapons to ensure, in a world stabilized by nuclear deterrence, that nuclear weapons will never be used."[15]

Unlike Manhattan Project chief Robert Oppenheimer, who made the famous remark about physicists "knowing sin," *The Space Children*'s weapons scientist is firmly in denial.[16] For Dr. Wahrman, anything that undermines

America's ability to maintain a pronounced strategic advantage against its foe is philosophically untenable. It is precisely this logic and sophistry that the scientist repeats at the film's conclusion. He pleads with the children, who have formed a physical cordon to prevent the colonel and his troops from attacking the creature. His argument is well intentioned but deeply paternalistic and patronizing. Gusterson's description of the nuclear scientists' central axiom is apt here, compounded by their living in "a different reality," isolated within a "total institution" under secrecy, segregation, and surveillance:

> In order for the scientists' central axiom—that nuclear weapons exist to save lives and prevent war—to be believable, nuclear weapons scientists must be convinced in their bones that deterrence will not break down; they must have internalised as an integral part of their feeling and thinking selves the conviction that the weapons really will not be used.[17]

Dr. Wahrman's seeming rationality is ultimately presented as flawed when he invokes the survival of the species, paradoxically premised upon deterrence from the threat of global annihilation.

> Children. I'm your friend. Now I wouldn't ask you to do anything that I didn't feel was necessary. Think of your parents; the people on the project. Your country may be in terrible danger. The *Thunderer* is useless. I don't think you know what you've done. . . . Colonel Manley has a daughter of his own. I have a son. We wouldn't ask you to do any more than we'd ask our own children. So please get away from that cave so Colonel Manley and his men can move in.

The soldiers begin to advance and the extraterrestrial emerges from the cave. The children collectively lurch forward while the assembled parents reel in horror at the unworldly apparition. As the colonel commands his troops to open fire, the earth shudders and is awash with light. Powerless, the group watches as the giant brain ascends into the heavens, reversing its earlier trajectory. All present look to the sky, following its flight.

> COLONEL MANLEY: I don't understand. Why did it destroy the *Thunderer?* Why? Why?
> BUD: It had to, because the world wasn't ready to do it.
> DR. WAHRMAN: The world? What do you mean, the world?

BUD: The children, all over the world, *they* did what we did, in other countries.

COLONEL MANLEY: You mean the warheads in Moscow and Prague and London, are all *useless?*

BUD: Yes.

ANNE BREWSTER: The world is having second chance . . .

Everyone turns and looks upward. The camera dollies back and cranes upward as the sound track swells with angelic music and a superimposed title displays a biblical passage: "Verily, I say unto you . . . except ye become as little children, ye shall not enter the kingdom of heaven" (Matthew 18:3). Hence, the actions of the children are narratively aligned with the typology of New Testament scripture, which provides both a prophetic resonance with and a moral justification for their actions. At the film's conclusion, the alien is discursively read as an emissary and agent of God's divine wisdom, like a mid-twentieth-century angel that delivers a sacred message and acts as a protector of the innocent.[18] Nevertheless, the assembled children are shown physically placing their lives on the line to defend the alien and bring about this cosmic harmony. They have become willing saboteurs to ensure global nuclear disarmament.

Twenty-five years later, *The Manhattan Project* improbably depicted a 17-year-old high school senior, Paul Stephens, challenging the doctrine of nuclear deterrence head-on by constructing his own atomic bomb, to be unveiled at a national school science fair in New York. A decade later, in 1994, real-life Detroit teenager David Hahn accidentally initiated a Federal Radiological Emergency Response Plan when local troopers searched his car trunk and believed he was carrying a homemade nuclear bomb.[19] Over a two-year period the 17-year-old boy scout managed to obtain sufficient radioisotopes such as americium, radium, and beryllium, and other nuclear materials, to build in his parent's garage—with written assistance from the Nuclear Regulatory Agency—a homemade neutron gun, and later, a crude breeder reactor. By the time state and federal authorities became involved and a crack counterterrorist Nuclear Emergency Search Team arrived at the Hahn family home in suburban Michigan, geiger counters were running high several hundred meters from the boy's garage. According to the Environmental Protection Agency, up to 40,000 neighborhood residents were potentially exposed to contamination of up to 1,000 times normal background radiation.

David Hahn's backyard experimentation seems the stuff of fiction, blurring the boundaries between narrative film drama and teenage determina-

The Manhattan Project (1986) features high schooler Paul Stephens (Christopher Collet, second from left) building an atomic bomb, mystifying both scientists and the military.

tion and inventiveness. As radiological expert Dave Minnaar from Michigan's Department of Environmental Quality asserted, safety policies and regulations never anticipated such a real-life nuclear drama: "It's simply presumed that the average person wouldn't have the technology or materials required to experiment in these areas."[20]

Unlike David Hahn, who had no ostensible political or ideological motivation for his nuclear hobby, the teenage prankster of *The Manhattan Project* is spurred into action after discovering a covert weapons laboratory has been established near his bucolic town in Ithaca, New York, which uses laser technology to refine and purify plutonium (Pu), giving it "twenty times the punch" of thermonuclear explosions. A visiting nuclear scientist, Dr. Mathewson, keen to date Paul's unmarried mother, ingratiates himself by inviting the boy to visit the MedAtomics Research Facility. After being given a radiation film badge to wear and scrutinizing the laboratory security system, Paul witnesses green plutonium jelly being processed by robots, but Dr. Mathewson denies the nature of the substance by asserting that the material is the less powerful isotope Americium 231. Outside the facility on his way home, the student notices what appears to be five-leafed clover.

Soon after, at his teenage girlfriend Jenny's house, Paul becomes incensed at the corporate and military deceit:

PAUL: There's only two uses for plutonium—in weapons and reactors, right? So if they're making reactors, why would they say it's medical? And if it's medical, why are they fooling around with plutonium? It doesn't make sense.

JENNY: Why would he invite you inside? It's crazy.

PAUL: So he's crazy. Look what he does for a living! He's hot for my mother. He figures I'm a dumb kid . . . plus which, he's got all these security clearances. I don't know what they are—Los Alamos, Livermore Labs, Oak Ridge. You know what they make at Oak Ridge? . . . Nuclear warheads!

After Paul shows Jenny a handful of five-leaf clovers, suggesting that the odds of this occurring naturally without chemical or nuclear mutation are more than a billion to one, Jenny demands that Paul tell the press, but Paul is dismissive of his girlfriend's suggestions: "It's a government lab, they're not going to let you in there. . . . What do you want to do, march on Washington?" This cynical comment demonstrates the teenager's contempt for both the mainstream media and peaceful protest as ineffective means to usurp the government and military-industrial complex.[21] However, Jenny is unrelenting in her disdain and challenges Paul's resigned complacency:

This isn't funny. Do you know what this is about? It's like, I don't know, when you read about Anne Frank, and you say to yourself, Jesus, why didn't they do something? The whole world is collapsing but they just sit around like, as usual. Maybe it will go away. But it *doesn't* go away. It gets *worse!* And nobody thinks about the future.

At this point Paul decides to take direct action, spurred on by his girlfriend's passionate evocation of genocide, apathy, and disavowal. After a lengthy series of vignettes depicting Paul studying publicly available nuclear implosion designs and easily acquiring the necessary technologies (including C4 plastic explosives) to make the device, he produces a fissionable metallic ball of plutonium from stolen laboratory gel and takes the unarmed device to New York. When the authorities discover the theft, Dr. Mathewson immediately suspects Paul and, uncannily prophetic of David Hahn's story, a nuclear search team locates traces of the radioactive material at a garage Paul had earlier rented. Initially, the military and FBI capture Paul and attempt to interrogate him, but a gang of science fair geeks help him escape with the bomb, as the national media portray Paul as a terrorist. Returning to Ithaca, he eventually negotiates with Dr. Mathewson, promising to hand over "the gadget" if the scientist signs a statement "about the lab—what it is, where it is, what happens inside—everything." Despite Mathewson's concerns over security clearances and prospects of jail for them both, Paul wins his concession. Meanwhile, Jenny uses her local grassroots community networking to spread the news about the lab and muster the locals into descending on the facility.

Surrounded by FBI snipers, Paul assembles the bomb, ready to detonate it, and ironically invokes the logic of deterrence and its binary stalemate in order to buy time. Mathewson finally persuades the teenager to hand over the device, but then surprisingly repeats the boy's earlier strategy by engaging in his own act of subversion, holding the facility hostage unless the boy is granted free passage. Once armed, however, the bomb's mechanism is tripped accidentally by an environmental surge and all present desperately try to prevent it from going critical. Paul, Dr. Mathewson, the military, and the FBI all work cooperatively to disarm the device with seconds to spare as a mass of local community activists, friends, and family swarm about at the facility gates and eventually gain entry, leaving the military to flee in helicopters. Improbably and unconvincingly, the scientists and soldiers abandon the laboratory, leaving its secrets and supplies of purified plutonium to "people power."

If the paradoxes of nuclear deterrence are presented through children developing their own weapons of mass destruction to demonstrate the secrecy and undemocratic activities of the military-industrial complex in *The Manhattan Project*, then a film released the same year, *Amazing Grace and Chuck*, promotes a pacifist alternative to individuals embracing these annihilating technologies and using them as instruments to force policy change.

Following an elementary school visit to a Montana ICBM silo, local schoolboy and promising Little League baseball pitcher, Chuck Murdock, questions a visiting congressman about why the missile crews are armed. In *WarGames* the opening sequence depicts the failure of a senior airman to follow orders and fire his missiles, despite the threat of deadly force from an adjacent officer. In *Amazing Grace and Chuck*, it is the mere concept of two men buried beneath blast-proof doors with handguns in charge of America's nuclear arsenal that disturbs the boy. Neither his father (an air force reserve fighter pilot) nor the congressman can explain to Chuck's satisfaction why such weapons and delivery systems exist.

So perturbed is Chuck by the visit and the implications of global cross-targeting with its associated megadeath that he withdraws from family and friends and suffers from vivid nuclear nightmares.[22] One weekend Chuck inexplicably refuses to play in a major ballgame. He explains to all concerned that he will not again play baseball until all the nuclear weapons are gone.

Chuck (Joshua Zuehlke) and Celtics star Amazing Grace Smith (Alex English) form an unexpected friendship in *Amazing Grace and Chuck* (1986) to promote world peace.

"I'm not sick. But I can't play because of nuclear weapons. It's my best thing and I have to give up something."

Chuck's story is treated disdainfully by the local newspaper, but the national press picks up on the quirky story. It is one which deeply affects an NBA basketball player, "Amazing Grace" Smith, who flies out to visit Chuck. So impressed by Chuck's resilience and strength of character in giving up his favorite thing, only to be pilloried by school friends, teachers, and community, the NBA star joins the boy, withdrawing from the league in order to move closer to Chuck's home town in solidarity.

Soon two of Amazing Grace's NFL buddies come to visit, and after meeting Chuck they also quit pro football mid-season. Like a contagion, sports stars all over the U.S. join the action, refusing to honor their contracts. Chuck's father battles with local contractors and his military peers, who argue that their livelihood is dependent on the current national security posture. So troubling is the protest movement that the president (Gregory Peck) visits Chuck and tries to persuade the boy to change his mind.[23] It's a telling exchange, with the elder statesman respectfully goading the child into abandoning his protest, suggesting Chuck's action (or inaction) will make it *harder* for bilateral arms negotiations to succeed between the superpowers.

But Chuck retains his "principles" and refuses to demur to the leader of the free world.

A mysterious and powerful industrialist, Mr. Jeffries, threatens Amazing Grace's manager, which ends in the basketball hero's murder after his plane is sabotaged. Devastated by the loss of his friend and the failure of the authorities to move on the arms issue, Chuck publicly announces to the assembled media:

> I had a friend. His name was Amazing Grace Smith. He was my best friend. I think he was the best basketball player that ever lived. All he wanted was for people to live, and now he's gone. He told me—and I've seen it—that there's death buried in the earth. Amazing said it would be a good thing if everybody stopped pretending the death wasn't there. If we stop playing, he said we could start playing when they took it away. And now he's gone, and the death is still there. . . . I don't want to talk any more.

With this he silently raises his left hand in salute and from that point refuses to speak. Like many *hibakusha* who fell victim to the atomic bombs at Hiroshima and Nagasaki, silence is a considered strategy that recognizes the failure of discourse to represent such issues and events.[24] Chuck's actions symbolically invoke what psychologists such as Robert Lifton and others have identified as "nuclearism"—denial, disavowal, and numbing—by repressing the consequences of imminent thermonuclear oblivion and maintaining "business as usual."[25]

At school the next day Chuck is berated and ostracized by his teacher, yet in solidarity at his treatment, the entire class leaves the room in silent protest to support Chuck's action. After the media reports on Chuck's protest, White House advisors describe the children's movement as global, similar to the conclusion of *The Space Children*, being repeated all over the world. The officials try various strategic spins to convince the president to intervene while expediently embracing Chuck's popularity. But the president adopts another course of action and secretly travels to Russia for a private summit with the Soviet premier. Together, they use the children's initiative to bypass their arms negotiators and draft a phased weapons reduction with "an immediate cut of fifteen per cent" over a "seven-year program to eliminate all nuclear weapons." The president soon greets Chuck, confident that his treaty will win over the boy. But the still silent and canny Chuck refuses to talk, his father suggesting to the president: "a lot can happen in seven years. You'll be out of office . . ."

Back in Washington, the despondent president is given devastating news:

WHITE HOUSE AIDE: Now the Joint Chiefs are telling us they can no longer guarantee a launch. The guys in the silo might shoot each other, or stick flowers in their guns. Every sign tells us that the Russians have the same problem. We have silent children around the world. Their parents are going on strike. Our allies, our enemies—all blaming us.

PRESIDENT: The people want their children back.

After a final emergency summit, the president once more visits Chuck and shows him a draft joint U.S.-Soviet declaration for the abolition of all nuclear weapons. Within a few months, before the world's media, the U.S. president, and the visiting Soviet premier, Chuck stands atop his local baseball mound, ready to pitch. He has won. In a fairy-tale ending, Chuck Murdock's nonviolent protest and personal abstinence (silence and sacrificing) bring about what 40 years of international diplomacy could not: the eradication of nuclear weapons from the planet.

In all of these films, the discursive power of persuasion by adults who argue for the continuance of genocidal weapons, deterrence, and mutual assured destruction for the benefit of national security and global peace is undermined by the impassivity, intransigence, direct action, or counterlogic of children who question the very assumptions that maintain such postures. More than 20 years prior to *Amazing Grace and Chuck*, *The Manhattan Project*, *Project X*, and *Terminator 2*, Jack Arnold's fantasy *The Space Children* advocated direct action by children in dismantling and destroying the accumulated nuclear arsenals worldwide. This was at the heart of the Cold War and amidst anxiety over atmospheric nuclear testing and the emerging space race. Thirty years on, toward the conclusion of the Cold War, *Amazing Grace and Chuck* clearly established personal, and then public, dissent by children with acts of individual and collective volition. There is no external (i.e., alien or superhero) catalyst for these determined acts of passive resistance and noncompliance. As such, these films provide a sobering and liberating representation of children and adolescents actively ensuring that a future exists for their generation. By exposing and resisting the complacency, denial, and fatalism identified as intrinsic to the military-industrial complex's cultural and economic hegemony, a small number of Cold War children's films provided alternative paradigms for action in and reflection on the atomic age.

NOTES

1. Most commentators place the end of the Cold War between 1989 and 1991. For an analysis of this theme in post–Cold War cinema, see Mick Broderick, "Is This the

Sum of All Fears? Nuclear Imagery in Post–Cold War Cinema," in *Atomic Culture*, ed. Scott C. Zeman and Michael A. Amundson (Boulder: University of Colorado Press, 2004), 125–147.

2. On the inuring effects of nuclear weapons, see Susan Sontag, "The Imagination of Disaster," in *Hal in the Classroom: Science Fiction Films*, ed. Ralph J. Amelio (Dayton, OH: Pflaum, 1974), first published in *Against Interpretation*, 1965.

3. Mick Broderick, *Nuclear Movies* (Jefferson, NC: McFarland, 1991).

4. From 1967 to the mid-1970s, various student-led U.S. counterculture groups such as the Yippies, the Weather Underground, and the Symbionese Liberation Army committed criminal acts (robberies, jailbreaks, murders) and sabotage in order to halt the American war effort.

5. On Agnew, see Henry Jenkins, "Introduction: Childhood Innocence and Other Modern Myths," in *The Children's Culture Reader*, ed. Henry Jenkins (New York: New York University Press, 1998), 21. On May 1, 1970, Nixon famously said of the antiwar student protesters, "You see these bums, you know, blowing up campuses, storming around about this issue." Three days later, national guardsmen shot dead four students at Kent State University, Ohio. See http://www.ichiban1.org/html/history/1969_1973 _vietnamization/13_sanctuary_counteroffensive_1970.htm.

6. Before Matthew Broderick came to typify the quintessential rebellious '80s teen in *Ferris Bueller's Day Off* (1986), the young actor prefigured this defining counter-establishment persona in *WarGames* as a video arcade champion with a wise-ass disrespect for educational authority.

7. Dyson is undoubtedly named after the gifted young Manhattan Project nuclear physicist Freeman J. Dyson, who, after working on many nuclear projects over decades, ultimately recanted his vocation after a "road to Damascus" conversion against weapons development and testing. See Brian Easlea, *Fathering the Unthinkable: Masculinity, Scientists and the Nuclear Arms Race* (London: Pluto Press, 1983), 155–163. Of course "Dyson" (die-son) also connotes the parental destruction of a generation.

8. In *It Came from Outer Space* (1953), a ridiculed amateur astronomer convinces a stranded party of shape-shifting extraterrestrials not to turn their nuclear energy device against the world. In *Tarantula* (1955), a demented atomic scientist uses human guinea pigs as subjects for his experimental radioactive growth serum, resulting in gigantism, with his laboratory animals and insects running amok. Similarly, *The Incredible Shrinking Man* (1957) shows how human exposure to radioactive fallout and pesticides can lead to a catastrophic biological change when the central protagonist exponentially diminishes in size to the point of subatomic transcendence. Another quasi-science fiction film, *The Mouse That Roared* (1959), comically depicts arms race politics and superpower brinkmanship with its zero-sum game of increasing weapons power to the point of continental destruction as a tiny European country captures the devastating Q-bomb. Hence, in the six years from 1953 to 1959, Arnold returned repeatedly to B-grade studio films that problematized atomic energy and its application as weaponry of mass destruction. Another key trope Arnold returns to is in providing empathy, if not sympathy, for the monstrous "Other," as aliens or inexplicable creatures.

9. Dwight D. Eisenhower, *Public Papers of the Presidents, 1960*, pp. 1035–1040, at http://coursesa.matrix.msu.edu/~hst306/documents/indust.html.

10. Easlea, 167.

11. Hugh Gusterson, *Nuclear Rites: A Weapons Laboratory at the End of the Cold War* (Berkeley: University of California Press, 1996), 98–97.

12. See Easlea, 167; and Gusterson, 97.

13. This line prefigures *Superman IV: The Quest for Peace* (1987), where Superman reproaches the Elders of Krypton, who urge him to leave Earth to its primitive wars and flee to other worlds, saying, "Sometimes there is more to learn from children than the wisest of men," before deciding unilaterally to disarm the world of nuclear weapons.

14. Gusterson, 49.

15. Ibid., 56.

16. On "sin," see Easlea, 157. For "denial," see Robert Lifton, "The Prevention of Nuclear War," in *The Psychology of Nuclear Conflict*, ed. Ian Fenton (London: Conventure Ltd., 1986), 77–89.

17. Gusterson, 57.

18. See Hugh Ruppersburg, "The Alien Messiah in Recent Science Fiction Films," *Journal of Popular Film and Television* (Winter 1987): 159–166.

19. See Ken Silverstein, "Tale of the Radioactive Boy Scout," *Harper's Magazine*, Nov. 1998, 17–22.

20. Ibid.

21. On nuclear cynicism see Spencer W. Weart, *Nuclear Fear: A History of Images* (Cambridge: Harvard University Press, 1988), 265.

22. On children's nuclear nightmares, see Henri Parens, "Psychoanalytic Explorations of the Impact of the Threat of Nuclear Disaster on the Young," in *Psychoanalysis and the Nuclear Threat: Clinical and Theoretical Studies*, ed. Howard B. Levine, Daniel Jacobs, and Lowell J. Rubin (Hillsdale, NJ: Analytic Press, 1988), 1–17; and John Mack, "The Threat of Nuclear War in Clinical Work: Dynamic and Theoretical Considerations," in Levine et al., 43–80.

23. The fictional character Chuck Murdock is in part inspired by the story of 10-year-old U.S. schoolgirl Samantha Smith, who wrote a letter to the new president of the Soviet Union, Yuri Andropov, in late 1982 expressing her concern over the prospect of nuclear war. In April 1983, Andropov replied and invited the girl to visit the Soviet Union. It was a propaganda coup for the USSR, and the embarrassed Reagan administration scrambled to maintain the moral high ground. An instant international celebrity, Smith died a couple of years later in a plane crash. Despite her successful interventions, Smith said: "Sometimes I still worry that the next day will be the last day of the Earth, but with more people thinking about the problems of the world, I hope that some day soon we will find the way to world peace. Maybe someone will show us the way."

24. *Hibakusha* author Sadako Kurihara explores the problematic of silence in "The Literature of Auschwitz and Hiroshima: Thoughts on Reading Lawrence Langer's *The Holocaust and the Literary Imagination*, Translated and Introduced by Richard H. Minear," *Holocaust and Genocide Studies* (Spring 1993): 91–96. As Peter Schwenger

has asked rhetorically in *Letter Bomb: Nuclear Holocaust and the Exploding Word* (Baltimore: Johns Hopkins University Press, 1992): "Has a language that is adequate to Hiroshima been found?" (13).

25. Robert Lifton and Richard Falk, *Indefensible Weapons: The Political and Psychological Case against Nuclearism* (New York: Basic Books, 1982), 103; and Weart, 256–266.

PART 2

POLITICS AND STYLE

CHAPTER 4

CHINESE "YOUTH PROBLEM" FILMS IN THE 1980S

The Apolitics of Rebellion

XUELIN ZHOU

In February 2004, Chun Shu, a Beijing teenage writer, appeared on the cover of *Time Asia*. Chun, along with another high school-dropout-turned-writer, Han Han, punk rocker Li Yang, and computer hacker Man Zhou, were described in *Time*'s lead article as the embodiment of disaffected Chinese youth and were labeled *linglei*, a word used to carry negative connotations of "a disreputable hooligan" but in the official dictionary defined as "an alternative lifestyle" (Feb. 2, 2004). While it is remarkable to see Chinese *linglei* youth in the cover story of a prestigious Western magazine, we should be aware that Chinese youth, whether they were *linglei* or mainstream, did not always occupy a large enough space in society for "an exercise in self-expression" or "a mannered display of self-conscious cool." Far from that, there had been extremely limited options for young people in terms of lifestyle. In the process of growing up, youngsters were invariably required to learn from their elders, with everything being arranged for them: lifestyle, leisure interests, behavior, and values. Throughout China's long history of social development, youth had remained largely in oblivion. One reason for this is that traditional Chinese culture tended to ignore this stage of human life by regarding aged people as children and young people as adults.[1] One advantage of this cultural outlook was to skip over the rebellious teenage period.

This "unity" of order regarding age patterns remained ultra-stable until the late twentieth century, when Chinese society was undergoing unprecedented tremendous change. Of all the strands that interweave to make up the period, the concept of autonomous youth is particularly conspicuous. The new generation thought and behaved in a different way from their elders.

They took a critical attitude toward social reality and formed their own subculture in antagonistic relationship to the establishment. This new cultural phenomenon shocked the more conservative sectors of society and has generated various interpretations, such as "juvenile confusion," "moral collapse," "spiritual vacuum," "political indifference," "generation gap," "post–Cultural Revolution syndrome," and so on.[2]

Globally, one problem in studying "youth culture" is how to define the term. "Youth" can be understood biologically, with reference to those who have not yet reached full sexual maturity, and to a period of radical transformation from dependent childhood to responsible adulthood. Sociologically, youth can be referred to as an intermediate phase of life in which the individual develops an autonomous personality and establishes a clear place in society. But a precise definition is never possible since youth, in terms of the conditions that determine the age of this stage, changes historically. Various components of social conditions, such as the development of education, employment patterns, disposable income, and even diet, all play a role in the shaping and reshaping of youth. Even the biological maturation of the body can occur earlier in some cultures than in some others. Despite the complexities associated with the word, though, "youth" retains its meaning in relative terms as a period "between," a period of transition, a period that is fluid and exploratory. Terms that crop up frequently in discussions of modern youth culture include the following: marginalized, flexible, transient, spontaneous, hedonistic, subversive, and nonconformist. This list of associations can be compared with a typical Western account such as Robert Chapman's 1953 essay "Fiction and the Social Pattern," which described the young adult years in New Zealand as a period of freedom between the controls of childhood and the conformity of adulthood:

> As soon as reaction becomes possible—when they start to earn between fifteen and eighteen . . . [their] reaction takes the form of a rebellion, which seems, but only seems, to be a rebellion against the pattern. Actually, to strike out against parental authority . . . to assert or experiment with other values and practices . . . this is the normal course over the ten years between seventeen and twenty-seven. A period of adolescent and post-adolescent *Sturm und Drang* seems to be an inherent part of cultural patterns deriving ultimately from the European complex; though not being a part, apparently, of all cultural patterns.[3]

For a long time, conventions in China regarded the ages 15 and 25 as the lower and upper thresholds marking the beginning and ending of youth, but

as recently as 1982 the duration was expanded to include the age group between 14 and 28.[4] This duration of 15 years can be further divided along the
lines of Margaret Mead's landmark *Culture and Commitment*, which speaks
of three different cultural styles: the pre-youth period (14–17), the co-youth
period (18–22), and the post-youth period (23–28).[5] Though the ages of the
young central characters in the films I shall be examining are never clearly
revealed, their background and experience as shown in the movies suggest
that they are living on the borderline of the latter two periods.

Film both reflects and helps to reshape society. In the late 1980s, China
saw the production of a multitude of "youth problem" films, such as *Sunshine and Showers* (1987), *Coffee with Sugar* (1987), *Samsara* (1988), *Masters
of Mischief* (1988), *Rock Kids* (1988), *Out of Breath* (1988), *Obsession* (1988),
Half Flame, Half Brine (1988), and *Black Snow* (1989).[6] Previously, little effort
had been made in Chinese cinema to explore in detail the lifestyle, emotions, and attitudes of these freewheeling young men and young women.
In these films, conventional heroes—workers, peasants, and People's Liberation Army soldiers—were replaced by angry and alienated youth, who
formed a new type of screen hero and emerged as a new déclassé stratum of
youth in contemporary China. The characteristics of these "new heroes" are
summarized by a veteran Chinese film critic as follows: First, they have a
low educational level. Because they passed their school years during the Cultural Revolution, when little schooling was available, they display an anti-
intellectual tendency. Their cultural inferiority complex manifests itself as
mockery and deflation of intellectuals (whether university students, writers,
or professors). Second, they either have no regular job or give up a profession to make their fortune as wheelers and dealers. Third, they are ultra-
hedonistic, adopting an irresponsible attitude toward life and tending to see
it as a mere game. Lastly, they disdain conventional moral criteria and social norms. They indulge in promiscuous sex, make money unscrupulously,
do whatever they want to do, defy the law, and behave like delinquents.[7]

In other words, the young people to whom critics like Shao Mujun allude
lived on the periphery of society, having neither respected social status nor
lofty ideals. (And they did not have aspirations to these things themselves.)
Coming from the chaotic years of the Cultural Revolution, they despised the
existing social order and orthodox morality. Their emergence on the silver
screen was not only indicative of a transforming society but also suggested
the coming of a "beat generation" in Chinese film. In many aspects, these
youth films provide a wealth of substantive images of socially and culturally
marginalized youngsters. The underlying argument of the present chapter
is that the emergence of these "youth problem" films, as an indication of a

Samsara (1988) examines the changing political and moral conditions for young people in China, such as Shi Ba (Lei Han) and Yu Jing (Tan Xiaoyan).

burgeoning youth culture, provides a touchstone of the tremendous changes occurring in China since the late 1970s.

This essay looks at Chinese youth's deviations from conventional values in the 1980s with particular reference to two "youth problem" films, *Masters of Mischief* and *Samsara*. I place their "rebellion" under scrutiny on two levels—domestic and social. But I conclude by arguing that the "rebellion" represented in these "youth problem" films is more of style than content in a progressively commercialized society.

Both *Masters of Mischief* and *Samsara* were based on the works of a Beijing popular writer, Wang Shuo.[8] *Masters of Mischief* was about the rise and fall of a Three-T Company (Trouble-shooting, Tedium-relieving, and Taking the blame)[9] set up by three unemployed youths. At first sight the company's name and the film's title may seem to contradict each other, as what the three T's refer to does not give the impression that these young men are "masters of mischief." But this ambiguity is soon removed as the story develops. A young doctor is too busy with his patients to date his girlfriend, so he asks the company to arrange a stand-in for him. A young self-proclaimed writer is worried because he has never won any literary award, so he turns to the company. The latter subsequently stages a fake (Three-T) literary award ceremony for him. A young wife is feeling depressed but has difficulty in getting hold of her husband as an outlet for her anger. In this case, the company sends a staff member to take the blame. A stout middle-aged man approaches them for help because all his life he "has never been able to do what he wants." He comes to the company with the hope that he can have a chance to slap Yu Guan, the company's mastermind, "two times, just two times!" After a series of such seemingly ridiculous events, the company is forced to close down because a customer who has employed them to look after his bedridden mother brings a suit against them for negligence. The film ends with an exaggerated mile-long queue of people outside the closed-down company's gate, all waiting their turn to be served.

Paul Clark succinctly sums up the storyline of *Samsara* as follows:

> The chief protagonist in *Samsara* . . . lives without a family: his parents, high-ranking cadres, have died. Shi Ba makes a living in the private sector greatly expanded by Deng Xiaoping's economic reforms of the 1980s. Like other entrepreneurs with social and political connections, Shi Ba dabbles also in some illegal business. Success brings threats of blackmail. Resistance to the demands brings a severe beating. From then on Shi Ba drifts. Refusing to join a friend in blackmailing foreigners, he marries Yu Jing. This relationship proves a disaster. One evening, in a macho act, Shi Ba throws himself off a balcony.[10]

Historically, "home" in the Chinese cinema had been dominated by a morally perfect father figure. A source of wisdom, the father functioned as an absolute authority "to preserve order and maintain structure."[11] His position was seldom, if ever, challenged. This ethical code guiding the power relationship between senior and young generations had cultural and historical roots. An important concept in the traditional Chinese culture was that of filial piety [*xiao*], which for hundreds of years had been a yardstick of morality by which the domestic power relationship was judged. In the early years of Confucianism, the concept of filial piety merely carried the connotations of innocent and sincere relations between father and children. This subtext was in subsequent dynasties distorted by a strong sense of hierarchy. According to an updated interpretation and requirement of the code, a son should completely obey his father. The position of a child within the domestic space was low—even his marriage was arranged by the elders of the family. Gradually, this ethical code, coupled with that of loyalty [*zhong*], became important principles of running a family as well as governing the state. By modern times, "filial piety" was synonymous with "absolute subordination" on both domestic and social levels.

Naturally, the "rebellion" initiated by the Chinese angry young men in the 1980s started from "home." In the immediate years following the Cultural Revolution, as Li Yiming observes, "both the critiquing of totalitarian politics and the longing for liberal politics were associated with a political mythology as symbolised by 'father.' He was either described as a totalitarian authority or portrayed as a liberal-minded leader."[12] Some early Chinese films of the New Era began to attack the deified representation of "father."[13] On the level of everyday practice, members of a younger generation had finally learned to use the domestic sphere as a space to express their discontent in the 1980s. The extraordinary authority of the father began to teeter, although he was unwilling to "step down from the stage of history." One task of these youth problem films was therefore to delineate the conflicts and contradictions arising from the increasingly large gap between members of young and old generations.

Shi Ba in *Samsara* was a typical "new hero," preferring an unfettered and unrestrained life. Believing himself a "free man," he did not like others, not even his mother, to interfere with his private life. On one occasion, he told his girlfriend what he thought of his deceased mother:

> My mum was a mother with Chinese characteristics. She always hoped that I could live the same life as everyone else. She believed it her responsibility to ensure me to live as meaningfully and significantly as she did. When others joined the army, she wanted me to follow suit. When the fashion changed to getting an education at college, once again, she wanted me to be among them. She always hoped I should join the Communist Party and marry another Party member. She spent her whole life arranging things for me, but she never bothered to ask me what I wanted to do myself. When I quit my job in extreme depression, she was so irritated that she went to join my father in the netherworld.

Yu Guang in *Masters of Mischief* was the only young adult with a living father in these youth problem films. A revolutionary veteran, Yu's father reprimanded his son for having set up a Three-T company, which, in his eyes, was absolute nonsense. What the three youngsters did was ludicrous to him —"If people like you are needed for troubleshooting for the public, why do we still need the Communist Party?" On one occasion (the only occasion) in the film, the father and the son have a face-to-face encounter, which is paradigmatic in its tit-for-tat conflicts between the junior and the senior, each of whom sees the world in his own way. This particular scene sheds much light on the generation gulf in a society experiencing profound changes in all aspects.

The scene opens with Yu's return "home." Earlier that day, Yu's father had been to the Three-T Company, arguing with a staff member there and urging his son to go back home, since he had not seen Yu "for a very long time." Yu opened the door only to find that his old man was practicing *qigong* by standing on his head. Later in the scene, when the father, in an attempt to understand his son's thoughts, asks, "What on earth have you been doing these days?" the latter only mimics the inquirer's head-standing behavior. This physical misplacement (with one character standing on his head while the other is talking) suggests that neither can listen to, not to mention accept, what the other has to say, stressing a lack of communication and comprehension between the father and the son. The old man's revolutionary belief and morality prove to be mere clichés for the young man to laugh at. For example, the father exposes his heart by saying, "You don't know how much I worry about you. You're a grown-up man now. Why do you still fool around everyday? You should think about your future and see how you can do something meaningful for the people and country." But his sincere words and earnest advice only became a target of ridicule, and the son asks in retort,

What on earth do you want me to say? Would you be happy if I called myself a bastard, a parasite? What the hell have I done to make you so unhappy? I didn't murder anyone, or set fire to any house. Neither did I go to the street to demonstrate. I've always behaved myself. Have I bothered anyone? I know you want me to look forward and determined, pushing out my shoulders and holding up my head with pride. I'd be a good boy in your eyes then. But isn't that kind of life a bore! All in all, I guess I'm a bit vulgar . . .

Yu's evaluation of his own way of doing things ("I'm a bit vulgar . . .") is a far cry from what his "fathers" expected him and his generation to be ("successors of revolutionary courses"). On the other hand, and on a social level, Yu's self-description as "a bit vulgar" demonstrates the surfacing of a "plebeian culture" [*shimin wenhua*] in a society that found itself being increasingly driven by consumerism. The 1980s to Chinese youth were a time when all sorts of ideas were mixed together, a time when the boundary between elite culture and mass/popular culture blurred. All that had been established was being challenged and questioned. While old rules were being destroyed, new ones were not yet being established. This sense of nihilism and hedonism is succinctly captured in the style of Wang Shuo–esque deconstruction in a scene from *Masters of Mischief*.[14]

The scene depicts a fashion show, with a huge T-shaped stage, across which a parade of cat-walking models represent main figures of the most significant social and political events in twentieth-century China. Here we see May Fourth students, warlords of the Republican period, old-Shanghai prostitutes, peasants, landlords, soldiers of the People's Liberation Army (PLA), Kuomintang generals (KMT), revolutionary workers, Cultural Revolution Red Guards, intellectuals, bikini-clad bodybuilders, rock 'n' roll kids, plus emperors and ministers from traditional operas. Initially, these people, belonging to different ideologies and classes, frown and scowl at each other. But when the rhythm of the background music changes to disco (an imported Western cultural form and a symbol of modernity and the open-door policy), headshaking turns into handshaking. The models dance to the fast beat, shoulder to shoulder, hand in hand, all in a sign of rapprochement. A traffic policeman stands among them and tries desperately to maintain order, but seems insignificant and helpless. The picture presented here is reminiscent of that delineated in the famed opening paragraph of Charles Dickens' *Tale of Two Cities*.

Standing at a crossroads and being devoid of a destination, Chinese youngsters would express their discontent and frustration by parodying what their elders had valued. Further, the essence of "plebeian culture" is badinage, parody, and earthiness. What received the ridicule and parody in these youth problem films covers a large spectrum: from education to literature, from art to fashion design, from Communist leadership to orthodox Marxism, from commercialism to modernism. One such "rebel" scene is from *Samsara*, in which a stone-faced PLA soldier guarding the national flag on Tiananmen Square is ridiculed by Shi Ba and his peers as a robot. The significance of the scene lies in its style and setting. In terms of style, the construction of the scene relies on the frequent use of POV shots and shot/reverse-shots, which presents a clear and sharp contrast between two different value systems: individualism and collectivism. Since 1949, individualism had been condemned as a decadent bourgeois ideology. Individual aspirations were given very little, if any, public space in the socialist discourse. But this ideology was reexamined (and reevaluated) in films such as *Samsara*.[15] In terms of mise-en-scène, Tiananmen Square is situated at the heart of Beijing, China's political, economic, and cultural center. No other place in China can provide Chinese youth with a more appropriate space to express their discontent and rebel against the establishment.

Despite the film's ridicule, parody, and even rebellion, *Samsara* did not portray Shi Ba's mocking of the established system as a deliberate scheme. Shi's act (of encouraging two girls to tease the guard) was, to borrow George Melly's words on the British "angry young men" movement in the 1960s, more "an immediate and spontaneous reaction to life at any given moment."[16] Like his *linglei* peers, Shi did not intend to transform the current social order or to propose a new one. This lack of political subversion can be understood on three levels. First, the masses never became an independent political power in the long social history of China. "Plebeian politics," either as a concept or in substance, never existed in Chinese discourse. The young rebels in films (as in society) were by no means unified but acted like "a plate of loose sand." Second, the established structure was so powerful that the masses could only "rebel" in the crevices of society. When they had a face-to-face confrontation with authority, they would withdraw. For example, in *Masters of Mischief*, Yu Guang was late for a date with a girl on Chang'an Boulevard. He tried to take a shortcut by leaping over the cycle railing (a defiant act) but was promptly spotted and stopped by a traffic policeman (a symbol of authority). To escape a fine (punishment from the authority), Yu had to pretend that he had just escaped from a lunatic asylum (marginalized sector of society). As in *Samsara*, the two girls were mocking the guard only within a maze of traffic railings (rules and regulations of mainstream society). Third, such a lack of political subversion was in the nature of the youth subculture itself. When youth rebelled against the dominant culture, they were at the same time seeking "a compromise solution" and were caught "between two contradictory needs: the need to create and express *autonomy and difference* from parents . . . and the need to maintain . . . the *parental identifications* which support them."[17] In order to "create and express *autonomy and difference* from parents," young people might stay uncommitted, refuse to decide on a formal career, and not give themselves fixed future goals to pursue,[18] but they would do little more than that.

Not surprisingly, these youth problem films managed to escape the censors' sharp scissors. In the eyes of the censors, these movies would not have much negative influence on audiences in political terms. Their significance, to quote Shao Mujun, lay more in the fact that they could "satisfy the audience's desire to explore the political and sexual taboos on the one hand, but not offend authority at the same time. They reflect social reality, but do not totally focus on the dark side."[19] Another Beijing-based film critic, Hu Ke, similarly observes: "*Masters of Mischief* was just like a standard product of the Three-T Company. It can relieve tedium for the audience and bring them cheerful laughter. In so doing, suppression caused by political and sexual taboos gets relieved to a certain extent. In the process, each audience member finds a socially harmless outlet to let off his unconscious aggressiveness and sexual desires."[20]

In a society rapidly moving toward consumerism, even the weak elements of political subversion expressed through youth in these films would soon dissolve. As a matter of fact, the trend was already visible in these films. Consider the opening sequence of *Masters of Mischief*, a collage of scenes around Tiananmen Square, an explosive juxtaposition of a variety of images which subtly capture the mood of an urban panorama and present a gallery of images picked at random from a rapidly expanding metropolis: bustling Chang'an Boulevard flanked by a concrete forest of modern-style buildings (some still under construction with cranes towering to the sky); vehicle flows in the middle of pedestrians and hordes of bicyclists; a floating population from rural districts mingling with urban residents and foreign tourists; the Five-Starred flags flying alongside the Union Jacks and the Stars and Stripes; voices through loudspeakers urging passers-by to view a *kung fu* film starring Jet Li and to visit Chairman Mao's mausoleum; instances of body piercing; rock 'n' roll dancers; sarcastic slogans on the T-shirts of punk youth. This sense of contemporaneity is emphasized by sounds and voices from the boulevard, the marketplace, and Tiananmen Square.

These images, including the sound track, displaced the conventional connotations of "square" (associated with the memory of revolution and the political movements of different historical eras) with apolitical and commercial elements. In fact, by the mid-1990s, the revolutionary connotations of "Tiananmen Square" had disappeared completely and "square" itself had been replaced by *plaza* (shopping mall or commercial shopping center).[21]

Often the question was asked: "What is left after [the urban hooligans] discard nobility, negate faith, mock ideals, and destroy social order and morality principles?"[22] These young urbanities would certainly not "idle away" their youth. While the protagonists of these youth problem films were in a vital sense refusing to conform to the established regulations of "adult society," they would find it hard resisting the temptations from a newly emerged consumer society in an increasingly globalized context. From this perspective, the angry and alienated youngsters portrayed in the 1980s youth problem films were the forerunners of the *linglei* youth covered by *Time* magazine in the new millennium.

NOTES

1. See Sun Lung-kee, *Zhongguo wenhua de "shengceng jiegou"* [The "Deep Structure" of Chinese Culture] (Hong Kong: Jixianshe, 1983), 394.
2. See Zhao Zixiang et al., "Qingnian wenhua yu shehui bianqian" [Youth Culture and Social Changes], in *Shehui kexue zhanxian* [Social Science Front], no. 4 (1988): 110.
3. Robert Chapman, "Fiction and the Social Pattern," in *Essays on New Zealand Literature*, ed. Wystan Curnow (Auckland: Heinemann Educational Books, 1973), 86.

4. This revision was proposed in the Eleventh National Congress of the Chinese Communist Youth League as the official age range for Chinese youth to join the organization; it can thus be regarded as the official duration of youth in contemporary China.

5. Margaret Mead, *Culture and Commitment: The New Relationships between the Generations in the 1970s* (New York: Columbia University Press, 1978), 13.

6. The term "youth problem" comes from the perspective of mainstream society. Discontented youth departing from established values tend to be regarded as causing problems for parents, neighbors, and officials. However, the use of the term in this essay does not indicate any value judgment on my part. Rather, it is a reference to the huge literature around this term (or set of issues) in the West since the 1950s, as well as in China today.

7. See Shao Mujun, "Why Did a Wang Shuo Cinema Craze Occur," *China Screen*, no. 4 (1989): 29.

8. For more about Wang Shuo and his popular writing on *liumang* [hooligans], see Geremie Barmé, *In the Red: On Contemporary Chinese Culture* (New York: Columbia University Press, 1999), 62–98.

9. This translation of the "Three T Company" [*santi gongsi*] is from Jing Wang, *High Culture Fever: Politics, Aesthetics, and Ideology in Deng's China* (Berkeley: University of California Press, 1996), 274.

10. Paul Clark, "Chinese Cinema in 1989," in *The Ninth Hawai'i International Film Festival* (Honolulu: East-West Centre, 1989), 40.

11. Li Yiming, "Shifu xingwei zhihou—Dangdai dianying zhong de jiating: Queshi yu buchang" [After Father Was Beheaded—Family in Contemporary Cinema: Absence and Compensation], *Dianying yishu* [Film Art], no. 6 (1989): 10.

12. Ibid.

13. A ready example was Chen Kaige's *Yellow Earth*. Its alternative and unconventional portrayal of the "father" generated hot debate.

14. The scene was not in the original novella but was added to the film "in order to convey social information, enlarge its influence and strengthen its power to criticize society." See Mi Jiashan, "Discussing *The Troubleshooters*," *Chinese Education and Society* 31, no. 1 (Jan./Feb. 1998): 10.

15. The director of *Samsara* was apparently not the only Chinese filmmaker to explore the subject. Chen Kaige, for example, also treated the issue—more thoroughly—in his 1985 film *The Big Parade*. For a substantial analysis of the relationship between individualism and collectivism explored in the film, see Zhang Jiaxuan, "Review of *The Big Parade*," *Film Quarterly* 43, no. 1 (Fall 1989): 57–59.

16. George Melly, *Revolt into Style: The Pop Arts in the '50s and '60s* (Oxford: Oxford University Press, 1970), 9.

17. Stanley Cohen, *Folk Devils and Moral Panics: The Creation of the Mods and Rockers* (St. Albans, England: Paladin, 1973), 26.

18. Charles A. Reich, *The Greening of America* (New York: Random House, 1970), 362.

19. Quoted in Wang Yunzhen, "Fang Mi Jiashan tan *Wan Zhu*" [Interviewing Mi Jiashan and Chatting about *Masters of Mischief*], *Dianying yishu* [Film Art], no. 5 (1989): 3.

20. Ibid., 8.

21. For a stimulating description and interpretation of the transforming process from *guangchang* [square] to *shichang* [market], see Dai Jinhua, "Invisible Writing: The Politics of Chinese Mass Culture in the 1990s," *Modern Chinese Literature and Culture* 11, no. 1 (Spring 1999): especially 31–35.

22. Yan Jingming, "Wanzhu yu dushi de chongtu: Wang Shuo xiaoshuo de jiazhi xuanze" [The Masters of Mischief and Their Conflicts with the City: The Choice of Values in Wang Shuo's Writings], *Wenxue pinglun* [Literature Criticism], no. 6 (1989): 90.

CHAPTER 5

THE AGE OF TRANSITION

Angels and Blockers in Recent Eastern and Central European Films

ANIKÓ IMRE

Anyone even vaguely familiar with Eastern and Central European films will notice their preoccupation with children and teens. Yet, "youth film," in the sense of a genre of films that *address* young people, is at best an emerging concept in postsocialist cultures. Similar to the way in which Hollywood's teen representations have changed over the decades along with the political climate,[1] adolescents have served as indispensable representational devices for Hungarian, Slovak, or Polish filmmakers engaged in processing the "moral panics" of their respective times. During socialism, child and teen characters, most often portrayed in dysfunctional school and home settings, where they were invariably humiliated and subjected to physical and psychological abuse, served as symbolic screens onto which the culture could allegorically project its own schizophrenic state—the psychological division between a sense of collective, national maturity derived from a Eurocentric cultural heritage, and the vulnerable, childlike condition to which Soviet colonization and socialist totalitarianism reduced national citizens.

The most common narrative pattern of such allegorical films is the boys' bonding and coming-of-age story. Protagonists of these films are in search of female care and male role models, a quest not lacking in uplifting moments but invariably doomed to fail in an era when idealistic energies bounce back from the glass ceiling of political control. Géza Radványi's *Valahol Európában* (*Somewhere in Europe*, 1947) or Miklós Jancsó's *A harangok Rómába mentek* (*The Bells Have Gone to Rome*, 1958), set during and immediately following World War II, both tell stories about rebellious boy groups. In Radványi's highly symbolic film, a group of orphaned and stranded "European" children turn to violence and crime to survive. Jancsó's teen boys face the ethical dilemma of whether they should join the war effort or not. Idealistic, they escape to an island that is both real and symbolic, where they form their own republic.

These plots are similar to that of Ferenc Molnár's turn-of-the-century novel *A Pál utcai fiúk* (*The Pál Street Boys*), considered a national classic and mandatory reading for all Hungarian students. The novel, as well as Zoltán Fábri's eponymous film adaptation (1969), depicts a war over a vacant lot— an urban island—between two gangs of teen boys.[2] The fight takes the life of the weakest link, the little Nemecsek. Melodrama shifts to tragedy when it turns out that the "island" will be taken away from the boys so it can be developed. Ultimately, this film is not so much an inquiry about adolescence as it is a parable about the senselessness of war. Jirí Menzel's well-known *Ostre stedované vlaky* (*Closely Watched Trains*, 1966) also has literary origins: it was adapted to the screen by Bohumil Hrabal from his own novel. While its bittersweet plot revolves around a bumbling teenage boy's sexual experiences under the guidance of a womanizing stationmaster, its allegorical concern, once again, is with the moral choices a man should make during wartime, under foreign military occupation. All of these films process the impossible ethical dilemmas presented to men as universal—ungendered human choices one has to make in situations when youthful idealism pushes against the political constraints of the historical moment. None of these films offer explicit critical commentary about the *gendered* nature of warfare and of its incentive, territorial nationalism.

The postwar East and Central European generation's decisive and unifying experiences were Nazism and the Holocaust, the unspeakable destruction of the war, and the subsequent socialist regime, with its own lasting moments of national trauma. However, the experience of children who were born or came to critical consciousness after the end of the Cold War—today's East and Central European teenagers—is crucially different from that of their parents and grandparents. It is safe to speculate that the generational gap that separates baby boomers in the U.S. from their children, variously nicknamed "screenagers," "slackers," or "Generation X,"[3] is not nearly as profound as that between parents who grew up in national isolation, under travel restrictions, centralized governments, and state-controlled media, in forced economic equality assured by relative poverty, and without democratic elections, and their children, who are growing up in a world where the very term "Eastern Europe" is becoming obsolete. This new world is characterized by a fast-growing divide between the rich and the poor, quickly rendering socialism a tourist attraction or nostalgic memory, yielding, somewhat reluctantly, to the multimedia seductions of postmodern consumer capitalism. At the same time, it is also a more colorful world than it used to be, bearing the impact of recent immigration flows and revitalized tourism, offering more choices not only when it comes to television channels but also in matters of identity politics.

East and Central European film industries, scrambling to get film production back on track after the near-total dissolution of the funding, distribution, and exhibition structure of national cinemas, and facing the new challenges of for-profit filmmaking on a national and international scale, went through their own "awkward age" in the 1990s. While filmmakers and the industry were busy trying to update their own values and redefine their national identities, transnational media swooped in with attractively packaged and easily adaptable products to fulfill and multiply teenage desires. The overwhelming popularity of Hollywood-made or inspired youth films, commercial television programs, video games, print magazines, and fan sites in the postsocialist region makes it evident that the products of global media have had much better success at tapping into teen fantasies and wallets than have national cinemas. Commercial television channels in native languages are the cinema's main competitors for youth viewership, churning out banal but widely popular soap operas, reality shows, talk shows, and game shows licensed and adapted from globally successful models.[4]

East and Central European cinemas have also made an inevitable turn toward the commercial, following tried-and-true recipes of genre films. While some of the comedies, romances, and occasional action-adventure flicks that have cropped up have achieved relative popularity, they still have difficulties resonating with the unique generational sensibilities of postsocialist screenagers. Given the lack of an indigenous youth film genre, then, I will offer a rudimentary typology of recent films that center on teen characters. My intention is twofold: to spark interest in further, interdisciplinary research on postsocialist youth media cultures and to contribute to a global understanding of the youth film genre, for which existing descriptions, based primarily on Hollywood products and American consumers, are inadequate.

ANGELS

In order to characterize a prominent group of East and Central European films about adolescents, I am borrowing the image of angels from "Gangsters and Angels," the Hungarian critic Sándor Turcsányi's article about Árpád Sopsits' film *Torzók* (*Abandoned*, 2001). Turcsányi argues that representations of innocent, ethereal, vulnerable, often orphaned[5] young people are central to understanding Hungarian—and, by extension, East and Central

European—cinemas and cultures. *Torzók* exemplifies the continuity that such real-symbolic adolescent figures, predominantly boys, have created between socialist and postsocialist teen representations. It is an autobiographical film admittedly made to process the director's own traumatic memories of growing up in the 1960s in an institution of parentless boys, thrown at the mercy of sadistic teachers.[6] The angel motif comes from the protagonist teen boy's somewhat sentimentally presented dreams, in which he flies off on angel wings to transcend his suffocating environment in search of a utopian family.

While there is no question about the truthfulness of the film's sordid depiction of an era, the allegorical relevance of the film remains attached to the past and is thus somewhat self-serving. It is also hard to look past the sense of personal psychological urgency that underlies the film: the boy protagonist is less important than the remembering filmmaker. The film's grim dialectic is a little outdated. The parallel between the prison-school and the outside world of totalitarianism is specific to a bygone historical era. The film's black-and-white aesthetic, with its eternal winter outside and dark rooms inside, the barred windows, the stereotypical opposition of cruel but victimized and good but suicidal teachers, its sentimental lyricism coupled with the relentlessly depressing storyline, can hardly count on audience success.

This is a film that has more in common with fin-de-siècle literary models of symbolically and also often literally imprisoned boy groups than with young people in the present.[7] However, it also provides a platform for reassessing certain suppressed aspects of earlier representations of boys; most important, its commentary about the continuity between male homosociality and homosexuality is more explicit than that of earlier models. The physical intimacy that the two main characters experience in the institution becomes the ground for unbreakable emotional bonds against the cruelty of the outside world. This bond is vital for the boys' survival in the conspicuous absence of female nurturing. The one female character, Marika, is more of an object of titillation than a source of comfort, to be peeped at while she is bathing.

Male intimacy and missing or uncaring mothers become increasingly conspicuous features in "boy films" of the 1980s and 1990s. In István Szabó's *Colonel Redl* (1984), based on John Osborne's play *A Patriot for Me*, as well as on the life of the actual, historical Alfred Redl, and set during the last years of the Austro-Hungarian Monarchy, the young Redl is sent to military school by his mother. As his family disappears from his purview for good, the young cadet falls in love with his handsome upper-class schoolmate—a lifelong love that is explicitly identified as homosexual only just before he dies. Sándor Pál's *Herkulesfürdői emlék* (*A Strange Masquerade*, 1976), another film set in the aftermath of World War I, features an angelic young soldier who cross-dresses as a female nurse in order to hide in a sanatorium from political authorities. While the film's allegorical concern is evident in the way in which its poetic cinematography depicts fear and claustrophobia, it has now become not only possible but also imperative to discuss how gender subversion and the suggestion of homosexuality are employed as tools to convey political subversion.

Iskolakerülök (*Truants*, 1989) centers on yet another group of boarding school boys. Their heroic geography teacher, played by popular Hungarian actor Károly Eperjes, accomplishes an impossible task: besides teaching his subject, he also needs to save a student from suicide, consistently reject the advances of a sex-hungry female colleague, and undo the work of a narcissistic mother unfit for parenting. This scenario is so unrealistic within a profoundly patriarchal society such as Hungary that the misogyny of the representation is almost too easy a target. One is prompted to search for more systemic reasons for such an intense need to assert masculine power and degrade femininities deemed threatening. The problematics of Sergei Bodrov's *S.E.R.* (*Freedom Is Paradise*, 1989), released in the same year, is remarkably similar: 13-year-old Sasha, whose mother died early and whose father is in jail, repeatedly escapes from the prison-like reformatory where he lives in order to search for his father. After several such attempts and many adventures, he manages to locate his father; the film ends on a note of hope inspired by the father-son reunification. *The Witman Boys* (1997) goes even further in blaming bad women for producing a miserable generation (of boys). Another literary adaptation, based on the fiction of fin-de-siècle modernist writer Géza Csáth, the film is a stylized, bleak rendition of the visceral Freudian adventures of two teenage brothers. After their father dies, their mother's hatred causes the boys to vent their frustration by torturing animals and indulging their growing interest in sexuality. A prostitute's warm embrace welcomes them to sexual bliss, but her love is costly. They murder their mother to get her jewelry and to secure for themselves a kinder mother.

There is a lighter, less tragic trend within the Eastern and Central European boys' coming-of-age group of films. The social symbolism of individual stories and the parallel between psychological and social upheaval are still on the surface, but the tone is bittersweet and the edge of tragedy is softened by humor. Emir Kusturica's early film, *Do You Remember Dolly Bell?* (1981) evokes nostalgia by its very title. The film is about Dino, a teenage boy, who lives in a household of brothers dominated by a tyrannical father. Dino becomes entangled in the world of petty crime and blackmailed into hiding a young prostitute, "Dolly Bell," in the family's attic. Dino and the girl fall in love and eventually stand up to her pimp in a romantically gratifying turn. The film celebrates, or retroactively constructs, an era of optimism and courage, when there were women to be saved from dumb criminals. The background is a nostalgic image of 1960s Sarajevo, remembered as a time when socialism was still in its full idealistic swing, and when Sarajevo was itself a swinging town, with all ears tuned in to Italian rock 'n' roll.

Obecná skola (*The Elementary School*, 1991), the Czech Jan Sverák's preparation for the Oscar-winner *Kolya* (1996), takes us back to immediate postwar times and to the school setting, but the theme and mood are updated to suit more contemporary, nostalgic viewer expectations. The war is already a sepia-tinted memory evident only in ruined buildings in the background and teenage boys' war games. In fact, the film opens with a visual trick that blurs the distinction between real war and boys' games by showing us documentary footage of battle, which turns out to be the boys' playful fantasy images. But the film is less interested in adolescent subjectivities than in the figure of the new teacher, the intimidating but enchanting war hero, Igor Hnizdo. Hnizdo arrives with a slightly questionable Partisan history and an irrepressible weakness for women. The boys, who have already destroyed the weak nerves of their female teacher, are impressed by Hnizdo's military garb, real pistol, and tough manners. However, he evolves into a true role model only after he reveals an artist under the uniform, whose real tools are his musical instruments and stories about the Czech national hero Jan Hus. The director's real concern seems to be with salvaging this Byronic East European artist-hero and his masculine ethos as a model for a new generation, recreated through the admiring eyes of adolescent followers.

Recent Hungarian variations on this theme are similarly invested in sustaining the bohemian-Byronic role model, whose very validity is thrown into question by the desperation with which he is being reinvented. In Róbert Koltai's popular films of the '90s, *Sose halunk meg* (*We Never Die*, 1993) and *Ámbár tanár úr* (*Teacher Ámbár*, 1998), adolescent boys are learning how to be men from the invaluable lessons that only likable and poetically inclined scoundrels of a previous generation can impart to them. While the earlier film rides the wave of postsocialist optimism and resurgent nationalism to popularity, the later one is bogged down by its own skepticism and a contrived romantic subplot between the lustful middle-aged teacher and a female student.

There are some crucial aesthetic differences between tragic-somber and comic-nostalgic films about teen boy-angels. The latter group of films, with its less demanding symbolic agenda, less realistically remembered historical memories, and more emphasis on the titillating sexual aspects of the teen-age transition, has proven to have much greater audience appeal. At the same time, the two groups embody different approaches to the same crucial problem: the pressure to redefine masculinities amidst the processes of the East and Central European transitions from state socialism to global capitalism. Both groups of films are eager to disavow their underlying concern with representing masculinity by distancing their plots from the ongoing gendered crisis of nationalism. Makers of "tragic boyhood" films tend to draw on literary models in order to universalize the boy's psychological transformation into a man. They evoke the allegorical monster of communism in order to nostalgically reclaim the public spheres of national politics and art as inherently masculine islands in the rising, emasculating sea of global consumerism. "Boyhood lite" films of the second group, while they are also invested in evoking sympathy for lovable, almost-extinct masculinities, take this unspoken mission less seriously. That is precisely why they are more effective at reaching entertainment-deprived East European audiences.

Neither group has a particular interest in addressing teen audiences. What is really at stake in both kinds of scenarios is not the desires of today's boys but the losses of yesterday's men: teachers and fathers who are struggling with their own coming-of-(middle-)age. Taken as a group, one can read these films as their makers' efforts to reconcile the contradiction between their own absent or inefficient postwar fathers and the inordinate public importance afforded to men and masculinity within Eastern and Central European nations. Their ultimate goal of revisiting masculinity in its protean, adolescent form is to redeem their own past and assert their own continued importance in a radically different present and future. Whether they celebrate the womanizing wisdom of middle-aged clowns or wallow in the self-pity of the national intellectual dethroned by the business entrepreneur, these films are mourning. They are mourning an era not too long ago when manhood was allegedly absolute and unquestionable, rather than a set of performances, and when women were content raising their children alone, and endlessly forgiving instead of threatening to break into politics and business.

This idyll of the past is, to a great extent, a wish-fulfilling projection of a situation that never quite existed. However, it is undeniable that the relatively isolated nationalisms of the socialist era were conducive to maintaining a suffocating masculinist order. It was unproblematic to represent allegorically the supposedly homogeneous social-political field of the nation as a boys' school or other kinds of homosocial playing grounds without even addressing the blatant omission or demonization of women and other marginalized groups. The prospect of rejoining Europe and the eruption of global capitalism into postsocialist nationalisms have brought more visibility and relative empowerment to many women, offering a greater variety of public identities than nationalism made available to them before. Most obviously and dubiously, women have been distinguished by the new commercial media as the primary consumers.[8] National media, in turn, have responded to the perceived feminine threat with a regionwide backlash.[9] It is hard not to see the string of films about boy communities striving to emulate men of the past as continuous with this defensive media backlash.

BLOCKERS

Some recent films have shown us the other side of public masculinities, placed firmly back in the present and in their domestic environments, deprived of their nostalgic glow, often in gendered confrontation with women and at a generational war with their adolescent offspring. It is no coincidence that this group of films has had better success at addressing adolescent audiences, who tend to be consumed by identity crises raging within their own personal spheres. In Eastern Europe, the socialist decades generated universal skepticism toward political action. The corruption of postsocialist party politics, made more conspicuous to the public eye in an era of media proliferation, has done little to revive civic enthusiasm. The adolescent population of the region appears to be especially apathetic toward matters of national and international concern.[10]

The first internationally recognized film that spoke of the unspoken lives of Russian teenagers was *Little Vera* (1988), a film best described as a perestroika melodrama. While the film gained notoriety because its onscreen nudity broke the representational rules of Soviet prudishness, its honesty about a family trying to survive in the dehumanizing blocks of flats omnipresent behind the Iron Curtain lent the film relevance far beyond the sensational, and crossed the boundaries of its national cinema. In *Little Vera*, as well as in the number of subsequent transitional adolescence melodramas, the feminizing effect of the transition finds representational expression in young female characters. The primary experience of the teen girls in these films is confinement, producing a desire to escape. The confinement is both physical, represented by the crammed living spaces in blocks of flats, and symbolic, manifest in suffocating families with abusive, alcoholic fathers and submissive, masochistic mothers. These are families whose members can only speak in agitated tones, always on the verge of verbal and physical violence.

Vera makes the choice to seek liberation in sexuality, spending her time

This Russian poster for the "perestroika melodrama" *Little Vera* (1988) features the title character (Natalya Negoda) in a remarkably salacious manner.

in bed—or on the beach, in the absence of domestic privacy—with her rebellious boyfriend, Sergei, who is despised by her father. After much violence, a suicide attempt, and the death of her father, Vera is no closer to escaping her victimized condition than she was at the beginning of the film. In an even more devastating version of Vera's story, *Lilya-4-Ever* (2002), the protagonist, 16-year-old Lilya, who lives in a rundown post-Soviet Baltic industrial town, does not even have a family anymore. Her single mother unexpectedly abandons her to join her boyfriend in New York. Lilya's situation goes from unspeakably bad to worse, rendered even more horrific by the film's documentary-like realism and the certainty that there are many actual girls in analogous situations.

Lilya is forced out of her small apartment into a filthy hole where, after being brutally cast out of school and block communities, she isolates herself from the outside world by sniffing glue and finding a younger boy, Alyosha, whose own abusive father forces him to live in the street, for a companion. Lilya soon resorts to prostitution to survive. Her fate seems to take a more fortunate turn when a dashing young man picks her up one night and promises to take her to Sweden, where he has "connections." After this omi-

In *Lilya-4-Ever* (2002), Lilya (Oksana Akinshina) suffers a terrible adolescence that leads to prostitution and suicide.

nous event, there is nothing to save Lilya from the traffic in naïve and hopeless Russian women. The director relentlessly subjects the viewer to such an escalation of suffering and humiliation that Lilya's suicide—introduced by her dream of an angel-winged flight with her only human connection, Alyosha—comes as a relief.

Teenage prostitution is also the theme of Wiktor Grodecki's three films, set in Prague. *Not Angels but Angels* (1994) and *Body Without a Soul* (1996) feature interviews with teen boy prostitutes in the streets of Prague. The look into their world is almost sensationally candid. The boys, most without families, fleeing to the city from crammed blocks of flats, sell their bodies predominantly for German tourists. The sex is unprotected and the living is precarious. *Mandragora* (1997), Grodecki's third feature film about teen prostitution, focuses on Marek, who tries to make it in Prague after running away from his small Czech town and tyrannical father. Within a short time, he winds up destitute, drugged out, and infected with AIDS, dying next to a public toilet. This is almost too much to bear, not the least because Grodecki's naturalistic treatment of sex and drug abuse, along with the stilted dialogue, verges on sexploitation. As Andrew Horton argues, the director's failure to go beyond shocking and simplistic moralization turns the film into a "mockumentary."[11]

The film that popularized the name "blockers" (*blokerski* in Polish) to describe an emerging group of lower-class postsocialist youth whose existence is defined by the depressing, faceless blocks of flats emblematic of the socialist era,[12] is the Polish Robert Glinski's recent black-and-white documentary-style feature *Czesc, Tereska* (*Hi, Tereska*, 2001).[13] Both the plot and the semidocumentary presentation are eerily similar to those of *Little Vera*: Tereska, who lives in a Warsaw tenement with an unemployed, violent, and alcoholic father and an uncommunicative, church-bound, factory-worker mother, has all her angel-dreams crushed by loveless circumstances. Under peer influence, she drifts toward cigarettes, alcohol, horny teenage boys, and petty theft. She strikes up a friendship with Edek, a handicapped factory doorman; when Edek reveals his own emotional-sexual desperation, she murders him. In Poland, the film became a much-discussed social document about a new generation of hopeless young people and rising adolescent crime. It also made international media news by virtue of the fact that the actress playing Tereska, whom Glinski found in an institution for juvenile delinquents and whose performance won numerous festival awards, disappeared after the film was completed to resort to her old criminal habits. They found her a year later and placed her in another institution.[14]

Glinski admits that the film was inspired by Polish newspaper reports about growing teenage violence and that he consciously situates his work in a realistic, documentary tradition.[15] Yet the degree of intimacy and permeability between life and fiction grows beyond the socially committed artistic desire to document slices of reality unseen by propaganda cameras and mainstream fiction films. It owes something to the global postmodernist aesthetics of media simulation that increasingly encompass postsocialist societies. Similar to Grodecki's *Mandragora*, Glinski's film has more to do with reality television than the filmmakers would have us believe. Even though the grim image of hopeless and murderous Polish Gen-X-ers is as true as the utter vulnerability of teenage prostitutes in Prague, they also make for newsworthy stories and ideal media spectacles. It is no longer possible to effect a neat barrier between noble artistic intentions and less noble journalistic intentions in the postsocialist media world.

The Hungarian Krisztina Deák's film *Miskolci Bonni és Klájd* (*Bonnie and Clyde of Miskolc*, 2004), currently in postproduction, is probably the latest case of sensationalized youth violence in point. The film narrates the recent criminal adventures of a real-life couple from the gray industrial town of Miskolc. Admittedly inspired by film and television models—hence the title—the couple has gone on a bank-robbing spree. After they eventually get caught, the man kills himself in prison, while the woman writes a memoir about their adventures. This makes her famous in Hungary, and their story is turned into an action-adventure thriller that promises to be rather profitable when released, not the least because its media-inspired real-life-turned-into-media reputation guarantees it a continued media spotlight.

I ♥ BUDAPEST

While films about "blockers" may not be the entertainment of choice for most Eastern and Central European teens, at least they engage with the actual lives of a significant group of "transitional" youth, even if their interest is often limited to shocking, media-worthy desperation. It appears that some acknowledgment of the particular postmodern ethics and audiovisual sensibilities of this in-between, "alpha-omega" generation[16]—the inheritors of socialist memories and the pioneers of a globalizing Eastern Europe—is indispensable for films in order to reach teen audiences at all. Director Ágnes Incze's first feature, I ♥ Budapest, is among the few recent films that have recognized this necessity.[17]

The film opens with the camera tracking along a beige-colored texture with vertical lining. It is impossible to tell if this is an aerial shot of wheat fields, an extreme close-up of a knit pattern, or something altogether different. As it turns out, this playful confusion about truth and appearances, or, more specifically, about the manipulative nature of mediated experiences, is a central theme of the film, evident in all of its registers. The credit sequence continues with a few shots that seem to be mocking TV commercials. Two women are shown from behind, walking hand-in-hand to a light techno beat on the sound track, introduced by close-ups on various body parts that feature the women's matching clothes items and accessories: platform shoes, jeans skirts, shoulder bags. When the camera cuts to a frontal long shot, the tone of satire overwhelms the commercial cool. The two women turn out to be a mother-daughter pair. The twin outfits emphasize the mother's less-than-glamorous figure next to the attractive teen daughter's, especially in the marked absence of supportive bras: the camera is mesmerized by breasts playfully bouncing to the extra-diegetic rhythm. The environment—a dirt road with power lines above—could still maintain the impression of a chic commercial until a bright-red truck intrudes into the frame from behind the women and covers them with dust.

As the ensuing brief dialogue informs us, mother and daughter are parting: the daughter, Anikó, is off to a new adventure in the capital. Escaping the backward, suffocating rural home to seek one's fortune in the city is a familiar theme from other East and Central European films. In this case, however, the daughter has a harmonious relationship with her plump but youthful mother, while no tyrannical father complicates the picture. Anikó is simply lured by her old high school friend, Mónika—whose promises of adventure and money can only be found in Budapest.

What follows in the rest of the film is summed up by an American reviewer this way: "What if *Dawson's Creek* took place in urban Hungary and all its stars were factory workers, sluts, and crooks!?"[18] It quickly turns out that it is not enough to be young and pretty to have fun in Budapest, and that Anikó's romantic idealism makes her profoundly unfit for the world of crime and prostitution that Mónika prescribes as the bitter pill to swallow in order to be able to afford push-up bras and attract wealthy boyfriends. Yet, Anikó does not end up a junkie or a prostitute, as the rules of other realistic teen representations would have it. The director manages to save some of her protagonist's idealism—even if this requires a flight from the street police into the realm of the fantastic in a magic car at the film's conclusion.

This film constitutes a refreshing new cinematic look at East and Central European youth precisely to the extent that it keeps its distance both from the gritty allegorical narratives of blockers and angels and from the glamorized soap-opera passion of *Dawson's Creek*. The film employs elements of both genres: Anikó and Mónika chat about Madonna's lifestyle, are obsessed with stylishly revealing clothes, and dream about a real man, but they are also shown doing demanding physical work on the assembly line of a factory, where an older woman, exhausted and desensitized by mere survival during socialism as a working-class mother and wife, instructs Anikó that she must "bear it; struggle on." While Anikó's relationship with Miki, the security guard, has its own satisfying romantic moments, there are just as many ways in which the film's realism punctures spectatorial idealism, sometimes quite literally: Miki gets a flat tire while on a secret job mission; while the couple wade into a lake one night to bond in the water, the camera, with help from a car's headlights, focuses on a sizable hole in Miki's underwear.

It is in the representation of gender roles that Incze's sense of humor most effectively creates a more true and up-to-date image of contemporary East European teens than the stereotypes offered either by local poetic-allegorical realism or global soap-opera realism. Anikó's girly naivete, small-town ideas of family idyll, and the nurturing role she assumes in relation to Miki ("you need to water him like a flower," she says in defense of her patience toward Miki's brutish masculinity to Mónika) are just as painful to bear as Mónika's increasingly desperate attempt to project an image of tough worldliness to support her denial about being exploited by a jerk of a boyfriend. The film makes it clear that the Budapest cool that Mónika compromised her way into is sustained by the glamorous allure of media consumption. Its temples are fast-food establishments with blinding neon lights and nightclubs where young drug lords greet each other with gestures borrowed from Hollywood youth films while cramming as many swear words as possible into their incessant cell-phone conversations.

But Anikó turns out to have an inner strength and wisdom, and Miki's uncivilized manners turn out to hide a sweet and loving personality, even though their happy union is only conceivable in this film in a car flying over the same unidentifiable beige pattern with which the film opened. Incze refuses to yield either to the pull of the local cinematic tradition of the past or to the glittery, imported media vision of the future. The former is often more concerned with finding a proper allegorical impression for the plight of the nation or the struggles of the intelligentsia during an ongoing historical crisis than with representing a unique generational identity, while the latter's stilted exaggeration of youthful self-absorption exploits the narcissism of teen viewers for better box office success. Ultimately, both approaches deprive teens of their generational agency. Of course, the price to pay for making films that reflect the postsocialist teen generation's peculiar confusions is the films' limited appeal outside of Eastern Europe. Yet, *I ♥ Budapest,* with its mocking commentary on how media globalization permeates both backward rural purity and rotten cosmopolitan hipness, is probably the closest to an indigenous youth film and a rich source of material about the generational sensibilities of postsocialist teens.

NOTES

1. See Timothy Shary, *Generation Multiplex: The Image of Youth in Contemporary American Cinema* (Austin: University of Texas Press, 2002), 3–11.

2. John Neubauer describes Molnár's novel as one of the first modern stories about teenage gangs. He discusses the novel's thematic continuities with contemporaneous European novels about adolescence and comments on the novel's allegorical critique of grown-up warfare—a characteristic feature of East and Central European films about adolescent boy groups. See Neubauer's *The Fin-de-Siècle Culture of Adolescence* (New Haven: Yale University Press, 1992), 52–55.

3. For a good introduction to studies of youth culture and the various designations applied to youth groups, see Jonathon S. Epstein, "Introduction: Generation X, Youth Culture, and Identity," in *Youth Culture: Identity in a Postmodern World,* ed. Jonathon S. Epstein (Oxford: Blackwell, 1998), 1–23.

4. On the post–Cold War restructuring of East European television, see Colin Sparks, "Media Theory after the Fall of European Communism," in *De-Westernizing Media Studies,* ed. James Curran and Myung-Jin Park (London: Routledge, 2000), 35–49; and John Downing, "Full of Eastern Promise? Central and Eastern European Media

after 1989," in *Electronic Empires: Global Media and Local Resistance*, ed. Dayan Kishan Thussu (London: Arnold, 1998), 47–62. For a description of new, "hip" programming on Hungarian commercial television, see László Hartai, "Vettem egy Maxot" [I Bought a Max], *Mozgókép és Médiaoktatás*, http://www.c3.hu/'mediaokt/input. Accessed on May 28, 2004.

5. To account for the frequency with which the motif of orphaned, maltreated, and abandoned children recurs in the Hungarian cinema of the 1970s and 1980s, Melinda Szalóky coins the term "orphan-nation" to designate a certain national "exilic consciousness," adapting Hamid Naficy's model. Melinda Szalóky, "Somewhere in Europe: Exile and Orphanage in Post–World-War-II Hungarian Cinema," in *East European Cinemas*, ed. Anikó Imre (New York: Routledge, 2005).

6. See Péter Mátyás, "Fiúk a rács mögött" [Boys behind Bars], *Filmkultúra*, http://www.filmkultura.hu/2002/articles/films/torzok/hu.html. Accessed on May 9, 2004.

7. See John Neubauer, *The Fin-de-Siècle Culture of Adolescence*, especially chapters 3 and 9.

8. See, for instance, Eliza Olczyk and Anna Twardowska, "Women and the Media," *Polish Women in the '90s*, http://free.ngo.pl/temida/media.htm. Accessed on March 2, 2004.

9. See Zillah Eisenstein, "Eastern European Male Democracies: A Problem of Unequal Equality," in *Gender Politics and Post-Communism*, ed. Nanette Funk and Magda Mueller (New York: Routledge, 1993), 303–330; Katalin Fabian, "Unexpressionism? Challenges to the Formation of Women's Groups in Hungary," *Canadian Woman Studies* 16 (1991): 80–89; Masha Gessen, "Sex in the Media and the Birth of Sex Media in Russia," in *Postcommunism and the Body Politic*, ed. Ellen E. Berry (New York: New York University Press, 1995), 197–228; Joanna Goven, "Gender Politics in Hungary: Autonomy and Antifeminism," Funk and Mueller, 224–240; Laurie Occhipinti, "Two Steps Back? Anti-Feminism in Eastern Europe," *Anthropology Today* 12, no. 6 (1996): 13–18; Vida Penezic, "Women in Yugoslavia," Berry, 57–77.

10. For a more detailed explanation, see Judith L. Van Hoorn, Ákos Komlósi, Elzbieta Suchar, and Doreen A. Samelson, *Adolescent Development and Rapid Social Change: Perspectives from Eastern Europe* (Albany: State University of New York Press, 2000), especially 3–58.

11. Andrew Horton, "Going Down and Out in Prague and Prerov: Wiktor Grodecki's *Mandragora*," *Kinoeye*, http://www.ce-review.org/kinoeye/kinoeye15old2.html. Accessed on May 17, 2004.

12. Melinda Szalóky identifies "a whole subgenre of housing-problem films in Hungarian cinema, including Béla Tarr's *Family Nest* (*Családi tüzfészek*, 1977), Zsolt Kézdi-Kovács's *The Nice Neighbour* (*A kedves szomszéd*, 1979), and Péter Gothár's *A Priceless Day* (*Ajándék ez a nap*, 1979)." Vera Chytilová's *Panelstory* (1979) is perhaps the most conscious attempt in Czech cinema to represent state socialism's control of identities through its emblematic space. See Szalóky, "Somewhere in Europe."

13. For reviews that mention the term "*blokerski*," see Uwe Rada, "Zwischen Kino und Wirklichkeit," *Die Tageszeitung*, Feb. 18, 2002, http://www.taz.de/pt/2002/04/18/a0201.nf/text. Accessed on Feb. 18, 2004; Wojtek Nerkowski, "Finding the Truth,"

interview with Robert Glinski, *The Warsaw Voice*, http://www2.warsawvoice.pl/old/v708/News04.html. Accessed on May 9, 2004.

14. See Nerkowski, "Finding the Truth"; and "Life Follows Art," *The Warsaw Voice*, http://www2.warsawvoice.pl/old/v708/News03.html. Accessed on May 9, 2004.

15. Nerkowski, "Finding the Truth."

16. The term "alpha-omega generation" comes from Van Hoorn et al., *Adolescent Development and Rapid Social Change*, 3–28.

17. It is significant that the film shared the award for "Best Debut Film" at the 2001 Hungarian Film Week with Ferenc Török's *Moszkva tér* [*Moscow Square*], another fresh and dynamic youth film set in Budapest, which dramatizes the 1989 political shift through the eyes of a group of graduating high schoolers.

18. Christopher Null, "*I ♥ Budapest*," http://www.filmcritic.com. Accessed on June 12, 2004.

▓ ▓

CHAPTER 6

THE SOUND OF THE SOUTH BRONX

Youth Culture, Genre, and Performance in Charlie Ahearn's Wild Style

KIMBERLEY BERCOV MONTEYNE

While it is hard to imagine a moment when hip-hop was not predominant in both urban and suburban youth culture, there was a time when it could be termed subcultural. In fact, even before MTV latched on to it as the next big thing, one of the first vehicles for hip-hop's entry into the mainstream in the early '80s was through the musical, in such films as *Wild Style* (1982), *Beat Street* (1984), and *Krush Groove* (1985). Although these films are in fact musicals, film historians have rarely tackled the way in which they employ the tropes of the genre in innovative and potentially transformative ways. Instead, criticism has tended to focus on the quality of their sound tracks and the street credibility of their performers. Through an analysis of *Wild Style*, I intend to show how aspects of the musical genre, traditionally associated with conservative American values regarding the integration of the individual within a community, have been taken up and transformed in order to present an unusually positive view about life in the South Bronx during the early 1980s. Within the guise of a conventional backstage musical, the film jettisons the conformist values of the genre and opens up radical narrative possibilities regarding the creative appropriation of urban space by teenagers and the validation of an emergent black and Latino youth subculture.

Jane Feuer has commented on both the necessity of using genre theory and its polemic in relation to the category of the American post-1960s musical.[1] For example, many musicals made in the '70s and '80s—produced following the breakup of the studio system and the genre's golden age—employed a critical appropriation of studio-era themes, songs, and characters in order to deconstruct the mythmaking machine of the American musical. Most notably, *Pennies from Heaven* (1981) and *All That Jazz* (1979) call into question the fantasy of entertainment as a positive and utopic force, thus working to demystify the "music man" figure of the studio era in various ways.[2] Feuer also notes that, paradoxically, many post–studio-era musicals conserved very traditional aspects of the genre and used historical quotation and traditional musical structures in order to "reconstruct" rather than "de-construct" the genre.[3]

Most of Feuer's examples of the 1980s teen reconstructionist musical are, as she notes, indistinguishable from the larger genre of teenpics.[4] This argument is very useful and compelling when applied to mid-1980s musicals such as *Flashdance* (1983), *Footloose* (1984), and *Dirty Dancing* (1987). However, it does not take into account the diversification of the teen musical during this period in terms of the restructuring of racialized urban spaces. Nearly all of Feuer's examples are drawn from very popular box office smashes (except 1979's *Rock 'n' Roll High School*) that conform to suburban white middle-class adolescent identification.[5] Yet, to be fair, she does give a nod to Spike Lee's *School Daze* (1988) and the racial diversity of John Waters' *Hairspray* (1988). Even so, there does seem to be room in this discussion for a more extended analysis of the possibility inherent in the '80s teen musical to engage with a racially diverse inner-city space of representation outside of white middle-class locales.

For example, contemporaneous with the films that make up the body of Feuer's analysis there was also a series of films aimed largely at an adolescent or young adult audience that defined itself *against* the predominantly white spaces and culture of the suburbs, instead staging the performative aspects of black and Latino inner-city street culture. Even in the previous decade a new vocabulary seeking to describe a specifically American urban youth-centered graffiti culture had begun to coalesce in print, for example, with T. Kochman's *Rappin' and Stylin' Out: Communication in Urban Black America* (1973) and Norman Mailer's *The Faith of Graffiti* (1974). This new cultural lexicon was also being explored in a wide variety of academic fields, including linguistics, studies of urban space, and folklore studies.[6] Following from this, the films *Style Wars* (1983), *Wild Style, Beat Street, Krush Groove, Breakin'* (1984), *Breakin' II: Electric Boogaloo* (1984), and *Rappin'* (1985) all provided alternative spaces in which to imagine this emerging inner-city, youth-driven street culture.

While I have grouped these films together in terms of their reordering of white middle-class teen musical spaces as predominantly black and Latino street performance sites, they all display radically diverse production conditions and markedly different aims. *Style Wars* was an unscripted documentary, initially airing on television, that took a somewhat ambivalent and paternalistic view of the growing graffiti practice and emergent urban youth culture in New York City, while *Krush Groove* was a musically exciting but ultimately unsatisfying attempt to loosely portray the life of record producer Russell Simmons, his label Def Jam, and his production company.[7] In the same vein of the latter film was *Beat Street* (produced by Harry Belafonte), *Rappin'*, and the *Breakin'* series. These films were more about music and having a good time, and for the most part backed by commercially driven funding, yet plot devices still often turned on issues of race and the struggle over urban spaces.[8] Charlie Ahearn's *Wild Style* was an independent "art" film, whose funding was derived primarily from European sources, most notably the West German television station ZDF and the United Kingdom's Channel 4. This film imagined an all-rapping, all-dancing, all-painting South Bronx where performance was intimately connected with both bettering the community and personal transformation.

Ahearn's film also sought to uniquely bridge two somewhat traditionally opposed modes of filmmaking, the documentary and the musical. The result was an intensely original docudrama that challenged contemporary media visions of the South Bronx as a social problem riddled with crime and drug abuse. This film also sought to transform the stereotype of the graffiti writer from a destructive teenaged "hood" to a sensitive young artist concerned with the integrity of his work. While the immense popularity of rap today has somewhat diminished the "otherness" of such notorious and legendary hip-hop locations as the South Bronx and Compton, a review of *Beat Street*, a less gritty film that also takes place in the South Bronx, reveals the absolutely "foreign" territory these films introduced in the early '80s. Jim Welsh, writing in '84, avows that "*Beat Street* is an agreeable picture once one gets over the culture shock, overflowing with a tremendous energy and inventiveness."[9] Clearly there is a crucial territory that needs to be addressed here, a space of difference captured by these inner-city teen musicals or teenpics that is only hinted at by Feuer in her brief reference to *School Daze* and *Hairspray*.

What links these films is the cinematic exploration of hip-hop culture—graffiti, rap, spinning and mixing records, break dancing—and the potential appropriation of hitherto "white" spaces of performance culture associated with the musical. I have chosen to focus specifically on *Wild Style* because it managed to suggestively evoke these aspects of hip-hop culture through the negotiation of "real" urban spaces while at the same time also largely conforming to the structure of the classical Hollywood musical. Thus, by placing this film in dialogue with Feuer's notion of the teen musical as reconstructionist, I argue that *Wild Style* also takes on larger issues haunting the musical since its birth, that of race and the appropriation of space through performance.[10]

WILD STYLE: GRAFFITI AS PERFORMANCE

Ahearn's film opens with an image of the word "graffiti" executed in the new "wild style" of urban script that supplanted the somewhat softer and more readable bubble-style letters of the late 1970s. We then see a rope thrown down an outdoor wall with the figure of Lee Quinones, real-life legendary graffiti writer and male lead of the film, scurrying down the wall. The camera then cuts to a close-up of the face of this young artist as we hear a subway screaming by, and the sound track breaks into a chunky hip-hop beat. These shots evoke the clandestine and dangerous nature of graffiti writing, or "bombing," at night in the city. Subway sounds permeate this scene (and the entire film), attesting to the pervasive sight and sound of the trains in the South Bronx. Most of the illegal writing of graffiti in the film also takes place in train yards at night, echoing these first few scenes.

In *Wild Style's* initial sequence, or prologue (these images precede the credits), Raymond (Quinones) is clearly located in the space of the outsider, the artist who must work covertly at night. We also see romantic lead Rose, played by Sandra Farbara (Quinones' real-life girlfriend), inscribing her name onto a wall beside Raymond. Like Quinones, Farbara "plays" a character based on her own experiences as a young graffiti artist. The documentary aspects of this film, while largely related to emerging hip-hop culture, also chronicle the actual relationship between the two stars of the film. The couple appears together in this initial sequence; once we are inside the actual narrative space of the film, however, we learn that they are no longer together. Thus, the initial shots in *Wild Style* function as a thematic introductory episode that is somewhat narratively disconnected from the film. It tells the viewer what the film will be about rather than locating any specific diegetic incident. This initial sequence, almost entirely accompanied by music and animated images, sets the tone of the film as somewhat playful, but also introduces us to the romantic plot and to the main character Quinones as a brooding young artist.[11] It also locates the urban as a space of performance, one which will be reincarnated many times as the film constantly reconfigures the space of the city through various modes of creative representation. In the sequence following the credits we are made aware of Raymond's graffiti identity, Zoro, as he paints an enormous image of the famed masked marauder on a subway car. We also see several Zoro images and tags around the city in a montage of images following this initial graffiti "performance." This

Wild Style (1982) combines rap music, break dancing, and artistic graffiti to explore urban youth culture.

secret identity will come to play a major part in the narrative of the film, attaching itself to conventions of the Hollywood musical in various ways. For instance, Raymond's identity is linked to both communal and romantic disharmony, a common threat to stability in the narrative of the musical. Raymond's "unmasking" will be followed by his integration into the community, a turn symbolized by his "appearance" in the final stage number of the film. It also coincides with his eventual romantic reunification with Rose. Thus, this process of "unmasking," or redirecting a "troubling" identity, found in such "classic" musicals as *Love Me Tonight* (1932) and *Top Hat* (1935), is employed in *Wild Style* to satisfy the generic demands of the musical for successful romantic pairing and integration into the community.

Although the image of graffiti is ever present in these first few shots, what is underscored in this initial sequence and indeed throughout the whole film is the presence of the body, the artist at work, rather than the work itself. Instead of focusing only on the finished piece, the film emphasizes how the act of performance can situate identity both through the circulation of art or performance and through the repetition of the performance. The throwing of the rope over the wall, signifying the breaking into and getting out of a prohibited space, is as much a part of the acts of graffiti, perhaps even more so, than the finished work. *Wild Style* makes it clear that performing *is* inscribing oneself into social space. Indeed, graffiti, rap, and break dancing as evoked in this film are about struggles over performance space both in terms of the cinematic dominance of historically white representational space and in terms of struggles between different groups in predominantly black and Hispanic urban communities.

A NEW COMMUNITY, A NEW HOME

Wild Style's "crews," or teenaged gangs, traverse the city like the train cars decorated with their graffiti art, and compete with each other through break dancing, rapping, and athletics. These competitions happen in many different city spaces: the club, the street, the basketball courts, as well as the train yard. This theme of competition and performance structures nearly every aspect of the film, yet is negotiated by the confines of the traditional Hollywood musical as it incorporates aspects of both folk and backstage musicals.[12] Film historian Rick Altman writes that the folk musical can be characterized by its emphasis on "family groupings and the home." He also argues that "in many cases the action of the film is entirely limited to the type of town where everyone is a neighbor, where each season's rituals bring the entire population together."[13] The notion of a communal or family audience is central to the structure of the folk musical because it provides a model for spontaneous performance. According to Feuer and Altman, the folk musical values the quality of the amateur over the professional and imbues everyone in the community with the ability to perform.[14] Being in the audience in a "folk" sense is participatory, a practice which erases any boundary between performer and audience. The essence of the folk musical in terms of performance seeks to tap into the desire to be a performer. Thus the constant permeation of performance space by the audience attests to the fact that the barrier to performance is in fact irrelevant.[15]

For example, Ahearn stages an integrated musical number on the front stoop of a home that clearly derives from a casual street encounter. We see the spontaneous song of the golden-era musical transformed into a rap performed by members of Double Trouble rather than the traditional nuclear family grouping. In this scene a young boy casually walking in the street stops to listen to their rap. He hears their "song" and remains transfixed, providing the audience for their doorstep performance. The camera focuses closely on the faces of the rappers for most of the scene. It then pans back to reveal the boy, our audience, dancing but also contributing to the number by snapping his fingers, keeping the beat. We hear the musical percussion of the young boy and we also hear the sounds of the city throughout the scene. Not only does the audience literally become a performer but the city as well participates in the number, underscoring the fusion of documentary and musical elements in the film. This scene presents a reconstruction and a reworking of the folk audience, the extended nuclear family, and the traditional locus of the folk performance: the home.

This performance by Double Trouble also emphasizes the folk characteristic of generational relations, the passing down of ritual and tradition to the youth.[16] Paradoxically, hip-hop in general and rapping in particular *is* youth culture rather than an older tradition to be passed down. It is a new mode of performance and tradition but one that initially included a positive emphasis on children and the community.[17] In this example both the performer and audience are drawn from the street. Just as nearly all the neighborhood members are shown to be talented at some aspect of performance, so all members of the community are shown to provide an audience for collective performance, from nighttime graffiti writing, to rapping, to break dancing.

The communal audience occurs in nearly all of the performance-oriented scenes in the film and Ahearn continually shows us that, as one break dancer or artist steps out of the limelight, he or she immediately becomes a member of the audience. Indeed, this permeable border is in fact built into the very practice of the break-dancing circle filmed in the Roxy nightclub. As one member leaves the circle another one enters, creating a continuous flow between performer and audience. We even see Raymond and Rose, the "stars" of the film, as merely two of the numerous clapping and cheering spectators. In every aspect of performance in *Wild Style*, both in the club and on the street, there is a continual regeneration and displacement of the community-based audience.

Just as Ahearn reworks and redeploys the traditional folk audience of the musical, so too does the conventional setting of the home undergo a radical transformation. As noted above, according to Altman, musical performance in golden-era folk musicals often takes place in a natural country setting or within the home. Yet, in *Wild Style* the streets and urban spaces of the South Bronx function as the community's *home*, their central locus for communication, socialization, and performance. Altman argues that in the Hollywood folk musical,

> the family residence, whether farmhouse, mansion, or humble flat, thus takes on a symbolic value, for it serves not only as the stable and constant backdrop of the folk musical's action, but also as a permanent reminder of the strength and stability of the American family and home.[18]

However, in *Wild Style* we rarely see the interior of the home; it has been displaced by the street and other urban locales that provide the backdrop for communal expression and bonding. Children play in the streets; people meet, converse, and perform on front stoops; groups convene to play ball on neighborhood courts; and an abandoned amphitheater is taken over by the community to be used as a performance space for amateurs.

Even when we do glimpse the spare interior of Raymond's home, it too has been covered with graffiti. In an early scene, after we first see Raymond painting his Zoro logo, we track our graffiti hero through the street. The camera follows Raymond walking at night and then tracks up slowly to reveal the shadowy façade of a brick tenement building. He then climbs into his home through a window, reminding us of the opening shots involving the rope climbing. Raymond encounters his brother Hector (a military man), who greets him with a gun as he condemns the state of his graffiti-covered room. Hector refers to Raymond's street art brought indoors as "fucking garbage" and advises him to "stop fucking around and be a man." Even though we see a conflict between two brothers, Hector clearly displays a paternalistic tone toward his younger brother, disciplining Raymond in what appears to be a home without a father. This sequence reinforces the theme of entering prohibited spaces and stages a confrontation between "authority" and youthful creativity. The conflict between Hector and Raymond is staged as a "showdown" between a figure of parental authority and a teenager, articulating the stereotypical problem of teenagers and their perpetually untidy rooms. This scene uses a cliché found in many representations of parent/ youth relations (in sitcoms, television adverts, and countless teen films) in order to open up a very radical and suggestive premise regarding the transformation of space through artistic intervention.

Interestingly, the camera prevents us from seeing the entire space of the cramped room. Ahearn only focuses on small sections of the space, dividing it up into artistic abstract components that isolate and emphasize the graffiti rather than the domestic function of the room. Susan Stewart has argued:

> Graffiti make claims upon materiality, refusing to accept the air as the only free or ambiguously defined space. The practice of graffiti emphasizes the free commercial quality of urban spaces in general, a quality in contrast to the actual paucity of available private space.[19]

This scene underscores the unstable and permeable border between the inside and outside, between legal and illegal spaces, and most dramatically, between the function of "home" and street. It also suggests that through the youth-driven creativity of graffiti, the confined blocks of tenement living can be imagined as fluid spaces that resist the uniformity and often overly constrained aspects of urban living.

The multicultural communal groups found in Ahearn's film also challenge the racially unified notion of home and community at the very heart of
the classic American folk musical, for example, the Judy Garland film *Meet
Me in St. Louis* (1944) or the all black cast of *Cabin in the Sky* (1943), starring Ethel Waters. Ahearn's film reconfigures the notion of "home" within
the musical, and an ever-present problem of inner-city life—the paucity of
domestic spaces—as a challenge to be overcome through the creative act or
performance of rap and graffiti. However, the use of folk musical devices also
stages a critique of contemporary urban problems that paradoxically upholds
many of the tenets of community propagated by the traditional folk musical.

"HOW FAR AWAY IS THE SOUTH BRONX?"

The golden-era folk musicals discussed by Altman often mythologized an
American past in which social order was predicated upon a racist set of social
relations. In films such as *Show Boat* (filmed in 1929, 1936, and 1951), an unproblematic antebellum past set the notion of a harmonious social order in
tandem with an imagined social space in which everyone knew their place,
racially speaking.[20] According to Altman, the folk musical often called up a
distant past in order to expurgate all of the unpleasant aspects of that past.
In contrast, *Wild Style* evokes a contemporary space of racial difference that
still incorporates aspects of the folk musical and demarcates a totally different culture from that of white middle-class America. Harlan Jacobson pref-
aced his 1983 interview with Ahearn by the following:

> There's something delirious about the camera as reporter, taking one
> into foreign waters, or behind enemy lines, or penetrating political cur-
> tains where the shape of the country on some schooldays map is the
> only image one has. True of China until 1972, true of Afghanistan until
> 1979, probably still true of Albania, and definitely true of the South
> Bronx today, twenty minutes from this typewriter.[21]

The temporal displacement may only be twenty minutes away for Jacobson, but the cultural difference is described as immense and completely
other, even foreign. The early '80s may have been when many aspects of hip-
hop culture "broke" in terms of underground and academic spaces, but the
music and images of black and Latino urban youth culture at this time remained marginalized in terms of mainstream representation, particularly in
relation to contemporary rap's biggest promoter, MTV. Craig Watkins argues
that MTV systematically excluded black performers from its play roster because of "market calculation and racism." He writes:

the executives postulated that because the network's primary target was white youth, the insertion of blacks into the format would alienate its predominantly white constituency and, most importantly, jeopardize the commercial viability of the network. Consequently, the decision to exclude blacks was not simply based on economics; it was also informed by the constellation of industry commonsense ideas and practices specifically reacting to and based on what *whites* would find pleasurable.[22]

Even though Ahearn's film does not contain any militant theorized critique of white culture, the critical significance of the film lies in visualizing and circulating images of inner-city locales and black and Latino youth culture outside of the spaces of crime news reportage.

The foregrounding of various spatial properties of the South Bronx also draws upon a long tradition of African American literature and film that uses the city as "a metaphor for African American experience."[23] Paula Massood has noted that "the hood" has represented both a dystopic and utopic trope in African American film production and representation. She argues that the use of the city as a signifier in African American visual and literary representation has helped "make visible" hitherto invisible spaces of urban life.[24] *Wild Style* underscores the urgency of representing the actual space of the South Bronx by the very fact that it is a documentary while also capitalizing on the positive creative forces of the city space through its continual showcasing of emerging urban youth culture.

THE "MUSIC MAN" IS A PAINTER

Although I am arguing that *Wild Style* is a musical, it is also true that the two main characters are not musicians or dancers but graffiti artists. However, this does not detract from the film's function as a musical. Many musicals take as their central character a "brilliant" but somewhat misunderstood artist that may be, but is not always, a stage performer himself.[25] Raymond is a conventional "music man" in the sense that entertainment and creativity are restored as a positive and utopic communal vision at the end of the film partly through his artistic intervention. However, the predominance of graffiti as a "backdrop" for the film has tended to shift the focus of analysis away from its musical aspects and toward its visual elements and basic romantic plot involving Quinones and Farbara.

Significantly, the conundrum of Raymond's "secret" artist identity of Zoro that we are made aware of in the opening shots is also one of the narrative devices that most emphatically links the film to the musical genre. His confidant and would-be promoter/manager, Phade, played by legendary recording and graffiti artist Fab Five Freddy, knows the real identity of Zoro because he used to paint with Raymond. A large part of the narrative involves the potential unmasking of Raymond as Zoro by both Phade and a white reporter, played by Patti Astor. This happens in various ways, including the introduction of an entirely white, predominantly female, and somewhat rapacious New York art world.

In *Wild Style* the potential co-optation of hip-hop culture is largely dealt with through an exploration of the relationship between street graffiti and the lure of the New York gallery. Young street artists, short on cash and tired of having their words and images covered in a matter of days, did in fact accept commissions to make graffiti artwork on canvas, as we see Raymond do, thereby completely erasing any communal or performative aspect of the piece.[26] This tense relationship between gallery work and the street artist takes up *the* theme of very early musicals—success in the "popular" arts at the cost of personal, familial, or communal loss. I would suggest that in many ways *Wild Style* captures the very problematic of the founding text of the backstage musical, *The Jazz Singer*. Like Raymond, Jakie Rabinowitz (Al Jolson), protagonist of *The Jazz Singer*, is torn between being a success outside of his community or remaining true to an "authentic" notion of culture. The two spaces of culture seem irreconcilable but through performance these differences are in fact magically erased in the final live concert scenes in both films. For Jakie, the appearance of his mother in the audience of his popular show attests to the potential integration of "authentic" and popular culture, while the final "rap convention" of *Wild Style* brings the popular and communal together unproblematically in an explosive neighborhood party. At the end of Ahearn's film we are unsure of whether or not Raymond will continue to paint in the street or in the gallery, but the final scene, by involving the community and a prospective way of "being heard" and "getting seen," seems to suggest that you don't need to choose between success and the community: you can have it all. Jean Fisher noted in 1984:

> Like the classical Hollywood musical, *Wild Style* is about everyone's desire to be a star, which, as is ironically acknowledged, is impossible to realize without validation and promotion by the mainstream culture, and consequently, exposure to the risk of exploitation; so far rap and break dancing have not been incorporated into white style to the extent of graffiti art.[27]

As I noted previously, the final performance of *Wild Style* also serves to facilitate another plot device of early musicals, the revelation of a "secret" identity. In Ahearn's film this scene of disclosure functions to reunite the troubled couple through a discussion of art production that is ultimately linked to the final stage "show" of the film. As in most backstage musicals, a successful show is equated with a successful romantic pairing. However, within the quintessential backstage musicals of the '30s, most notably the Warner Bros. cycle starring Ruby Keeler and Dick Powell, the two protagonists and potential romantic couple in the narrative were almost always seen together on the stage by the end of the film in at least one stage production number.[28] *Wild Style* rewrites this ending as Raymond's involvement in the show entails painting the "set" of the disused amphitheater rather than singing and dancing. Raymond's painting of the stage design is captured by Ahearn as a performance, a "solo" act in the space that will become the final hip-hop show of the film. Initially Raymond is unhappy with his work, a design that evokes themes of artistic alienation. Rose and Raymond come together to discuss the direction of this present work as Rose convinces him that "it's not about you, it's about the performers." With this in mind, Raymond repaints the space as an emblematic star in order to represent the future "stars" of the show—the community. This transformation from personal to communal representation also coincides with the final romantic coupling of Raymond and Rose. The concluding show is a raging success, and in one of the final moments of the film we see Raymond perched on the top of the amphitheater, integrated into the spectacle of performance without literally being on stage. Like earlier musical conventions, romantic pairing is linked to Raymond's successful "performance" and integration into the community.

SINGING, DANCING, AND BASKETBALL

Not only does *Wild Style* borrow structural devices from the musical, it also directly quotes from previous musical film sources. Ahearn filmed one of the most successful sequences of *Wild Style* as an homage to Robert Wise's *West Side Story* (1961). However, rather than presenting the problem of urban communal divisions as violent warfare between racial groups, represented by the "American" Jets and the Puerto Rican Sharks in Wise's film, Ahearn constructs a city space of performance across racial divides in which all of *Wild Style*'s "crews" are racially mixed.[29] This homage, shot in an inner-city basketball court, features rival "crews" Cold Crush and Fantastic Five engaging in a competitive rap session while performing a stylized dance-inflected basketball game. The reference to *West Side Story*'s opening shots of New York's Spanish Harlem are very specific, from the use of urban basketball courts to the decisive snapping of fingers that anticipate the number. Furthermore, the inscription of "gang" territory is marked in the much earlier film by graffiti as well. However, the films radically differ in their appraisal of the potential sublimation of violence into performance. In Wise's film the initial balletic encounter between the Jets and the Sharks ultimately ends in an explosion of frenetic violence, with the staging of an all-out "rumble," while the competitive performative aspects of *Wild Style* suggest that the potential for youth gang violence can be fully suffused through its redirection into creative forces.

In fact, the desire to transform the potential brutality of youth gang interactions into nonviolent and creative manifestations is largely how hip-hop culture actually emerged. Afrika Bambaataa and other former gang members created the Bronx-based Zulu Nation, "a loose organization dedicated to peace and survival," to promote performance and hip-hop as a creative way to end violence between youth gangs in inner-city neighborhoods.[30] David Toop writes that early performance venues for hip-hop culture such as dances "helped bring former rival gangs together. In the transition from outright war the hierarchical gang structure mutated into comparatively peaceful groups, called crews."[31] *Wild Style*'s basketball rap is an example of this potentially radical transition, uniquely situating this emerging aspect of inner-city youth culture within the generic boundaries of an integrated musical number.

I would argue that Ahearn's "basketball number" is a fully integrated musical number in many ways. First, the transition from speech to song as a natural occurrence arising from the plot is certainly in place or even made irrelevant since rapping is already directly derived from everyday speech. Individual members of the "crews" answer back and forth to one another in increasingly challenging rhymes directed at both individuals and the gang as a whole. Second, the aspect of youth gang or "crew" competition is the overarching theme of *Wild Style*, so the motivation for the scene is in fact already inscribed in the film through many displays of creative competition by the time this number occurs.

There is much more camera movement in this scene than in other parts of the film. Quick camera cuts follow the trajectory of the ball through the concrete spaces focusing on the players (rappers) and also on the audience, a chorus line of young female rappers commenting on the two crews. The space of musical performance and the documentary space of the city are completely fused and inseparable in this sequence. As the camera follows the ball it also becomes distracted by the rapping chorus and follows them, revealing the surrounding spaces and faces of the inner city. Interestingly, the sustained focus on a musical performance, rather than preventing "documentary aspects" from entering in to the screen, facilitates their inclusion.

CONCLUSION

While the "basketball number" can be considered as a "traditional" integrated number, it also challenges the supposed narrative links assigned to the integrated musical performance by Altman.[32] If, as Altman argues, the musical number functions to reconcile two mutually exclusive terms introduced in the plot of the film, how do we address a film in which none of the "stars" of the plot are musical performers? Perhaps the two stars are not musical performers, but what I have been trying to suggest is that the sense of performance in the film suffuses every aspect of it. Living in the South Bronx is described *as* performing for the teenagers and young adults in Ahearn's film. The difference between Raymond and Rose and all others in the film, however, is somehow significantly reduced because according to the film everyone can be captured as a performer. Also, placing Raymond and Rose within the audience when they are watching other performers diminishes the viewer's distance from the "stars" of the film.

This "flattening out" of the distance between stars, supporting actors, and spectators also underscores the documentary aspect of the film. Even though *Wild Style* was a totally scripted documentary drama, Ahearn's camera also spends a great deal of time filming urban spaces that don't necessarily further the plot. The street and the everyday encounters of urban life are in many ways the "stars" of the film.[33] Thus the two main integrated musical sequences entirely leave out our main characters and at moments the power and space of the street totally encroaches on the narrative territory of the film. *Wild Style* in fact deliberately democratizes these spaces, creating a productive generic "tension" that seems to permeate the criticism of this film.[34] If documentaries have historically been concerned with everyday life and the exposition of various problematic or unacceptable social conditions, the musical has been largely concerned with spaces of fantasy, imagination, and various forms of utopian desire.[35] However, it is also true that many musicals do acknowledge social problems in their narrative while also transcending these social constraints through song and dance.[36] *Wild Style* brings these two spaces together in an inventive way that imagines a progressive social space of performance with the power to transcend the racial and social problems of inner-city life.

While Ahearn received a great deal of criticism for what was seen as "whitewashing" negative aspects of the South Bronx, namely heroin and violence, it could be argued that the film capitalizes on the most important theoretical aspect of the musical: to imagine what an idealized community might feel like, or at least what it might look and sound like.[37] Most importantly, the film emphasizes the positive and energetic force of inner-city youth culture in this process. While it unproblematically dissolves the tension between commercial success and communal participation in the final scene for the young performers, Ahearn's film overwhelmingly underscores the power to be found in noncommercial spaces of creativity associated with early hip-hop and black and Latino youth culture in the early '80s. *Wild Style* validates both performance and visual representation as a means to transform the "real" geographical spaces of the city, suggesting that hip-hop, and perhaps youth culture more generally, occupies a prominent place in the progressive reordering of communal relations.

NOTES

1. Jane Feuer, *The Hollywood Musical* (Bloomington: Indiana University Press, 1993), 124. Feuer, in her discussion of 1980s musicals, writes that the classic model of genre theory is problematic for understanding genre within a postmodern context. Classic genre theory, she contends, does not allow for reading against the grain of the text. She critiques Rick Altman's formulation of genre as an inadequate methodology for reconstructionist musicals because it fails to "explain how resisting readers may transform musicals." Rick Altman, in his 1999 *Film/Genre*, revises some of his own pioneering work on genre study, highlighting the bricolage, or "genre-mixing" aspect, of many post-1960s Hollywood films. Altman argues that post-1960s Hollywood films often deliberately stress genre conflict, for example by mixing "comedy into action films, with the wise-cracking tough guy becoming the modern genre-mixing equivalent of the singing cowboy." He argues that this "genre mixing" is part and parcel of a postmodern sensibility, but is also quick to point out that early Hollywood had attempted it. Altman describes the products of these early efforts as "a small number of genres combined in an unspectacular and fairly traditional manner." Rick Altman, *Film/Genre* (London: British Film Institute, 1999), 141.

2. James Hay, "Dancing and Deconstructing the American Dream," *Quarterly Review of Film Studies* 10, no. 2 (Spring 1985): 106–107. Hay writes of the male leads of "deconstructionist" musicals of the '70s and '80s that "these post-modern music men are unable to orchestrate narrative resolution in their films because they are hopelessly driven by libidinal impulses . . . They do not perform full, rounded roles as did their precursors, but rather complex characters whose darker natures are foregrounded and discourage intense audience identification or admiration."

3. Feuer, 123–138.

4. Feuer, 125. Feuer also writes that "the teen *musical* is not a genre in the sense that Thomas Schatz defines it in his book *Hollywood Genres*, that is, a community of

interrelated types. Nor does it precisely fit Rick Altman's definition of genre as a set of semantic elements that coalesce into stable syntax. However, the 'teenpic,' broadly speaking, may be considered a genre in both of these senses." Feuer notes, however, that some films, like *Rock 'n' Roll High School*, point to the polemic of this distinction in that they traverse the semantic locales of the teenpic but use the structure of the musical in an ultimately subversive way (135).

5. *Flashdance* is different from most of the other films discussed by Feuer because it is located in an urban setting rather than the suburbs. It could also be argued that the film does raise class issues; however, these tensions are ultimately magically erased by the end of the film as *Flashdance*'s protagonist, played by Jennifer Beals, gains access to an upper-class dance conservatory and a white-collar hunk. This transcendence of class anxieties through romantic coupling closely follows the pattern of the 1930s "fairy-tale musicals" of Jeanette MacDonald and Maurice Chevalier.

6. Folklore studies in particular provided some very early analysis and discussion of hip-hop culture. The journals *Folkculture Forum* and *Western Folklore* in particular began writing about black urban youth culture in the '70s and early '80s. Of interest to this paper is Sharon R. Sherman, "Bombing, Breakin', and Getting' Down: The Folk and Popular Culture of Hip-Hop," *Western Folklore* 43 (Oct. 1984): 287–293, which provides a critical analysis of *Style Wars* and *Wild Style*.

7. David Toop, *Rap Attack 2: African Rap to Global Hip-Hop* (London: Pluto Press, 1984), 164. In his critique of this film, Toop writes that "in the years to come, like the rock and roll features of the '50s, the only reason for watching will be the brief musical performances—in this case by L. L. Cool J, Run-D.M.C. and the Beastie Boys."

8. The plotline of *Breakin' 2: Electric Boogaloo* involves the potential destruction of a black community recreation center by what Leonard Maltin has called "a toothy WASP developer who could rate a centerfold in *Forbes*." Leonard Maltin, *Leonard Maltin's 2004 Movie and Video Guide* (New York: Signet, 2003), 175. *Rappin'*, starring Mario Van Peebles, centers on a poor urban community that struggles to prevent a wealthy developer from turning community members out of their homes to make way for a redevelopment project.

9. Jim Welsh, "Beat Street," *Films in Review* 35 (Aug./Sep. 1984): 435.

10. Richard Dyer, "The Colour of Entertainment," *Musicals: Hollywood and Beyond*, ed. Bill Marshall and Robynn Stilwell (Exeter: Intellect Books, 2000), 28. In speaking about the classic Hollywood musical, Dyer writes, "Whites in musicals have a rapturous relationship with their environment. This may be confined to the utopian moments of the numbers, but then they are the reason why we go to see musicals. The potentially colonialist nature of this is suggested not only by the way whites stride down streets as if they own them (which in a certain sense they do) and burst all over other locales (which they don't), but also in the way the cultures of the colonized, as perceived by whites, are incorporated into the fabric of the numbers' music and dance."

11. The visual underscoring of this "brooding" romantic aspect of Quinones is somewhat forcefully stated in an opening shot that frames his face in the darkness

behind the grid-work of a chain-link fence. The shadows play on his face, and the connection between urban spaces and his identity is not only revealed in his bodily performance, but is literally inscribed on his face by the chain enclosure of the train yard.

12. Rick Altman, *The American Film Musical* (Bloomington: Indiana University Press, 1987). For a detailed discussion of both the folk and backstage musical, see chapters 7 and 8.

13. Altman (1987), 273–275.

14. Feuer, 13–15. In speaking of the appeal inherent in the "amateur" performer of musicals, Feuer writes that "amateur entertainers can't exploit us . . . because they *are* us." She argues that the staging of a professional performer as an amateur in a film erases the financially exploitative aspect of the film industry and, in speaking of folk musicals, that "the creating of community within the films cancels out the loss of community between Hollywood and its audience."

15. Feuer, 3. Feuer makes this argument about nearly all golden-era musicals. She argues that the permeable border between the audience and the performer in the film addressed the tension between the loss of the live performance in theater and the "dead" celluloid space of film: "The Hollywood musical as a genre perceives the gap between producer and consumer, the breakdown of community designated by the very distinction between performer and audience, as a form of cinematic original sin. The community seeks to bridge the gap by putting up 'community' as an ideal concept."

16. Altman (1987), 274. In discussing films of the mid-forties such as *Meet Me in St. Louis*, *Oklahoma*, and *Carousel*, Altman writes that "the multi-generational family . . . becomes permanently fixed as a standard element of the folk musical."

17. The title track of *Wild Style*, "Wild Style Subway Rap," performed by Chris Stein of Blondie and Grandmaster Caz, includes the lyrics "Everyone has a talent on the earth and you can take it or leave it for what it's worth. No matter how hard things may seem you've got the potential, fulfill your dream. With the future it's up to us to make our homes rate an A+. Let your mind be pure and free to create, use the beat in your heart and ink to be great. Word, that's what it's all about, I'm gonna do my thing and won't let nothing else hold me back, strive to be #1 always. That's the same thing I told my little brother, he said he wanted to drop out of school, and I had to tell him, you gotta push . . . push."

18. Altman (1987), 275.

19. Susan Stewart, *Crimes of Writing: Problems in the Containment of Representation* (Oxford: Oxford University Press, 1991), 217.

20. Linda Williams, *Playing the Race Card: Melodramas of Black and White from Uncle Tom to O. J. Simpson* (Princeton: Princeton University Press, 2001), 136–186. Williams argues that the showboat in this film is representative of both interracial amity through performance and racial exclusion and banishment in its narrative space. The themes of racial harmony are suggested within interracial performance yet the structures and hierarchies of both performance and narrative constantly appropriate black suffering and black loss into the service of lament and nostalgia for a past that valorizes white political and social power.

21. Harlan Jacobson, "Charles Ahearn interviewed by Harlan Jacobson," *Film Comment* 19, no. 3 (May/June 1983): 64.

22. S. Craig Watkins, *Representing: Hip-Hop Culture and the Production of Black Cinema* (Chicago: University of Chicago Press, 1998), 180–181.

23. Paula Massood, "Mapping the Hood: The Genealogy of City Space in *Boyz N the Hood* and *Menace II Society*," *Cinema Journal* 35, no. 2 (Winter 1996): 85.

24. Massood, 88. Massood (quoting Charles Scruggs, *Sweet Home: Invisible Cities in the Afro-American Novel* [Baltimore: Johns Hopkins University Press, 1993], 18) writes that the cityscape of the hood film "has been mythologized as both a utopia—as a space promising freedom and economic mobility—and a dystopia—the ghetto's economic impoverishment and segregation. . . . The process by which this duality is examined is by placing on the screen those fragments of the city which have been previously made invisible or erased and by 'focus[ing] on space not defined by American urban maps.' In the process, the films work toward a re-presentation in which the specificity of South Central L.A., Watts, Bed-Stuy, Red Hook, and Harlem undergo a process of rearticulation, making visible—from invisible city to the hood."

25. Gene Kelly plays a painter in the musical *An American in Paris* and Dick Powell plays a burgeoning musical writer in *Dames*.

26. This theme is taken up in the documentary *Style Wars* as well as the film *Basquiat* (1996), which chronicles the rise to fame of graffiti artist Jean-Michel Basquiat in the early '80s.

27. Jean Fisher, "Wild Style," *Artforum International* 22 (April 1984): 84.

28. See for example *Dames* (1934) and *Gold Diggers of 1933* (1933).

29. Ellin Stein, "Wild Style," *American Film* 9, no. 2 (Nov. 1983): 50. Although Ahearn somewhat dismisses the relationship between *Wild Style* and *West Side Story*, many thematic and stylistic connections are very apparent, particularly in this musical number. Ellin Stein quotes Ahearn as stating, "I didn't want to make *West Side Story*, although I love that movie. This is more like *On the Town*, a populist musical."

30. Toop, 57.

31. Toop, 14–15. Toop also writes that "competition was at the heart of hip-hop. Not only did it help displace violence and the refuge of destructive drugs like heroin, but it also fostered an attitude of creating from limited materials. Sneakers became high fashion; original music was created from turntables, a mixer and obscure (highly secret) records; entertainment was provided with the kind of showoff street rap that almost any kid was capable of turning on a rival."

32. Altman (1987), 16–27. In describing the relationship between the plot and performance numbers in the musical, Altman argues that "the plot . . . has little importance to begin with; the oppositions developed in the seemingly gratuitous song-and-dance number, however, are instrumental in establishing the structure and meaning of the film." Altman poses this argument predominantly in terms of problematic gender roles and identities. He suggests that the structure of the musical reconciles two mutually exclusive terms, creating a "concordance of opposites."

33. Karen Jaehne, "Charles Ahearn: Wild Style," *Film Quarterly* 37, no. 4 (Summer

1984): 3. Jaehne quotes Ahearn as stating that "I neither glorified nor dramatized these people. I tried just to create a situation where they could perform."

34. Fisher, 85. The author writes that "in some respects, despite its assembly of original and articulate talent, *Wild Style* represents a missed opportunity to establish an 'alternative movie' in the spirit of its own subject matter, or to open up a serious debate on the impulses that generate a subcultural network of codes and on their ambivalent relation to a wider cultural context. With the exception of a few panning shots of the semi-derelict landscape of the South Bronx and passing references to the origins of subway graffiti, *Wild Style* does not attempt to function as social documentary." I am not sure what the "missed opportunity" is, since the film shows members of a notoriously bleak and oppressive social space responding positively to the challenges this space presents. Part of the rhetoric of early graffiti was, contrary to most mainstream culture, communal beautification.

35. Richard Dyer, "Entertainment and Utopia," *Movie* 24 (Spring 1977): 2–13. Reprinted in *Hollywood Musicals: The Film Reader*, ed. Steven Cohan (London: Routledge, 2002), 20. Dyer writes of the musical that "two of the taken-for-granted descriptions of entertainment, as 'escape' and as 'wish-fulfillment,' point to its central thrust, namely utopianism. Entertainment offers the image of 'something better' to escape into, or something we want deeply that our day-to-day lives don't provide. Alternatives, hopes, wishes—these are the stuff of utopia, the sense that things could be better, that something other than what is can be imagined and realized."

36. Most representative of this relation would be *Gold Diggers of 1933*, where we see the poverty of depression-era New York as well as the fantastic spectacle of song and dance in a series of Busby Berkeley production numbers.

37. Stein, 49–50. The author writes that "Ahearn readily admits . . . he soft-pedaled some negative aspects of life in the South Bronx. 'I veered away from the violence,' he says. Another all-pervasive feature of ghetto life missing from the movie is heroin, the neighborhood's most self-prescribed form of escape."

PART 3

YOUTH AND INNER-NATIONAL CONFLICT

■ ■ ■ ■ ■ ■ ■ ■ ■ ■ ■ ■ ■ ■ ■ ■ ■ ■ ■ ·■

CHAPTER 7

OUT OF DEPTH

*The Politics of Disaffected Youth and Contemporary
Latin American Cinema*

LAURA PODALSKY

Over the past decade or so, there has been a proliferation of films from a variety of Latin American countries about disaffected youth, among them *Rodrigo D: No futuro* (1990, Colombia), *Johnny Cien Pesos* (1993, Chile), *Madagascar* (1994, Cuba), *Pizza birra faso* (1997, Argentina), *Amor vertical* (1997, Cuba), and *Amores perros* (2000, Mexico). Although tales of youthful alienation have been a cinematic staple in many countries since the 1960s, many of these recent Latin American films depart from the older models by privileging the perspective of working-class and lower-middle-class subjects and, in so doing, harshly indict societies riddled by mundane acts of violence, exploitation, and emotional brutality. Whether in the form of *Rodrigo D*'s blaring punk sound track or *Amores perros*'s dazzling camera work and editing, these films attest to the affective charge of everyday life for young adults.

These films should also be placed within a much larger discursive network as they resonate with concerns voiced elsewhere by both conservative and leftist critics about the depoliticization of young people, the decreased moral authority of schools, and the deleterious effects of media culture. There are clear analogies here to the critique of the so-called Gen-Xers that has been carried out in the U.S. since the early 1990s. However, as numerous critics have reminded us, "youth" is a sociopolitical category constituted by a variety of intersecting discourses (legal, psychological, sociological, filmic) and solidified by the work of numerous institutions (the state, schools, families). Hence, discussions about youth and the representation of youth must be situated historically and geographically in particular times and particular spaces.

Gael García Bernal on a French lobby card for the popular Mexican film *Amores perros* (2000), known in French as *Amours chiennes*, and in English as *Love's a Bitch*.

In Latin America, particularly in the Southern Cone, discussions of "today's youth" are often inflected, in one way or another, with debates about the region's recent political history. In the mid-1980s, commentators like Miguel Bonasso, Mario Marcel, and others noted the key role played by Latin American youth in redemocratization efforts. By the 1990s, others would designate contemporary youth as a "lost generation"—a product or residue of the long years of dictatorship—and characterize youth culture, whether discussed in terms of the proliferation of video arcades and mall culture or the practice of "zapping" (quickly scanning TV programs with the remote control), as the most trenchant signs of the triumph of neoliberalism.[1] In Cuba, discussions about contemporary youth have been framed differently—but similarly situate today's youth as a measure of the legacies of the past, in this case, the promise (or failed promise) of the revolution. Such recurrent commentary on "the problem of today's youth" tell us less about young adults themselves than about the way in which youth has functioned as a sociocultural category. As critical educator Henry Giroux points out, youth has long functioned as "a metaphor for historical memory and a marker that makes visible the ethical and political responsibility of adults to the next generation" and thus has served as a useful "symbol of how society thinks of itself and as an indicator of changing cultural values" (10).

When talking about youth and film, we are clearly discussing a wide range of productions. There are clear differences between Argentine films like *Picado fino* (1993–1996), a very low budget, stylistically experimental film, and *No sabe, no contesta* (2002), a more mainstream narrative; and between Mexican films like *Por la libre* (2000) and *Perfume de violetas, nadie te oye* (2001). The differences between films such as these are a question not only of mode of production and formal characteristics, but also of their targeted audiences. While it may be less reasonable to talk about "youth films" as critics do in the U.S. (where 18- to 24-year-olds are an established niche market), there are signs that some Latin American producers have been trying to nurture a local equivalent.[2]

With those differences in mind, the central concern of this essay is examining the affective play of particular films—that is, they way in which they articulate, evoke, and deploy emotion. More specifically, I want to unsettle other analyses that would suggest that these contemporary films are merely a postmodern reworking of the alienation characteristic of European and some Latin American films about youth from the 1960s. Rather, this essay will argue that at least some of the recent films register what Raymond Williams called "structures of feeling" that question (and at times disrupt) dominant discursive formations. In order to do this, I will briefly analyze recent films from two different countries that in many ways depart from the representation of youth in other contemporary films made in their respective countries: from Argentina, *Picado fino* and *La ciénaga* (2000), and from Cuba, *Nada* (2001) and the short *Un pedazo de mí* (1990). Despite their many differences, these films share a common discursive tactic: they inscribe contemporary affective disjunction in terms of depth perception. As I will illustrate, *Picado fino* is a film about surfaces, about the absence of "in-depth" affective connections between family members and between lovers. It is a film that seemingly registers a postmodern "waning of affect"—an interpretation that I will contest in the following pages. Unlike *Picado fino*, *La ciénaga* is a film about what lies underneath the surface of perceptible reality. With numerous deep-focus shots resplendent with color, Lucrecia Martel's film registers the pregnant emotions percolating below the surface of everyday life that strain against their representational containment. The Cuban film *Nada* shares an interest in superficial reality with *Picado fino*, but it becomes a means to bring into relief the affective textures of everyday life and to bridge the communicative distance between its protagonists. In contrast, the short *Un pedazo de mí* characterizes the crisis of youth in terms of the hollowing out of emotional spaces, an articulatory practice also evident in the works of Ismael Peralta, a young Cuban painter, and in Pérez' film *Madagascar*.

The comparative nature of this analysis serves a number of purposes. Among other things, it suggests some of the ways in which "youth" has been articulated differently in different parts of Latin America. Furthermore, it highlights how representations of youth relate to differential socioeconomic conditions, specific historical trajectories, and local institutional genealogies. In the case of Argentina, I will situate the films in relation to the "explosion" of films by younger directors (the "New New Argentine Cinema" that emerged in the mid-1990s), as well as to a particular discursive legacy in which youth were defined as guerrillas or subversives. In the case of Cuba, I will locate *Un pedazo de mí*, a film made under the auspices of the Asociación Hermanos Saíz, and *Nada* in relation to the institutional crisis of ICAIC (the Cuban Film Institute), which has been producing films about youth by "not-so-young" directors, and to a dominant trope resulting from the notion of Cuba as the site of the perpetual revolution: youth as eternal (and, at times, martyred) militant epitomized in the figure of Ché Guevara.

OF SURFACES AND PLANES

Standing on the margins of the new independent Argentine cinema, Esteban Sapir's *Picado fino* is a unique film that gestures toward the past even as it distinguishes itself from both previous and contemporary films about young adults. Set in the city of Buenos Aires, the story revolves around Tomás, a young man from a working-class family who is ostensibly looking for work after he discovers that his girlfriend Ana is pregnant. Frequently shot in close-ups that cut across rather than frame his face, *Picado fino* tells a tale of social disconnection in which every search lacks direction and human relationships are void of affective grounding.

Like other contemporary Argentine films about young adults, *Picado fino* resonates with the themes of communication and desire reminiscent of the "first" Nuevo Cine—that is, films from the early 1960s by directors like David José Kohon, Simón Feldman, and José Martínez Súarez.[3] The storyline of Sapir's film bears a remarkable similarity to the first episode of Kohon's *Tres veces Ana* (1961), in which a young, unmarried couple grapples with news of the young woman's pregnancy. And, both films utilize the urban mise-en-scène to articulate the subjective constraints experienced by their protagonists. Yet their differences are also startling. Whereas in *Tres veces Ana* the problem of communication was a matter of finding the words to overcome affective distances between two subjects, in *Picado fino*, there is monologue in place of dialogue. In the opening café sequence of Sapir's film when Ana tells Tomás that she is pregnant, alternating frontal close-ups of each character articulate their affective isolation as their stilted, monotonal dialogue underscores their disconnection:

> ANA: How quickly things change, Tomás. In a few days, the results. I'm not sure, but what are we going to do?
> TOMÁS: It's not important what we do. Today I've lived a hundred times. I'm tired of this monotony. What are we going to do? What everybody does.
> ANA: What does everybody do?
> TOMÁS: What everybody does. What does everybody do?[4]

This interchange is markedly different from a similar café sequence in *Tres veces Ana*. In the earlier film, a two-shot "held" the two young adults together even as their conversation about the impossibility of her having their child—continually overlaid by the sounds of clinking dishes, chatter about the most recent soccer match, and the honking of cars—signaled their unraveling as a couple. In *Tres veces Ana*, the young couple's desire for each other, frustrated by socioeconomic limitations, was unambiguously present. In *Picado fino*, desire is ephemeral, something that helps pass the time.

The differences between *Picado fino* and *Tres veces Ana* might suggest that the newer film (and others that are less formally experimental, like *Sábado*, or the appropriately titled *No sabe, no contesta*) articulate a postmodern sensibility. The alienation of the 1960s has been replaced by ennui and irritation and the subject has become fragmented (evident in the off-kilter framing of *Picado fino*). There is now a glory in surface play, rather than in plumbing the emotional depths of individuals—a difference visible in the film's proclivity for frontal shots, extreme close-ups, and overhead shots as well as in the absence of master shots to anchor the protagonists, and the spectator, in a given place. By cutting across the character's face and flattening out the pro-filmic space, *Picado fino* points to the fragmentation of the subject while its lack of master shots speaks of the subject's dislocation. Thus, it might be argued that in its depiction of young characters as destabilized and directionless subjects, *Picado fino* registers the irrelevance of politics to Argentine youth and, even more broadly, the impossibility of future social transformation.

Yet, I do not find this explanation entirely satisfactory. In the first place, the apathy of *Picado fino*'s young protagonists stands in direct contrast to the insouciant playfulness of the film itself, which uses a variety of techniques, including graphic inserts and asynchronous sound, to comment ironically on the characters' actions. In the second place, *Picado fino* is one of many works by young filmmakers that have exploded onto the Argentine scene over the last decade to revitalize a somewhat stagnant national film industry. Many of these filmmakers have emerged from the numerous film schools that were established in the early 1990s. As noted by many Argentine critics, their films are not united by a dominant stylistic tendency or by a larger political or filmic project (as with the "first" New Latin American Cinema).[5] Indeed, when provoked in interviews to comment on their own work, the latest group of young cineastes strenuously disavows any interest in political or social commentary.

Rather than take the filmmakers at their word, we must situate their work in relation to the way in which youth has been constructed in Argentina since the 1960s. In his fascinating work on rock music in Argentina, Pablo Vila has discussed the way in which the category of "youth" became synonymous with "lo sospechoso" [the suspicious] starting around 1974–1975, during the second Peronist administration (255). In the following years, after the coup that would install the Proceso de Reorganización Nacional (1976–1983), a hard-line military junta that carried out the campaign of terror known as the Dirty War, this association hardened to the point that "the social space occupied by young people in those terror-filled years was absent, negated, a 'no-place'" (258). According to Vila, this "no place" resulted not only from the actions of the military, but also from those of other institutions of civil society like the political parties and trade unions (258–259).[6] While youth could not be represented by (or represent themselves through) such institutions, they also disappeared from other discursive sites. Advertising agencies removed all young adults from commercials and replaced them with young children "smiling, freshly scrubbed, and, of course, totally obedient" (Guillermo O'Donnell cited in Vila, 258–259). In this context, the rock music scene became the dominant site through which young people could construct and negotiate their identity as youth during the initial years of the dictatorship (256).

Yet, by the mid/late 1980s, rock was no longer necessarily an alternative cultural space and, as big producers made in-roads, many bands turned their attention for the first time to the "body, pleasure, and entertainment" (265). Around the same time, access to cable TV increased and malls proliferated, and commentators increasingly saw these shifts as contributing to the de-politicization of young people. It is now commonplace to characterize contemporary young adults as apathetic, indifferent to the horrors of the recent past, and lacking a sense of social solidarity as well as any totalizing view of society.[7] It should be noted that many scholars do not "blame" young adults for their apathy and lack of sociopolitical commitment, but rather see the "apolitical sensibility" of contemporary youth as a result of the failures of social institutions (schools, the family) and the larger political apparatus[8] as well as of the seductive powers of "postmodern culture," often defined as the unfettered power of the marketplace.[9]

While the increased commodification of all aspects of everyday life is certainly troubling, these analyses often betray an underlying urge to resuscitate older models of the political and, in so doing, pay insufficient attention to the sociocultural work carried out by the new "sensorially laden" cultural practices favored by young adults. Films like *Picado fino* and *La ciénaga* as well *Sábado* and *No sabe, no contesta* are part of a youth culture "constellation" that includes other affectively charged works—from the ironic politics of the punk-ska band Todos tus muertos to the grunted screels of the heavy metal A.N.I.M.A.L. to the *escraches* practiced by HIJOS, a group composed of young adults who lost their parents during the Dirty War.[10] If the latter's street performances are more readily identifiable as political acts, their emotionally packed, tactical interventions are nonetheless, like the recent films, remapping what might be considered political.[11]

If *Picado fino* is not political in any traditional sense (particularly when compared to the New Latin American Cinema), it does comment on class relations, globalization, and the legacies of the dictatorship. The film situates the emasculating, dead-end factory job held by Tomás' father in direct relation to the forces of globalization, evident in the omnipresence of U.S. media and entertainment products, from old reruns of *Batman* to Tomás' video games, whose English terminology ("Insert Coin," "Extended Play," "Round II," "Game Over") are appropriated by the film itself and used as graphic inserts to provide ironic counterpoint to the actions of the characters. Although *Picado fino* antedated the December 2001 meltdown of the Argentine economy, the film ably anticipated the critiques that would be leveled against neoliberal policies and globalization in the aftermath of the crisis that led to the downfall of five presidents in a number of weeks—namely their exacerbation of socioeconomic inequalities.

Perhaps even more significant, if more subtle, are the film's references to Argentina's past. In one of his job applications, Tomás lists his birthday as May 25, 1973, a date significant on several levels. May 25 is Argentina's independence day, a date commemorated in the name of the central plaza of the nation's capital: Plaza de Mayo. Born on that date in 1973, Tomás becomes a symbol of the failure of the dreams and promises associated with independence and, more succinctly, of the political failures of the second Peronist government (1973–1976) as well as the infamous Proceso. By selecting 1973 (rather than, say, 1976) as the date of Tomás' birth and "hiding" the reference in the detail of a single shot, *Picado fino* eschews facile political denunciations to concentrate on the effects of such political legacies on contemporary urban youth. In Tomás' world, there are no "real" heroes, only dubbed, parodic imitations like Batman, and the signs of what must be done are mixed and ambiguous at best. This is quite some distance from the reification of the martyred Ché and the Manichean worldview expressed in the classic *La hora de los hornos* (*The Hour of the Furnaces*, 1966–1968) of the New Latin American Cinema. Yet, the call to "wake up" is ever present in the insistent ringing of an alarm clock and the persistent imagery of a crying baby.

Before discussing the sociopolitical significance of *Picado fino*'s affective play, I will examine the representation of young adults in another Argentine film: Lucrecia Martel's much celebrated *La ciénaga*. Although Sapir worked as a cameraman on Martel's previous short, *Rey muerto* (1995), while he was putting together his own film, *La ciénaga* is notably different from *Picado fino* in stylistic and narrative terms. Martel's film features exuberant colors instead of black-and-white footage and a depth of field almost entirely absent from Sapir's film. Whereas *Picado fino* centered almost exclusively on the experiences of Tomás, *La ciénaga* chronicles the lives of two families: one, led by Meche, owns the Mandrágora (The Mandrake), an estate that grows red peppers, and the other, led by Tali, lives in the nearby town, La Ciénaga (The Swamp). Nonetheless, as argued below, as in *Picado fino*, the subjective experiences of youth become the ultimate measure of more generalized social decay.

La ciénaga traces the interactions between the two families from the day of Mecha's accident by the side of the pool at the Mandrágora (where she falls on broken wineglasses in a drunken stupor) to the tragic death of Tali's youngest son Luciano (Luchi) on the patio of their home in La Ciénaga. Although the wounds on Mecha's chest are the most recent, her children are the ones that have the most telling injuries and bear the most visible scars of familial and social decay. Joaquín, her youngest son, lost an eye while hunting in the nearby mountainside three years before; Vero, her teenage daughter, has a half-circle scar on her chin from some unknown accident in the past; and José, her eldest son, comes home bruised and beaten one night after getting into a fight during carnival. Yet, the scars are something more than signs of parental disregard, as the film is quick to point to the children's own unthinking cruelties, which contribute to their injuries: Joaquín's love of shooting small animals and his pitiless gaze on the dying cow; Vero's racist treatment of Isabel, one of the family's indigenous maids, and her boyfriend

In *La ciénaga* (2001), children of various ages gather around a pool and witness the antics of their parents.

El Perro; and José's harassment of Isabel. Indeed, the film has a refreshingly unsentimental approach to the children and young adults that are at the center of the plot.

Of all of Mecha's children, only Momi, her youngest daughter, does not bear any visible signs of injury, and it is precisely this character whose subjective state is privileged by the film. As a film about what lies underneath the surface of daily life, about that which is not immediately visible and yet is nonetheless detectable, *La ciénaga* characterizes the 15-year-old Momi as the only one to sense the latent forces ignored by the other characters. In a key sequence, Momi dives into the family's stagnant pool as the other children lounge around the deck. Framed in a prolonged long shot from the other side of the pool, her plunge draws stupefied reactions from the other children, who wait and wait for her to reappear, their lack of response underscored by a delayed reverse shot of the putrid surface of the water. The scene functions as an effective metaphor for Momi's compulsion, unique among all the characters, to penetrate the surface of the dirty reality ignored by others. To some degree, the film's critique of familial and social decay is keyed to Momi's "psychic fall" from sensitive teen to emotionally numb young adult.[12]

Joaquín (Diego Baenas) is a scarred and half-blinded child in *La ciénaga*.

Through the many scenes in which Momi stands as witness to the actions of others, *La ciénaga* suggests that the young girl somehow sees more than the other characters. Momi is different from her mother, Mecha, whose willful blindness is symbolized by the sunglasses that she wears inside the house and by her failure to schedule the cosmetic surgery that would give Joaquín a prosthetic eye. Momi's sensorial acuity goes beyond the merely visual. Unlike her father, Gregorio, and her sister, Vero, both of whom recoil from what they find to be offensive body odors produced by the oppressive summer heat, Momi rarely bathes. Told that she smells by others, Momi only showers after Isabel admonishes her for jumping in the fetid pool. In these and other ways, Momi functions as a key register of the film's "disquieting materiality."

As intimated above, one of the most notable means by which the film creates this sense of density or "materiality" is the sound track. In a recent interview, Martel underscored the "youthful" perspective produced by the film's complex sonic density:

I always felt more confident with the sound than with the image. One thing that seems important to me about *La ciénaga* is that although there was no clearly defined narrator, which was a very big risk, the point of view of the narrator was not going to be me as an adult but me as a girl. When you're a child perhaps there are lots of things you don't understand, but you're much more perceptive . . . In cinema, the most tactile, intimate thing you have to convey is sound. The sound plunges into you; it's very physical. And to be faithful to that childlike viewpoint, I worked with the idea that the sound could tell more than the image, including more than the words. (Monteagudo 74; translation from original article)

The point here is not that Momi is Martel's stand-in narrator, but rather that the film is trying to endow the spectator with the perceptive powers of the child. The sound track deliberately interweaves low-, medium-, and high-frequency sounds through the inclusion of distant thunder or airplanes, conversations, and the buzzing of different insects, respectively (Peña, Felix-Didier, and Luka 121). This density or multiplicity of sonic material "floods" the spectator and becomes that which s/he cannot ignore. As Martel says, "In the cinema, you can close your eyes but you can't stop listening" (122). Through this sonic density, the film "tunes" the spectator, like a piano, to vibrate in the correct key, to be able to interpret the cadences it taps out. The words of the characters become muffled and less distinguishable and the spectator, like a child, pays more attention to the tones and pitch of ambient sound to understand what is truly going on. Martel has said that *La ciénaga* "belongs to the genre of the 'desperate scream'" (123). It is this affective charge that lasts beyond the film's tragic ending.

And, indeed, it is *there* that one finds the politics in this ostensibly apolitical film about disaffected youth. Although references to the dictatorship are entirely absent from *La ciénaga*, its legacy is present in "this tension between an ominous past and an indecipherable present" (Quintín 115). Martel herself has noted that the films of the 1990s from first-time filmmakers register the Dirty War and the "disappeared" as "densities" or "knots" (Peña, Felix-Didier, and Luka 123). Unlike films like *La historia oficial* (1985) and *Sur* (1988), made immediately after the end of the dictatorship, which discussed the repression directly, the more recent films eschew explicit political denunciations:

What one feels is that the topic has lost its explicit, timely political charge and what has remained is the human, dramatic charge, the historical weight of all of that happened, the guilt, the lack of atonement . . . the absence, because everyone is missing someone, whether someone close to them or not. All of that has a strong presence on what is happening today. (Martel in Peña, Felix-Didier, and Luka 123)

La ciénaga registers that presence by evoking in the spectator a childlike sensibility, not as return to innocence, but rather as a way to access the affective legacies of the dictatorship. The film calls upon the spectator to plumb the depths that lie below the surface of today's civil democracy.

In sum, rather than putting forth a totalizing vision of societal reform, films like *Picado fino* and *La ciénaga* mobilize the affective legacies that have been ignored by the legalistic mechanisms of the so-called truth commissions and diverted by public performances of commemoration. As argued by Nelly Richard in relation to postdictatorial Chile, the rush to produce consensus after the "return to democracy" has "rationalized" politics.[13] Addressing the crimes committed by the military government became reduced to a legal investigation, subject to the rules and regulations of court systems that had proved entirely bankrupt under the dictatorships that ruled the Southern Cone during the 1970s and 1980s. In Argentina, the trauma was "summed up" by the *Nunca más* report and "dealt with" when President Raúl Alfonsín, the man who took office immediately after the military government and who promised to restore the country's democratic system, declared the "Punto Final," an arbitrary date after which no further legal actions could be initiated for crimes committed during the military government. The pragmatism of such political maneuvers has coincided with the public "appropriation" of emotion whether in the feature story on the Mothers of the Plaza de Mayo on the cover of *Gente* (Argentina's version of *People* magazine), the media's repeated attention to the bloodier aspects of the military's repression, or the appearance of a former torturer and his victim on a TV talk show (Kaufman, 17–18, 23; Kaiser, 500, 502–503). Through emotional appeals to the most heart-wrenching and sensationalistic aspects of the military's repression, such media reports complement the legalistic approach to the crimes of the Dirty War. Both tendencies divert attention away from more in-depth examination of Argentina's political history and ongoing economic inequalities as well as from particular affective legacies—anger, guilt, complicity, mourning—that cannot be easily untangled.

Although *Picado fino* and *La ciénaga* do not address such issues explicitly, they do articulate emergent structures of feeling that signal less a simple "waning of affect" or the affective paralysis of young adults than a renegotiation of modes of sociopolitical engagement. By adjusting the spectator's depth perceptions, they force us to adopt a new type of sensibility—one that cannot ignore the emotional charge of history marginalized in the rationalized realm of traditional politics and, at the same time, one that does not subsume cognition under purgative outburst.

OF SEAWALLS AND SCAFFOLDING

The following section offers a contrasting view of how youth is being formulated in contemporary Cuba. Whereas in Argentina there has been an explosion of filmmaking activity by younger directors in recent years, in Cuba these types of productions are both less numerous and less "visible." This "absence" is the result of a number of circumstances, among them, the economic difficulties starting in the 1990s that have sharply curtailed ICAIC productions and, perhaps even more important, the production bottleneck at ICAIC. In the process, a whole generation of filmmakers who are slightly younger than or contemporaries of "consecrated directors" like Tomás Gutiérrez Alea (1928–1996) and Humberto Solás (b. 1941), including Juan Carlos Tabío (b. 1943) and Fernando Pérez (b. 1944), had extended "apprenticeships" and began to make their first feature films while in their forties. Tabío (who collaborated with Alea on his last two films, *Fresa y chocolate* [1993] and *Guantanamera* [1995]) and Pérez have since inherited the mantle of Alea and Solás to become Cuba's most prolific and, in the case of Pérez, celebrated filmmakers. Curiously enough, many of the films of both of these directors have demonstrated a particular preoccupation with young adults: in the case of Tabío, *Se permuta* (1984), *Plaff* (1988), *Fresa y chocolate* (1993), and *Lista de espera* (2000); in the case of Pérez, *Clandestinos* (1987), *Hello Hemingway* (1991), and *Madagascar* (1994).

The structural bottleneck at ICAIC has had an even greater impact on the subsequent generation of filmmakers, which includes Jorge Luis Sánchez (b. 1960), Enrique Alvarez (b. 1961), Juan Carlos Cremata (b. 1961), Arturo Sotto (b. 1967), and Humberto Padrón (b. 1967). Although their work has found institutional support through the state-supported Escuela Internacional de Cine y Televisión in San Antonio de los Baños and alternative artistic organizations like the Asociación Hermanos Saíz, these "babies-of-the-revolution" have had a hard time breaking into feature filmmaking. Despite the many provocative shorts that emerged around 1990, like Enrique Alvarez' *Sed* (1989), Juan Carlos Cremata's *Oscuros rinocerantes enjaulados* (1990), and Jorge Luis Sánchez' *Un pedazo de mí* (1989), *El fanguito* (1990), and *Dónde está Casals* (1990), it would be at least 5 to 10 years before these no-longer-quite-so-young filmmakers would be given the opportunity to direct feature films.

The personal production histories of these 30- and now 40-something directors have led them in a variety of directions over the last 10 years; their works are not stylistically similar and they do not share a common vision of society. Nonetheless, they do offer a perspective on youth that is different from that of older directors, and they engage in interesting ways with contemporary debates over the "crisis" of Cuban youth. According to diverse social scientists from the island, today's young adults are quite distinct from earlier generations of youth, valorizing as they do access to dollars over professional fulfillment, and rock stars over national heroes (Oneida Pérez et al., 264–265). As discussed by María Isabel Domínguez García, demographic shifts and the slow-growing job market have created a series of problems for the incorporation of young adults into society (226–227). Even though young adults (who by the late 1980s represented one third of the total population) are better educated than ever before, they tend to be unqualified (or overqualified) for the types of jobs that are available— for example, those in the service sector oriented toward attracting foreign currency (tourism) and those in agriculture and fishing (230–231). The re-orientation of the Cuban higher educational system toward professional and technical specialization has not occurred quickly enough to address this problem (233–235). At the same time, the criteria for social mobility have been changing rapidly; increasingly, those who have access to dollars (regard-less of their educational background and job category) are viewed as more privileged (240–241). Given these material conditions, the ideology of col-lective solidarity has been less than persuasive for young adults, as well as others, who are drawn to individualistic pursuits and espouse materialist values (Gómez, 120; Oneida Pérez et al., 258, 262, 264–265; Romero et al., 359–360).

Frequently tracing this generational shift to the difficulties of the Special Period, these studies define the "problem" of contemporary Cuban youth in economic terms. Nonetheless, they also unfailingly see the issue in moral and emotional terms as a crisis in values and dissident affective states (Ro-mero et al., 335–336, 338–339; Gómez, 123, 140–141; Oneida Pérez et al., 256). Despite their often sympathetic reading of the situation of young adults, many of the recent studies by social scientists reassert an older model of (sac-rificial) youth and moral rectitude epitomized by the figure of Ché Guevara (Gómez, 140–141; Romero et al., 340–341). At the end of her article, Domín-guez García draws a distinction between three "types" of youth: those who are strongly nationalistic and tie their personal aspirations to those of so-ciety (like Ché); those in an "intermediary" sector, who exhibit some social commitment, but who are pulled toward individualistic pursuits and react passively to the current situation; and, finally, those in an "opportunistic sector," characterized by deteriorating moral values and purposeful consumerism (242). Domínguez García's typology has been quite influential, drawing support from other scholars like Romero et al. (345, 347) and reverberating in films like *Plaff* and *Lista de espera* with protagonists who are or become emblematic of the first category. Yet, this type of "diagnosis of social ills" does not acknowledge either the failure of Ché's preferential model of moral over economic incentives (discarded by the Cuban state itself as a principle of economic policy by the late 1960s) or the possibility of a different type of politics that eschews systematic rupture in favor of the type of social mobilization imagined in Juan Carlos Cremata's *Nada*.

Like Arturo Sotto's *Amor vertical*, *Nada* reworks the broad gestures characteristic of Cuban comedies to depict alienated young adults in more subtle terms. The film follows the misadventures of Carla Pérez, a petty bureaucrat working in a neighborhood post office who spends her days stamping letter after letter with an official government seal. When a spilled cup of coffee leads her to open one of the letters in order to dry it off, Carla becomes fixated on the idea of rewriting the often tersely phrased missives that cross her desk to call forth all their affective potential and, in so doing, help people communicate with each other more effectively.

In this simple plot, the film situates young people like Carla as the means by which the fragmented nation can heal through the search for and expression of "lost" or repressed emotion. Cremata's work juxtaposes Carla's editorial interventions, which infuse the epistolary form with lyrical expressions of love and suffering, with the packaged emotionalism and stifling bureaucratic speech of the "older" generation. At home, Carla becomes drawn to the show of Professor Cruzado, a TV psychologist who hands out trite advice and tells his audience to "paste on a smile" and move forward, beyond their heartache. At work, she faces the empty rhetorical flourishes of the omnipresent bureaucratic signage ("Don't monkey around, work"/"No mariposees, produce").[14]

In the face of such exhortations as well as the excessive emotional displays of absurd *telenovelas*,[15] Carla's acts of rewriting are figured as a type of guerrilla-like, bottom-up insurgency. The film often crosscuts between scenes of Carla rewriting the letters in her apartment with those depicting the people who will receive them. In one such sequence, a close-up of Carla's hand tracing letters on a blank page dissolves into a medium long shot of an older man walking down a sidewalk staircase. Subsequent shots depict the man in his daily routine—playing dominoes with friends in the park, answering his door to receive his daughter's letter from the postman, picking up a bottle of milk and walking along the *malecón*—as Carla's breathy voice-over reads the words of heartfelt longing that she has written to replace the daughter's mundane complaints about her life in southern Spain:

> Your life and mine only exist in memories. They only meet in memories, but [then there's] daily life, the boredom, the pleasure, the time that flies by without giving us time for our memories, and even if it's true that one doesn't go looking for those memories, they pop up again. . . . It hurts not to see you, Dad. I wonder what are you like now, who you are without me there. Memory is an animal that . . . eats, sleeps, and wakes up and when it does, without wanting to, it wounds our soul and all that we are.

In the middle of this montage, as the man reads the letter, an extreme close-up highlights a single teardrop rolling down the sheet of paper. In sequences such as this one, *Nada* depicts Carla's reformulations as liberating acts releasing authentic emotions pent up by mundane routines and calcified familial bitterness.

Cremata's *Nada* articulates a clear, age-based critique of an older generation that has failed to address the affective costs of revolutionary struggle—particularly, though not exclusively, the pain of separation through immigration and exile. Like the older man in the scene mentioned above, Carla, too, feels the loss of family members—in her case, her parents, two opera singers who left Cuba for the United States who send her periodic postcards from Miami featuring overweight women on the beach, sirens of capitalism and symbols of complacent consumer culture. The film's opening sequence captures Carla in an overhead shot as she talks in voice-over to her absent parents, saying, "You didn't do anything to me. Nothing at all" [No me hiciste nada. Nada]—a claim that the film itself (whose very title echoes her words) questions.

Nada is in many ways an effort to respond to nothingness and disavowal in its attempt to revivify "true" or "authentic" emotion. Yet, in contrast to traditional articulations that characterize authenticity in terms of depth, Cremata's film encounters what it is looking for in the surface of things. As mentioned in the opening of this article, *Nada* shares *Picado fino*'s interest in surface play, albeit in a very different way. Whereas the Argentine film favors frontal shots and disjunctive editing, the Cuban film employs overhead shots and scratches the surface of the film stock. Among other effects, these devices tend to flatten the screen and play with the realism of the pro-filmic space.

Together with the film's black-and-white photography, they call attention to the tangibility of emotional states and the textures of reality. When the older man stands on the *malecón* at the end of the sequence mentioned above and the camera cranes up, in slow motion, to an overhead shot, the film encourages the spectator to perceive the textures of that moment. The chipped surface of the seawall and the pockmarked sidewalk stand in for the grating emotional wear of familial separation. Yet, as the camera cranes down again, on the other side, to frame the man looking out over the wall toward the oncoming waves and the distant horizon, the shot also captures the underlying love and longing for reconnection, signaled by the man's gaze in the direction of Spain, that the rewritten letter has brought to the surface. Throughout the extended crane shot, we hear the continuation of Carla's voice-over:

> On some days your face appears more sweet; on others, more bitter, but it is always there, essential, silent, eternal, urgent. There are times when I'm dying to talk with you, to hear your voice. . . . There are days when you are God, Dad, and that bridges the distance between us . . .

Rather than attesting to the waning of affect, *Nada*'s preoccupation with the surface of things gestures toward the way in which emotion weighs on everyday life.

The film's call for "affective mobilizations" to draw together the Cuban people—figured here not as a function of the nation-state, but rather as an imagined, paraterritorial, affective affiliation—appears to offer one solution to the dilemma of contemporary Cuban cinema as articulated by Cuban critic Juan Antonio García Borrero. In his recent book *La edad de herejía*, García Borrero characterizes 1990s cinema as stylistically innovative, but plagued by individualistic navel-gazing (176). Attributing such solipsism to a number of factors, including the crisis of the Socialist bloc, the fall of utopias, and, on a more immediate level, the lack of vigorous debate among the island's filmmakers, García Borrero calls on the younger filmmakers to recapture a sense of collectivity and to propose new utopias (173, 177–178). And, this is precisely what *Nada* does in the end when Carla renounces the lottery slot that would allow her to leave Cuba for the United States. In so doing, she acknowledges what her mail-carrier boyfriend César has written to her in a letter prior to her departure: "People leave without ever truly getting anywhere. . . . If everybody leaves, nothing changes . . . nothing at all." Her decision reconfirms the well-established revolutionary exhortation to find personal fulfillment through commitment to the larger social good and, at the same time, reasserts the joyfulness of such an endeavor. In the final sequence, a yellow butterfly scratched onto the surface of the film (a recurrent motif) flitters around the head of Clara and César as they sit on a hill overlooking the ocean and playfully discuss what it means to be Cuban. Even as Carla's decision to stay signals her recommitment to the collective body, the butterfly mocks the bureaucratic exhortation to work and not screw around ("No mariposees, produce"). And her pleasured sighs as César makes love to her remind us that to be Cuban is to laugh, have fun, and take it all in stride. Unfortunately, in this final gesture, *Nada* falls back into line with the recuperative moves of traditional Cuban comedies and fails to address seriously the shortcomings of the revolution, forestalling, rather than challenging, the siren call of global consumer culture.

It is perhaps significant that one of the most radical depictions of contemporary Cuban youth appeared 11 years earlier in Jorge Luis Sánchez' film *Un pedazo de mí*. The film offers a refreshing perspective on young adults by examining the subjectivity of that "third" sector critiqued by Domínguez García and written out of most mainstream films. This 15-minute short presents interviews with a number of so-called *frikis* [freaks], young men marginalized by society who love heavy metal and other types of hard-driving English-language rock music. In key moments, as the sound track plays Jimi Hendrix, Pink Floyd, and other rock legends, the film uses black-and-white footage and a revolving handheld camera on wildly dancing bodies to capture the liberating charge of the music. As counterpoint, the sparse mise-en-scène marks the young men's sense of alienation and marginalization as they walk through half-finished apartment buildings or construction scaffolding on the streets of the city. Attesting to the economic hardships experienced by these young men (*prior* to the onslaught of the Special Period), the film's hollowed-out urban landscape speaks, in quite poetic ways, about their feelings of emotional isolation and abandonment and about the absence of affective ties to their own families or to the larger society. In another particularly lyrical sequence, a slow tracking shot leads us down a hallway and into a room with a rocking chair and crib void of human presences.

Youth here—unlike in other Cuban films—holds a metonymic rather than an allegorical charge. In other words, *Un pedazo de mí* does not offer us a totalizing trope of Cuban society wherein young adults function *merely* or *primarily* as a symbol of future possibilities and potentialities. Nor does it suggest that the experiences of this marginal(ized) sector of young adults is somehow representative of all Cuban youth. Rather, the documentary situates the young men as an important, if ignored, part of a larger whole. The film's vacant cityscape and unoccupied buildings recall the symbolism of Sara Gómez' now classic *De cierta manera* (1974), yet in the context of 40 years of revolution makes much less sweeping proposals for change. In registering the young men's feelings of emptiness and thwarted yearnings, the mise-en-scène serves as a simple reminder to take care of one's house and the individuals who live in it.

This short does not "recuperate" the young men by showing how they have come to recommit themselves to the revolution. Although it documents their love of their homeland in their testimony ("I'd never leave," insists one of the young men), the film does not offer a tale of redemption through their eventual incorporation into the social body. Instead, *Un pedazo de mí* labors to deepen the spectator's understanding of the young protagonists' painful disconnect from society and to validate their truncated desires for familial affection. The film does not subsume personal desire under one's commitment to the social good, nor does it dismiss the affective resonance that rock music holds for young adults as an expression of superficial consumer desire or antirevolutionary activity (a perspective held over from the radical nationalism of the late 1960s and early 1970s, when all rock music was considered inherently neocolonialist). In its dogged attention to subjectivities, it rallies against the dominant articulation of youth as eternal militant.

I want to conclude by taking a brief look at similar debates about contemporary U.S. youth cultures that will help clarify the specificity of Latin American youth formations. In his article "'. . . And Tomorrow Is Just Another Crazy Scam'," Ryan Moore examines the "progressively nihilistic, exhausted, and ironically distanced character of much of [U.S.] youth culture and link[s] that 'structure of feeling' with the downward mobility of the middle class and the cultural condition we have come to know as 'postmodernity'" (253). According to Moore, the "fall" of the white middle class has unsettled the narratives of progress and upward mobility that have dominated U.S. culture since World War II and deeply influenced the socialization of white, suburban youth (259–261). This discursive break has been accompanied by a "fundamental rupture between affect and ideology" that has made the investment of affective energies in larger ideals "arbitrary at best" (254–255). The recent focus on the apathy or "aggressive indifference" of young adults is also the result of the contemporary influence of prosperous Baby Boomers who were in their twenties in the 1960s, as suggested by Lawrence Grossberg. Now in their sixties, the Boomers wish to retain the characterization of youth that emerged in the 1960s as the template through which to see all subsequent generations of youth (35, 40, 43; also cited in Moore, 265). The lack of faith in political commitments and social causes exhibited by contemporary 20-somethings conflicts with the narratives of progress and social mobility that were embraced by the 1960s counterculture as much as by the mainstream "conservative" culture it rebelled against (Moore, 259–260).

This quick overview of the U.S. case provides several interesting contrasts to the situation in Latin America, where the legacy of earlier generations of youth, and the revolutionary 1960s, is quite distinct. While there are clear differences between Argentina and Cuba, the Latin American revolutionary movements, which to a great degree defined youth at that time, had greater structural impact on their respective societies than did the U.S. counter-culture. If only in the case of Cuba did the insurgency lead to a full-scale revolution, armed guerilla movements in Argentina and elsewhere success-fully destabilized political institutions and, more indirectly, economic struc-tures. Or at least this was the dominant perception that right-wing groups appropriated to justify the numerous military coups that took place in Brazil (1964–1984), Chile (1973–1989), Argentina (1976–1983), and elsewhere. Per-haps today's critiques of contemporary Latin American youth can be traced to the shared revolutionary legacies or, more to the point, to the worries of a revolutionary generation who are now in their fifties and sixties and are looking back on the failures or limitations of their own youthful projects. Yet, given this often-bloody historical context, it is much more problematic for the Latin American contemporaries of the U.S. Baby Boomers to lay claim to a heroic past of transformative "resistance."

As demonstrated in the previous pages, recent Latin American films about young adults (often made by young or "youngish" adults) are deeply informed by this earlier generation of youth and specific historical legacies. The Cuban films respond to the notion of youth as eternal militant symbolized by the figure of Ché Guevara and the moralistic orientation spawned in the early days of the revolution that subtends contemporary discussions of society. In a markedly different context, the Argentine films engage historical lega-cies and contemporary political debates tangentially, through gestures and metaphors. Unlike recent U.S. films, these Argentine films and others from Mexico and Brazil do not display a simple nostalgia, but rather a "nostalgia for nostalgia."[16] Taken together, these representations of youth are quite dif-ferent from the ones in the U.S., which are marked, according to Moore, by "the inability to locate oneself or even one's class in a historical, narrative fashion" (261). Such differences directly bear on the way in which the above mentioned Latin American films play with questions of depth and affect. As Moore (via Frederic Jameson) notes, the sense of "temporal fragmentation" evident in U.S. youth culture "is directly related to the crisis of affect in post-modernity insofar as history and narrativity are precisely the type of 'depth models' whose apparent evaporation has paved the way for the contemporary liberation of feeling" (261). Whether through the "presence of depth" (*La ciénaga* and *Un pedazo de mí*) or "superficial play" (*Picado fino* and *Nada*), these Latin American films of disaffected young adults register the weight of history even as they contest, to greater and lesser degrees, the legacies of earlier formations of youth.

NOTES

1. Sarlo, 18–23, 41–55, 57–73. See also her *Tiempo presente: Notas sobre el cambio de una cultura* (Buenos Aires: Siglo XXI, 2001), 79–91.

2. In the case of Mexico, Televicine's productions are a case in point. Starting in the early 1980s, this branch of media conglomerate Televisa began to produce feature films that combined pop music and entertainers like Luis Miguel, Lucerito, and later Gloria Trevi and Yuri to draw younger viewers. Although the commercial success of such films is uneven, recent statistics point to the importance of young adults as a market sector in Latin America. In Brazil most cinemagoers are between 14 and 25 years old, and it is this audience that has drawn the interest of global capital like Warner Bros. and Diler Asociados, who have collaborated on a number of films starring Xuxa ("Muy Caliente: Hollywood Majors Team up with Latin Film Producers," *Variety*, April 1–7, 2002, A2).

3. See the articles in Fernando Peña's edited volume *60/90 Generaciones* (2003) for further comparison of the work of filmmakers from these two eras.

4. Translations provided by author, unless otherwise noted.

5. See the articles in Horacio Bernades, Diego Lerer, and Sergio Wolf, eds., *Nuevo cine argentino: Temas, autores y estilos de una renovación* (Buenos Aires: Ediciones Tatanka/FIPRESCI, 2002) and Callegaro and Goldstein for some of the earliest "hard copy" studies of the new independent cinema. Consult the archives of the on-line journals *FilmOnLine* (www.filmonline.com.ar) and *El Amante* (www.elamante.com) for even earlier coverage.

6. For an example of the vision of youth promoted by the repressive military government, see the illustration reproduced in Diana Taylor, *Disappearing Acts: Spectacles of Gender and Nationalism in Argentina's Dirty War* (Durham: Duke University Press, 1997), 195.

7. See Jabbaz and Lozano, 99, for a summary of such comments and Trigo, 309–310, for an overview of similar critiques of contemporary Uruguayan youth articulated by both those on the Right and the Left.

8. See for example Jabbaz and Lozano, and Guelerman.

9. Martorell, 137–138. Beatriz Sarlo provocatively shifts the terms to argue that youth functions as an allegory for today's marketplace, characterized as it is by "rapid circulation and . . . accelerated obsolescence" (43).

10. HIJOS are most well known for their public acts of denunciation staged in front

of the homes of individuals presumed to have been part of the Proceso's repressive apparatus who have never been brought to justice. See Martorell and Kaiser for more in-depth analyses.

11. Indeed, they might be reworking notions of the public sphere and perhaps of civil society itself. This possibility is mapped out by Paolo Carpignano et al. in their article on talk shows and "the public mind," where they suggest moving away from the notion of civil society as constituted by institutions—political parties, unions, and so on—toward one "consolidated in the circulation of discursive practices" (119).

12. By the end of the film Momi will lose her ability to penetrate the surface of reality. Returning from town, she will join her sunglasses-clad sister Vero on the pool deck, in a scene reminiscent of the opening tableau of the drunken adults, having failed to see the miraculous appearance of the Virgin on the town's water tower, which had attracted so much attention in news reports seen throughout the film.

13. Richard further suggests that the political realm has become simply another site of market logic: "The consensual model of 'democracy of agreements' formulated by Chile's transitional government (1989) signaled the shift from politics as antagonisms—the dramatization of conflict ruled by a mechanism of confrontation—to politics as *transaction:* a formula of pacts and their praxis of negotiation" (27). See also Kaufman, 15, 20–22, 26, for similar arguments in the case of Argentina.

14. The imagery of the original Spanish phrase (literally translatable as "Don't flit around like a butterfly, work") becomes significant later on when butterflies begin to appear on screen.

15. The inclusion of the *telenovela* provides one of the film's funniest and sharpest critiques of the stagnancy of Cuba's audiovisual productions and their calcified notion of youth. Coming on right before Professor Cruzado's show, the *telenovela* features an old nun with wrinkled features who cries out about the impossibility of love even as she throws herself against the dapper young hero, dressed in nineteenth-century garb. The setting and the age difference of the two protagonists recall Humberto Solás' *Cecilia* (1982), which featured a thirty-something Daysi Granados in the title role of the teenage mulata and the much younger Spanish actor, Imanol Arias (b. 1956), as her lover. The allusion is particularly noteworthy as Granados herself appears in *Nada* as Carla's vicious boss, the rigid Cunda Severo.

16. Kathleen Newman, "Cinemas of Solitude after the Lettered City," unpublished paper presented at the annual conference of the Latin American Studies Association (LASA), Dallas, March 2003.

■ ■

CHAPTER 8

BIRDS THAT CANNOT FLY

Childhood and Youth in City of God

SONIA CRISTINA LINO

In the first sequence of the Brazilian movie *City of God* (2002), with *pagode*[1] music in the background, we see slums and a group of people in a party mood getting ready to cook a few chickens. With vibrant images and rhythm, the audience is introduced to this situation from the perspective of one of the chickens that is waiting to be cooked. Held by the foot, the chicken watches as another chicken is killed and plucked. The visible anxiety of the animal is underlined by the fast editing and the *pagode* rhythm, which gets increasingly faster, reminding us of a music video. Suddenly, the chicken escapes. Running through the narrow streets of the slums, it avoids the traffic and the people chasing it, young men carrying knives and firearms, yelling angrily because of the instinctive rebellion of the animal. They are the organizers of the party, and are immediately identified by the Brazilian public as the drug barons of the slums, who, in that precise moment, see their power defied by a chicken.

Managing to alter momentarily the fate that awaits it, the chicken is suddenly stranded between its hunters and a young black man with a frightened expression who is carrying a camera. He is the narrator of the story, nicknamed Rocket, and he has, in his own turn, the police chasing him. The police aim their guns at the drug dealers and vice versa. Between them are the chicken and Rocket. The scene is freeze framed and, in a flashback, Rocket starts to tell the story that will explain this moment in his life, starting with the history of the City of God [Cidade de Deus] slums where he was born. The same sequence is shown at the end of the movie, followed by the outcome of the story.

This initial sequence synthesizes the feelings of Rocket and of the other young inhabitants of the slums who are introduced by him: young people as scared as chickens, amid armed hunters and/or famished people, legal or illegal, that threaten each other's lives to hold on to power and assure survival for a little longer. Just as the runaway chicken gains another chance for survival, so Rocket finds his momentary "escape" in photography.

I analyze here how this movie introduces the survival strategies and life perspectives of the poor young slum inhabitants, making an analogy with the representations and meanings associated with chickens in Brazilian culture, as well as the cinematic elements used by the director that allow the establishment of such an analogy.

CITY OF GOD AND THE DISCUSSIONS GENERATED BY THE MOVIE

City of God is based on the 1997 book of the same title, written by Paulo Lins.[2] At that time it caused a controversy in the academy, starting a discussion that alternated between its literary value and its political-documentary[3] aspect. Five years later, when the movie was released, the controversy re-emerged and was strengthened by the film's publicity, reaching beyond the academic milieu to the general public. Aesthetic, sociological, and political questions were raised in various analyses of the movie, luring millions of people to the theaters. The public responded promptly to the publicity that urged audiences to see a big-screen representation of the daily violence common in Brazilian cities.

The growing urban violence in Brazil had been approached by the media as a fight between two worlds. On one side, the institutional world, the territory of "normality" and of the law, which regulates the urban and consumer order, whose institutions were being threatened by organized crime. On the other, the city outskirts and slums, inhabited mostly by African Brazilians and/or migrants from the Northeast, spaces of material, educational, and moral poverty.[4] However, in the last two decades, the limits of this social-spatial rift have become less defined.

Since the '30s, with the quest for a national cultural identity led by the state, we have seen an "overlapping of spaces"[5] from a cultural production standpoint. Throughout recent decades, this overlap reached into cultural consumption patterns because of the development of mass media. At the same time, in an inverse direction, with the strengthening of the globalization process, we can perceive a deepening of social-economical differences. So, while the cultural industry expanded itself horizontally, identifying individuals through their capacity to consume the same goods advertised in the

Violent crime is a way of life for youth in the Rio de Janeiro enclave that is the setting for *City of God* (2002).

audiovisual media, social and economic differences have grown, making it impossible for most to have access to material goods. If identity through citizenship was not a reality, the search of identity through consumption remained an option.[6] However, this option could not be shared by the majority of individuals, who were still economically marginalized.

In the presence of these transformations, a new kind of violence emerged, one that was defined not only by the violent act per se, but also by its motivation. It was a kind of violence used to acquire material and symbolic goods that could assure some identification with the constituted powers, legal or not. The primary characteristic of this new kind of violence was that it became a means to reach social-economical ascension, social recognition, and power. Crimes that had been committed as the last resort for survival and to minimize social inequalities—such as small thefts or con tricks that characterized the "vagrant life" of the '50s and '60s described by Antonio Candido and exalted by Roberto DaMatta[7] as traits of the Brazilian cultural identity— lost their potency to the crimes of the international drug-dealing market, which did not hesitate to use all resources of physical and moral violence to achieve power.

The beginning of these transformations dates back to the 1970s and 1980s, a time that coincides with the urban reforms in Rio de Janeiro that moved slums from the Southern Zone of the city to regions farther from the city center and the coast. During this removal, Cidade de Deus was created. The movie is thus about the consequences of this removal and the subsequent abandonment of the slums by public authorities, as well as the negligence toward its inhabitants and the growth of violence.

City of God is a well-crafted movie, with an aesthetic that in some moments is similar to a music video and in others reminds us of an action movie. These techniques, however, are used to tell a story that deals with sensitive issues in this moment of Brazilian history, such as misery, urban violence, the lack of social policies, and corruption. It was exactly around these characteristics—a "clean" and realistic aesthetic to deal with "dirty" and taboo issues—that the main controversy generated by the movie revolved. When referring to *City of God*, professor and movie critic Ivana Bentes[8] included it in a list of movies that, according to her, create a "cosmetic of hunger,"[9] that is to say, movies that promote a "spectacularization of violence" through the association of marginalized themes and characters with modern aesthetics and techniques aiming to conquer the international market.[10]

In terms of its aesthetics and narrative, many voices were raised to support the movie. As an example, I cite an article published by the newspaper *Folha de São Paulo*, in which the movie critic José Geraldo Couto, without disagreeing with many criticisms of the movie, prefers to underline the "astounding vigor and extreme narrative competence"[11] expressed in the script and in the excellent direction of actors, as well as the social importance of the young group of actors that came from the slums and played different roles in the movie. According to the critic, "all these conquests—not to mention the skillful assimilation of advertising and music video techniques with essentially cinematic narrative purposes," would be obscured by the adoption of the "cosmetic of hunger" label.[12] To these aesthetic comments were added sociological criticisms that accused the movie of presenting the slums as a violent space enclosed in itself, adding to the stigmatization of its inhabitants. The use of children in scenes that portrayed graphic violence was also criticized.[13] As a matter of fact, the director did not make any concession in showing children being co-opted by drug dealers in exchange for money and protection. In one of the most talked-about scenes, we see one of the drug barons, Little Zé, in a ritual of initiation to crime, commanding a child to shoot smaller children because their small thefts were attracting the police to the slums and getting in the way of his business.[14]

In 2004, when the film was nominated for four Oscars, aesthetic and social-political discussions reemerged in the media. On this occasion, in an open letter published by the site "Viva Favela,"[15] author Paulo Lins defended the book and the film, claiming that both were fictional works that allowed for a free interpretation of reality. Besides, he claimed that his responsibility was to seek the imagination of those who are socially segregated.[16] This raises the question of which cinematic choices were made to portray what Lins had called "the imagination of those who are socially segregated," and I argue that the images of the chicken in Brazilian culture were chosen to portray this imagination.

Chickens have many representations in Brazilian culture. In cookery, the chicken is popularly associated with special occasions or with the "Sunday lunch"; in the Afro-Brazilian religions, the "macumba chicken" is offered to spiritual entities in *candomblé* and *umbanda* ceremonies. Chickens were in fact brought to Brazil by Portuguese settlers. The animal was first mentioned in the *Pero Vaz de Caminha Letter*,[17] sent by the scribe of Pedro Álvarez Cabral's fleet to the king of Portugal, Dom Manual. In this letter, Caminha describes the voyage and the first contact with the people that inhabited the newly discovered land, noting that the Indians were very friendly, although the same could not be said of the first contact between the Native Brazilians and the animals brought by the Portuguese.[18] Since then, the chicken has appeared, with different connotations, both in educated and popular language.

Some of the most common derogatory expressions used in Brazilian Portuguese are: *galinha morta* [dead chicken]—apathetic, cowardly, and weak person; *homem* or *mulher galinha* [chicken man or chicken woman]—a person that has affective or sexual relationships with many others at the same time; *ladrão de galinha*—a swindler that, due to his intellectual and moral incapacity, can't devise great schemes, playing petty tricks on others. We can also find words associated with chicken, such as *cacarejar* [to cackle]—to talk fast and repetitively; *ciscar o assunto* [to scratch the theme]—to beat around the bush; *chocar* [to hatch]—to take long to do something.

There are plenty of negative expressions in colloquial Brazilian Portuguese that use the image of chickens. However, the chicken can also be associated with the idea of work. It is seen as a productive, submissive, and servile animal that remains linked to the home and circulates within the yard since its wings do not allow it to see the world from another perspective. It is the symbol of the "good worker" that produces throughout his whole life to fulfill the nutritious or commercial needs of his "boss," and that, when the production comes to an end, becomes food.

ESTABLISHING AN ANALOGY

We find a striking image of a chicken in a Brazilian movie poster for *City of God*. The poster alludes to the first sequence of the movie, with its image of

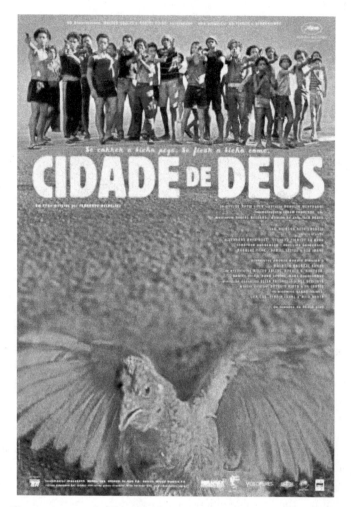

The Brazilian movie poster for *City of God* features a significant image of a large chicken.

armed teenagers and children above the title and a chicken below, its wings spread, apparently trying to fly. The sentence used as a subtitle calls our attention: *Se correr o bicho pega, se ficar o bicho come* [If you run, the beast will get you; if you stay put, the beast will eat you]. It's a popular Brazilian proverb used in reference to problems that cannot be solved and whose consequences are negative and inevitable. This makes us associate the escape of the chicken with an attempt that sooner or later will be frustrated. The strong colors and the shades of yellow and terracotta suggest a certain rusticity usually associated with "tropical heat." The references to the chicken and to its multiple cultural and linguistic meanings are more common in Latin America, especially in Brazil and Mexico.

As we watch the movie, the association between the chicken's attempt to escape in the opening sequence and the story of Rocket becomes inevitable. Just as the chicken tries to escape the fate that awaited her, running through the narrow streets of the slums before ending up in a pan, so Rocket tries to escape the violence of the drug traffic that controls the "City of God." The use of the popular proverb strengthens the suggestion of an understanding of the movie based on the visual element of the animal in the poster. On the other hand, this association concerns mainly the Brazilian public, or the public familiar with Brazilian culture, which relates to the situations shown in the movie.

In a poster created for the North American market, we see a different approach. The reference to the chicken is replaced by a photo showing Rocket on the beach, being kissed by Angelica, a girl that does not live in the slums and who will be the boy's first love. The popular proverb is replaced by a sentence: "15 miles from paradise . . . one man will do anything to tell the world everything." The emphasis is put on Rocket, and the poster establishes the distance between the audience and what they will see in the movie. The young man becomes the main character who will manage to break the cycle of violence that surrounds him and blow the whistle on the atrocities perpetrated in a space that exists outside the lives of the audience: the slums.

The poster also strengthens the idea of the coexistence of two worlds, the "tropical paradise" of Rio's Southern Zone coast and the chaotic and lawless inferno of the slums. The poster used in the Brazilian market, by contrast, suggests a link between the characters and the audience through the continuity of both images (young men with guns and the chicken), and the association between the proverb and the images. The international poster suggests the opposite effect: the delimitation of two universes, "paradise" and "slums," in two images separated by the text. The narrator/hero that appears in the text would be the only link between these two spaces. The audience is placed in a position far from the story that will be shown in the movie. That is to say, the upsurge of violence and the dismal living conditions in the slums due to the drug traffic, which are the main themes of the movie, are placed in a space outside the lives of the spectators, to whom this reality is conveyed exclusively by Rocket's courage to narrate the story. (Other posters were created to publicize the movie in other markets, but the image of the chicken is present only in those used in Brazil and in some other Latin American countries.) Besides the initial sequence in which the animal is shown, another explicit reference to a metaphorical meaning of

The North American poster for *City of God* places more emphasis on Angelica (Alice Braga) and Rocket (Alexandre Rodrigues).

the chicken is the character Knockout Ned (Mané Galinha in Portuguese), suggesting that he is a "dead chicken" [galinha morta],[19] meaning an inexpressive, mediocre person.

In *City of God*, the narrative is characterized by its circularity, expressed in the recurrence of dangerous and unsafe situations to which the characters are exposed in the slums. Few scenes take place outside the slums, and of these, most are indoor scenes, giving an idea of the boundaries imposed on the characters by the lack of perspective. Among the techniques used in the

movie that suggest such an effect, we can point out the initial sequence, repeated at the end of the movie, in which the camera moves through scenes
clockwise and back to a starting point; the use of flashbacks; the introduction of characters that will become part of the plot only later, making the
spectator go back in time within the story to identify them. These are movements that go back to a starting point in a journey that repeats itself like the
movement of a boomerang.

These techniques, emphasized by the use of just one narrative point of
view—Rocket's—begin and end the story. It is through his point of view that
other stories are introduced. Even using stop motion and divided screens in
many moments and showing incidents from the perspective of other characters, it is Rocket who tells the story. After all, Rocket grew up in the slums
and, like most of the young people of his generation, found himself divided
between a life of poverty, resignation, and social exclusion, on the one hand,
and the violent criminal life led by most of his childhood friends, on the
other. Refusing to accept these two options, he tries to break the cycle of
poverty and violence in which he grew up and to change his destiny through
photography.

The death of his brother, Goose, when Rocket was still very young, influences his decision to look for an alternative in his life. His first contact with
photography happens during a news report about a homicide in the slums. In
that moment, Rocket notices that it is possible to look at life from a perspective different from that of a victim or a villain. However, in order to do this,
he must break his link with the vicious circle of the slums, an environment
in which the only two options are those previously discussed and one that,
ironically, Rocket will manage to expose, but not to change. When he chooses
not to show a picture of a policeman being bribed by a drug dealer, Rocket
makes a movement in two directions: he manages to leave the slums, but he
does not manage to reach the safety he desires and to outline the spaces of
order and disorder, of law and crime. His life is still menaced by other powers
whose limits do not lie within the space of the slums.

In the stories of his childhood friends that have become drug dealers, such
as Little Zé, Benny, Carrot, and Knockout Ned, the link that unites the characters is the association between social respect in adult life and the exertion
of physical violence and crime as forms of power and survival. An example
of this link is the dialogue with Steak and Fries, a boy that tries to convince
the drug dealers that he can be part of the gang: "I smoke, I sniff, I have already killed, I have already robbed, brother . . . I'm a good man." Or in the
previously mentioned scene when Little Zé puts a gun in a child's hand and
tells him to shoot the smaller children to prove whether he is able to be part

of the gang. It is a kind of initiation ritual not only into crime, but also into a new phase in life in which the passport is the substitution of a real gun for a toy gun.

The moment that marks the transition from childhood to adult life for the main characters is the conquest of the first drug-dealing point by Little Zé. He refuses to be called by his childhood nickname, Little Dice, and chooses the new nickname by which he will be called from that moment on, Little Zé. His coming-of-age is represented by increasingly violent scenes. His aging process and his power are represented by a sequence of scenes portraying slaughters that he leads. Present as a highlight in the movie trailer, these scenes also mark the turning point in the history of the slums, when a new generation of criminals takes control of the drug traffic and reorganizes it using corporate techniques. Power and money become mixed, and unlimited violence becomes the means to attain them.

As the violence and the power of drug trafficking increase, an ever-growing number of children feel attracted to it.

CHILD 1: The business is drugs, you know?

CHILD 2: If you want to be a dealer, you have to start as a mule.

CHILD 1: This mule story is bullshit. It takes too long to win the confidence of the bosses and work your way up to management.

CHILD 2: How are you gonna do? You gotta wait until they die . . .

CHILD 1: I'm out of it! You gotta do as Little Zé did. You gotta leave everyone behind and that's it!

This power of life and death is not only exerted over the rest of the slum's population, but is also the condition for survival of the drug dealers themselves. The money made with the trafficking and the exertion of violence allows Little Zé to keep his leadership and to survive the corrupt police officers. Although the motives for these actions are different, the trait that unites the characters involved in drug trafficking is the fact that they choose crime while still in their childhood years. The exception is the character of Knockout Ned, who becomes a criminal during his adult life because of honor and not power. After witnessing his fiancée being raped by Little Zé, Knockout Ned looks for revenge, associating himself with a rival gang.

This episode allows us to see two important aspects. On one hand, the absence of any state-sponsored system of justice in the slums, which is why Knockout Ned seeks his own. On the other hand, the immaturity of Little Zé, who demonstrates difficulty relating to the opposite sex. He may appear victorious in his first drug deal through the force of his gun and his use of fear, winning the respect of the other inhabitants of the slums, yet the same guns are not enough to secure him his affective and sexual coming-of-age. Such sexual immaturity becomes a strong feature of all the characters and is the element that reminds us of how young they really are.

Social and emotional maturity is out of synch for Rocket too. He feels an ongoing platonic love for Angelica, a white middle-class teenage girl he will never be able to reach, just like the safety and the freedom outside the slums. Rocket will manage to have his first sexual experience only when, believing that his life is at risk, he spends the night out of the slums, in the apartment of a journalist who publishes (without his consent) the picture of Little Zé he had taken. Sexuality for the young people in the movie is always associated with dangerous situations. Goose dies by the hands of his lover's husband, Little Zé relates to the opposite sex only by force, Knockout Ned witnesses his fiancée's rape, Rocket has his first sexual experience only when he thinks his life is at risk. The only character who is affectively and sexually mature in relation to his age is Benny, who dies before he can fulfill his adult life dreams.

Finally, the lack of alternatives is represented by an almost total lack of reference to spaces outside the slums. When shown, these spaces are indoor sets.[20] Critics interpreted this as an attempt to limit to the scope of the slums: the causes and effects of the violence caused by the drug traffic.[21] I analyze the absence of outdoor scenes and open spaces, which becomes more evident throughout the movie, as a representation of the limits imposed on the development of these youngsters by the growing violence around them. Their perspectives are limited by insecurity and fear and are represented by indoor sets and by the verticalization of the slums. At the same time that the violence increases, the shots become more closed and the experiences of the youngsters are left at the mercy of the powers at war. Forced to live with a reality that is very far from the bourgeois ideal of a naïve childhood and an adolescence full of discoveries, the movie shows young people who grow up having to strike a balance between the doubts and uncertainties of their age and an environment that asks them to make daily vital decisions, an environment in which the verbs "to live" and "to survive" are mixed up, an environment that shocks the spectators, who, after leaving the theaters, have to face those images in the streets and corners of their cities and towns.

Young people have to adapt to blurred boundaries, with their wings as mere ornaments, as is the case with chickens, who cannot fly as high as birds and see the world from other angles. Just like the chickens, they have lost their ability to fly away from their predators and have adapted to the routine of domestic life, waiting for their fate to be accomplished. They learn to live with predatory powers, whose orders and disorders do not follow any logical path or set of rules that may allow them to take a flight higher than that of daily survival. As little children they already learn that "if you run, the beast will get you; if you stay put, the beast will eat you."

NOTES

This essay was translated into English by Marcello Lino.

1. Popular and contemporary musical rhythm with roots in the samba—a new style of samba.

2. Paulo Lins, *Cidade de Deus* (São Paulo, Cia. das Letras, 1997).

3. Paulo Jorge Ribeiro, "Alguns impasses da crítica cultural contemporânea: *Cidade de Deus*," *Interseções. Revista de Estudos Interdisciplinares* 5, no. 1 (2003).

4. This dual and complementary image is expressed by the great number of reports based on statistical research, academic or commissioned by the media, that indicate the spatial advance of crime rates to urban areas that until then were middle-class strongholds.

5. I use "overlapping spaces" here to analyze the Brazilian cities as Edward Said uses "overlapping territories" and "intertwined histories" to describe the colonial relationship of the nineteenth century.

6. Néstor Canclini, *Consumidores e cidadãos* (Rio de Janeiro: UFRJ, 1997).

7. João Cezar de Castro Rocha, "Dialética da marginalidade. Caracterização da cultura contemporânea," *Folha de São Paulo* Caderno *Mais*, Feb. 29, 2004, 4–8; Roberto DaMatta, *Carnavais, malandros e heróis* (Rio de Janeiro: Zahar, 1978); Antonio Candido, "A dialética da malandragem," *Revista do Instituto de Estudos Brasileiros*, no. 8 (1970): 76–89.

8. Ivana Bentes, "Estéticas da violência no cinema," *Interseções. Revista de Estudos Interdisciplinares* 5, no. 1 (2003): 229; Ivana Bentes, "Estéticas da violência e cultura nacional," in *A Missão e o grande show*, ed. Ângela Maria Dias (Rio de Janeiro: Tempo Brasileiro, 1999), 101–127; Ivana Bentes and M. Herschmann, "O espetáculo do contra-discurso," *Folha de São Paulo* Caderno *Mais*, Aug. 18, 2002, 10–11.

9. Paraphrasing the expression "aesthetic of hunger," coined by Glauber Rocha in the '60s.

10. Ivana Bentes, "Estéticas da violência no cinema," writes:

We have gone from the "aesthetic" to the "cosmetic" of hunger, from "an idea in the head and a movie camera in one hand" to the steadicam, the camera that "surfs" the reality, the signal of a discourse that values what is "beautiful" and the "quality" of the image, or also, the mastery of the classical technique and narrative. An "international popular" or "globalized" cinema whose formula is a local, historical or traditional theme and an international aesthetic. . . . We are going through a moment of infatuation with this other social reality, in which the voices of those who are outcast begin to conquer space in the market: in literature, in music (funk, hip hop), speeches that reflect the daily lives of the inhabitants of the slums, of the unemployed, subemployed, prisoners, drug addicts, a "diffused" group of outcasts that reached the media and is portrayed by it in an ambiguous way. (229)

11. José Geraldo Couto, "Cidade de Deus questiona produção nacional," *Folha de São Paulo. Folha Ilustrada,* Sept. 7, 2002, 6.

12. Ibid.

13. Criticism by sociologist Alba Zaluar and by rapper MV Bill published by the press upon the release of the movie.

14. For a discussion of such violence, see Amnesty International, "Dossiê Rio de Janeiro: Candelária e Vigário Geral 10 anos depois," London, Sept. 28, 2003 (originally published in *Jornal Zero Hora, Porto Alegre,* June 17, 2002).

15. At http://www.vivafavela.com.br.

16. Paulo Lins, "Carta aberta," published by the websites Viva Favela—www.viva favela.com.br—and Cinema em Cena—www.cienam.art.br/variedades-textos.asp? cod=20: "Obviously neither the movie nor the book follows faithfully the history of crime in Cidade de Deus, otherwise it would be a documentary or a History book, respectively. These two works are based on a given social reality to 'shed light on our misery', make politics, change the world. . . . I am committed to what is real in the work of art and not immediately with the historical reality that we want to change. . . . There is nothing strictly new in the movie *City of God.* Everyday the news throws on our faces the chaos in which we live. . . . It's just that the press doesn't have the same power to move and surprise people that a work of art has. Maybe this is the reason of the controversy. . . . As a writer, I had a commitment to reach for the imagination of those who are socially segregated, to be credible, to warn people about what the awful income distribution in Brazil is doing, to incite the creation of forums on racism, abandon of the elderly, negligence of our children by the government, widespread violence, police arbitrariness and corruption, to question the lack of public, social and cultural policies."

17. Pero Vaz de Caminha, scribe of the fleet led by Pedro Álvarez Cabral, which reached Brazil on April 22, 1500, writes to the King of Portugal, Dom Manuel, a letter narrating the voyage as well as the physical and human characteristics of the land they had discovered. During the nineteenth century, after independence, the letter gained importance and is considered the first official document of the country.

18. Pero Vaz de Caminha, Letter to King Dom Manuel. Adaptation by Rubem Braga: "A chicken was showed to them and they didn't want to touch it; afterwards, they took it, frightened."

19. Lins, 1997.

20. The only places outside the slums shown in the movie are the beach, the supermarket, the newspaper building at which Rocket works, and the home of the journalist where he takes refuge after the pictures of Little Zé are published. Still, with the exception of the beach, these places are shown from inside.

21. Couto, "Cidade de Deus questiona produção nacional."; Bentes, "Estéticas da violência no cinema," 234.

CHAPTER 9

PORTRAYING MUSLIM YOUTH IN EGYPT AND INDIA

"Worship None but Allah and Be Dutiful and Good to Parents"

CLAUDIA PRECKEL

Islam embraces many principles and ideas about childhood and Islamic/ Muslim education, which differ according to historical time period and region (Barazanji, 406). All of these schools of thought aim at shaping children's characters in line with the Islamic worldview. Islamic families are entitled to educate their children in order to allow them to follow the Quran and the sayings of the Prophet Muhammad. Tradition encourages young people to "Worship none but Allah (alone) and be dutiful and good to parents" (Sura 2, Verse 83). During recent years, the Quranic mandate of obedience to Allah and obedience to parents has brought a growing number of young Muslims into conflict with their parents. Young people, for example, perform the daily five ritual prayers, whereas their parents do not. Muslim daughters want to wear the veil, whereas their parents disapprove. This conflict between the generations is further fueled by radical, "Islamist," or "fundamentalist" groups. They even stress that obedience to parents has to be secondary to obedience to Allah. Throughout the Muslim world, Islamic revivalist groups are having a growing influence on Muslim youth, as they consider youth welfare one of their main duties. Many Muslim filmmakers from several Muslim countries have reacted to the threat of fundamentalism to society. In this essay I want to analyze the depiction of young Muslims in two very different countries, Egypt and India. Despite differences in culture, social circumstances, and religious interpretations, both countries face the rise of (even violent) Muslim activities.

SYNOPSIS OF THE FILMS

Both films in my analysis show the immense influence Islamic radical groups have on teenagers. The first film, *al-Abwab al-moghlaka* (*The Closed Doors*, Egypt, 1999, Arabic), portrays the life of young Mohammed in Cairo. It is the first feature film directed by Atef Hetata (b. 1965), who is a student of Egypt's well-known director Youssef Chahine (b. 1926) (Fawal). Hetata himself is the son of two renowned Egyptian intellectuals: his father, Sherif Hetata, is a famous civil rights activist, and his mother, Nawal El Sadaawi (b. 1931), is one of the most popular feminists and female rights activists in Egypt (Malti-Douglas; Roger). Like his parents, Atef Hetata fights constantly against the growing influence of Islamic fundamentalism in Egypt.

Al-Abwab al-moghlaka is set during the Second Gulf War (1990–1991), when Iraq invaded Kuwait. Mohammed's father has divorced his wife, leaving 15-year-old Mohammed (Ahmed Azmi) alone with his mother Fatma (Sawsan Badr). Mohammed's brother Salah left Cairo some years earlier in order to work in Iraq. He has not been heard of since the Iran-Iraq War.[1] Fatma has to earn some money for her son and works as a maid for a rich Lebanese family. Mohammed strictly disapproves of this, as he considers them to be materialistic, westernized, and decadent. He also fears that Fatma's employer may sexually harass his mother—a fear which later turns out to be justified.

Mohammed attends high school because his mother wants him to become a pilot. But life at school is hard. The classes consist of almost 50 boys each. The teachers hardly know their pupils' names and are always ready to punish them. Mohammed does not have any friends at school, mainly because his parents are divorced. Thus, Mohammed feels alone, and he does not have anyone to talk with about his awakening sexuality. He feels intrigued by almost every woman near him, even by his mother. Mohammed is confused by his feelings and tries to find a new orientation. When Hasan, one of the teachers in his school, tells him that a certain mosque is offering courses for the preparation of examinations, Mohammed joins the radical group of young men in the mosque. He hopes to find understanding, sympathy, and explanations for his sexual desires. Indeed, Shaikh Khalid seems to be an ideal father figure to Mohammed, as he seems to be both gentle and a man of great moral values. Shaikh Khalid tells Mohammed about the impurity of his sexual desires, especially when his mother is involved. He further advises Mohammed to show responsibility toward his mother as well as for his own life and to marry at a very early age. Later, he even arranges a marriage between Mohammed and one of his relatives, and between Fatma and one of his supporters.

At the same time, Mohammed is attracted by another group of young men: the street children of Cairo. With its population of almost 16 million people, Cairo is the biggest city in the Middle East. The number of street children is constantly growing, a fact which is heavily criticized in the film. Mohammed befriends a young dropout named Awadine. Awadine persuades him to play truant from school. The boys go to the cinema instead, or hang around in cafés watching the street life. They also work as street vendors. Awadine becomes the only friend Mohammed ever had. Mohammed considers his new life on the streets to be exciting and full of a freedom he has never known before. On the other hand, he knows that this is not the life his mother or Shaikh Khalid wants him to lead. His mother is afraid that Mohammed may become a criminal because of the bad influence Awadine has on him. After meeting Awadine for the first time, she tells Mohammed that she would prefer that Mohammed go to the mosque. Later, when she finds out that Mohammed has completely come under the influence of the Islamists, she definitely regrets her earlier wish.

When Fatma finds out that her own son wants to force her into a marriage, she is extremely shocked, because she has other plans. She has begun to meet Mohammed's teacher, Mansour (Mahmoud Hemida), at school. Mohammed is shocked as well as jealous: he tells his mother not to leave the house without a veil and forbids her to work. He tries to find further "Islamic" rulings stating why she should not go out on the streets and contact Mansour. When Fatma refuses to obey these "Islamic" rulings and begins a love affair with Mansour, the situation escalates and ends up in a tragedy: Mohammed kills Fatma and Mansour.

The second film, Khalid Mohamed's *Fiza* (India, 2000, Hindi), is about the tragedy of the middle-class family Ikramullah in Bombay, consisting of the widowed mother (Jaya Bachchan), her daughter Fiza (Karisma Kapoor), and Fiza's brother Amaan (Hrithik Roshan). The film opens six years before the main action; the family idyll is destroyed one night in 1993 when communal riots shock the city of Bombay, following the destruction of the Babri mosque in Ayodhya (Noorani). Amaan follows a friend's call to the street and is involved in Hindu-Muslim fights. He vanishes into the darkness and disappears. When the story resumes six years later, Amaan is presumed dead, but his mother and Fiza still believe he is alive and will return one day. Fiza, who has graduated from college and plans to be a journalist, one day believes that she sees her brother on the streets and decides to search for him. She finds him in a camp in Rajasthan which is used as a base for terrorist activities. Fiza persuades him to return with her to Bombay, but problems arise. Amaan cannot reintegrate into his former life and again joins the *jihad* group. Khalid Mohamed wants to show that the problems that the Muslim youth have might drive them into terrorism. Hindu as well as Muslim young people face the same situation in modern India—unemployment or violence. In the end, young people like Amaan have to realize that religious sentiments and communalism are only exploited by political leaders betraying the masses. By the end of the film, everyone in the Ikramullah family except Fiza is destroyed.

RADICAL MUSLIM GROUPS

Fiza focuses on the dispute between India and Pakistan over the Kashmir region, which is divided by a "line of control." The conflict started in 1947 after the partition of the Indian subcontinent into two independent states: India and Pakistan. The conflict further escalated in Indian-controlled Kashmir in 1989, and since then, the activities of several Muslim radical groups have increased. These groups[2] try to justify their fight as *jihad*—"Holy War"—in the name of Allah. The male protagonist Amaan is shown joining such a group. At the end of the film, he even takes part in the attempted assassination of a Hindu politician. The depiction of the Indian Muslim groups suggests that these groups are fighting for mere worldly, political goals and not for religious, ideological aims. Neither do we see any religious teachers preaching to the masses.

The fundamentalism of the Egyptian Islamists is of another kind (J. Clark 2004). The Egyptian groups like the Jama'at al-Islamiyya and the Islamic Jihad want to violently overthrow the present government of President Mubarak, whom they see as corrupt, impious, and influenced by the capitalist West. Their aim is to replace his government with an Islamic state. The Islamists glorify the armed struggle to achieve the modern "caliphate" even if it involves using terrorism. The groups of Shaikh 'Abd al-'Aziz and his student Shaikh Khalid are depicted as totalitarian because they reject everything that does not fit in with their interpretation of Islam. They have huge circles of adherents who meet in the local mosques. Sometimes, big gatherings take place in a mosque outside Cairo. Both *shaikh*s preach against the West, with its bad influences like "pornography, alcohol and capitalism." Mohammed is further told to eradicate evils and errors in Egyptian society. Here a Quranic verse (Sura 3, Verse 110) is hinted at, saying that every individual has the right, or rather the duty, to command goodness and to remove vices wherever he finds them (*amr bil maruf wa-nahy 'an al-munkar*). Mohammed tries to live this Quranic principle, even when it brings him into conflict with his mother. At the beginning of the film, Mohammed disapproves of the fact that his mother is working for a rich Lebanese family, but he would not dare to ask his mother to give up this job. The rich Lebanese family has adopted many things from the "Western" lifestyle: they eat fast food, drink alcohol, and wear blue jeans. Mohammed considers this to be inappropriate for Arab/Muslim families. But the most disturbing thing in Mohammed's eyes is that Fatma's employer owns a second flat in which he meets several women. He asks Fatma to clean this flat regularly, but his ulterior motive is to start a sexual relationship with her. Fatma plainly rejects this, and gives up her job. Although she clearly does not approve of her employers' lifestyle, she asks Mohammed: "How can we judge them?" Mohammed does not want to answer this, but later, when he seems to be brainwashed by the Islamists, he wants to impose his beliefs by force on everyone, even on his mother.

In spite of these differences between the two films, both portray young men as ready to die or even kill for the Islamic cause, using violence and terrorism. Further, both films suggest that the repressive system of society is to be blamed: children, as well as women, are victims of (male) violence of different kinds. There are few positive male figures that can guide young men in the right direction. This is the reason why it is easy for Islamist groups to exert an enormous influence on young people.

STRONG MOTHERS—ABSENT FATHERS

The families portrayed in these two films suffer from a loss of their father. Father Ikramullah died several years earlier, and his daughter Fiza is full of bitterness as a result. She tells her mother: "He died—and he left us here to die behind him." It becomes clear that she considers her family incomplete and suffers from the absence of a strong father figure.

Mohammed's father is still alive yet has left the family for a younger woman. Although Mohammed sees his father regularly, he feels left alone: his father only offers superficial comments and is not prepared to answer his son's questions concerning life, his future, or even sexuality. Thus, Mohammed is left without any male guidance or male role model. This is the reason why the group around Shaikh Khalid seems to be so attractive to young men: the *shaikh* has a soft and gentle voice and seems to know everything about life. He offers guidance to all young men who feel lost. The inner circle of the group consists of men, whereas women (daughters and wives) are only entitled to be married to followers of the group and to give birth to the next generation of followers. They further have to share the religious interpretations of their husbands.

Both films show that there is an enormous pressure on women and children. Because of the worldwide economic crisis, a growing number of women and young people have to work in order to sustain their families. *Al-Abwab* depicts the serious problem of unemployment in Egyptian societies and how it creates trouble among family members. In both films, the mothers and children work and thus carry the burden of the whole family on their shoulders. At the same time, everyday life is full of repression: for example, there is a lot of military drill at school. The classes consist of 50 pupils or more, and only those who pay for additional lessons will pass the examinations. There is no place for creativity, individual support, or intellectual freedom in the school system. On the contrary, children have to put up with punishment and humiliation from their teachers, as well as from their classmates. As a consequence, Mohammed will not find any support or understanding of his problems. Although his classmates are the same age and have the same questions about sexuality, nobody will help him.

VIOLENCE, SEXUALITY, AND SEXUAL ABUSE

Although the majority of Indian films are love stories, the depiction of sexuality on screen is not common, since there is strict censorship. Even kissing sequences are only hinted at. Still, several other possibilities by which sexuality is conveyed in Indian films do exist (Gokulsing and Dissanayake, 78; Garga, 196): for example, dancing sequences and even "wet sari scenes." In these scenes, the female body is exposed on screen, but it remains a visual object of male desire. Only recent films like *Jism* (*Body*, Amit Saxena, India, 2003, Hindi) show self-determined female sexuality on the Indian screen, and this film was controversial.

In the past, in the majority of Indian films, women were portrayed as modest and chaste, and only "reacting" to male desires. The image of women has recently changed toward a more active role, as women are no longer submitting to men. In the 1970s, a new kind of film came to the screen portraying sexual violence against women. *Insaaf ka tarazu* (*The Scales of Justice*, B. R. Chopra, India, 1980, Hindi) and *Zakhmi Aurat* (*Injured Woman*, Avtar Bhogal, India, 1988, Hindi), among others, came to be known as "rape films" (Garga, 199; Rajadhyaksha and Willemen, 446),[3] since their main motif was sexual humiliation and female revenge for male violence. Of course, rape itself was only hinted at. These films can clearly be seen in a context of feminist activities in India following some terrible incidents of rape (Gokulsing and Dissinayake, 106). The intention of these films was to stress that women were no longer helpless victims of male violence.

Although public attention was then drawn to the fate of female victims of sexual violence, Bollywood films continue to imply that female life in India is not free of sexual violence even in the 2000s. For example, when Fiza applies for a job, she is sexually harassed. The boss of the company tells her: "You are an attractive girl. Let me meet you in the evening. Dinner. I'll make you very, very happy." Thus, it is clearly underlined that some men still consider women to be helpless objects. But Fiza does not consider herself to be a victim. She shouts at him, telling him to keep his thoughts to himself, and even throws a pail of water in his face.

Indeed, in India there has been an increase in the public awareness of both the sexual abuse of women and child sexual abuse. For example, Grace Poore released her documentary *The Children We Sacrifice* in 2000,[4] a film which was shot in India, Sri Lanka, Canada, and the U.S., showing "the universal crime of incestuous child abuse through the prism of South Asia." This film definitely challenges the image of a safe and happy childhood and stresses the betrayal of children which happens in numerous families.

The director of *al-Abwab* portrays children not only as victims of sexual violence, but also as perpetrators. Mohammed, for example, enacts sexual violence on two occasions. In one scene, he meets a girl of his own age who brings him some tea. She belongs to the group (and may be a relative) of Shaikh Khalid. She is completely veiled, wearing even a black veil and black gloves. Mohammed asks the girl for her name, but she seems to be very shy and does not answer his question. Then Mohammed asks the girl to take away the veil, but she refuses. After having asked her for the third time, Mohammed simply tears away the veil in front of her face. In the Islamic world, veiling of women is strongly connected with erotic and sexual desires. In the eyes of the Islamists, a veil is more than a piece of cloth: it is a symbol of a woman's virtue and honor. Thus, tearing away the veil is tantamount to taking away her honor. Thus, Mohammed's action can be interpreted as an act of violence. On the other hand, another interpretation seems to be possible: seeing a ("naked") face may be considered something human. Whereas the other men of the Islamist group remain anonymous and without an identity, we get to know this girl's name: Samaa. She does not remain an anonymous veiled girl, but becomes a visible human being with a name. The subtle message thus might be: tear down the veils of Islamist Islam, and what you get is a soft (female?) Islam of the human kind.

The second time Mohammed becomes a perpetrator of sexual violence is when he sexually harasses his neighbor, Zeinab. Mohammed feels very much attracted to her, but he also feels contempt for her because of her lifestyle, her open-mindedness, and her sexual allure. At the beginning of the film, Mohammed believes Zeinab to be a nurse, but later he finds out that she is a prostitute who is supporting her unemployed husband. When Mohammed finds out that Zeinab is a prostitute, he tries to make her feel guilty because of her conduct. For example, he tells her about a woman who was murdered by her own husband because she had a love affair with another man. Zeinab, on the other hand, does not take Mohammed seriously. She tries to provoke him by sexual allusions or remarks concerning Mohammed's masculinity. Only when she learns that he is under the influence of the Islamists does she take him seriously; she is shocked and even begins to fear him. When Mohammed realizes that his mother is meeting his teacher, he tries to find out where Fatma is. He goes to Zeinab's flat, shouts at her, punches her, and starts to kiss and touch her. Zeinab does not offer any resistance, but does not further encourage him. It seems as if she is used to this situation from her "job" as a prostitute.

The problems of children who become victims of sexual violence, however, are also the main subject of several other Arabic films, such as *Rih as-sadd*[5] (*Man of Ashes*, Nouri Bouzid, Tunisia, 1986, Arabic). The film tells the story of Hachemi, a young Tunisian woodcarver. On the eve of his arranged marriage, Hachemi is tormented by flashbacks from his youth. He and his best friend, Farfat, were both sexually abused by their employer, and Farfat has been defamed as a homosexual by people from their village.[6] Hachemi feels guilty about the whole situation and considers himself to be inadequate for the role of husband. His father does not want to understand his problems and even beats him. Hachemi and Farfat try to get away from their problems and go to a brothel. There, some other men are joking about Farfat's "homosexuality" and "missing masculinity." In his anger, Farfat runs through the streets with a knife in his hand, searching for his childhood tormentor. When he finally finds him, he stabs his former employer to death. *Rih as-sadd* is an impressive film about several taboos in Tunisian society: homosexuality, child abuse, and prostitution (Shafik, 259).

It is important to see that most films do not blame religion/Islam for violence and sexual abuse, but rather the patriarchal systems of those societies. Violence and fanaticism are interpreted as the consequence of the exaggeration of masculinity.

EXAGGERATION OF MASCULINITY

In the film *Fiza*, the protagonist Amaan undergoes a significant masculinization (Dyer 1992). In the beginning we can see Amaan laughing and joking with his mother and his sister. He is interested in the aesthetic aspects of

Indian star Hrithik Roshan showing a hypermasculine persona in *Fiza* (2000).

art and painting. We can also see him laughing. In these scenes, the female side of Amaan is stressed, and thus there is a "feminization" of his body. This means that Amaan/Roshan, with his masculine body but soft heart, is the object of female erotic desire (Preckel 2003a). Later he is even shown as a vulnerable man and as a victim. His laughing at the beginning of the film can be interpreted as a kind of passiveness and thus as a symbol of "dangerous" feminization since a man always has to be active (Horst and Kleis, 108; Kirkham and Thumin). To counter this feminization of Amaan/Roshan, the hero is shown to have lost this ability to laugh in the middle of the film. After Amaan returns to Bombay, he sees a comedian in a park. Instead of joining the laughing audience, he starts to fight two villains who disturb the scene. This is the point where the process of Amaan's masculinization starts.

This masculinization reaches its definitive climax when the male protagonist prepares himself for the *jihad.* Amaan/Roshan can be seen performing martial arts as if he had not done anything else since his childhood. He is perfectly handling the *nunchako* [two sticks connected by a chain or a rope]. This creates an aura of invulnerability and control (Preckel 2003b, 221; Shary 2002, 72). His muscles and physical abilities are the embodiment of masculinity [*rajuliyat*]. Hrithik Roshan clearly follows the tradition of actors like Sylvester Stallone or Arnold Schwarzenegger — especially when he wears the same type of clothes, namely armless shirts, or the quasi-obligatory "muscle-shirts." Masculine control over his own body is further underlined by the black *ninja* mask, which plays an important role as a symbol for terrorists. Some other symbols for the (Islamic) masquerade of the *mujahidun* are the *kaffiyya*, the traditional Palestinian head wear. They are, on the one hand, a sign for the pan-Islamic solidarity; on the other hand, they are a symbol of the rebellion against injustice. By means of these symbols, the male protagonist undergoes a process of anonymization and dehumanization.

Not only does Amaan/Roshan undergo this process, but so does the female protagonist, Fiza. After Amaan vanishes, she is no longer enduring her role as a victim of male violence. She decides not to submit to her fate [*qadar*] like her mother does but starts actively searching for her brother. Fiza's masculinization is further illustrated when she is harassed by two villains and finds the will to fight them, saying that she is no longer a weak and uninformed [*be-shurur*] woman. She even throws a bottle filled with acid at them. This masculinization is additionally seen in the clothes Fiza wears. At the beginning of the film, she is dressed in the traditional *shalwar-qameez*. Later, during the search for her brother, she wears jeans and a blouse. Then she dances in a disco in a trendy and fashionable leather outfit, and thus demonstrates that she wants to have the same freedom men have, even to flirt with whom she wants and when she wants.

The development of Fiza's character is foreshadowed by the choice of her

Amaan (Hrithik Roshan) and Fiza (Karisma Kapoor) confront their different cultural expectations in *Fiza*.

name. In Arabic, *"fiza"* means wideness and openness, so perhaps it is a symbol for her open-mindedness. This indeed is the description of Fiza at the beginning of the film. In Arabic the name normally is pronounced Fidâ, which echoes *"fidâ,"* which means "to ransom" or "devoting oneself to save another." It is this word which is used as a synonym for assassin or suicide attack in an Islamic context. In *Fiza*, the female protagonist devotes herself to the search for her brother to preserve national integrity, and finally sacrifices her personal happiness and that of the family by killing that brother (Preckel 2003a).

The climax of Fiza's masculinization is finally reached when, at the end of the film, she takes the machine gun and kills Amaan, who does not see any further positive possibilities in his life. The message of the film is that terrorism is the escalation and even exaggeration of masculinity. Aggression and violence proceed from male members of the Muslim community. The excessive lifestyle of male Islam makes men, as well as women, victims. Out of the feeling of despair, women also undergo masculinization and commit acts of violence and destruction. The result is that traditional family values are destroyed and the intact family is no longer durable. The implication is that with the destruction of the family, the survival of the whole nation is endangered. The film definitely offers no solution to the conflict, except escaping from the world by committing suicide—which, by the way, is forbidden in Islam.

There are several parallels between *al-Abwab al-moghlaka* and *Fiza*. Although Mohammed does not have exceptional physical features, as Amaan does, one can say that he undergoes a masculinization, too. His masculinization can be seen in his physical features first. At the beginning of the film, Mohammed looks like a boy. Especially in his face, one can see his soft features, which remind us of a boy. These features have completely vanished by the end of the film. His features become hard, and he dresses more like a typical Egyptian adult than as a boy. For example, he leaves aside his sneakers (Western symbols), which are a present from his father. But Mohammed's masculinization is primarily psychical. He is convinced that he has to assume all responsibilities for his family. He also wants to reverse the roles of the one who has the authority (parents) and the one who has to obey (child). Shaikh Khalid further stresses Mohammed's "duty" to be a man who is able to care for a family. This means that Mohammed should observe his family members and correct their behavior when necessary. Mohammed and his mother start to argue about this: he tells her that she should not leave home, and if it becomes necessary, she should be veiled. He shouts at her: "A woman who is not veiled will be an hung up by her own hair and burn in hell. God told all women not to leave home. Thus, you are a sinner." When Fatma tells her son to obey her and to stop talking like that, he says: "I definitely will not obey. Obedience is not accorded to a sinner." At this point of the story, Mohammed is more likely to obey his interpretation of Islam than to obey his mother.

CONCLUSION

Although *al-Abwab al-moghlaka* and *Fiza* have different approaches to the depiction of Islamic fundamentalism, they both give a vivid picture of how young Muslims suffer from a system of oppression, humiliation, sexual violence against women, and corruption. Ultimately, the protagonists of both films realize that they were betrayed by their religious leaders. They were told to act—even to kill—in the name of religion. But they have to see that Islam does not sanction acts of terrorism or violence. In both films it is stressed that Islamic fundamentalism is strongly connected to excessive masculinity. Consequently, terrorism is seen as an escalation and exaggeration of masculinity,[7] and aggression and violence stem from male members of the Muslim community. Due to the resulting disruption of traditional family values and the destruction of the nuclear family itself, Islamic values like "Worship none but Allah and be dutiful and good to parents" cannot be maintained—even in Islamic societies. The doors of open-mindedness and humanity are shut by some radical people, who believe they have solutions for all social and political problems in their countries. In their films, Khalid Mohamed and Atef Hetata issue a plea for reopening these doors and for giving young Muslims a chance for a better future.

NOTES

1. The Iran-Iraq War was commonly referred to as the Persian Gulf War until the Iraq-Kuwait conflict in 1990–1991, which came to be known as the Second Gulf War, and later simply the Gulf War. The first conflict lasted from September 22, 1980, when Iraqi troops invaded Iran, until August 20, 1988. The war was caused by disagreements over the border between the two countries. It was also a conflict between the Republic of Iraq, under the leadership of Saddam Hussein, and the Islamic Republic of Iran, under the leadership of Ayatollah Khomeini. More than 1 million soldiers are said to have been killed during the war. For further reading see Morris M. Mottale, *The Origins of the Gulf Wars* (Lanham, MD: 2001); and M. El-Azhary, ed., *The Iran-Iraq War: Historical, Economic and Political Analysis* (New York: St. Martin's Press, 1984).

2. The three main groups are the following: Hizb ul-Mujahideen, Lashkar-e-Toyeba, and Harakat ul-Mujahideen. Beside the removal of India from Kashmir, they

are fighting for the enforcement of a rigid form of Sunni Islam (Sreedhar and Manish; Akbar).

3. In this context, several European/American productions are also worth mentioning as they were on screen at the same time: *Thriller-en grym film* (Bo Arne Vibenius, Sweden, 1974) tells the story of mute prostitute Frigga, who is raped and later takes a bloody revenge. The figure of one-eyed Frigga was taken as a model for the killer Elle Driver (Daryl Hannah) in Quentin Tarantino's recent *Kill Bill* (2003–2004). *Extremities* (Robert M. Young, U.S., 1986) is about Marjorie (Farrah Fawcett), who takes revenge on a man who has invaded her home and raped her.

4. See the official Web site of the documentary at http://www.shaktiproductions .net/tcws.html. Shakti Productions also released a film on domestic violence under the title *Voices Heard Sisters Unseen*.

5. For further reading see Jarrod Hayes, "A Man Is Being Raped: Nouri Bouzid's *Man of Ashes* and the Deconstruction of Sexual Allegories of Colonialism," in *African Images: Studies in Text and Cinema*, ed. by Maureen N. Eke, Kenneth W. Harrow, and Emmanuel Yewah (Trenton, NJ: Africa World Press, 2000), 73–88.

6. For the depiction of adolescent homosexuality in American cinema, see Shary (2002), 238–246, and Shary (2005), 94–99.

7. This view is also shared by Anand Pathwardhan in his controversial documentary *Father, Son, and Holy War* (1996).

■ ■

CHAPTER 10

PROJECTING A BRIDGE FOR YOUTH

Islamic "Enlightenment" versus Westernization in Turkish Cinema

SAVAŞ ARSLAN

MEHMET: You behave like a young Viennese girl. You are learning western music: Bach, Beethoven, and Strauss. Why?

LEYLA: It is very simple: I like Vienna and the Viennese.

MEHMET: But you are not Viennese. You are from Istanbul. You are a Turk. I cannot understand why one would learn somebody else's music without learning one's own.   FROM A CONVERSATION IN THE MOVIE *Memleketim*

Popular Turkish cinema, known as Yeşilçam, peaked in the 1960s and 1970s in a complex context; it needed to respond not only to the hegemony of Hollywood but also to the complex realities of Turkish political and social life. Founded in 1923, the Republic of Turkey made a radical break with its formidable predecessor, the Ottoman Empire, by constructing a republican state based on Western models. An extensive program of reforms rooted in European models and French laicism changed the alphabet from Arabic to Latin script, westernized the calendar, and outlawed Islamic forms of dress, including the red hat known as a fez (itself a product of nineteenth-century westernizing reforms) and the full-body veil worn by women. Structural changes such as legal and educational reform were made tangible and visible through signs of everyday life, including writing and dress. State programs reformed the arts, discouraging traditional Ottoman forms in favor of a synthesis of Western and folk traditions. Yet this centralized program could not completely reform the populace in its image. Rather, the reality of Turkish experience during the twentieth century became an uneasy bridge between East and West, between Turkey's centrally projected modern identity, based in cities and remarkably secularist, and the traditional and religious practice persisting in the periphery. While many ideological groups agree that Turkey must forge a bridge between East and West, the type of bridge has always been a contested issue. In addition to the bridge forged by the central government in the field of culture, a variety of alternative bridge projects came from both the left and right sides of the political spectrum. But with all of these projects, youth has been taken as the river that runs under the bridge—a river that might be changed with dams, bridges, or by merely rerouting its flow. Countering the republican cultural projects, one such alternative project for a bridge came from the conservative religious right. Far from Islamist in the sense of a fundamentalist vision, the four films discussed in this essay are about a religious bridge for Turkish youth who find themselves at a moment of choice between Western and Eastern cultural and religious values.

The Turkish director Yücel Çakmaklı says that his entry into the film-making business was marked by the "double reality" of modern Turkey, which oscillates between West and East. He explores this theme in his 1975 film *Memleketim* (*My Homeland*), a romance between a medical student raised in rural Turkey and a rich girl from Istanbul who meet in Austria, where they are attending university. In Çakmaklı's words, these two young people "meet there and in the meantime [the filmmakers] explain the problem of westernization . . . for the first time in Turkish cinema, cultural dichotomy is the obstacle before their union."[1] The film begins when Mehmet (Tarık Akan), a medical student investigating the effects of recreational drugs, meets Leyla (Filiz Akin), a conservatory student captivated by Western culture. He wanders toward a group of her friends, who are singing to the accompaniment of a guitar, playing a John Sebastian tune. She asks in English if he is Turkish, to which he responds that he is from China; then she begins to tease her friends by claiming that they are both Afghani. Innocent as the repartee seems, it sets the film in a context where the non-West has no identity in the eyes of the West and the westernized. Thus Mehmet, eager to return home to serve his people, comes to criticize Leyla for rejecting her roots. Together, they tour Austria, stopping at museums commemorating Ottoman incursions into the area. Salzberg, birthplace of Mozart (who composed *Rondo Alla Turca*), becomes the backdrop for their discussion of the relative merits of Turkish and Western culture. The museums, of course, present the Turks as invaders, while for Mehmet they symbolize the historic might of the empire. As they travel, the sound track shifts between limpid examples of classical music and powerfully heroic Turkish folk songs that celebrate historic battles against Europe. Leaving for Turkey, Mehmet criticizes Leyla for behaving like a Viennese girl, uprooted from her own culture.

Unlike Mehmet, who plans to heal his countrymen, she plans to bring Western classical music to Turkey, thus diluting local culture. Up to this point, the film follows the structure of a melodrama, the primary genre of popular Turkish cinema; however, the sexual tension that has mounted between them is suddenly cut short as he departs for Turkey and she remains in Austria. There, Leyla finds herself in an identity crisis without him. She soon returns to Turkey, delights her grandmother by learning Turkish music, and goes in search of Mehmet. By the time she gets to him, it is too late: he is already married to a properly Turkish woman. The experiment in a dual reality has thus irretrievably failed; it is this danger, on a national scale, which the film is designed to underscore. The two projects of identity building imposed on young people are both on the same contested terrain, carrying the tensions of cultural westernization at different levels. *Memleketim* and the other three films to be discussed here overtly go against the promise of republican ideology through the use of a popular language—film—which, unlike other modes of artistic production in Turkey, was not directly mediated by the state.

It is this concern with the "dual reality" of modern Turkey that characterized the projects of the political left and the conservative, or Islamist, right in the 1960s and 1970s. As aptly put by Kemal Tahir, with reference to Marx, the two sides of the dichotomy denote two different worldviews: "The issue we call westernization was called 'The Eastern Problem' by Westerners" (131). Thus the makers of the Turkish state adopted the imperialist problem of formulating the East in the image of the West, reproducing the imperialist ethos within a nationalist ideology. Tahir proposed that the path against the ills of westernization should pass through socialism; Turkish Islamists shared this revulsion against the West. Necip Fazıl Kısakürek argues that the West has the mind and rationality to conquer *this* world, but it lacks the "spirit" of the East (224). For him, the technology and reason of the West will solve everyday problems but not the ills of any society, which can only be eliminated with the introduction of Islamic ideology. Even though the means of these projects differ, the longing toward a bridge of social engineering is hardly different in structure from that of the republican ideology of westernization that it opposes. In all of them, the prescriptions might have been different, but the younger generation was seen as being at the center of each project; youth would elevate Turkey above its current state.

Turkish popular cinema emerged despite the plans of the educated elite, whose projects disregarded tradition and ethnicity in favor of nationalist modernization programs. In their picture of positivist social engineering, seeking the path toward uplifting Turkey to the level of European civilizations, there was no place for Islam and traditional culture. As Abdullah Cevdet, a late Ottoman intellectual, wrote, "There is no other civilization: Civilization means European civilization and it must be imported with its roses and thorns" (quoted in Halman, 24). This importation was not limited to the sociopolitical and economic realms, but also involved a redefinition of arts and culture. One of the founding fathers of the cultural policies of the Turkish Republic, Ziya Gökalp, outlined what he considered to be the "essentials of Turkism" in his book of the same title. For him, the arts had to be strictly defined along the lines of Western conceptions such as humanism, high art, canons, conventions, originality, authenticity, and artistic creativity. Gökalp deemed Western genres and a modernized version of traditional folk genres appropriate for the construction of Turkish arts while disparaging Ottoman and Islamic genres. For example, Gökalp first delineates three types of music available in Turkey in the 1920s: Eastern music, Western music, and folk music. Then he claims that Eastern music is what is foreign to Turks, while folk music belongs to the Turkish *Kültür* [culture], and Western music to the new civilization of Turks. Thus genres like classical Ottoman music were ignored while Western classical music and opera, along with modernized versions of folk music, were favored. The new national culture had to be disseminated to all of the regions within the borders of Turkey, regardless of local ethnic identities.

It is not, then, very surprising that Necip Fazıl Kısakürek disparaged him as a "Durkheim thief" whose Turkism was completely against Islam (78). Kısakürek situated himself in opposition to Western culture, including the modernization or polyphonization of Turkish music through Western models, which had been one of Gökalp's projects. Given this frame, Gökalp's and Kısakürek's differences constituted a debate on what is a thorn and what is a rose: the West, or Islam? In spite of this public debate, the issue tackled by *Memleketim* was never directly addressed by the social engineers of the republic. In this vacuum, popular works like *Memleketim* emerged, taking on issues already ideologically coded in other art forms. As will be seen below, popular Islamic films also responded to such modernization projects by repeating the binaries set by the republican projects, such as East and West, traditional and modern. Instead of eliminating cultural modernization or social engineering projects imposed upon the people (with youth as a particular target), the films discussed here articulate a line of thinking similar to that of Necip Fazıl Kısakürek, basically repeating these dualities.

The film *Memleketim* takes its name from a famous pop song of the era reflecting the nationalist mood of the mid-1970s, following the war in Cyprus. This pop song has a Western musical infrastructure, which Çakmaklı normally disparaged as anathema to the national and Islamic character of his audience, but he decided to use it because it suited the mood of the film. This reflects the tactics of popular cinema exploiting any available tool. Nonetheless, the film's sound track mirrors the stress between Western classical music (Mozart's Austria) and Ottoman religious and classical music. Such a contrast goes back to the qualities of *essence:* while Gökalp talks about the "essentials," Çakmaklı talks about an "essence" that we lost and to which we must return. And though these notions are opposed, with "essentials" evoking the West, and "essence" evoking a lost Turkish past, both ideas refer to the project of creating an East/West bridge. For Çakmaklı, Turkish essence has been lost because the westernization programs and the westernized popular cinema brought about a different form of life and a cultural rupture. In other words, this problem of essence is attached to the originary mythos of the nation-state: it is a problem of origin. In this respect, all of the films dealt with here (and a handful of other Islamic films) propose an alternative national essence that is opposed to the republican one, vying with each other by utilizing youth as the tabula rasa of nation building. Republican projects firmly established the importance of a nationalist education by introducing two national holidays assigned specifically to children and youth; the Islamic films of Yeşilçam also work on this supposedly empty and contested terrain through popular films that deal with the enlightenment of young people who end up choosing the proper path of tradition and Islam out of their dichotomous personal experiences. In other words, the priorities set by the republican regime in relation to the education of youth toward nation building is, in structure, reproduced by these popular films.

Memleketim was not alone in constructing a filmic critique of the westernization project. *Birleşen Yollar* (*Merging Paths,* 1970), *Gençlik Köprüsü* (*The Bridge of Youth,* 1975), and *Yalnız Değilsiniz* (*You Are Not Alone!* 1990) provide similar examples of this trend. While the first three films come from the golden age of Yeşilçam, the fourth is from the end of this style of filmmaking.[2] While I will take these films as indicative of sociopolitical and cultural changes in the 1970s and 1980s, I should also note that the number of Islamic films made in Turkish popular cinema is limited. Yeşilçam relied on genres such as melodrama, comedy, and action, and it also produced various remakes of Western films, as well as sex comedies, in the second half of the 1970s. The first three films discussed here (all from the 1970s) did relatively well at the box office in comparison to the melodramas and comedies of the period. The fourth film, *Yalnız Değilsiniz,* was a relative box office hit in a period when popular filmmaking in Turkey was in severe difficulties and a lot of film theaters had closed.[3]

Consider that *Birleşen Yollar* came out in 1970, when Yeşilçam cinema peaked in terms of production (around 300 films a year), and that *Memleketim* and *Gençlik Köprüsü* came out in the mid-1970s, a time when both political extremism in Turkey and sex comedies in Yeşilçam were on the rise. In the 1980s, Turkish films were mainly produced for the video market in Turkey and in European countries, where Turkish immigrant workers created a high demand that in the 1990s would be met by Turkish satellite television stations. The success of a few Islamic films in the late 1980s and the early 1990s is important in that, with a couple of other films, they brought about a fresh approach to filmmaking; they also reflected change in terms of political Islam. The 1980s marked the start of the integration of Turkey into global capitalist markets and a relative process of democratization. At the same time, migration from rural to urban areas started to affect Turkey's urban culture, putting republican cultural projects centered in big cities into a serious crisis. Far from a radical Islamism, this mainstream movement consisted of a democratic response to religiosity which the militant secularism of republican reform had consistently rejected. Within this context, *Yalnız Değilsiniz* deals with the problem of the headscarf in the public sphere, an issue that emerged in the mid-1970s and became a significant political issue more than a decade later. Turkish laicism, much like its French counterpart, does not allow the headscarf in schools and governmental institutions. This film deals with the struggle of female students who choose to express their faith by wearing headscarves.

All these films feature a series of binary oppositions: traditional/modern (traditional medicine versus modern medicine); Islam/laicism (religious nationalism versus ethnic or leftist nationalism, and religious education versus the republican education system); East/West (Ottoman and Islamic versus Western musical genres; traditional or religious locales versus nightclubs and bars); rural/urban (apartment/townhouse or shantytown); Islamic enlightenment versus decadence (religious books, mosques and praying versus partying, gambling and drinking); low class/high class;[4] and male/female. The first element of these oppositions is favored, whereas the second elements are represented negatively through a melodramatic opposition between good and evil. While Çakmaklı's *Memleketim* breaks away from the melodramatic resolution of the heterosexual pairing, his *Birleşen Yollar* revolves along the lines of melodrama, much like the novel it is based on. The endings of *Gençlik Köprüsü* and *Yalnız Değilsiniz* present obvious messages directed toward the spectators even though the films themselves develop along the lines of Yeşilçam melodramas. The laying out of the above oppositions in the Islamic films of the era is not very different from the film lan-

The poster for *Yalnız Değilsiniz* (1990) focuses on the film's consideration of the sensitive issue of the headscarf for young Turkish women.

guage of Yeşilçam, despite the relative politicization of issues beyond melodramatic narration.

While this point might be read as a particular reflection of a mode of filmmaking which entered into so-called alternative filmic practices, the lines defining gender and youth relations are remarkable in the Islamic films of Yeşilçam. While most of these films are about young people trying to figure their way out of existential crises, the "true path" they espouse is surprisingly unclear. All of these films involve a heterosexual relationship building up between the protagonists through a series of binary oppositions that separate them. Many of the obstacles before the resolution deal with issues similar to Yeşilçam melodramas: good characters are flawless while evil characters, such as decadent parents, try to prevent the marital relationship and the Islamic enlightenment of their children. Above all, what is interesting in these films is the gender of the character who goes through a process of enlightenment: all of those who are enlightened are young women. This might be read in relation to a patriarchal culture: almost all of the republican reformers and Yeşilçam filmmakers were male, including all of the Islamic filmmakers. Then, it might be argued that the gender of the filmmakers led them to further define the terrain of cleanness through young females instead of young males. What seems more important is related to the politics of dress codes. In terms of male clothes, the Western-style suits are generally accepted by the Islamists, too. However, given the politically symbolic status of the headscarf, and curiously not of the full body veil, which is uncommon in Turkey, and against the relative laicism of the republican regime, it is easier to reflect on an Islamic political theme through the sign of the headscarf.

Dress reform has always been an arena characterized by sharp gender differences. While the westernization of dress for men required them to replace fezes and turbans with hats, and baggy trousers with European suits, this sartorial shift did not go against religious stipulations. In contrast, the elimination of the veil from the public sphere directly opposed Islamic traditions of the physical seclusion of women in the public sphere. Although today some forms of male dress, such as a collarless shirt worn without a tie or a particular type of beard, may represent Islamist politics, their relatively subtle inflection makes their restriction difficult.[5] Thus the politics of Islamist dress codes come to be enacted through women, for they are openly affected by the stipulations of the republican reforms, and their choice to wear a headscarf is understood as a blatant disregard for enforced secularism. As a result, Islamist men can attend school, while women are stopped at the doors of public buildings, including schools, for wearing a headscarf. Ironically, the forced secular feminism of westernization has thus created an oppositional Islamist feminism among women fighting for their right to religious expression. While men can thus function in a "dual reality" of the public and private sphere, women come to submit doubly, first to a religious patriarchal order of their own choice, and second to a state order which refuses their right to education by banning wearing headscarves in schools, thereby relegating them to more poorly paying employment. They are doubly silenced, first by the regime and second by the traditional tensions of their lifestyle.

Although Islamic films attempt to problematize these issues, their success is questionable in terms of both method and content. Often regarded as propaganda, and quite influential among their audiences, these films none-theless rely on the mainstream melodramatic tactics of Yeşilçam as well as on promotion of social engineering akin to that of the republican state. They reproduce the dialectical formations of the stresses between indigenous culture and westernization. In this regard, the working of the Islamic alternative, sharing the structure of republican projects, opts for an "essence" set by the male filmmakers. Because of this repetition of republican cultural tactics and mainstream filmic discourse, Islamic films have not produced alternative texts that might go beyond formal ideological constructs—instead, as will be seen below, they are the products of a male-dominated popular film-making industry filled with patriarchal prescriptions.

Birleşen Yollar is based on Şule Yüksel Şenler's best-selling novel Huzur Sokağı [The Street of Inner Harmony], which has some loose autobiographical elements about the writer's own Islamic enlightenment. The film's graphics (on the cover of the DVD through which it circulates today) underline the conflict between the two separate worldviews of its young protagonists. The film starts with Bilal (İzzet Günay) studying for his graduation exams in an old lower-middle-class Istanbul neighborhood marked by townhouses from the nineteenth century. Life in the neighborhood is pictured as happy, much like the idyllic south of D. W. Griffith. But the entry of modern apartments brings in upper-class residents, threatening the inner harmony of the neighborhood. Is this the threat of modernization and westernization, or is this a threat brought in by the new upper-class residents? Indeed, even though the filmmakers see it as only based on the degeneration of a cultural essence, it is the threat of modernization, which is all about breaks and divides in relation to tradition as a whole, with its sociocultural and economic makeup.

The traditional Istanbul neighborhood is also threatened by a rich girl, Feyza (Türkan Şoray), who is a resident in the new apartment building. Not surprisingly, as in many social issue films or even melodramas of the era, class distinctions are emphasized by showing two breakfast tables: one is resplendent with the excesses of a continental breakfast, and the other is as basic and simple as possible. And, as in the romance depicted in Memleketim, Feyza's friends start partying, an activity characterized by thick smoke, heavy drinking, and dancing to Western pop and rock songs. As indicated above, this is the generic theme of popular melodramas that constructs the insurmountable obstacles between the two main characters through a number of binary oppositions: high/low class, urban/rural, and so on. Crosscutting and the portrayal of the rural, low-class character in the mise-en-scène of a party are keys to depicting this opposition. If the promise of melodra-

matic text is the achievement of heterosexual romance through a deal between the economic might of the upper class and the authentic culture of the
lower class, Islamic films have a general tendency to depict upper-class characters as being in search of something beyond their decadent life. In other
words, they enact the Pygmalion story, common in popular melodramas, in
reverse.

In such a search, Feyza makes a bet about one of her friends, a classmate of Bilal, that she will make him come to her birthday party and dance
at the party. Romance is laid out in romantic comedy fashion; movement
toward the climax of play—the birthday party scene—is slowly constructed
through the cultural clash between Bilal and Feyza. Yet the contrast is off-
set by Feyza's interest in Ottoman court music and her love for her grandmother, who wears the headscarf and prays continuously. So Feyza's self is
divided between an upper-class, westernized look (makeup, perfume, music,
dancing) and a traditional, lower-class one (simplicity, her grandmother's traditional attire). Feyza's divided self is thus the battleground, and eventually
her playful side gives way to her other self, which is enlightened by Islam.
This is a slow process, in which Feyza first covers her head with a hat and
then with a headscarf, and then she begins to wear properly modest clothing.
However, the birthday party changes everything: first Bilal proposes marriage and Feyza accepts, but then Feyza's friends tell Bilal about the plot. As
Bilal leaves, despite Feyza's deep apologies, the melodrama heightens. Feyza
marries a rich businessman who turns out to be a gambler and a criminal;
Bilal marries a lower-class woman. Feyza later gets a divorce and devotes
herself to religion and to her daughter, while Bilal's happy life comes to an
end with the death of his wife, who leaves him alone with his son. Years
after Feyza's enlightenment and her pursuit of a simple life, which she creates without any support from her family, her daughter coincidentally meets
Bilal's son, who has become a doctor and treats Feyza. Before her death, Feyza
sees her daughter married to Bilal's son, and thus the rift between Feyza and
Bilal is healed. The melodramatic narrative of this film comes in part from
the novel, partly from the director's long history as an assistant director in
Yeşilçam, and also from the scriptwriter, Bülent Oran, who wrote several
hundred popular film scripts.

It is not surprising that the filmmakers who produced *Gençlik Köprüsü*
claimed that they had eschewed the trappings of popular cinema in order to
make a genuine Islamic film. Their critical attitude toward popular cinema
also involved an attempt to revolutionize the filmic environment in Turkey,
echoing the discourse of leftist filmmakers and critics. The film was directed
by Salih Diriklik, but it was written and made possible by a wider group

of filmmakers to which the director also belonged: the Akın (Raid) group, some of whose figures, like Abdurrahman Dilipak and Ahmet Ulueren, later became columnists for daily newspapers. Another member, Mesut Uçakan, made numerous films, including *Yalnız Değilsiniz.*

According to the cover of the *Yalnız Değilsiniz* DVD, the film tells how a young girl is stigmatized by leftists for writing an essay with a conservative Islamic perspective in the period preceding the 1980 military intervention, when political extremism was at its height. The message and political stance of the film seems clear from the outset, leaning toward Islamic conservatism set against republican ideology. With the mention of leftists on the cover of the DVD, the issue becomes even more complicated as the Islamists attempt to conflate the socialist left with republican reformers. Also central to the film is the development of romance between members of different classes—in this case, two couples. Again, a lavish, upper-class life is contrasted with a lower-class life through the depiction of romantic relationships. The film opens in front of the gate of Istanbul University, showing an enormous triumphal arch that ties Ottoman westernization in education with Western architectural forms, and repeating the Yeşilçam convention of identifying university students by locating them on campus. Beyond the two initially introduced romantic relationships, the film centers on an essay written by Emine (Birtane Güngör), who covers her head except at school, where the headscarf is forbidden.

The tension develops via the contrast between two different contests: a pop music contest which Mine (Necla Nazır) will attend and an essay contest which Emine will attend. The pop music contest, organized by a daily titled *Zilliyet,*[6] represents decadent westernization, while the essay contest ("Our Youth and National Goals"), organized by the Islamist MTTB (the Association of National Turkish Students), represents the true path (the Akın group was linked to the MTTB). Similarly, the names of the two high school students contrast West and East: Mine is a comparably modern name while Emine is the name of Mohammed's mother. Moreover, like other Islamic films, the film uses Ottoman music in the sound track, counterposed with westernized pop music performed by Mine. So, as Mine starts singing a cover of a famous pop song of the 1970s, Emine starts reading her essay: "The Turkish youth is in a big crisis and depression. This is not a physical or psychological crisis; it is a result of the absence of a moral and spiritual education. This education requires that they be freed from the complexes of westernization and directed to our own sources." The film thus articulates the central issue as a problem of lost essence, and as the contest between true origin and bastardized westernization. Both of the contestants become winners, but not surprisingly, their respective successes lead them to starkly different ends. Mine's *zilli* [immoral] path is supported by her republican teachers, but it leads her into the depraved world of nightclubs; Emine's true path is stigmatized by her republican teachers because of her participation in a contest organized by an Islamist association.

This theme of opposite cultures and lifestyles is reinforced by several secondary themes. The history teacher claims that Cyprus belongs to the Turks, and he opposes Turkish culture to Western culture, which is based on Greek and Roman cultures. The literature teacher, by contrast, identifies the founders of world civilizations as Sophocles,[7] Plato, and Aristotle. But against this westernized teacher, a student claims that the ancient Greeks were barbarians, and another says: "We saw what kind of a civilization they have in the Cyprus issue." Further, the students react unenthusiastically to the comedian-like teacher's explanations about the ancient Greeks who produced the earliest texts on humanism and historical materialism.

Like *Birleşen Yollar*, *Gençlik Köprüsü* depicts the murder of an Islamist student, a friend of Emine and Mahmut (Salih Kırmızı), by a group of leftist students that includes Mine's boyfriend and Mahmut's nephew Abdullah (İlhan Kasap). Following Abdullah's arrest, Mahmut, who has lost his friend and whose nephew has been arrested, starts to run aimlessly through the streets of Istanbul as he searches for some sort of divine order that can stop the political murders among his peers. The film closes with his words: "I am searching for an order, one that is in all respects part of me!"

The early 1970s melodramas gave way to the politically extremist years of the late 1970s, and the 1980 military intervention led to an authoritarian regime in the early 1980s, bringing with it significantly unequal distribution of capital in the late 1980s. With these developments, popular Turkish cinema went into sharp decline, with drastically fewer films and theaters. In this period, a few films, including some Islamic ones, briefly served as reminders of the glory days of popular cinema. One of these films was Çakmaklı's *Minyeli Abdullah* (1989), which created some euphoria before Mesut Uçakan's *Yalnız Değilsiniz*. The message of *Yalnız Değilsiniz* is evident from its alternative titles: *Serpil'in Hüzünlü Hikayesi* [*The Sad Story of Serpil*] and *Başörtüsü Dramı* [*The Headscarf Drama*]. The film was advertised with the following phrase: "She had only one wish in life, to live according to her faith." *Yalnız Değilsiniz* relates the story of a young girl who finds herself in an identity crisis which leads her to a "return to the Origin." While *Gençlik Köprüsü* seems to introduce the headscarf problem through an isolated instance, *Yalnız Değilsiniz* reminds us that the sad story of Serpil is shared by many Muslim students. This politicization of the headscarf as a symbol has become a hotly debated subject since the 1980s. Moreover, the distinction between *Muslim* students and others has been emphasized particularly by assigning the *non-Muslim* characteristics to *other* Turks. But this othering is indeed a reversal of the republican regime's othering of all threats to the unity and integrity of the regime, such as Islamists, leftists, and Kurdish nationalists.

Yalnız Değilsiniz repeats the general frame of binaries that are integral to other Islamic films and also Yeşilçam melodramas. During the opening credits, the concrete streets of an apartment block complex are torn into pieces by a growing sapling, and then the film starts with Serpil riding her bike in a similar apartment complex in Istanbul. This modern Istanbul is full of the vices of global capitalist society: ads for La Femme women's stockings and a Turkish beer, the storefronts of Wendy's hamburgers and Mudurnu Fried Chicken, a Turkish version of KFC. Passing through such vices, Serpil decides to buy dates from an old street vendor for breaking the fast in the evening. As she returns back to her upper-class apartment complex, she goes to the room of her sick grandmother (Nevin Aypar). Her grandmother is treated by traditional herbal drugs, and Serpil, who is a medical student, criticizes her for not trusting in modern medicine.

As in other films, Serpil's father (Murat Soydan) has a mistress, and her mother, Seval (Nilüfer Aydan), loves gambling. As her anatomy class leads her into deep thoughts about death, her friends keep partying, drinking, and doing drugs. But she also has a couple of religious friends: Salih (Efkan Efekan) and his headscarfed fiancée, Gülğen (Nur İncegül), who tell her about death as a reunion with the divine beyond the materialism of this world. Serpil's conversations with them also expose her to Gülğen's dilemma about the headscarf, which is forbidden in the school. Eventually, Serpil buys some Islamic books, despite the disapproval of her parents, who go to the parties of westernized Turkish elites and talk about the advantages of good relations with the U.S. and the E.U. In the meantime, Serpil's grandmother passes away while praying, and this leads Serpil to think more about death. Then she tries one of her grandmother's headscarves. In an existential crisis, she decides to learn more about herbal drugs. This leads her to a medical doctor, Murtaza (Haluk Kurdoğlu), who happens to be the uncle of Salih. She learns from Murtaza that, beyond the realm of modern, synthetic drugs, there is a metaphysical connection between sickness and treatment.

Opposed to Serpil's first steps toward Islamic enlightenment, her parents ask Serpil's cousin Füsun (Funda Birtek) to warn her about the dangerous path she is headed toward. Füsun, a "nonbeliever," is about to start a feminist association called Free Woman and asks Serpil to work with her. But

Serpil is in a state of deep thought about herself and existence; she keeps seeing her grandmother in her dreams. Eventually, her search leads her to the existence of Allah and she starts praying and covering herself with a headscarf, as well as with loose-fitting clothes. Her mother decides that she has lost her mind and thus needs professional help. After her parents put Serpil in a new private clinic, she becomes the advertising image for the clinic in a newspaper: "Victim of religious reactionaries, Serpil went mad." The last moments of the film repeat the opening sequence: a girl on a bike rides in the streets before stopping in front of a street vendor to buy dates. But this time, the girl is different—hence the name of the film: *You Are Not Alone!*

Nonetheless, the young girls of Islamic films are all alone in their struggle to wear the headscarf in schools. They do not even get much support from young Islamist men, who do not have to contend with prohibitions against their attire. Neither do the girls get support from their Muslim friends, and their westernized parents are against them. A central family figure in these films is the grandmother, who is very influential. The figure of grandmother stands for traditional Turkish life and for the Ottoman culture as valued by Islamic films. The grandmother represents the rupture created by the republican reforms, which replaced the Ottoman definition of identity based on Islam with a national identity. The great divide created by the modern nation-state in a path toward westernization produced the corrupt upper-class parents of these young girls; their grandmothers were less influenced by the republican reforms, for they were born before the founding of the Republic of Turkey. But the strong influence of the grandmother serves as a restoration of the missing link, reclaiming the true origin and essence based on an Islamic identity. Both the headscarf that their grandmothers wore and the lifestyle that they had were part of a supposedly "original" state of tradition that cannot be retrieved except in the form of nostalgia. It is because of this divide that the headscarf has become a political symbol for the Islamist films of the post-1980 period.

Despite historical changes and despite the differences between filmmakers, these later films still repeated storylines of the earlier films by Yücel Çakmaklı. Mesut Uçakan, who was involved in *Gençlik Köprüsü* and who directed *Yalnız Değilsiniz*, claims that his films are distinctly different from Yeşilçam films and the films of Çakmaklı. For him, Çakmaklı "seems to be referring to national values, especially to Islam, with a fantastic good will, and this is mostly confined to show a mosque or to call for praying." But for Uçakan, Islam should be represented "as an active way of life and a deep system of thought" (166). Moreover, he claims that his films are not pure Islamic films which you can make only in a regime where Islam infuses everyday life. Instead, he says that his films involve "the necessary and conscious compromises of a transition cinema" (in Tosun, 36). Yet another definition of post-1980 Islamic films comes from Abdurrahman Şen, who characterizes them as "white cinema," which is "respectful to religion, language, traditions and conventions of our nation and which preserves and disseminates them" (162). In the early 1990s, at a time when Yeşilçam was generally thought to be dead, white cinema was proposed as a solution to the demise of Turkish cinema in general, but it did not turn out to be as successful as it was intended to be.

Nevertheless, all four films studied here, whether national, transitional, or white cinema, share a commonality in terms of their filmic language and narratives. Despite their attempts to be different from popular Turkish cinema, they are basically melodramas. The two later films may differ from the earlier films by Çakmaklı, but Islamic films in Turkey made from the early 1970s to the early 1990s that deal with the enlightenment of young people all share the same opposition to modernization and westernization, including laicism. They do not offer an alternative to republican reforms so much as a general resistance to them. At the same time, these films seem to inadvertently reproduce the very conditions they seek to resist: they are the projections of predominantly male filmmakers or intellectuals that aim at exerting the proper sociocultural and political programs over the masses, and in this specific case, over young women, who are seen as the blank sheets of yet-to-be inscribed projects.

NOTES

1. From an interview with the author on Aug. 3, 2002.

2. In the 1990s, with the start of the "New Turkish Cinema," popular cinema in Turkey went into a serious crisis and changed its form because of private broadcasting companies, television series, and other new forms that made film available outside of theaters.

3. Following the 1980 military intervention, the number of films and film theaters decreased heavily, which led to a severe stagnation in popular cinema until recently.

4. When I asked Çakmaklı about class conflicts in his films, he responded, not very surprisingly, that he focused on the lifestyles of his characters but not on their class backgrounds, which would put him dangerously close to the leftists. This disinterest in class issues turns into an open encampment against the leftists in *Gençlik Köprüsü*.

5. Interestingly enough, the current prime minister of Turkey, Recep Tayyip Erdoğan, refuses to wear tuxedos for national or international meetings. Instead, unlike other presidents or prime ministers, he wears regular suits with ties.

6. A similar pop music contest was organized by a national newspaper, *Milliyet*,

which means "nationality"—the Arabic word "*millet*" means nation. However, the filmmakers render this name into *Zilliyet* with a play on the Arabic word "*zillet*," which means inferior or lesser, so *Zilliyet* comes to mean inferiority or lesserness. Moreover, *zilli* [literally, having or being with bells] is a curse that means "immoral woman."

7. Interestingly, the teacher says Sophocles instead of Socrates, and this must be a slip caused either by the Akın Group or by the actor who played the literature teacher.

PART 4

NARRATING GENDER AND DIFFERENCE

CHAPTER 11

NARRATING THE FEMININE NATION

The Coming-of-Age Girl in Contemporary New Zealand Cinema

MARY M. WILES

The storyteller takes what [she/he] tells from experience—[her/his] own or that reported by others. And [she/he] in turn makes it the experience of those who are listening to [the] tale. . . . In every case the storyteller is a [wo]man who has counsel for [her/his] reader . . .

WALTER BENJAMIN, "THE STORYTELLER," IN *Illuminations*

Filmmaker Vincent Ward remarks, "Childhood is a common theme in New Zealand writing. Perhaps this is due to the relative newness of the national identity, and 'rites of passage' stories reflect this coming of age" (70). This essay explores the parameters of the girl's coming-of-age story in contemporary New Zealand film, beginning with an analysis of Ward's *Vigil* (1984) and then turning to Niki Caro's recent *Whale Rider/Te kaieke tohora* (2002). In both films, the landscape serves as a correlative to the emotional states of its adolescent inhabitants and is transformed through their capacity to re-envision it—and themselves—through storytelling, fantasy, and role-playing. These fantasies of girlhood are also narratives of nation: each film reworks the dominant themes of New Zealand nationhood, replacing the active male pioneer with the imaginative, tenacious female storyteller whose coming-of-age can be understood as the allegorical re-envisioning of national evolution (Molloy, 154).[1] In each film, haunting images of a primeval world elicit our nostalgia for an innocent, pure state that becomes metonymically associated with girlhood; in each film, the residual effect of colonial dominion is allegorically resonant in an experience of traumatic loss that transforms the girl, her family, and/or her community; in each film, the girl's personal evolution is perceived to be at once the result of this primal loss and its resolution.

The first New Zealand film selected to screen in competition at Cannes, *Vigil* was hailed at the time of its release as a sign of New Zealand film's coming-of-age. *Vigil* opens as a narrative of loss. Residing in the windswept hills of the remote Taranaki valley, 12-year-old Lisa "Toss" Peers watches from the kitchen window as her father, Justin, sets ablaze some pyres of still-born lambs. Entranced by the fire, Toss anticipates the possibility of an adventure with her father and slips past her mother to join him as he trudges off toward the hills. Inspired by filmmaker Alexander Dovzhenko's portrait of Russian peasantry in *Earth* (1930), Ward silhouettes father and daughter against the diagonal horizon line formed where the sharp incline of the Taranaki hills meets an unremitting sky. During their ascent, a menacing windstorm suddenly sweeps through the valley, blinding Toss, smothering her cries, and separating her from her father and his flock. The sudden separation and moment of blind panic during the storm provide a portent of imminent tragedy. As the sky clears, they discover a lamb that has become separated from the flock and pinioned below in a steep mountain crevice. As Toss watches from the opposite hill, her father slides down to retrieve it. There is an uneasy hesitation, then the sound of rocks giving way; suddenly, Justin slips and plummets to his death below. Toss stands immobilized as his final cry echoes through the hills. This primal loss profoundly affects the girl's story and transforms the life of her family, composed of her mother, Liz, and grandfather, Birdie. The film chronicles a complex coming-of-age story which is told primarily from Toss' highly imaginative point of view. In her movement toward puberty, her father's fall becomes a correlative to her own emotional state as she teeters on the threshold between an immobilizing fear of utter loss of control and the pleasure of self-possession.

Following the funeral, one senses the peculiar quietude of the farmhouse inhabited by Toss and her mother, the sparsely furnished rooms of which open out to a remorseless sky that seems to offer no solace. The empty home as locus of trauma serves as the allegorical site for a conception of the nation that, as feminist theorist Maureen Molloy observes, "places women, hearth and home at the center or foundation and, at the same time, on the periphery of the civil state" (160). She bases her observation on Sigmund Freud's discussion of the *heimlich* (homely)/*heimisch* (native), terms that in German can convey security, familiarity, and intimacy, or, inversely, the gruesome, ghostly, and occult.[2] This dual sense of the *heimlich*, Molloy argues, "recapitulates the immanence of the unhomely in the home for women" (160). In her provocative analysis of New Zealand films released in the 1990s, Mol-

loy revisits the Freudian uncanny to substantiate her argument that "the uncanny is the feminine, the doubling, merging, unbounded, archaic unpre-
dictability neatly encapsulating not the home, nor simply the mother's body,
but the problematic that the female presents to the Western notion of the
unified bounded self" (155). Exploring its implications in the representation
of the nation, she further maintains that "the lack of boundaries, surety, and
the return of the archaic make [the uncanny] also a powerful expression of
the postcolonial nation" (160). Molloy's association of the uncanny with the
feminine enables us to explore the unique configuration of the coming-of-
age girl within the context of the postcolonial nation.

The mirroring that the film establishes between Toss and her mother invokes the doubling that is associated with uncanny feelings (Freud, 234).
Grief-stricken, Liz shares an unspoken understanding with Toss. She quietly
remarks that she wants her daughter's hair to be tied back in "shiny, smooth,
clear sharp lines" in imitation of, but different from, her own unkempt, wavy
strands. Liz quietly sews a ballet tutu for her by the light of an open window
and later, one afternoon, dons tights to model graceful dance movements for
her daughter when they practice side by side in the barn. Toss is easily distracted from ballet, however, and races outside dressed in her tutu and knee-
high rubber galoshes to see one of Birdie's miraculous new mechanical con-
traptions put in motion. Throughout the film, Toss moves back and forth
between the centrality of her mother's home and the periphery of the remote
Taranaki hills, as easily as she shifts between the names "Lisa," a derivative
of her mother's name, "Elizabeth," and "Toss," a nickname connoting her
tousled, cropped hair. Mirroring Toss' bodily oscillation, Liz' loyalty wavers
throughout the film between a determined will to preserve her home in the
rural hills and the desire to move to an urban location that offers the allure
of Western metropolitan culture.

The structure of doubling that characterizes Toss' relation with her
mother also defines her evolving relation to Ethan, a poacher whom Birdie
hires to help out on the farm after the funeral. Toss first spots Ethan through
the lens of her binoculars in the moments just before her father's fall, watching him move stealthily up an embankment to retrieve two lambs that have
gone astray, just as her father is descending the embankment. It is thus
through Toss' point of view that the spectator is introduced to Ethan, who
serves as Justin's "double," an uncanny occurrence that Freud claims happens when there is a "repetition of the same features or character-traits or
vicissitudes" (234). In this scene, the phenomenon of "the double" serves
as "an uncanny harbinger of death," foreshadowing Justin's fall; however, as
Freud notes, "the double" can serve conversely as an "assurance of immor-

In *Vigil* (1984), we watch Toss (Fiona Kay) watching the poacher, Ethan (Frank Whitten).

tality," or as Otto Rank observes, "an energetic denial of the power of death" (in Freud, 235). Through her binoculars, Toss isolates the uncanny space that repeats the nonview of her father's traumatic disappearance, which is marked by the hollow repetition of his echoing voice through the void. Ward uses the binocular lens to distinguish Toss' perspective from the adult world around her, and sound is also especially significant in creating the adolescent girl's perspective. Ward states that he wanted his character to hear the world, "muffled, unclear, then suddenly rent by the scream of a hawk or the thud of a knife into wood, sharp and lucid, reverberating down the valley like the echoes at Chartres" (72).

Instances of animistic thinking emerge repeatedly within the film to efface the boundaries between what is human and what is mechanical (Freud, 240). The family tractor is almost an automaton, fleeing across an open field as though attempting to show its human observers that it possesses a mind of its own and that it can, according to Birdie, "send out little miniatures of itself that hit your eyeball and explode—flash." Such occurrences in the film conform to what Homi Bhabha calls moments of the "cultural uncanny," which arise when cultural "non-sense" surfaces within a scientific, rationalist economy (136–137). This interrelation between "scientific rationalism and archaic 'belief,'" Molloy argues, provides Bhabha with the means to analyze the cultural dissonance produced in postcolonial nations (157). It is the girl's point of view that in *Vigil* becomes the locus of archaic, primitive beliefs, including the belief in the omnipotence of thoughts and in the magic that ensues (Freud, 240). Toss believes that she may have made Ethan appear by magic in her binocular lens and thus attributes certain superhuman powers to him. She recounts to her mother that Ethan possesses magic powers, like a prince emerging from what Gina Hausknecht terms "the deep forest of female adolescence" (36).

Toss' initial encounter with the poacher betrays a violence that foreshadows the increasingly sexual nature of his relation to her mother. Eager to help in the business of docking and tailing the lambs, she approaches Ethan, who is sharpening his knife. Reacting on impulse, Ethan unflinchingly cuts the lamb that Toss is holding in her arms, and its blood splatters across her face. She swoons from the shock, reeling beneath the force of such visceral violence. The "first blood" that Toss later smears across her face like war paint replicates the red lipstick that Liz is circumspectly applying in her bedroom mirror before welcoming Ethan to their noonday meal. In anticipation of Ethan's initial gesture of seduction, Liz preens before her mirror; Toss subsequently repeats this by creating a duplicate dressing room inside a gutted car that sits abandoned at the site of her father's fall. Toss strips to the waist while gazing at her own reflection in the mirror, her exposed torso doubling her mother's in a later scene in which Liz strips to the waist, reclaiming her sexuality by soliciting the poacher's advances. Perched in a nearby tree, Toss is privy to their impassioned gestures and cries. Afterward, Toss watches while the two ferociously devour leftover scraps of meat, while sharing unintelligible utterances.

It is through Toss' eyes and ears that we experience the home as *unheimlich*. At night, Toss lies in her bed, where she dreams of a duel between Ethan and her father. Armed with swords, both men ride fiercely through the bleak landscape like medieval Knights of the Round Table. Ward remarks, "The set had a medieval feel, as if we were seeing it through Toss's eyes after she had been influenced by Grimms' Fairy Tales" (73). Ward's choreography actualizes the intensity of Toss' Oedipal relation to Ethan and her mother and later is echoed in the primeval forest dreamscape of Christine Jeffs' *Rain* (2001), where 13-year-old Janey secretly seduces her mother's lover, an itinerant boatie and photographer whose charismatic appeal recalls that of the poacher Ethan.

The cyclical progression of the four elements—fire, air, water, earth—that marked the film's opening scenes continue to modulate Toss' emotional movement toward maturity. As night falls, torrents of rain assail the old shed

Toss creates an unusual dressing room in *Vigil*.

where Toss and Birdie huddle together. Toss soon drifts into an uneasy sleep and has another unsettling dream. Hearing the menacing sound of approaching horses' hooves, she revisits the barn, where farm equipment has acquired a mysterious life of its own. Suddenly, Ethan drops down from the sky and assails her head with electric sheers, recalling the celebrated dream scene from E. T. A. Hoffmann's tale in which the child Nathaniel dreams that the Sandman takes "red-glowing dust out of the flame with his hands" and then attempts to sprinkle it into his eyes (91). Toss screams and wakes up suddenly, carefully touching her head to ascertain that it is still in place. Feeling a moist sensation, she reaches under her jacket and, when she extracts her hand, sees that it is covered in blood. Frightened, she alerts her grandfather to the fact that she is dying. When Birdie flatly replies, "Aren't we all," Toss wraps herself in a blanket and goes outside to stand alone in the rain. Framed in profile, she ceremonially removes the woolen hood that has protected her head and masked her face; she quietly opens up the blanket to cleanse her body of menstrual blood. This solemn moment marks Toss' acceptance of her body as the site of her struggle with her environment (Boudreau, 44). It figures centrally in her complex rite of passage, doubling the bleak funeral scene in which her mother, emotionally denuded, cries silently in the rain at her father's grave.

The following morning, Toss watches from the window as Ethan beats on the shed door in an attempt to say good-bye to her before he drives off. Watching as his car crashes across the broken gate separating their farmhouse from the world outside, Toss blinks several times, as though to confirm that her final vision of Ethan is truly no longer a vision and that she has stopped fantasizing. His departure, which doubles her inaugural loss of her father, allegorically demarcates the traumatic period of readjustment experienced by New Zealanders, who, divested of their privileged trade relation with the British in the mid-1970s, were subsequently forced to adapt to their new ambivalent status (Molloy, 167). Ethan's return to the devastated farm family in the role of a "poacher," the shady "double" of the dead symbolic father, must be viewed as the working through of traumatic loss within the parameters of an ad hoc matriarchal unit. Like those New Zealand farmwives who at the time were assuming more active roles in the farm business, Liz playfully reminds Ethan following their lovemaking, "I might as well make use of you while you're on the payroll." Toss' loss of "double" vision in the final scene corresponds to her loss of dual fathers and so confirms her affirmation of self. As the girl's coming-of-age story revolves around her shifting relationship to the two fathers, Justin and Ethan, it offers us an allegorical re-envisioning of national evolution moving beyond the sanctuary of the past into the uncertain future.

Vigil represents a departure from earlier New Zealand films where, as Martin and Edwards point out, physical engagement with the environs of the new country represented a rite of passage to manhood (48). In Ward's film, the innocent body of the adolescent girl is interfaced with a primordial New Zealand landscape that, while appealing to our nostalgia for an archaic, primitive past, discloses the inevitability of a new postcolonial identity. As the family farmhouse recedes on the horizon, Toss hesitates momentarily but then proceeds down the road, following the elevated mobile home that is pulled along behind Birdie's repaired tractor. This closing scene is reiterated in the final scene of *Rain*, where we share Janey's uneasy perspective as she journeys down the road away from the world of childhood, marked forever by the sense of responsibility she shares with her mother for her younger brother's death at the beach. In *Vigil*, Ward captures the secret world of the adolescent girl in a film that questions the dominant representations of New Zealand nationhood by refocusing our attention on the female storyteller. The female teller of tales continues to figure prominently in recent New Zealand films, such as Brad McGann's *In My Father's Den* (2004), where world-weary war journalist Paul finds a reflection of his former self in 16-year-old Celia, a spinner of tales, like he is, who plans to renounce her small-town life in central Otago and realize her literary ambitions in Europe.

Like *Vigil*, Niki Caro's *Whale Rider* provides a legend of loss transformed. During an interview at the TriBeCa Film Festival, filmmaker Caro stated, "I was actually very inspired by New Zealand films in my growing-up years. It was Vincent Ward's first film, *Vigil*, and his short films that opened up a whole new world for me. And it was a world I could move around in" (in Kehr, E1: 23). Caro's film opens with a peaceful seascape on the eastern coast of New Zealand and the deep blue marine world inhabited by the whales, who connect the Ngati Konoki tribe of Whangara to the sacred traditions of their ancestors. According to Maori legend, their tribal ancestor Paikea rode into the village on the back of a whale. The film story begins with the birth of Pai, who is named after her ancestor Paikea and so represents the end of a long line of tribal chiefs. Like *Vigil*, the film opens with a narrative of loss. Pai suffers the traumatic loss of her twin brother and her mother, who both die in childbirth. Grief-stricken, her father, Porourangi, departs for Europe to pursue a career producing modernist sculpture, leaving Pai behind with her paternal grandfather, Koro, the Whangara village chief, and her grandmother, Nanny Flowers. The film story recommences 12 years later, chronicling the coming-of-age story of the girl Pai.

The film is an adaptation of Witi Ihimaera's novel in which the girl's coming-of-age story acquires the mythic dimensions associated with the tale of an ancient bull whale. Pai's early loss parallels that of the whale, who, years earlier, faced abandonment when sharks savaged his mother in the shallows of Hawaiki. The calf's mournful crying was heard by the whale rider Paikea, who succored him and entered the sea playing a flute. Many years later, the ancient bull whale remembers his master's flute music as a "rhapsody of adolescence" (17). The novel explains that the male voice of the whale rider, Paikea, possesses a supernatural quality that allows him to communicate with the whales and command them. In the film adaptation, the whale rider's supernatural ability to *interlock* with nature is articulated predominantly through the female voice. Pai's voice-over narration introduces us to the family and the events surrounding her birth. At the film's beginning, Pai's voice seems to emanate from a murky blue depth that is coincident with that "glassy sea known as the Pathway of the Sun," thus associating the girl's voice with a primeval moment prior to the creation of Western civilization (Ihimaera, 16). The remainder of the film works to restore to the woman's voice its mythical dimension and thus accomplish its harmonization within the patriarchal assemblage of Maori culture, which had effectively excluded it.

While Pai's grandmother, Nanny Flowers, serves as a constant source of strength and wisdom, Pai's life is profoundly affected not only by the loss of her mother at infancy but also by the emotional absence of her grandfather, who remains bitter about the death of his grandson, whom he regards as the sole legitimate heir to the chieftaincy. When his firstborn son, Porourangi, returns home from Europe for a rare visit, Koro meets with him in the *whare whakairo* [carved meeting house] and reproaches him for his neglect of traditional Maori customs, admonishing him for failing to complete the carving on his *waka* [sacred canoe], which he began before his departure. During a slide presentation of his recent work, Porourangi adds insult to injury when he confesses to his audience of curious spectators that he is involved with a German woman, Ana, who is pregnant with his child. Koro becomes enraged with his son's refusal of family tradition and fumes that Pai is of no use to him. Porourangi later asks Pai if she would like to return with him to his new home in Germany, and initially, Pai agrees to accompany him. When the day of their departure from Whangara arrives, Koro watches from the window of their home and comments to Nanny, "When she was born, that's when things went wrong for us." Depleted and childless, the Apirana house is haunted by a colonial presence that continues to inhabit private space, "rendering it the most unhomely place of all" (Molloy, 164).

Pai is not only excluded from her grandparents' home—which clearly is neither *her* home nor strictly *theirs*—but also from the public spaces of the meetinghouse and chief school. Summoned home by the mystical sounds of the sea, Pai stands at the threshold of the meetinghouse, where she greets her grandfather. Immersed in conversation with other male elders in their search through sacred books for answers to the community's dilemma, he sternly replies, while barely looking up, "Not now, Pai." The meetinghouse that traditionally served as a venue for intertribal gatherings and political debate, according to Jeffrey Sissons, also served as the site where the elders met to discuss responses to colonialism (36). While the meetinghouse clearly serves as the focal point of the Whangara settlement, it forecloses the feminine voice, thereby reinforcing the sense of the unhomely in the home for women. Pai is also denied admission to Koro's chief school, where he provides the Maori boys of the community with training in the rituals and customs of their tribe. When the boys arrive at the *marae* [ancestral meeting place] for their initial lesson, Nanny summons Pai for the opening *karanga*, which Maori feminist Kathie Irwin describes as "the first call of welcome to all who have gathered, the living and the dead" (14). Despite Koro's protests, Nanny begins the *karanga* standing in the porch of the meetinghouse. Historian Anne Salmond observes that such women, widely admired for their clear, strong voices, are known in their *iwi* [tribe] as "bugles" (127). Pai then replies to her grandmother from the visiting side and, following the tradition of the *pai arahi* [leaders over the threshold], leads the boys who process to the *marae tea*, the central space between the hosts and guests during a welcome. Yet Koro insists that Pai sit behind the men rather than among them, thus prohibiting her participation. Gender division on the *marae*, as Salmond points out, is based upon the principle that men are *tapu* [sacred], whereas women are *noa* [common] (127). A woman can only stand to speak on the *marae* if her birth is so high that her *mana* [prestige] overrides her *noa* status, and, as Salmond notes, this rare occurrence is possible only in certain tribes (127).

Although patriarchal tradition embodied in her grandfather's prohibition prevents Pai from participating in the traditional *whare whakairo* and chief school, her primordial oceanic home provides her with shelter and offers her an alternative space to fashion a feminine identity. The sea and its creatures remain inaccessible to her grandfather and his male students, however. Still searching for a future chief, Koro takes the boys to an isolated inlet where he throws his *rei puta* [whale tooth] pendant into the ocean. He tells them that they must dive and retrieve it, for the one who finds it will become chief. Koro is devastated when none surface with it and blames Pai for their failure, insisting that she leave their home. From the dark still solitude, Koro calls on the ancient ones. His lament is drawn from that of Paikea, who had called on the ancient ones when his canoe sank. It is Pai's nondiegetic voice-over recitation, however, that usurps the supernatural authority of the male voice in this scene, informing us that the ancient ones are not listening. Pai's mystical capacity to *interlock* with nature recalls the supernatural strength of another New Zealand swimmer, Alex Archer, who in filmmaker Megan Simpson's *Alex* (1993) overcomes personal loss to win selection for the 1960 Olympic Games in Rome. The film shows how Alex's unique relation to the sea and its creatures provides her with exceptional power and speed in the pool, thus enabling her to triumph over her British rival, Maggie Benton. Newcomers to New Zealand, the cosmopolitan Bentons are portrayed as colonial usurpers who embody the potential threat of ferocious international competition. As in *Whale Rider*, the film's opening and closing scenes connect Alex's coming-of-age story with the spiritual trajectory of the primeval creatures that guide her. Indeed, Pai's forceful voice-over, which resists colonial or patriarchal domination, echoes that of Alex at the film's close: "I've always known that in another life I was or will be a dolphin. I leap over and through the waves, free and triumphant."

Pai's destiny, along with that of the Ngati Konoki tribe, is assured when

Lauren Jackson plays the title role in *Alex* (1993), the story of an inspiring New Zealand girl.

she reclaims her connection to her ancestress, Muriwai. While seated with her granddaughter in the *waka* overlooking the ocean, Nanny explains to Pai the significance of her matriarchal lineage: "You have the blood of Muriwai in your veins, girl." Muriwai's story provides the feminine counterpart to that of Paikea. At the time of the Great Fleet, Muriwai and the sisters of the Matatua canoe sighted a good landing place at Whakatane (Irwin, 15; Salmond, 149).[3] The men disembarked to explore this inviting place, but Muriwai and the others were left aboard the canoe (Salmond, 149). Treacherous tides dislodged the canoe, which proceeded to drift out to sea. Usually, only men were permitted to paddle a canoe, but in the moment of immediate danger, Muriwai took up a paddle and, according to Salmond, cried out, "Let me make myself a man!" (149). She commanded her crew and managed to paddle the Matatua to safety, saving them all from certain destruction. Muriwai's deeds are the source for the *"kawa wahine,"* which Irwin describes as "a women's etiquette amongst the tribes descended from Muriwai . . . highborn women in the direct line from Muriwai have held the right to speak on the *marae"* (15). Pai's *whakapapa* [genealogy] would clearly place her among those privileged few.

In the face of her grandfather's prohibition, however, Pai is forced to call to the ancient ones from her father's *waka*. Balanced on the periphery of

Pai (Keisha Castle-Hughes) calls to the ancient ones from the *waka* in *Whale Rider* (2002).

the coastline, the forgotten *waka* serves Pai as an alternative home, which connects her to the sea, her true spiritual abode. Pai's transformation of the abandoned canoe into a space of feminine performance recalls Toss' conversion of the deserted auto into a girl's vanity. In each film, the girl's private performance space permits her to formulate a feminine identity through role-playing apart from the preconceptions and prohibitions of patriarchal society. This private space that each girl inhabits not only serves to commemorate the mythic past, which is allegorically expressed in the loss of family members and/or community, but also allows her to look ahead to the unforeseeable future. Pai's destiny is clear when she later retrieves the magical whale tooth ornament from the ocean floor; the sounds of the ancient ones guide her to it and thus assure her ascendance to the chieftaincy. In her unique ability to transform the village landscape through the traditional gestures, language, and songs of the Maori, Pai usurps the traditionally male role of the storyteller and rewrites the initial scenario of loss as a narrative of resistance.

The final scene shows Pai, like her ancestress Muriwai, take command of the *waka*, restoring it to its position of pride. Seated in the center beside her grandfather, Pai is surrounded by a crew composed of the male members of the Apirana family and Maori community, who together move gracefully in time with the rhythmic chant she provides as they paddle the craft toward the Pacific rim. Here, Pai plots her own future course and that of her people with the pronouncement, "I am not a prophet, but I know that our people will keep going forward, all together, with all of our strength." Pai's mystical connection to the sea offers her a powerful vision of personal destiny, which retells her traumatized past and that of the Maori community as a story of self-possession within the postcolonial landscape of New Zealand. This solemn moment serves as a mythic site where the past becomes the present, where the natural environment blends with the supernatural and where a broken male lineage is restored in its association with the feminine.

In both films discussed, girls use fantasy, storytelling, and myth to generate landscapes in which they do figure, in part as a response to those cultural and/or familial landscapes in which they do not. The fairy-tale tropes and tribal myths that inform the girl's story in *Vigil* and *Whale Rider*, respectively, are rooted in an oral folk tradition and, as feminist historian Marina Warner notes, are passed down from generation to generation (34). While invoking oral folk tradition, the girl's story in each film offers a redemptive fantasy, which may entail collusion with structures of oppression, as in *Whale Rider*, or involve strategies of resistance, as in *Vigil*. One might argue that these films fabricate an escapist vision when compared with such recent New Zealand films as Lee Tamahori's *Once Were Warriors* (1994) and Harold Brodie's *Orphans and Angels* (2003), which address grim urban realities such as racial violence and domestic abuse, alcoholism, and drug addiction, which the contemporary girl must confront in the city. And yet, the girl capable of determining her own place within the postcolonial landscapes depicted in *Vigil* and *Whale Rider* is missing from the dark cityscapes predominant in Tamahori and Brodie's dramas, and she is severely curtailed within such New Zealand films as Jane Campion's *The Piano* (1993) and Peter Jackson's *Heavenly Creatures* (1994), where, as Molloy convincingly argues, the feminine creative impulse is effectively shattered (154). Clearly offering an alternative to these pessimistic national narratives of the 1990s, *Whale Rider* returns to the triumphant tale of girlhood evident in *Alex* and *Vigil*, in which the implicit promise of a new feminine nation becomes apparent in the ascendant figure of the coming-of-age girl. *Whale Rider* continues to demonstrate the "opening toward the new" already discernible in *Vigil*, where, in Julia Kristeva's terms, uncanniness allows us to move beyond our own fragile boundaries and "tally with the incongruous" (188). In each film, the girl assumes the traditional role of the storyteller, revealing a distinct vision and voice that ensure her active presence in the discourses of emergent nationalisms.

NOTES

1. This analysis is conceptually indebted to Maureen Molloy's examination of Peter Jackson's *Heavenly Creatures* (1994), Jane Campion's *The Piano* (1993), and Lee Tamahori's *Once Were Warriors* (1994) in "Death and the Maiden: The Feminine and the Nation in Recent New Zealand Films," in which she addresses the films as "fantasies of femininity that are simultaneously narratives of nation" (154).

2. Maureen Molloy draws on Freud's discussion of the different shades of the word "*heimlich*" that include its opposite, "*unheimlich.*" Freud states: "Thus *heimlich* is a word the meaning of which develops in the direction of ambivalence, until it finally coincides with its opposite, *unheimlich*" (226).

3. Philip Armstrong's compelling discussion of *Whale Rider* underlies much of my thinking about this film throughout this essay. Armstrong maintains that the film offers us a formal rhetoric of Maori cultural survival, which opposes images of preservation and stasis to images of change and movement.

CHAPTER 12

GENDER, RACE, FEMINISM, AND THE INTERNATIONAL GIRL HERO

The Unremarkable U.S. Popular Press Reception of Bend It Like Beckham *and* Whale Rider

SARAH PROJANSKY

The fact that U.S. popular culture pays attention to girls is certainly not a new phenomenon; nevertheless, I would argue that representations of girls have significantly intensified since the mid-1980s. For example, since as early as 1923, when *Time* began publishing, girls appeared on the cover of that magazine once per year in most years; but, starting in 1986 they appeared several times nearly every year. In the 1990s, new television shows centering on girls included *Clarissa Explains It All* (1991–1994), *The Secret World of Alex Mack* (1994–1998), and *The Mystery Files of Shelby Woo* (1996–1999). All three aired on the children's cable station Nickelodeon as part of their explicit attempt to break new ground in children's programming by representing girls as central figures in shows aimed at a mixed-gender audience.[1] By the late 1990s, shows featuring girls proliferated on the networks, with, for example, twins Tia and Tamara Mowry in *Sister, Sister* (1994–1999), music star Brandy as *Moesha* (1996–2001), and Melissa Joan Hart (formerly of *Clarissa*) as *Sabrina, the Teenage Witch* (1996–2003). Shows such as *Buffy the Vampire Slayer* (1996–2001), *Joan of Arcadia* (2003–2005), and *Veronica Mars* (2004–) followed. Relevant films include, for example, *Clueless* (1995), *Pocahontas* (1995), *Harriet the Spy* (1996), *Mulan* (1998), *Bring It On* (2000), *Girlfight* (2000), *Lilo and Stitch* (2002), *Real Women Have Curves* (2002), *Thirteen* (2002), *Ella Enchanted* (2004), *Mean Girls* (2004), *Ice Princess* (2005), and *Herbie: Fully Loaded* (2005).

Also in the late 1990s and early twenty-first century, a spate of new magazines for girls appeared, including *Teen People* (1998–), *Cosmo Girl!* (2000–), *Elle Girl* (2001–), and *Teen Vogue* (2001–).[2] While *Seventeen* (1944–) had previously dominated the teen and preteen market, the titles (and content) of these new magazines make explicit their link to women's magazines, while simultaneously declaring this industry's heightened attention to girls as a specific target market and as formidable consumers in their own right. Also in print media, Mary Pipher's best-selling book, *Reviving Ophelia: Saving the Selves of Adolescent Girls* (1995), made "Ophelia" a well-known metonym for contemporary girls' angst. In the wake of *Reviving Ophelia*, several books addressing girls as "troubled" have emerged, including *Odd Girl Out: The Hidden Culture of Aggression in Girls* (R. Simmons 2002) and *Queen Bees and Wannabes: Helping Your Daughter Survive Cliques, Gossip, Boyfriends, and Other Realities of Adolescence* (Wiseman). There has been a spate of "anti-Ophelia" books, as well, which argue that girls are more resilient and resourceful than Pipher would suggest and that angst is not so much a syndrome as one part of the experience of girlhood (e.g., *Ophelia Speaks: Adolescent Girls Write about Their Search for Self* [Shandler], *In Your Face: Stories from the Lives of Queer Youth* [Gray], and *Yell-Oh Girls! Emerging Voices Explore Culture, Identity, and Growing Up Asian American* [Nam]).

I would argue that collectively these representations (among many, many, many others) reveal a recent form of what Michel Foucault calls an "incitement to discourse," in this case about girls.[3] While some of the discourse worries that girls are troubled, that "the media" or "popular culture" is to blame for much of girls' supposed difficulties, and that girls need protection —not attention—from the media, concomitantly, contemporary popular discourses provide a continuous discussion and surveillance of girls, expecting them to "live large" (Harris) in the public eye and, of course, proliferating those very media depictions of girls about which they worry. In other words, anxiety discourse incites an endless supply of more discourse—whether anxious, defensive, or celebratory—about girls. Collectively, these discourses figure girls in complex and contradictory ways: as vulnerable, yet powerful; as endangered, yet dangerous; as violated, yet wholesome; as spectacular, yet ordinary; as childlike, yet adultlike. Anita Harris has summed up these contradictory binaries by putting contemporary representations of girls into two categories: "can-do girls" and "at-risk girls."[4]

Within this context, at the turn of the twenty-first century, several international films featuring girls as heroes have become runaway hits in the United States, including *Run, Lola, Run* (1998, Germany), *Amelie* (2001, France), *Bend It Like Beckham* (2002, U.K.), and *Whale Rider* (2002, New Zealand). These films have crossed over from a more typical, to-be-expected short art house run to lengthy art house runs in multiple cities *and*, more significantly in terms of box office, to "mainstream" multiplex screens throughout the United States. For example, late in the summer of 2003, in my hometown of Champaign, Illinois (not far from Peoria), *Bend It Like Beckham* and *Whale Rider* were both playing at the same local multiplex, *Whale Rider* on what the multiplex has explicitly dubbed their "art house" screen[5] and *Bend It Like Beckham* on one of their unnamed "regular" screens. The next week *Bend It Like Beckham* continued its run, while *Whale Rider* moved to a regular screen elsewhere in the theater and another "art film" took its place for the requisite one-week run. Almost simultaneously, a poster for the upcoming video/DVD release of *Bend It Like Beckham*[6] went up in a prominent place in the window of my local video rental store. A month or so later, the poster for the upcoming video/DVD release of *Whale Rider*[7] went up. The two posters continued to sit side-by-side throughout the fall of 2003, inviting passers-by to rent these films and vicariously experience what reviews of the films overwhelmingly call "girl power."[8]

On the one hand, it is entirely unremarkable that the U.S. marketing campaigns for two films in the early twenty-first century simultaneously drew on girl power discourse about two very "can-do" girls to define and sell their films. It is even somewhat unremarkable that both were international films.[9] After all, both were hugely successful in their home countries, internationally, and on the festival circuit[10] prior to opening in the United States. In fact, *Whale Rider* is the most successful New Zealand film to date, and *Bend It Like Beckham* is the "top-grossing British-financed and distributed film ever" (Turan, March 12, 2003) and the first British film by a "nonwhite Briton" to become the top-grossing film on the British charts (Alibhai-Brown). In short, by the time these films came to mainstream U.S. theaters, they were as close to a sure bet as any nonblockbuster could be. On the other hand, it is worth remarking on the fact that, unlike *Run, Lola, Run* and *Amelie*, these two films center on girls of color who, during the course of the film, explicitly address issues of racialization and minoritization in the context of national and neocolonial identities.[11] And, reviews of the films in the U.S. press celebrate and even highlight this fact. For example, in the case of *Bend It Like Beckham*, the U.S. reviews focus the majority of their attention on Jess, played by Parminder Nagra (who is Indian British), despite having the opportunity to center on (or at least pay equal attention to) her co-star/sidekick Jules, played by Keira Knightley (who is Anglo British).[12]

This focus on two international films featuring confident and powerful girls of color challenging racism and sexism in their daily lives is unusual and potentially transformative or even disruptive in the context of U.S. popular culture. Nevertheless, in this essay I argue that the *ways in which* the reviews maintain this focus contribute to the continued displacement of U.S. girls of color. It is as though the comfort with seeing and addressing racism and sexism abroad and the full embrace of these films and their girl heroes stand in for a potential critique of racism and sexism or analysis of race and gender in a U.S. context. Collectively, the press coverage has a self-congratulatory tone about it: it addresses race, and even racism, gender, and even feminism, and celebrates the "overcoming" narratives the press itself finds in the films, all the while drawing the reader's attention to this broad-minded perspective.

The coverage, then, follows a typical "saving Other women from Other men" (Addison) logic, implying that things may be bad "over there" and we must support the girls who are doing something about it, but things must be better here, especially because we can recognize these "problems" and cele-brate the girls who overcome them. Both Erin Addison, in her discussion of *Aladdin*, and Ella Shohat, in her discussion of media coverage of the early-1990s United States war against Iraq, point out that white men function as saviors in the respective narratives. In this case, the film *Whale Rider* re-fuses this narrative and *Bend It Like Beckham* resists it.[13] I argue here, how-ever, that the press coverage itself steps into the role of white savior of Other women from Other men/cultures, using reviews of the films to complete this narrative.

I base this argument on a review of national U.S. press coverage of these films from their emergence in the international film scene in mid- to late-2002 through the summer of 2004, when I completed this research. I should be clear that this is not an argument about audience, extrapolated from the reviews. Rather, I am interested in examining how the U.S. popular press' positioning of these films is itself both productive of particular readings of the films and supportive of two interconnected cultural narratives, in par-ticular: one about the backwardness of Other cultures in comparison to the rationality of U.S. culture and the other about the supposed benevolent ac-ceptance of gender equality such that, while feminism may still be neces-sary elsewhere, the United States is beyond any need for feminist activism or analysis. The United States is thus safely postfeminist, and happily so, in that having supposedly evolved to this point means it is safe to celebrate "girl power" films such as *Bend It Like Beckham* and *Whale Rider*. Simul-taneously, the celebration of these films reinforces the implication that the United States is, indeed, in a postfeminist moment.[14] I develop this discus-sion by exploring three themes that emerge consistently in the press cover-age: a definition of the films as ahistorically authentic, a claim for the uni-versality of the films' stories, and a disavowal of the relationship between the films and their (potential) feminism. While these certainly are not the only themes in the press coverage, they are dominant ones, and they appear consistently across time and across discussions of both films. Furthermore, they work together to produce the version of U.S. benevolence I am describing here. I turn now to an analysis of each of these themes, in turn.

THE TIMELESSNESS AND AUTHENTICITY OF "OTHER" CULTURES

Defining a film as authentic and timeless is one way to distance it from the contemporary United States. For example, several reviews of *Bend It Like Beckham* attribute the film's supposed realism to the fact that the film's director is Sikh, as are her characters, and grew up in the same area of London where the film takes place. One review states that "there is a reality underneath *Bend It Like Beckham*'s easy humor, an impeccable sense of milieu that is the result of [the director] knowing the culture intimately enough to poke fun at it while understanding its underlying integrity" (Turan, March 12, 2003). Here, the collapse of the director with the film in the service of producing an authenticity authorizes someone from the outside of the supposedly authentic culture to take pleasure in laughing at that culture without risking critique for denying the film's/culture's "integrity." The "authentic" director, after all, provided the humor in the first place.

Reviews sometimes specifically couch arguments ascribing realism to the film through references to food, implying the "authenticity" and attractiveness (even if the overall review is negative) of the culture in question. These reviews literalize what bell hooks calls "eating the other": representing an exoticized other as desirable and profoundly possessable/consumable for a white subject. Building on hooks' work, Laura Ann Lindenfeld argues that some U.S. films that focus on race and ethnicity offer "a form of 'culinary tourism' . . . [in which] the white spectator can safely visit the world of the ethnic other and consume this food and family in a comforting, inviting, vicarious environment" (205). The reviews of *Bend It Like Beckham* exhibit this idea of "culinary tourism" with great delight.[15] For example, one review comments that "[the film has a] light-as-Indian-bread content and tone" (Toumarkine) or, more disparagingly, "[Jess' mother's] . . . shtick is as tired and unsalvageable as a week-old pakora" (Zacharek). One headline about several Indian films, not just *Bend It Like Beckham*, is titled: "Bollywood Flavor Curries Brit Favor" (Dawtrey). Here, "Indianness" is collapsed into one thing, such that there is no difference between Indian-made films (which *Bend It Like Beckham* is not) and Indian British films (such as *Bend It Like Beckham*), and that one thing can then further be reduced to food: in this case, the ubiquitous "curry." At least two reviewers take the discussion of food so far as to reveal their literal desire to eat the other. The more positive

Jess (Parminder Nagra) employs her football teammates to help dress her in formal attire for her sister's wedding in *Bend It Like Beckham* (2002).

(although perhaps more shockingly ethnocentric) of the two reviews claims "all ethnic comedies feature scenes that make you want to leave the theater and immediately start eating, and *Bend It Like Beckham* may inspire some of its fans to make Indian friends simply so they can be invited over for dinner" (Ebert, March 12, 2003).[16]

If *Bend It Like Beckham*'s realism comes at least partly from a conflation of "Indianness" with "Indian food," *Whale Rider*'s authenticity comes at least partly from a well-worn cultural association of indigenousness with landscape and the physical body, also available for consumption. In her discussion of another context—the scholarly debate over the "authenticity" of *Nanook of the North* (1922)—Fatimah Tobing Rony points out that whether the film is praised or condemned for its construction of authenticity, "in both cases, what is ignored is how *Nanook* emerges from a web of discourses which constructed the Inuit as Primitive man, and which considered cinema, and particularly Flaherty's form of cinema, to be a mode of representation that could only be truthful. I am not so much interested in whether or not Flaherty was an artist or a liar, but in taxidermy and how *the discourse of authenticity has created the film*" (301, emphasis added). While no debate emerges in the reviews of *Whale Rider*, their discourse of authenticity follows the pattern Rony describes and produces a particular circumscribed reading of the film, as well as an objectifying anthropological gaze. In particular, reviews of *Whale Rider* take both the location shooting and the Maori actors (both professionals and locals who had not acted previously) to be evidence of the film's "unmistakable authenticity" (LaSalle). One review says that the film "vibrantly *showcases* authentic Maori culture—the cast is exclusively Maori" (Calder, emphasis added).[17] The film also "opens a *window* into the indigenous Maori community and its traditions" (Tarabay, emphasis added). In these two examples the film functions as a passive display of culture ("showcase," "window") available for the viewer to gaze at unwatched, as a voyeur. Yet another review claims "*Whale Rider* is almost anthropological in its details" (Butler), defining the film not as a display to be gazed at but rather as an object to be mined for evidence of cultural authenticity.

All of these examples, in addition to reducing the meaning of culture to a static thing to be consumed/observed/mined, also reveal tautological thinking. The logic goes something like this: "I saw it in a movie that comes from/ is made by someone of that culture; I don't see those images everyday outside *my* back door; thus, it sure seems authentic/realistic; therefore, it must be authentic/realistic." For some, that tautology leads to a desire to consume the other, as in: "let's go out to eat" or "let's take a tourist trip to a beautiful land."

In many of the discussions of both films, this "authentic" Indian and Maori culture, respectively, is taken to be, by definition, patriarchal. This association of authenticity and patriarchy then displaces gender issues to elsewhere. Again, it is an unquestioned tautological assumption of the reviews that the specific attitudes toward girls and women, and views of girls and women expressed by the fictional characters in the film, do in fact represent the actual views of the entire (assumed to be unified) cultures in question, and have always represented their views. For example, one review calls Jess' parents in *Bend It Like Beckham* "traditional disapproving parents" (Bernard) who "are adamant about holding on to their traditional Sikh ways" (Gleiberman).[18] One review offers a slightly less negative version of traditionalism, while still nicely revealing the logical leaps these articles make as they connect "cultural tradition" to "patriarchal attitudes": "[these are] parents who, while not hidebound traditionalists, nonetheless think sports are an improper pastime for an almost-grown teenager with marriage and university to think about" (Scott). Here, implicitly it is a slightly (although not "hidebound") traditional attitude to believe that sports are improper for girls. This claim is made as though "we all know" that girls do not, have not, never have, (never will?) play/played sports in "Indian cultures," but do, of course, play sports in "our" culture, presumably without any fear of reprisal or discrimination.

Even the fact that, in *Whale Rider*, Pai's grandfather and grandmother *disagree* about the role of girls as leaders (he thinks it's a bad idea; she thinks it's a good idea) does not deter the critics from assuming that it is the grandfather's view that reveals the "truth" of Maori beliefs, despite the film's developed depiction of, for example, the grandmother as a key leader in the community and Pai's female teacher as a key figure for the perpetuation and interpretation of cultural traditions and the community's history and present. A typical claim in reviews of *Whale Rider* is that "tradition dictates absolutely that a girl, no matter how capable or involved, cannot fill [the] position [of leader]" (Turan, June 6, 2003).[19] One review states quite explicitly the assumption that "the beliefs that Koro [the grandfather] holds to are ones handed down for centuries" (Pickle). Headlines often draw on this theme, as in "Beauty and the Beast Called Tradition" (Whitty) and "Girl Battles Exotic Culture's Bias" (Gillespie).

More starkly, even the fact that many articles report that Keisha Castle-Hughes (who plays Pai) learned to fight with taiaha sticks (which only men are supposed to handle) during the making of the film, thereby providing one specific example of the adaptability and complexity of the culture in relation to gender, functions in these reviews only to reinforce the idea of timeless patriarchy. In one interview, for example, Castle-Hughes says: "The men, the Maori warriors, used to fight each other with [the taiaha sticks], and the whole purpose of Pai doing it [in the film] is because girls aren't allowed to. Even to this day. When I learned to use taiaha, I found it funny at first. I was like, 'I shouldn't be doing this,' but I had heaps of support. And we did some Maori chants and things so that it was possible for us to do the fighting" (Karan). This story reveals both that Castle-Hughes was able to use the taiaha sticks in her work and that there are "chants and things" within her community that address the possibility that a girl or woman might want to or need to use taiaha sticks. This story could be read to reveal that gender in this culture is neither static nor simplistic. The reviewers, however, report the story as evidence of the supposedly timeless rule that girls are not allowed to use the sticks. The culture = patriarchy = not modern = ahistorical = not-us/U.S. equation is so powerful that the reviews seem not to see the contradiction between Castle-Hughes' actions (using the sticks) and her claim (that girls do not use the sticks).

A few reviews mention the 1987 book on which the film was based, and report that the author, Witi Ihimaera, wrote the story after two significant events: first, his experience of seeing a whale swim up the Hudson River while he was in New York; and, second, his daughters' observation that there

Whale Rider presents Pai as an extraordinary young heroine. Keisha Castle-Hughes became the first performer under 20 to earn an Oscar nomination for Best Actress.

were very few stories available to them that had female heroes. One unusual article quotes Ihimaera saying, "having the girl [Pai, in the film] ride the whale, which is also a symbol of patriarchy[,] . . . was my sneaky literary way of socking it to the guy thing" (Richards). The process of Ihimaera having conceived of and written the book, and then the book's subsequent phenomenal success in New Zealand, show, of course, that culture does change and that the "patriarchy" of the culture is not an unchanging given that never faces challenges. But few articles mention this background, and this is the only article I found in which Ihimaera makes the point that the whale, itself, is a symbol of patriarchy. Thus, this apparently more subtle reworking of tradition and gender taking place over time through the life of the novel and now the life of the film is lost in the discussion of the film as a timeless story of girl versus authentic patriarchy.

UNIVERSALITY

While one might consider the kind of exoticization and construction of an ahistorical cultural authenticity I describe in the previous section to be the opposite of a claim that the films are "universal"—how can the films be both about a specific exotic/delicious/patriarchal culture *and* about all cultures at all times (i.e., universal)?—in fact these two different kinds of representations depend on and support one another. Once a culture is fixed into a static, ahistorical authenticity and thereby separated from any specificity of particular social changes that may take place over time (such as Castle-Hughes' use of the supposedly for-men-only taiaha sticks or Ihimaera's hugely popular critique of what he defines as "the guy thing"), it is only one step further to claim that the experiences represented in that decontextualized culture can really apply to anyone.

Reviews often support their claim for *Bend It Like Beckham*'s universality by associating it with *My Big Fat Greek Wedding* (2002). For example, one review claims "the comforting message at the heart of these ethnic comedies is that parents are comically impossible in any language, faith or nationality, but they will love and support you no matter what foolish notion gets into your head" (Bernard). Here, the specificity of a (fictional) Sikh immigrant experience in London, U.K., compared to a (fictional) Greek immigrant experience in Chicago, U.S.A., disappears and the story comes to be about "anyone." We all, after all, presumably have a language, a faith, and a nationality. One review claims universality, but seems to limit it to children of immigrants: "Jess, like children of immigrants everywhere, must figure out how to gain acceptance in two worlds" (Bernard). In a U.S. context, however, where the vast majority of readers of this paper presumably are children (or grandchildren or great-grandchildren, etc.) of immigrants, the reviewer invites us to associate ourselves with Jess, to claim her story as a universal story, without having to address the messy specificities of any particular immigrant and/or colonial story.

Reviews of *Whale Rider* often quote Niki Caro (the director) as saying, "The more specific you make it . . . the more universal it is. . . . We are all human and this film talks about things that are relevant everywhere" (e.g., Calder). While some reviews provide more specific quotations from Caro about what the "things that are relevant everywhere" are (e.g., "generational conflict" and "girl power" themes [Munoz]), most often they simply reproduce her claim about universality. The reviewers themselves also claim the film is universal, saying things such as "[the film's] familiarity is . . . part of the movie's power: here's a story from halfway around the world that somehow connects with the heart of viewers of almost any culture" (Caro).[20] While most reviews remain vague about the source of the universalism, some reviews are more specific about "how" the film connects with other viewers: for example, through a "coming-of-age" story (Anonymous; Hornaday) or "a tale of tradition and evolution, or intractability and acceptance" (Pickle).[21] Each of these more specific universal themes, however, remains dissociated from any specific cultural or national identity or experience. The films' supposed universalism, then, encourages U.S. audiences to associate their own experience with an abstract globalism that displaces the specificity of local and particular experiences in either New Zealand or the United States.

IT'S A GIRL POWER MOVIE, BUT BETTER!

Overall, the reviews' representation of these films as ahistorical, authentic, and universal tales helps to explain the larger comfort with the films in U.S. popular culture. They may tell stories about girls, those girls may be powerful and in control of themselves, and they may even confront racism, sexism, and the legacy of colonialism in their lives, naming and challenging it, but they do so outside of time, against an othered patriarchy and in a universal space that is neither uncomfortably here nor obtusely there. These films potentially could be read as offering a more confrontational and explicit feminist perspective than many of the other girl power films to which the reviews compare them. Nevertheless, the reviewers read the films more in the opposite direction, depoliticizing the films, paradoxically, through an explicit discussion of feminism.

To be fair, some of the reviews do simply claim and celebrate aspects of *Whale Rider* that either they define as feminist or can be understood to fit within a loose definition of feminism. For example, reviews sometimes quote Castle-Hughes as saying that "the most important thing about this movie is that it shows girls can do anything. Every girl is brought up to think they are not good enough to do this or that, but I realized that girls can do anything" (Munoz).[22] Many reviews see "female empowerment" (Gire; Stuart; Macdonald, May 31, 2003; Kenny; Nuckols; Morgenstern) in the film.[23] The film also apparently includes "some lovely you-go-girl moments" (Schwarzbaum). One review is titled "Girls Just Want to Be Maori Tribal Leaders" (Strauss), and yet another headline claims "This Girl, She Goes!" (Hornaday).[24]

Many more reviews, however, identify these elements of feminism or girl power only to claim that *Whale Rider* is somehow better than that vague thing called feminism. For example, one reviewer claims that "while *Whale Rider* is a doozy of a female-empowerment fantasy, it's mercifully free of any feminist smugness" (Ansen).[25] One review mentions both *Whale Rider* and *Bend It Like Beckham*: "As did *Bend It Like Beckham*, *Whale Rider* pulls off its girl-power message without coming off as predictable or self-righteous"

(Gillespie). Another review is more specific about what exactly is wrong with feminism when it claims that "*Whale Rider* . . . transcends its standard structure [in which "a girl tries to prove her value in a male-dominated society"] by plunging you into the lives of distinct, lovingly created characters" (Caro). Presumably that "standard structure" is both feminist and problematic for not providing those kinds of characters. For another reviewer, feminism is curiously separate from heroism: "Although I came into *Whale Rider* assuming that it was a film in which a girl challenges the patriarchy and fights to become accepted as a leader, Caro's movie has not a feminist agenda, but a heroic one" (Rickey).[26]

At least two reviews make the link between the "it's better than feminism" claim and the supposed deracialized universalism in the film. For example, one reviewer writes: "Refreshingly, *Whale Rider*—much like the recent *Bend It Like Beckham* or *Real Women Have Curves*—takes a more elegant approach to its feminist salvo, raising its sensibilities above cheap hyperbole, thus allowing for deep universal appreciation" (Weinkauf). Another reviewer writes: "When [the grandfather] Koro instructs all the first-born sons of the tribe in ancient warrior arts, or when the men and women of the village labor together to save a group of beached whales, or when cinematographer Leon Narbey simply lingers on the silhouettes of massive wood carvings against the clouds, *Whale Rider* emits a far deeper and more powerful pull than it does when it surfs the popular swells of chick rule" (Schwarzbaum). In these two reviews, while the film itself may have feminist elements, feminism, presumably, is not universal. However, "authentic" girls of color, carefully separated from the specificity of the reader/reviewer/viewer's present, are universal. In this way feminism remains lily-white (thereby allowing, of course, for an implicit critique of it for its whiteness and social disconnectedness). Furthermore, girls of color, such as the heroines of these films, remain more closely linked to their race and/or culture than to their gender. Thus, feminism is dismissed (including any feminism that one might actually read in the films), gender and race are separated (even though one might easily read Pai and Jess to be expressing intersectional feminist perspectives on the embeddedness of both gender and race in their lives),[27] and cultural difference can be celebrated as nonthreatening.

Other reviews are even more hostile toward feminism and/or girl power. In these reviews, praise of *Whale Rider* as an exception works in tandem with—as if as a justification for—misogyny directed toward other films and other women or girl characters. For example, one reviewer writes that "Castle-Hughes avoids the teeth-gnashing, righteous indignation of most adolescent-rebellion fantasies."[28] Another review claims that "the lush remoteness of the landscape [serves] as an entrancing contrast to the sugar-rush, you-go-girl empowerment of programmed pandering like *The Lizzie McGuire Movie*, whose tweener heroine flails her arms and bats her eyes as if she were sending distress signals" (Mitchell). These irritating girls who "flail their arms" in their attempts to be assertive are specifically from the United States. For example, one reviewer writes that *Whale Rider* is "a far cry from American movies, where the soon-to-be-teen would be slamming out of the house and jumping on the back of a Harley." The review then quotes Castle-Hughes as supporting this point: "'I know a lot of kids act out, but honestly everyone in New Zealand is respectful to their elders'" (Pearlman). In this confused quotation, Castle-Hughes simultaneously admits that "a lot of kids act out" and claims that New Zealand kids never act out. Thus, while I would like to think this was not Castle-Hughes' point, the reviewer is able to insult U.S. girls (for being resistant, for "acting out") by praising Castle-Hughes, her character, and the film for general passivity, despite the fact that Pai is anything but passive.[29]

Reviews of *Bend It Like Beckham* are a little more comfortable with embracing the film as feminist, perhaps because this is a much milder feminism than the explicit "girl power" feminism many reviews find in *Whale Rider*. Much of the acceptance of the feminism in *Bend It Like Beckham* appears in one- or two-sentence descriptions of the film's narrative. For example, one review describes the film this way: "The film, a romantic comedy, tells the story of a gutsy young woman, Jess, who has grown up in a loving family of tradition-bound Indian immigrants; though happy in England, they remain loyal to their culture of hard work and arranged marriages. But Jess . . . has other ideas" (Alibhai-Brown).[30] Making the presence, but ultimate irrelevance, of feminism explicit, another reviewer writes that "a girl is no longer considered a tomboy for being interested in sports. . . . No, Jess' roadblocks come from her more traditional Indian parents who still have old-world expectations for their daughters—expectations that most definitely encompass school and marriage but not anything like sports" (Baltake). Each of these examples softens the possible feminist reading of the film by opposing the idea of a girl's independence to cultural tradition. Thus, the reviews imply that the whole world—except "Indian culture"—is already feminist, completely comfortable with girls playing sports; thus, this is a gentle film about an Indian girl bringing the already accepted feminism of the outside world into her tradition-bound household.

Several reviews talk about the metaphor of "bending" as an explicitly mild version of feminism, often quoting Gurinder Chadha (the film's director) or Nagra to do so. For example, in an NPR interview Chadha says, "I found [bending the ball] to be a fantastic metaphor for my film because . . . with us, with girls and women . . . often we can stand at the end of a picture, we can see our goal and we, too, have to kind of twist and turn and bend the rules a little bit to get to our goal. And that works. And then also since the film is about an Indian girl . . . it was important for her to bend the rules as opposed to break the rules."[31] This is a safe, soft, painless feminism. And, importantly, it is safe, soft, and painless because of its explicit connection to that timeless, patriarchal, authentic Indian culture. Thus, in the U.S. context, the feminism is even safer in that it is only still necessary in "other" cultures. In the United States, as most of the reviews report, we *already* have girls' soccer and Mia Hamm. We are past a need for feminism, and thus these films are quaint ways for us to celebrate the fact that we have evolved, that we can take a story or two about a girl who defies patriarchal rule (in the literal sense of her father or grandfather) to achieve her own dream.

CONCLUSION

In this essay, I have tried to read against the grain of the reviews, when I can, and I have alluded to potential readings of the films that see them as offering specific feminist, antiracist, and/or anticolonialist perspectives. Thus, an implicit argument of this essay is that *Bend It Like Beckham* and *Whale Rider* have disruptive potential more akin to "smaller" films[32] such as *Girls Town* (1996), *Girlfight* (2000), or *Real Women Have Curves* (2002)[33] than to the blockbuster mega-marketed *Pocahontas* (1995).[34] But the (arguably unexpected)[35] blockbuster nature of these films' exhibition, ironically, works in contradistinction to that potential as the reviews fold the film into standard narratives about ahistorical, authentic distant cultures. This is not an either/or argument: either the films have disruptive potential or they do not. Rather, my purpose here is to detail the way in which the U.S. popular press reception of the films was able to make sense of the economic success—which in and of itself was highly disruptive—of these films by reading them into a contemporary globalized context in which the imagined U.S. moviegoing public is open-minded about and accepting of the racialized experience of historically colonized people elsewhere. Specifically, the way the U.S. popular press did this was through the figure of the better-than-feminist girl from elsewhere: the nonheroic heroine who rejects ahistorical patriarchy and embraces the global fantasy future in which girls ride/save whales/their culture (*Whale Rider*) or have mega-careers as athletes in—where else?—the United States (*Bend It Like Beckham*).[36]

In short, what I am arguing here is that the reviews of these films produce particular versions of authenticity, timelessness, consumability, universality, abstract globalism, and feminism in relation to each other in ways that thereby produce a more knowing, more evolved stance for the U.S. audience in relation both to U.S. girls and to other cultures, in this case Maori of New Zealand and Sikh of London. The result is the denigration of U.S. girls and the exoticization of the films' main characters and the actors who portray them. This is all produced through a collective voice that yells, "we're better feminists than feminists!" and "we're so comfortable with racial and national difference that we can appreciate these films!"

Certainly, this discourse of "saving Other women from Other men" is not new; this discourse of other cultures as authentic, timeless, and exotic is not new; and, this discourse of claiming the present of U.S. popular culture as having evolved past the need for feminism—in other words, as postfeminist—is not new: hence, the suggestion in my title that this press coverage is unremarkable. Nevertheless, these discourses emerge in the context of what I describe in the introduction to this essay as an incitement to discourse about girls in contemporary U.S. popular culture. Thus, my goal here has been to reveal the racial and national dimensions of this historical moment of worship, fear, and regulation of girls, as well as of what it means—in the United States—to be "a girl."

NOTES

1. As one Nickelodeon executive put it in an interview with Ellen Seiter and Vicki Mayer, "There aren't any more girl protagonists than boy protagonists [on Nickelodeon]. It just feels like a lot because we have some. We care less about gender in our programs and more about kids. Our demographic research shows that boys will watch programs with girls protagonists, so we've shattered that myth" (125).

2. As of January 2005, *Teen Vogue* absorbed the older *YM*, http://www.adrants .com/2004/10/conde-nast-sucks-ym-into-teen-vogue.php. Accessed November 4, 2004.

3. Anita Harris uses Foucault's concept of "incitement to discourse" slightly differently from how I am drawing on it here. She suggests that all the public anxiety about girls leads to an incitement to discourse *from* them: "Young women's thoughts, emotions, bodies, voices, and private spaces are all invited into the public arena, and this display is linked to successful living. . . . [This is] a time . . . when surveillance regimes take the form of incitement to speak" (149–150).

4. For related overviews of girls in contemporary popular culture, also see Meenakshi Gigi Durham, "The Girling of America: Critical Reflections on Gender and Popular Communication," and Frances Gateward and Murray Pomerance's introduction to their anthology, *Sugar, Spice, and Everything Nice: Cinemas of Girlhood.*

5. They have only one such screen, and the entryway is literally labeled with a sign that reads "art house."

6. Released Sept. 3, 2003.

7. Released Oct. 28, 2003.

8. The poster taglines are, for *Whale Rider*, "In the way of the ancients, she found a hope for the future"; and, for *Bend It Like Beckham*, "Who wants to cook aloo gobi when you can bend a ball like Beckham?"

9. It is worth pointing out in this context that the dialogue in both these "foreign" films is spoken primarily in English.

10. Both films won audience awards at various festivals. *Whale Rider:* People's Choice Award, Toronto; World Cinema Audience Award, Sundance; Audience Award at Rotterdam and San Francisco International. *Bend It Like Beckham:* second place as People's Choice, Toronto; Audience Award, Locarno International; Special Jury, Marrakech International.

11. From time to time in this essay, I make brief claims about potential readings of these films, as I do here by suggesting that *Whale Rider* and *Bend It Like Beckham* address minoritization, racialization, and neocolonialism. However, because this essay focuses on the U.S. popular press reception of the films, it would be disruptive to pause and develop a full analysis of the film texts, themselves, in order to support my claims. Rather, I will offer brief examples either in the body of the essay or in the notes in order to gesture toward these potential readings. So, for example, I would point out that *Whale Rider* is explicitly concerned with the potential loss of Maori culture as a result of the history of colonialism and that Pai (the central girl character) delivers one-liners—such as "Maori women have got to stop smoking; we've got to protect our childbearing properties"—that articulate this concern. In *Bend It Like Beckham* one scene draws a parallel between being Indian in London and being Irish in London, emphasizing the shared experience of minoritization and the legacy of colonialism. After Jess is thrown out of a game for starting a fight and her coach (and budding love interest) Joe yells at her for "overreacting" to the fact that the other player fouled her, Jess says: "She called me a Paki, but I guess you wouldn't understand what that feels like, would you?" Joe responds: "Jess, I'm Irish. Of course I understand what that feels like." After this exchange, they embrace.

12. I should point out that I am assuming Knightley is Anglo, based in part on appearance (a problematic approach) and more substantially on the fact that, unlike for Nagra, the press does not address Knightley's racial or ethnic identity, thereby implying that she is Anglo or at least white, an unremarkable racial identity in the context of the U.S. popular press. She is never quoted as stating how she self-defines racially. Knightley got plenty of press coverage of her own, of course, especially after the release of *Pirates of the Caribbean* (2003). For example, she was on the cover of the April 2004 *Vanity Fair:* "She's 18, Taking Hollywood by Storm, and Still Living with Her Parents. Keira Knightley: Isn't She Lovely?" Nevertheless, the overwhelming majority of articles focused specifically on *Bend It Like Beckham* center on Jess/Nagra.

13. *Bend It Like Beckham* does offer a white-but-Irish male coach and the U.S.-but-female soccer league as savior-like figures, but neither fully embodies the white male

savior role. As Therese Saliba points out in the context of U.S. representations of Arab women, however, there is a "white women saving brown women" narrative that parallels/updates the "white men saving Other women from Other men" narrative. *Bend It Like Beckham* arguably accesses and perpetuates this second narrative through its representation of the chance to go to the United States to play soccer—first in college and then hopefully professionally—as the ultimate achievement for Jess (and Jules).

14. See chapter 2 of my book, *Watching Rape: Film, Television, and Postfeminist Culture*, for a fuller definition of postfeminism.

15. Anita Mannur calls for a more complex understanding of the representation of food in texts produced by Indian Americans, and other Asian Americans, beyond a critique of the fact that "in the popular imagination Asians are inextricably linked to their foodways" (56). In this case, however, I focus on reviews that are not written from an Indian American perspective and that, I would argue, tend to simplify—rather than complicate—the relationships among race, ethnicity, and food.

16. Also see Edelstein.

17. This is not actually true. At least one actor (and, significantly, her character) is apparently not Maori: Pai's father's girlfriend is a blonde German.

18. Also see Toumarkine (March 2003) and Ebert, March 12, 2003.

19. Also see Dawtrey.

20. Also see Ansen and Gire.

21. Also see Cruz.

22. All but one of the reviews that quotes Castle-Hughes in relation to the feminism in the film suggest that she embraced and celebrated that feminism. One article, however, an interview between Donna Karan and Castle-Hughes, quotes Castle-Hughes as rejecting the need for the feminism represented in the film.

> KARAN: Now, *Whale Rider* is very much about a girl not being heard. Do you feel that way in your real life?
>
> CASTLE-HUGHES: No, not at all. I feel it's kind of the other way around. Like, boys are kind of unheard.
>
> KARAN: Really? Why do you feel that boys aren't being heard?
>
> CASTLE-HUGHES: Well, I don't know. I just don't feel that because I'm a girl I have a disadvantage, really.
>
> KARAN: You feel very equal?
>
> CASTLE-HUGHES: Very, *very* equal. Yes. (Karan, 95)

23. Also see Strauss.

24. Also see Macdonald, June 20, 2003.

25. Also see Chordas.

26. Also see Ebert, July 2, 2003.

27. For example, Pai strives—even though she is a girl—to be a leader precisely in order to resist the legacy of colonialism, and Jess encounters and explicitly confronts both racism on the pitch and sexism from her team's umbrella organization.

28. Also see Chordas.

29. Also see Kleinschrodt.

30. Also see Rainer.

31. Cited in Mills.

32. Obviously, the "size" of a film is relative and subjective. I am making a distinction here based on box office receipts, the number of screens on which the films showed, and the number of articles that appeared in the popular press. While *Whale Rider* grossed nearly $21 million and *Bend It Like Beckham* grossed over $32.5 million in U.S. box office receipts, *Real Women Have Curves* grossed less than $6 million, *Girlfight* grossed just over $1.5 million, and *Girls Town* grossed less than half a million. At its peak, *Whale Rider* was showing on 556 screens nationwide and *Bend It Like Beckham* on 1,002 screens; *Girlfight* made it up to 253 screens and *Real Women Have Curves* made it up to 163 screens (www.imdb.com). On a quick search of Newsbank, I found 95 articles about *Real Women Have Curves*, 20 articles about *Girlfight*, and 9 articles about *Girls Town*, while I found 154 articles about *Whale Rider* and 161 articles about *Bend It Like Beckham*.

33. For an example of the kind of disruptive potential I am thinking of here, see Mary Celeste Kearney for a discussion of *Girls Town* as a film that values feminist themes and "subvert[s] the two-gender system that grounds ideologies of not only patriarchy and heterosexuality but also liberal and cultural feminism" (140).

34. For example, Derek T. Buescher and Kent A. Ono offer a powerful critique of *Pocahontas* that challenges any claim that the film is politically progressive. They write: "The film employs the discourses of environmentalism, feminism, and multiculturalism to recuperate the colonial story. As a result, the film illustrates intersections of race, class, gender, and environmentalism within neocolonial rhetoric, a newly told old story" (151).

35. Both *Whale Rider* and *Bend It Like Beckham* opened on *fewer* screens (*Whale Rider:* 9 screens, *Bend It Like Beckham:* 6 screens) than both *Girlfight* (28 screens) and *Real Women Have Curves* (55 screens).

36. Ironically and sadly, the Women's United Soccer Association folded in September 2003, toward the end of *Bend It Like Beckham*'s run on U.S. screens.

CHAPTER 13

PACHYDERM'S PROGRESS

MURRAY POMERANCE

A poem is a petition.   THEO'S FATHER, IN *The Dreamers*

ADOLESCENCE

Age grading is a widely distributed feature of human societies. The alloca-tion of rewards and responsibilities, the designation of dependent groups, and the differentiation of rights and obligations on the basis of age is wide-spread among communities primitive and advanced, ancient and contempo-rary alike. Most typically, two broad categories are to be found, defined in mutual exclusion: childhood, a zone of technical incompetence and spiri-tual innocence; and adulthood, a zone of capacity, knowledge, moral duty, and ethical maturity. Between childhood and adulthood there is often imag-ined to lie a boundary of sorts, traversable in ways that can be ceremonially demarcated and publicly signified (typically through a puberty rite). When technological and social change are particularly rapid, as happened at the time of the Industrial Revolution, for example, machines learn to do work and come to replace human adults in the economy. Thus is created, under social arrangements where some people are forced to market their labor power for sustenance, a relatively intensified competition for work in an ever-shrinking workplace. It becomes thinkable to delay the onset of adult-hood, that period of life when the responsibility to work and the rewards of working fall—usually in some unequal measure—upon the shoulders of the socialized. While in feudal society youngsters who were "children" only days before might well have become "adults" and have found themselves working in the fields beside their parents as full-fledged members of the "adult" class (might, indeed, have married and themselves borne children at the age of 14 or 15), the labor competition of early capitalism (when mechanical systems began to assist, and then assimilate, labor) now provided the foundation for an age hierarchy among adults. The youngest of them—in some societies, the most physically fit—could be held off from demanding the jobs their parents wanted by means of an institutionalized redefinition of their strengths and powers, a reappraisal of their condition of embodiment, and a recalibration of their historical state, that grounded them in a special period (or moratorium) after childhood but prior to adulthood: adolescence.

If they were physically mature, something could still be said for the unpreparedness of adolescents to handle challenges now considered socially significant rather than personal and experiential: to leave awkwardness behind and develop smooth, fluid, and deft interpersonal skills; to attain some philosophical "understanding" or "knowledge" of one's world; to become confident and capable of chastity and other honors; to learn loyalty and fealty, and so on. The emotional *sturm und drang* that would fall upon eager young people held off from meaningful participation in their social world could itself be used to legitimate that holding off, according to a rationale that would in fact praise rationales and the ability to live strictly by them. If adolescence has certainly existed since the middle of the nineteenth century, it was around a hundred years later that, as Doherty (34–40) has pointed out, it became a commodity to be marketed and consumed—marked as the domain of "the teen-ager" and consumed often by teenagers themselves—and thus a mainstay of the capitalist economy of exchange, overproduction, and mass consumption. With the postwar creation of "teen-agers," soon enough they became targets of a "teen market"—teenpics, teen clothing, teen music, teen literature, teen imagery, and teen counseling—and thus came a bevy of professionals equipped, so it was claimed, to handle "teen problems." Teen life became increasingly problematic, requiring an institutional solution.

HIGH SCHOOL

The single overriding monument of capitalism, as regards age grading, is the high school, an institutionalization of the conceit that adolescents are particularly in need of an education designed especially for them and modified to address their peculiar needs and sensitivities (induced by the hegemony). Capitalism and mass technological society needed the high school as a holding pen for young people for whom, though they could surely copulate and endure the rigors of the workplace just as well as their parents, a base of operations was not yet legitimated in society. Curricula were developed in the early twentieth century often on the pretext of preparing young people (at least, boys) for college education. School became an elaborate delaying mechanism for those who needed the opportunity to—as Edgar Z. Frieden-berg defined the purpose of education—"understand the meaning of their lives, and become more sensitive to the meaning of other people's lives and relate to them more fully" (221). By the middle of the twentieth century, it was certainly not, as Friedenberg (and others) took pains to point out, so much the purpose of high school to educate young people incarcerated there by virtue of the mandatory school attendance laws that were, and remain, rife in the United States, as to make inevitable the learning of certain core assumptions:

> The first of these is the assumption that the state has the right to com-pel adolescents to spend six or seven hours a day, five days a week, thirty-six or so weeks a year, in a specific place, under the charge of a particular group of persons in whose selection they have no voice, per-forming tasks about which they have no choice, without remuneration and subject to specialized regulations and sanctions that are applicable to no one else in the community nor to them except in this place. So accustomed are we to assuming that education is a *service* to the young that this statement must seem flagrantly biased. (41–42)

All this at least partly because, for Friedenberg, "adults are incompetent to design, or too grossly impaired emotionally to accept and operate, a so-ciety that works" (249). Given that high schools served first and foremost the needs of the industrialists and managers (and now the megacorporations) that wanted to cheapen the labor they used in order to increase their own profits and were eager and willing to increase unemployment to do this, the challenge of making it possible for young people to see themselves and their world with increased clarity and fashion a response to their lives with in-creased perspicacity and articulateness was simply not near the top of the agenda. In greater and greater numbers as the sexual revolution of the 1960s wore to its close, adolescents simply had to be kept from exploding, kept from themselves, kept from their world, and kept out of the job market as long as possible.

This is the context in which the great American high school developed, a complex, by the 1960s, in which "nothing is provided graciously, liber-ally, simply as an amenity, either to teachers or students, though adminis-trative offices have begun to assume an executive look" (Friedenberg, 44). It was built upon the infrastructure of publicly funded physical plants from the 1930s and 1940s and a faculty body culled essentially out of the shabby-genteel middle class. During the Second World War, more and more women became teachers. The high school was renovated in the 1970s according to modern (Fordist) factory principles, its teaching staff now augmented by the inflection of vast numbers who saw themselves as professionals, not citizens subject to a calling, and who looked to bureaucracy as an organizational salvation, to rules and moral entrepreneurship as a means of social control, to psychological manipulation, streaming, and dossier keeping as pieties (see Cicourel and Kitsuse), and to the control of youthful enthusiasm—sexual, athletic, you name it—as the surest pathway to peace and freedom. The buildings, especially in the white middle-class suburban world, came to be vast and lavishly equipped, not only with test tubes and Bunsen burners and security-tagged library books but also with vice principals' offices, study halls, soon enough computer terminals, and hermetic cafeterias in which, later in the century, as a result of contracts cupidinously signed by desperate local school boards across America, nutrition-free preparations from high fructose corn syrup would routinely take the place of nutritious food (see Critser).

ELEPHANT

One such facility is Columbine High School in Littleton, Colorado. Well in advance of the massacre there between 11:40 a.m. and 4:00 p.m. on April 20, 1999, to which Gus Van Sant's *Elephant* (2003) is something of a response, the high school in America had become an early model of the "security zone" that Mike Davis writes about in *Ecology of Fear* (359–422). Characterized by diffuse moral proscriptiveness, heightened perception (often augmented technologically through surveillance mechanisms), characterological stratification (profiling), centralization of authority, extended record keeping, and an *in loco parentis* attitude, and rigorously symbolized by the omnipresence of (frequently uniformed) agents of control, the security zone of the high school, shown already well developed in Frederick Wiseman's *High School* (1968; see Grant, chapter 2), was designed not only to make young people's physical mobility difficult—except in well-monitored routines—but also to keep certain persons out while others were accorded special privileges, and to make it impossible for students to use the space freely for relaxation and pleasure. Much like an airport, the average American high school from the mid-1960s onward was a sterile and hard-surfaced environment, easy to clean and watch, with prescribed traffic patterns and little room for privacy, idiosyncrasy, sexuality, spontaneity, or unfettered expression. Given

Eric (Eric Deulen) and Alex (Alex Frost) cleaning up their act in *Elephant* (2003).

the application of Fordism to education by this time, it is hardly surprising that the high school was also, often, enormous, a facility for processing the intellect, skills, and personalities of thousands of young people simultaneously and thus a warrant in itself for techniques of crowd control.

This, at any rate, is the place in which we find ourselves as the characters of *Elephant* are methodically introduced, one particular sequence beautifully establishing the quality of the contemporary high school as a security zone free from the human touch. A pair of enjambed traveling shots, occupying together six minutes and eight seconds of screen time, begins on a playing field with a fixed camera looking out at a swath of grass bordered by some autumnal trees in the distance. A line of girls is visible all the way across the field, doing calisthenics. Near the camera more girls run past, a particularly gawky one of these, Michelle (Kristen Hicks), stopping suddenly to look up at the sky in wonder and then resuming her pace in slowed motion. Boys are playing football in two small squads, moving out of the camera frame as they advance up the field. One of these, Nathan (Nathan Tyson), needing to leave, enters the frame, bends, picks up a red sweatshirt and pulls it on, adjusts it, and heads off. We dolly after him as he walks through some trees to the school building. His shirt has a white "+" on the back, and the word "Lifeguard." Nathan has medium-length dark hair, heavy brows, and a compact build. He walks with an easy rhythm, as though himself a camera dolly gliding confidently and beautifully through experience. The ground dips down a slope and the camera stops, watching as he continues to walk away. Smaller and smaller he becomes as we see him approach and then enter the building through a side door.

Immediately now we pick him up inside, this time so close behind him that his head fills the frame. He walks away from us enough to be in medium shot again, turning onto a staircase and walking up toward a set of lambent windows; turns again and continues mounting the stairs, now on the second floor; glides down a long corridor lined with lockers; turns in a brightly lit atrium; heads for some brightly lit glass doors that lead out onto a patio walkway linking to a second building; walks toward, and passes, some boys skillfully break dancing; enters the other building; turns to pass three girls chatting—they freeze when they see him, one lifting her hand to her mouth in suspended excitement; turns back and keeps walking down the corridor, where he meets Carrie (Carrie Finklea), who is clearly attached to him. They kiss briefly and head into a large office suite where Nathan asks a secretary for a permission slip to leave the school.

Watching this, we sense where Nathan is at each instant, what is around him, what direction he has chosen, how his relatively unconstructed, shapeless, and more feelingful body movement outside is slowly recomposed as he soberly heads back to school routine. We can easily imagine that Nathan and his classmates spend their days modulating between loose, erotic, engaged behavior outside under the sky, and restrained, orderly, timetabled, extraordinarily guided activity required inside. We have an illusion of freedom: by means of the playing field, the school permits free bodily play, but only if it is safe, bounded, and timetabled. The large corridors make Nathan's movement, as he makes his way alone, almost dreamlike in its lack of press and constraint. But the smooth camera movement suggests the efficiency of the internal "road" and "traffic" system (a special dolly was constructed to facilitate this movement, especially around corners and in tight spots [Thomson]): that there is room here for hundreds of students to move between classes at the same time, for a vast circulation in which the personality can easily hide, or get lost. That Nathan does not struggle as he glides can mean he is one of those who are very accustomed to being constrained in this place.

What this sequence seems like on the screen is something else again. The activity is filmed to be nondramatic, in the sense that protagonists are not isolated by the camera or lighting and the visual field contains no object of particular focus. In this way, given a static camera, the kids tend to hover and float before the lens, rather than being chosen and "grasped" by the director's gaze. A tranquil music track underpins the entire length of this two-shot sequence, specifically, the Adagio Sostenuto from Beethoven's Piano Sonata Op. 27 No. 2, "Moonlight," recorded with low amplitude so that it is heard, mixed with the voices of the kids on the playing field or the normal corridor sounds in the school, as a distant subtext of the seen moments. Since this particular piece of music has a continuing, even unearthly, motility, like the movement of clouds scudding across the sky (that we see at the opening and closing of the film in extended shots), it tends to position the happenings we watch in terms of an all-abiding and overarching Nature or Cosmos, a Universe of happenings all of which may be taken to be involving and fateful. There is a feeling of emptiness, weight, unfolding probability, intensified by the smoothness with which the story proceeds.

The effect of the lighting and music, as well as of the respectfully distant camera position, is to detach the students from their engagements with one another and with the place, to turn them into moving parts that are energized and interrelated within the context of a surrounding mechanical system. No matter what the kids are doing, their activity and relationships are less important by far than their separation from the place, from one another, and from the meaning of their actions. The sense we have most powerfully, in this telling sequence but also throughout the film, is of what Patrice Blouin calls "incredible lightness" (13)—too much space, space in which the eye cannot focus, space through which one glides along as though borne by a systemic conveyor belt. "Losing the device of cutting," Van Sant had learned from Miklós Jancsó, "starts to make it less display-oriented and more of an account" (Thomson, 64).

Other sequences are arranged in the same disconnected, even hallucinatory, way. Elias (Elias McConnell), a photographer, wandering through a park and shooting snaps of a boy and girl, then encountering John (John Robinson) for a brief moment of conversation and a photographic opportunity; Michelle being told by her gym teacher that she must wear shorts in the future; John catching a ride to school with his inebriated father (Timothy Bottoms), receiving a reprimand for being late, passing through the office where Nathan and Carrie are getting exit permits, running into Elias in the hallway and posing for him while Michelle slinks by. All these intersecting lines of interaction lead us to suspect we are watching a single substantial reality from a number of points of view, as though moving around a sanctified object or space. Death will enter this setting, taking many of these young people. In all of this the dialogue is curtailed, or arcane, or abashed, or absent, so that one has the feeling these students know one another only from seeing and passing one another day after day, and do not really use language to understand their world or their friends in a way that transcends the superficial.

"Hey, are you going to the concert tonight?" John asks Eli, and Eli responds, "No, I can't, my parents are being bitches this week," and they move on, Eli to his darkroom, John to exit the building, where he sees Alex (Alex Frost) and Eric (Eric Deulen) entering with huge gym bags in their hands. Later, following the tale of Alex and Eric, we will come to know what is in the gym bags. "Hey, what are you guys doing?" asks John. "Just get the fuck outta here and don't come back," is Alex's answer. "Maybe shit's going down."

The bubble of individual experience disconnected from the social floats not only out of space but also out of time. Through a fluid and self-referential editing structure, Van Sant moves us forward and backward temporally, leading up to the few moments—here experienced from multiple points of view—in which Alex and Eric enter the school. Their gym bags contain automatic weapons, and they have come here today to commit mass murder. But earlier, in Alex's basement, we saw him practicing Beethoven's "Für Elise," a paragon of sensitivity and innocence almost lulled by his own performance. The camera slowly pans around the room, catching walls covered with pinned-up drawings, his bed strewn with papers, a radio, a sound system, a drawing of an elephant, a television with rabbit ears. "That's awesome," says Eric, flopping onto Alex's bed and picking up his laptop to play a computer game in which he uses an automatic weapon of choice to shoot people in the back. Alex switches to the "Moonlight" sonata, somewhat too forcefully perhaps, now seen from directly behind. Like the victims in the computer game and like Nathan walking down the corridor, the pianist is a human cipher, a head on a torso, not an expressive face. Together the two boys sit on the couch and visit www.guns.usa.

In its attention to detail in the scenes with these boys—Eric's wifebeater T-shirt as he guzzles milk at Alex's breakfast table, his way of demurely yet foxily smiling at his chum—and in the scenes with the other kids, the film posits a kind of canniness on the part of the students, a hipness to the sexual, political, and cultural surface which CNN routinely gives us as a picture of the world in which we live. Nathan and Carrie have an "appointment"—she is presumably pregnant, perhaps by him; John is rather too accustomed to parenting an irresponsible childlike father. This is a world where adults have abrogated some basic responsibilities, where high-caliber weapons are easily available to one and all by way of the Internet, where mediated documentary history sweeps past kids' eyes without causing them to digest its meaning, where sex is everywhere and yet feeling is curtailed, where language is inexpressive—and through it the kids move as though guided from the outside. "What is learned in the high school," writes Friedenberg, "or for that matter anywhere at all, depends far less on what is taught than on what one actually experiences in the place" (40). The abbreviated conversations we hear are themselves part of the format of obedience and acquiescence learned in the hyperefficient school system: given the pressures of the timetable and the number of locations each student must touch during the day, intensive conversations merely hold things up, merely lead to detention slips.

I am writing of this film in a way that will perhaps seem eccentric to those who, having seen it or heard about it, have been convinced it is principally about school violence—specifically, a kind of analytical memorial to the Columbine catastrophe. Indeed, as finally Alex and Eric do in fact terrorize the school, murdering many students and employees, the film can easily be understood as Van Sant's presentation of the various intertwined factors any of which might be taken to have "caused" such a horrible event while, at the same time none of them, "psychological or sociological, suffices on its own to tip the scales of violence" (Blouin, 15): that the killers were known as "dorks," "loners," and "outcasts" who "spoke German to each other, listened to German techno music and were fans of Adolf Hitler"; that they were "constantly insulted and harassed"; that they "linked their home computers and for hours played violent video games"; that the police did nothing in response to early warnings; that parents didn't know who their own children were; that the police, and adults in general, "had no warning" (*Rocky Mountain Daily News*). But I take *Elephant* to be a statement, first and foremost, about the condition of experience in the contemporary high school: a depiction of that socially organized environment as, indeed, the perfect setting for such an atrocity, a setting designed to educate the spirits of American youth toward the disaffection and detachment we see so bloodily exemplified by Alex and Eric's actions. That high school is the epitome of a capitalist social structure that has foregone sensation and pleasure, poetry, affect, philosophy, and experience for commodification, regulation, packaging, manipulation, indoctrination, and profit. The corridors through which Nathan softly parades are ideal for target practice; the persons we see and move past here are nothing but figures against the ground. If they become targets, gruesomely, this school was already designed for such transformation: in the official rationale, any student without a hall pass and outside of class could be spotted (targeted) and policed with ease. Alex and Eric can hardly be seen as responsible, alone, for what they do in this powerful context. Significantly, as we shall see, *The Dreamers* offers a very different portrait of what youth can be.

It is only in Alex's house that Van Sant's camera ceases to relentlessly prowl forward through its story. Here, while the boys play together in Alex's basement room, while they sleep, while they eat breakfast in the kitchen,

while they watch the documentary on Nazism in the living room and receive their gun shipment, while they practice shooting in the garage, and
while they shower together, the camera explores the space they inhabit but
essentially frames them as situated, comfortable, engaged, and static. In the
school, by contrast; in John's father's car; and in the school playground, the
camera finds the children of America in ceaseless motion forward, jogging,
racing, pacing, slinking, searching. As metaphor, this suggests that viewed
from an institutional perspective, the American young are to be understood
as moving toward the future. Rather than hinting that young people really
are this way, the film places their ceaseless progressiveness in the context
of the high school, developing that forward motion as a way of responding
to the constraints of the institutional space. By already in 1912 Max Scheler
had written in his extended essay, "On the Phenomenology and Sociology of
Ressentiment" (2003), this commentary on youthful "progress":

> The ideas of "progress" and "regression" are not drawn from an em-
> pirical observation of the phases of life as such—they are selective
> yardsticks which we apply to ourselves, to others, and to history. Jean-
> Jacques Rousseau was the first to protest against the pedagogical theo-
> ries which consider childhood and youth as mere precursors of matu-
> rity. Leopold von Ranke rejected the childish liberal belief in historical
> progress in the following magnificent sentences: "Such a 'mediated'
> generation would have no significance of its own. It would only be im-
> portant as a stepping-stone toward the next generation, and it would
> have no direct relation to the divine. However, I affirm that every epoch
> is directly related to God, and its value does not lie in what it engen-
> ders, but in its very existence, in its own self." The desire for progress
> corresponds to the view rejected by Ranke . . . (33–34)

What Ranke rejects, writes Scheler, is exactly the view that young people are
valuable not for what they are but for what they are in process of becoming,
in short, a view that rejects youth. This *ressentient* view withholds or blocks
a "free resignation" that is vital to proper growth since it is a healthy "renun-
ciation of the values proper to the preceding stage of life. Those spiritual and
intellectual values that remain untouched by the process of aging, together
with the values of the next stage of life, must compensate for what has been
lost. Only if this happens can we cheerfully relive the values of our past in
memory, without envy for the young to whom they are still accessible" (37–
38). In the American high school is a thoroughgoing and institutionalized
envy of the young, which manifests itself as a situated pressure for them to

grow up and be judged by standards hardly proper to their stage in life, while at the same time failing to offer them the responsibilities or rewards of adulthood. What Friedenberg once called "the dignity of youth" is hard for young people to achieve or celebrate in a system that persists in moving them forward and away from what they truly are (yet forward to a kind of nowhere).

Edgar Z. Friedenberg's argument in *Coming of Age in America*, that the high school is essentially a mechanism for denying young people liberty, that the ideal high school student is one who acquiesces to the *ressentient* demands of the system, finds echo in a statement about Dylan Klebold and Eric Harris (the models for Alex and Eric in *Elephant*) made by Lee Andres, the choir teacher at Columbine, the day after the shootings: "They were extremely bright, but not good students." Being a "good student" is not related in the high school to intelligence or creativity. It is related to heading purposively toward the next classroom, finding the correct hallway, getting a pass from authorities before you take your girlfriend to the doctor, curtailing a moment of horseplay while posing for a photograph in order to move on and get to detention on time. At a telling moment, alone briefly in a lounge and a little strained from being "good," John breaks into tears. His girlfriend Acadia (Alicia Miles) walks in, approaches him, quickly kisses the side of his head and moves on to sex education class, leaving him to recuperate with the generalized belief that everything will be better at some point in the future. John, indeed, is one of the people who survives.

THE DREAMERS

If murder and mayhem were Alex and Eric's dream, albeit a social and cultural nightmare, the two are at least capable of dreaming through, not merely pacing through, their lives. Equally oneiric, and rooted in sexual passion rather than a commitment to revolutionary violence, is Matthew (Michael Pitt), the protagonist of Bernardo Bertolucci's *The Dreamers* (2003). A high school graduate meandering through Paris in 1968, he is obsessed with film, one of those who sits as close as possible to the screen at André Langlois' Cinemathèque Française in order to "catch the images before anyone else does." He befriends, and is soon adopted by, two other young people apparently committed in the same way, Theo and his twin sister Isabel (Louis Garrel, Eva Green), children of a French poet who married an Englishwoman (Robin Renucci, Anna Chancellor). When the parents go off for a seaside vacation, the children take over the Parisian apartment de luxe, with its faded moss green walls and high ceilings. Matthew, deeply sensitive but modest and shy, is fascinated to see the twins' intimacies. Then, progressively, they initiate him into the secrecy of their bond, playing a cinema-charade game where they must identify beloved movies from a scene mimed by one of them. Matthew and Isabel fall in love, but she is bonded a priori to Theo, who is always "in" her. When Theo loses the movie charade game, Isabelle forces him to pay the forfeit of masturbating in front of her and Matthew. Later, when Matthew loses, Theo forces him to make love to Isabelle in his presence. Spending all their time together, the three become inseparable, until, in a raucous climax, they are awakened in the middle of the night by a mob chanting in the street outside. Running out to join in the protest—it is the time for the revolution of the young!—they are carried in the throng, chanting "Dans la rue! Dans la rue!" Theo joins a coterie preparing a Molotov cocktail, and Isabelle runs up to help him. Matthew is terrified, thrown into a paroxysm of philosophical agony. "*We* don't do this!" he pleads to Theo. "We do *this!*" And he seizes the boy and kisses him with abandon on the mouth. Aghast, frozen, Theo pushes him off and goes back to preparing the bomb he will hurl at the cordon of police who are shooting tear gas and preparing to charge. Matthew turns and goes back—back, presumably, to his other life, his American life, or perhaps, his truly revolutionary life in which battles are fought with passion and the flesh, not slogans and firebombs, in which, as Theo's father wrote, "a poem is a petition."

Adolescence is surely, among other things, a time of boundaries: between the self and the other, between the self and the world, between one's own self and the self others (and other systems) would impose. For Matthew, who might later, and still alone in a hostile world, become the alcoholic father of John in *Elephant*, 1968 is the moment when the threshold of loneliness is crossed and love is found for the first time. Trying to write to his mother in his dingy hotel room one night, Matthew cannot find words. When in the morning he awakened by a phone call from Theo inviting him home for dinner, it is as though a curtain of lead has been lifted from his eyes and the streets of Paris are all ashine in poetic reverie: at dinner, when she leans over the table to kiss him goodnight, Isabelle's hair catches in the candle flame and for an instant sparkles in the darkness like fireflies before Matthew tenderly snuffs it out. Escorting him to the bedroom which will be his, Theo winds through long labyrinthine corridors lined with his father's books; as the two stand together looking at the room, for Matthew the excitement of his new friendship with Theo, the proximity, the quality of the French boy's style and character, are all like a musk in the air. The kids spend their days arguing about film, dreaming of film. Was Chaplin better than Keaton or Keaton better than Chaplin? "Do you know what Jean-Luc Godard said about Nicholas Ray?" asks Theo. "Nicholas Ray is the cinema!" In this film,

Theo (Louis Garrel) and Matthew (Michael Pitt) cleaning up their act in *The Dreamers* (2003).

such a statement has profound resonance, not merely articulating a critical point of view or adumbrating a young man's knowledge of textual sources, but giving a sense of what it would be like to be invested in film so passionately and fully that it would be imaginable that cinema were a world, not a commodity; that one might *be* cinema itself. Together, Isabelle, Theo, and Matthew are alive, indeed scintillating with life. One of the qualities of youth that Rousseau and von Ranke point to is exactly this *bouleversement,* this sense of being overturned by awareness of, and hunger for, other people, the hunger Matthew feels for his new French friends and that Bertolucci's camera positions us to feel at his side. The youth of *Elephant* do not give appearances of feeling this hunger.

Bertolucci's recollection of 1960s youth, then, finds a poetic spirit entirely absent in our brutal present-day hegemony. A particularly profound scene involves Isa, Theo, and Matthew's attempt to outpace the three protagonists of Godard's *Bande à part* as they race at breakneck speed through the Musée du Louvre. We see the trio tearing through the exhibition rooms, fluttering past an old guard who tries to catch them as though they were so many butterflies, racing past the Winged Victory of Samothrace, shouting and breathless. Intercut with these spectacularly reconstructed shots are precisely matching shots from the original Godard film, so that the edited sequence represents exactly the prolongation of the earlier film into contemporary time, the replication of the 1960s experience, the loving memory of cinema's—at least New Wave cinema's—ebullient youth. This is Berto-lucci's way of saying, "Our values may endure." Now, Matthew is completely adopted by the delirious twins. "One of us! One of us!" they chant, from Tod Browning's *Freaks*, as they march off in a unity of desire and mutual understanding. In the very next shot, it is pouring rain. Matthew is crossing a boulevard toward the camera, to the sound of Bob Dylan singing "Queen Jane Approximately." His stride is charged with the music, as though he is inside it, and we are joined to him, also "One of us!"

Most revealing of the difference between *Elephant* and *The Dreamers* is their treatment of sex. Surely what has changed since 1968, beyond the face of our social order—Watergate, home computers, the Internet, crack cocaine, AIDS, the oil crisis—is the meaning of our sex. It is now perfunc-tory, even a form of exercise. Rather than languidly bathing in the rich pres-ence of our friends, as the kids in *Dreamers* do, we take brisk showers, as in *Elephant*, and entertain glancing contacts, shards of touch and affect. Every-one who can write a sentence is educated about sex, to the point of tedium, and sexual identity is bandied about as a basis for politically correct inter-personal relations. In a film such as *The Dreamers*, indeed, it can be shown unexpurgated and in full flower; even—as we see from Theo, who fries eggs while his sister is penetrated by Matthew—be watched being watched. In the late 1960s, sex was still a mystery, and so in being physically close with our friends we were leaving ourselves and finding the world. For Matthew, then, the American teenager whose educational institution is 1968 Paris, the ménage with Theo and Isabelle is life changing, no matter how it turns out in the end. When he lies naked with the two of them through the night in a tent Isabelle has concocted in the living room, with candles burning and bottles of Burgundy half consumed all around, Matthew has learned what feelings are.

Worth considering are the two scenes of cleansing that, in a way, center both movies. Theo, Isabelle, and Matthew share a bathtub in a long sequence, smoking marijuana and arguing about film and politics as they blush with one another in the suds. While they do not see the world in precisely the same way, it is evident that, vulnerable to one another's touch in this confined space, the three of them have come literally to embody the loss of discrete-ness and individualism that real social involvement implies. Each has pro-jected the self outward in an embrace—an embrace that crosses the bound-aries of gender and class, nationality and political belief, merging strangers through the love of art and the love of love.

In *Elephant*, by contrast, Eric and Alex shower together before suiting up to go out for the kill. Alex has stripped and stepped into the shower stall, is standing under the running water running his hands through his hair. Eric enters, removes his underwear, opens the stall door and steps in. "I've never been kissed," he says matter-of-factly, so Alex leans forward and kisses him, awkwardly drawing him close. Swiftly we cut, and they are loading guns into the car. These are two who have not, to be sure, known the kind of love that Matthew is shown in Paris. But more, they have transcended the body entirely. The blunt physical connection, which in 1968 electrified Matthew, is here a simple ritual, a moment no more profound than wiping a fleck of dirt off one's arm. So it is that some young people are dreamers of unities while others prepare invasion, invasion to obliterate the past. "I think," said Bertolucci (Wachtel, 93), "that film should be a way of communicating with young people, who seem to have a total loss of memory."

CHAPTER 14

BOYS WILL BE MEN

Teen Masculinities in Recent Spanish Cinema

SANTIAGO FOUZ-HERNÁNDEZ

YOUTH AND CHILDREN IN SPANISH CINEMA

Films about youth have been prominent in Spanish cinema of the last three decades. Data suggest that in the early 1990s youth went from media underrepresentation to overrepresentation and, according to Trenzado Romero, the "profession" most widely represented by male characters in the Spanish cinema of the 1990s was that of the "student," even if the narrative was completely unrelated to the world of education (99–100).[1] Young people between 15 and 29 years of age represent a quarter of the Spanish population and, judging by the *Revista de estudios de juventud* [*Journal of Youth Studies*], published quarterly by the Instituto de la Juventud [the Youth Institute], the field of youth studies is enjoying a period of great productivity in Spain.[2]

Among the most widely recognized post-Franco cinematic representations of Spanish youth are the iconic *Tigres de papel* (*Paper Tigers*, 1977) and Almodóvar's debut film *Pepi, Luci y Bom . . . y otras chicas del montón* (*Pepi, Luci and Bom*, 1980), both set around the time of the first democratic elections.[3] The early 1980s films of Eloy de la Iglesia—which focused on the world of drugs and delinquency—and, in the 1990s, Montxo Armendáriz's *Historias del Kronen* (*Stories from the Kronen*, 1995), are also generational landmarks from their respective decades.[4] Yet, the films that I will analyze here are perhaps more indebted to the long tradition of children narratives in Spanish cinema that goes as far back as Buñuel and that includes classics such as the religious *Marcelino Pan y Vino* (*The Miracle of Marcelino*, 1955); the political *El espíritu de la colmena* (*The Spirit of the Beehive*, 1973), which uses the point of view of a girl (Ana Torrent) fascinated by cinema to create an allegoric picture of post–Civil War Spain; and the controversial *Cría cuervos* (*Raise Ravens*, 1976), a sharp critique of the Francoist model of family seen through the eyes of a girl (also played by Torrent). In the early 1990s, two dark dramas by Basque director Juanma Bajo Ulloa are also noteworthy: *Alas de mariposa* (*Butterfly's Wings*, 1991), in which a girl jealous of her little baby brother smothers him to death; and *La madre muerta* (*The Dead Mother*, 1993), the story of a little girl traumatized for life after witnessing the murder of her mother. The rural period dramas *Secretos del corazón* (*Secrets of the Heart*, 1997), in which a child discovers that his father killed himself probably as a result of the semi-incestuous relationship of the child's mother and his uncle, and *La lengua de las mariposas* (*Butterfly's Tongue*, 2000), which illustrates the tragedy of the Spanish Civil War through the story of a troubled child and his Republican school master, are also classic examples. Among the most recent examples are *Eres mi héroe* (*You're My Hero*, 2003)—set in the Spanish transition—and the hospital drama *Planta Cuarta* (*The Fourth Floor*, 2003), which focuses on the lives of young cancer patients. Although there is no room here for a discussion of the latter film, it is worth mentioning its interest to this essay, not only because of the familiar young cast (one of the featured actors, Juan José Ballesta, is also the main character in *El Bola*, which I analyze later) but also for its themes of adolescent male friendship, loyalty, tragedy, and the body, which will be the pillars of my discussion.

Foreign audiences will be more familiar with the child characters in the psycho thriller *Los otros* (*The Others*, 2001)—where two traumatized children are victimized by a repressive and psychotic mother (played by Nicole Kidman); or the various child characters who often appear in flashbacks and who are a psychoanalyst's dream in many Almodóvar films, such as *Laberinto de pasiones* (*Labyrinth of Passions*, 1982); *Tacones lejanos* (*High Heels*, 1991), and, more recently, *Todo sobre mi madre* (*All About My Mother*, 1999) and *La mala educación* (*Bad Education*, 2004), to mention but a few. Needless to say, this frequent use of the child's perspective suggests a national preoccupation with the Oedipal which lends itself to many sociohistorical readings, oriented to the past (infantile regression) and to the future (ongoing process of maturation). These compatible interpretative poles are perhaps best exemplified by the work of Marsha Kinder, who has argued that this obsession with children and Oedipal narratives reveals a latent discourse about unresolved issues of the traumatic Spanish past (197–275), and Marvin D'Lugo, who sees the use of a child's viewpoint as suggestive of a much-needed process of maturation of older versions of Spanish communities (he makes the point with reference to Catalan identity in Bigas Luna's *La teta i la lluna* [*The Tit and the Moon*, 1994]], which must move from an inward-looking nationalistic fixation "toward a Europeanized Spain of the future" (205). While the historical and political relevance of the films studied in this chapter is undeniable and could inspire many allegorical readings about the Spanish nation, my main concern here relates to wider issues of gender and sexuality, such as male friendship and adolescence, "probably the period of greatest insecurity in the life course, the time when the young male becomes most vulnerable to peer expectations, pressures and judgement," as Messner puts it (199).

TURN-OF-THE-CENTURY COMING-OF-AGE FILMS

The three films chosen for discussion here focus on male teenagers struggling with their gender and sexual identities, and all share aspects of context, narrative, and production which contribute to form a representative and cohesive unit of analysis. All three films have been commercially successful in Spain and have been well received by the critics and by the Spanish Academy.[5] Furthermore, these three films were produced at the turn of the century (1998–2000) and, importantly, by young directors in their early thirties.[6] Finally, unlike many of the films mentioned above, the films that I am about to analyze have a markedly urban (two of them are set in Madrid, and the third near Barcelona) and markedly contemporary setting.

Barrio (*Neighborhood*, 1998) tells the story of three teenagers from a depressed area of Madrid who suffer the consequences of their families' poor, tragic, and, in one case, repressive and violent background. *El Bola* (*Pellet*, 2000), also set in Madrid, focuses more closely on the tragically ubiquitous issue of domestic violence in Spain, here affecting a 12-year-old boy who becomes a victim of the extreme physical and psychological violence exerted by his repressive father (a reminder of the "old" Spain of the dictatorship) but who finds refuge in the warmth of a new school friend and his liberal, young parents (representative of the "new democratic Spain"). Finally, the two young protagonists of *Krámpack* (*Dani and Nico*, 2000) come from a much better off (Catalan) background. The lush surroundings of Dani's family's beach house and a few ephemeral moments of sexual pleasure with his friend Nico (they engage in mutual masturbation—which they call "krámpack") help to make their sexual identity struggle much more bearable. Yet, while Dani is in love with Nico, Nico is in love with a girl who is also on holiday in this coastal town. Eventually, and partly due to Dani's friendship with an adult gay man, the summer proves a beneficial, life-changing experience for both boys, and their different sexual tendencies do not seem to get in the way of their friendship.

FATHER FIGURES

According to a survey carried out by the CIS (Spanish Centre of Sociological Research) in 1999, 80 percent of young Spaniards between the ages of 15 and 29 live at their parents' home and 60 percent live off their parents' income (42 percent exclusively so). Recent studies suggest that the age of emancipation of young people in Spain continues to increase due to the high cost of housing and instability of jobs (Requena, 1–13). Spanish critics such as Monterde (1993) and Trenzado Romero (1997) have argued that the family setting features so prominently in Spanish cinema due to its multifunctional narrative potential. As Trenzado Romero puts it, the family setting provides discourses of "power, submission and transgression . . . emancipation, maturation, initiation to sex, confrontation of old and new customs and economic cells of production and reproduction" (100–101, my translation). Fernando León de Aranoa's own debut film, *Familia* (*Family*, 1997) is, as its title suggests, a clear example of this. Spanish television has also exploited the narrative potential of the family unit, with hit series such as the early 1980s *Verano Azul* (*Blue Summer*, TVE-1), an important referent for *Krámpack* given its summer and coastal setting; the 1990s series *Médico de familia* (*Family Doctor*, Tele 5); *Compañeros* (*Peers*, Antena 3); and *Al salir de clase* (*After School*, Tele 5), among others.

The three young men of *Barrio* (León de Aranoa's second feature film) all come from dysfunctional working-class families who live in a modest barrio of Madrid.[7] Manu (Eloy Yebra) is the target of constant jokes and abuse from his two friends because he does not have a mother (she is apparently dead). His father, a former Metro driver who had to retire early due to problems with alcohol, lies to him regarding the whereabouts of his absent elder brother, apparently a busy businessman who in reality—as Manu later discovers—is a heroin addict who lives under a bridge and relies on their father to bring food for him on a daily basis. Manu's friend Javi (Timy Benito) lives in a nuclear family, but their daily family lunches are characterized by constant arguments between his miserable parents, the silent but mildly intrusive presence of his deaf grandfather, and the invasive noise of either his sister's salsa music or the television news.[8] His parents eventually separate after the mother reports an episode of domestic abuse (a central issue also in *El Bola*) but, as Marsh notes (169), his father's oppressive presence becomes even more intense when he decides to live in an old caravan within the con-

Barrio (1998) explores the lives of three friends in Madrid who appear entrapped by their social and class surroundings.

fines of the neighborhood. The familial tensions eventually provoke Javi's breakdown, later accentuated by the tragic destiny of his friend Rai (Críspulo Cabezas).

The presence of Rai's family is less prominent, with the exception of his elder brother, who is presented, on the one hand, as a heroic father figure (he has a job as a security guard, which is associated with power and the law, he has a nice-looking girlfriend, and apparently a good sex life) and, on the other hand, as an antihero responsible for some of Rai's misfortunes (he uses him as a drug dealer). In one scene that I will refer to later, Manu and Javi masturbate while watching Rai's brother have sex with his girlfriend through one of the security cameras at his workplace. Toward the end of the film, the three friends watch a couple have sex in a car, later discovering that the girl in the car is Javi's sister. These voyeuristic scenes are reminiscent of Manu's gaze when he discovers his drug-addict brother about to shoot up, subtly linking the claustrophobic atmosphere of the setting with the equally claustrophobic dependence on the family. As the director has said, the boys' financial and emotional dependence on the family—a function of their age and not the barrio in itself—is an important cause of their problems (*Barrio* DVD). The film also seems to suggest that the lack of role models available to these boys within their families will also affect their identities. Just as Rai is about to have his first romantic date (with Javi's sister), he dies a victim of his delinquent tendencies (and also a victim of a sick society—the neighbor who shoots him is a paranoid policeman obsessed with being a target of terrorism). Javi breaks down, unable to face his situation at home and the death of his friend, while Manu is shocked by a sudden awakening to life's harsh realities, represented by the unknown sides of his brother; the mulatto babysitter, who is associated with tenderness and nurturing at the beginning of the film but with casual sex at the end; or Rai's drug dealing. The story that started with the boys' dreams about women, sex, holidays, and cars ends with a series of events that will undoubtedly result in a fast growing-up process.

The presence of the family is even more crucial in *El Bola*. Pablo's family represents an older model of the family in Spain: the father works all day at his own modest business, helped by Pablo (Juan José Ballesta); the mother is a devoted housewife, and the grandmother also lives in the house.[9] As in *Barrio*, the presence of a grandparent (here suffering from incontinence) is a source of tension between her son and her son's wife as well as a vivid reminder of the futility of life and youth.

During most of the film, Pablo suffers his father's abuse in silence, only daring to admit it to himself and others when he graphically describes it

Pablo (Juan José Ballesta, right), the title character of *El Bola* (2000), watches intently as Alfredo's father (Alberto Jiménez) plies his tattooing skills.

to a police officer in the very last scene, thus marking his final liberation and maturity. There are clear contrasts between Pablo and the "new kid on the block," Alfredo (Pablo Galán), who is introduced by a teacher halfway through a class; wearing a bright orange hat, he awakens much curiosity among his peers. Alfredo's family is portrayed as the new, young, and liberated type of post-Franco, European family. In contrast with the cluttered, dark, heavy, and traditional furnishings and atmosphere of Pablo's family home, Alfredo's home is light, spacious, and modern, simply decorated with functional modern furniture. By all accounts both parents treat Alfredo as an equal, including him in various outdoor activities with their friends and generally allowing him a healthy level of freedom. Pablo's father owns an old-style tool shop, while Alfredo's dad is a passionate tattoo artist. From the beginning, Pablo observes Alfredo and his family with exotic fascination. Unlike Pablo's friends, he resists peer pressure and refuses to take part in their favorite and risky pastime (crossing the railroad track just seconds before a fast train is about to pass). Perplexed by Alfredo's individuality and difference, the other kids react typically, by insulting him and questioning his masculine identity and his sexuality.[10] As director Achero Mañas notes on the DVD commentary, conservative audiences would be quick to link the tattoo artist and hash-consuming dad (who hides his tattoo when he visits Pablo's family) to a dark narrative twist, and yet he is the picture of wholesomeness in contrast with the abusive and frustrated old man. As with Manu in *Barrio*, Pablo's family life is marked by tragedy: his elder brother died before Pablo was born, apparently in a car accident (although he might have been killed by his father). The anniversary of his death is marked by a solemn and sombre ceremony at the cemetery. It appears that death is a taboo in his family and the father uses his dead son as a way to exert more psychological pressure on Pablo, who is constantly and negatively compared to him. In contrast, Alfredo's family and friends discuss with him the illness and death of his godfather. The fatherhood embodied by Alfredo's dad is a positive, modern, and democratic alternative to the old, repressive ways of Pablo's father, which are reminiscent of fascist Spain. At the end of the film, after his worst battering ever, Pablo escapes home and is found in a park by Alfredo and his dad. Despite the advice of a friendly social worker, Alfredo's dad keeps his previous promise to protect Pablo, and it is suggested that Pablo will never return to his father. The pathetic picture of the repentant, powerless, and trembling abuser is contrasted with the confident and caring manner of the "new" father holding Pablo and covering him with his coat.

Krámpack provides a contrast with the other two films, not only because the main character, Dani (Fernando Ramallo), comes from a much more privileged background (his father runs a publishing business, they have a

Nico (Jordi Vilches) and Dani (Fernando Ramallo) enact masculine rites while confronting their sexuality more than they expected in *Krámpack* (2000).

huge house with a swimming pool and a maid), but also because the parents conveniently go on holiday at the very start of the film, leaving their son and his visiting friend Nico (Jordi Vilches)—whose parents we never see —to their own devices. While other adults fill the parental roles, they have a rather open approach to life. The maid (a liberated French woman) asks Dani's friend Nico to take her out to parties with them; the English teacher (actually Spanish) admits to Dani that she had a lesboerotic friendship in her adolescence and has liberal views on sex, reluctantly consenting to Dani's intimate encounter with her gay friend (who is about twice the boy's age). In the meantime, the "real" parents are on a trip to Egypt, thus further separating the world of the adults from that of the boys and yet, the "foreign" and feminine influence of the maid and the teacher contributes to the boys' critical reorientation toward the macho and conservative ways of Francoist Spain and their further integration into the more modern gender attitudes of Northern Europe.

MASCULINITY AND FRIENDSHIP

Hammond and Jablow trace the dramatization of male friendship to the classic Gilgamesh epic (discovered in the late nineteenth century), adding that even the biblical friendship of David and Jonathan and the story of Achilles and Patroclus in the Iliad had much earlier oral antecedents (245). As they note, these narratives often refer to close and devoted friendships between two men in agonistic settings and are common in Western literary tradition—including, as Hammond and Jablow also note (252), the Spanish medieval classic *Cantar de Mio Cid* as well as Cervantes' masterpiece novel of the seventeenth century, *Don Quijote*. In these stories, male friends openly declare their feelings to each other, stand together against all difficulties, and relegate family relationships to a secondary place. The concept has survived through the centuries and has also been celebrated in contemporary comics, television series, and in film, resulting in the popular Hollywood "buddy movie" genre. In non-Western societies, tribal rituals to mark same-sex friendships have been and still are common, and friendships between men are highly valued (see Sherrod, 231 and 237).

Drury Sherrod has argued that postindustrial Western societies have transformed the logistics of this type of male friendship, now damaged by the competitive nature of the job market (231). Eve Sedgwick (1990) has also described how the "homosexual panic" of contemporary Western societies has undoubtedly had an impact on the level of intimacy that exists in heterosexual male friendships. One of the striking features of the three films discussed here is precisely the emphasis that all three narratives place on male friendship (an aspect highlighted by all three directors in the respective DVD interviews). In *Barrio*, despite the narrative investment in their separate families and problems, the mise-en-scène often celebrates the boys' friendship by framing them together in memorable moments that depict them fantasizing about women, sex, travel, or cars, providing a sheer contrast with those darker scenes in which they are seen in their separate contexts, at home with their families (Javi), at work (Manu), or confronted by the police (Rai). Despite various cruel jokes about Manu's dead mother, Rai's useless jet ski—he won it after cheating his way into a contest—and Javi's saucy sister, the strength of their friendship becomes transparent at the end of the film, when Manu and Javi embrace and try to comfort each other about the loss of Rai.

In *El Bola*, Pablo's superficial and competitive relationships with his old school peers are contrasted with the sincerity and depth of his relationship with Alfredo. Pablo's schoolmates know that his father hits him but do nothing about it (other than gossip among themselves). Their daring game is based on competitiveness, confrontation, and risk (all traditional male traits). These relationships follow the classic pattern of male friendships, often based on common interests, group activities, and frequent laughter and put-downs, as opposed to the intimacy and conversation that characterize friendships between females (Sherrod, 220–222). Pablo actively seeks Alfredo's friendship, following him home after his first day at school and later finding out his exact address and visiting him spontaneously. Their clear and deep connection is confirmed during a visit to an amusement park. The various rides are exciting for both of them but not really risky, becoming a safe substitute for the railroad track game that Pablo used to practice with his mates earlier in the film. After the rides (the rollercoaster being a symbolic reference to the difficult times they are about to experience), they have something to eat together and enjoy having a chat, something that Pablo did not experience with his school acquaintances. Their friendship goes from strength to strength, provoking the jealousy of the other kids. When Alfredo refuses to take part in the suicidal game, the other boys react by typically questioning his sexuality, saying that Alfredo is probably "a poof like his godfather" (who has just died of AIDS). They also question his masculinity, challenging him to a game and provoking him by saying that he has no balls. Alfredo's reply is telling: "It is not that I have no balls, I just think it is a pointless game." Alfredo's friendship and the support of his family are instrumental for Pablo's emancipation from his abusive father, not only by offering refuge but also by providing emotional support and an alternative model to the macho masculinity that he sees at home and in the other kids.

During the casting for *Krámpack*, director Cesc Gay had in mind classic screen male friendships: "Redford and Newman, Lemmon and Matthau, Laurel and Hardy, Delon and Belmondo" (Renoir). Originally a play set within the confines of a flat, and mostly about homosexuality, Gay changed the setting (remarkably bright and exterior in the film) and, importantly, the focus (from sexuality to friendship), as well as the ages of the characters (which were lowered from 20-something university students to 16-year-olds) (as noted by Armengol). Nico's arrival and departure conveniently frame the film as a summer experience that will probably not be repeated, but which has been crucial in the maturation process of the two boys. Nico's heterosexuality is made clear from the start, when he flirts with a French girl on the train, and reinforced at the end, on the train back, when he looks at another girl tourist who sits in front of him. In the coastal town where they presumably spend most summer holidays together, Nico seems more interested in spending time with Elena (Marieta Orozco—who plays Javi's sister in *Barrio*) and discovering sex with her than in cultivating his friendship with Dani. Elena's presence becomes a threat for Dani, who gradually requires more from his friend than their sporadic and apparently meaningless mutual masturbations. The triangle between the two boys and Elena follows the conventions of many classic literary male friendships, in which the female element disturbs the homosocial pleasure of the two men (see Sedgwick 1985, 21–27). Dani goes out of his way to hinder Nico and Elena's relationship. Eventually, the boys come to realize that sex and friendship are best kept separate and, as the story of the English teacher suggests, their friendship will probably survive the transition into adulthood, but the physical element is likely to disappear.

VULNERABLE BODIES

As I have already mentioned, the secondary but memorable presence of death and old people is a key reminder of the futility of youth in both *Barrio* and *El Bola*. In *El Bola*, Pablo helps his mother wash his grandmother but looks away while he holds her in the shower. His family's attitude to the body and death is very different from Alfredo's; the latter discusses his godfather's illness, and at one point the whole family and some friends joke about farting in the car. They have a tactile relationship with the boys which contrasts with Pablo's father's distant nagging and aggression. The behavior of Pablo's father reveals a denial of his emotional ties with his son but also a crisis of the old patriarchal model.[11] This crisis is particularly evident in *Barrio*, where Javi's mother seems to be the one ultimately wearing the trousers, not only by imposing the presence of her father in the family but also starting most of the arguments and eventually reporting her husband's violence and having him evicted.[12]

Also important for this study are the scenes of masturbation that take place in both *Barrio* and *Krámpack*: the discovery of sex is a rite of passage that in both films transgresses the limits of the private to become an act of public pleasure. In *Barrio*, the scene seems to confirm that for the boys sex is experienced as an anticlimactic and out-of-reach fantasy. Having examined the sex ads of a newspaper with a bitter sense of humor, and having used all their cash on a frustrating call to a sex phone line (only to suddenly get cut off), now their masturbatory pleasure (already mediated by the security cameras, through which they can see Rai's brother and his girlfriend) is interrupted by Rai's gun-in-mouth Russian roulette game.[13] The Russian roulette is an anticipation of Rai's real death by gunshot, but the flirtatious play with the phallic gun in his mouth and its visual reference to fellatio is also part of a feminization process of his body throughout the film. Were it not for the arrest and police interrogations about drug dealing, one would be led to assume that Rai's dark dealings with the mysterious middle-aged man who follows him around in a car could be of a sexual nature. Both Manu and Javi refer to him in feminine terms on several occasions, touching his long hair and jokingly suggesting that he sells it to be made into wigs or dolls' hair (Manu) or calling him *"guapa"* (nice-looking girl) when he wears a wreath around his neck at the cemetery. If we accept one of the implicit precepts of Mulvey's gaze theory (1975), the feminization of Rai would be consistent with his objectification throughout the film: he is the only boy to be shown bare-chested (in bed), and the vulnerability of his body is made clear through his obsessively risky behavior (through his delinquent activities) but also metaphorically with the Russian roulette and his walks on tightropes (actually walls or wires found lying on the floor), in one case with a premonition just before his death. This vulnerability is also heightened by his continual references to death: his jokes about Manu's mother, his stories about seeing a drowned man on *Baywatch,* and his story of having been born dead. Drowning becomes a metaphor for his inability to escape the claustrophobic barrio and, ironically, the interior city of Madrid, but also for his powerlessness and eventual death.

Despite the lack of scenes of any sexual nature in *El Bola,* Alfredo's father's job as a tattooist and Pablo's physical suffering provide many opportunities for the boys to discuss and draw attention to their own and other bodies. Various shots depict Pablo as if overcome with fascination as he stares at photographs of Alfredo's dad tattooing a client. When Alfredo explains to Pablo that tattoos hurt the most in the bony areas, Pablo reacts by saying that his penis has no bone and "I bet it hurts like hell" there. As Mañas acknowledges (*El Bola* DVD interview), Alfredo's tattoo (done by his dad in a loving ritual) offers a sharp contrast with Pablo's bruises, also done by his father but in a very different context. When Alfredo's dad invites Pablo to witness how he tattoos his son, Pablo's gaze at his friend's body mirrors that of Alfredo when he accidentally discovered Pablo's bruises earlier on. Both children are symbolically marked by their father, but Pablo's marks represent hatred and frustration, whereas Alfredo's tattoo is a symbol of love, growing up, and bonding with his dad. When Pablo has to miss school due to a particularly bad battering, his father tells his teachers he has tonsillitis, unknowingly revealing the very sick nature of his action and its physical consequences. Ironically, when Pablo arrives back at school, the teacher is giving a lesson on bodily functions such as circulation and excretion. Like Rai in *Barrio,* Pablo talks about the inescapability of death and even his desire to be cremated (he does not want to be buried in a hole, like his brother),[14] and his vulnerability is also marked by powerful metaphors, such as his calling himself "Pellet." The pellet (the small metal ball that he carries around as an amulet) symbolizes his being kicked around and abused by his father and his school friends, his lack of control over himself and his destiny. Notably, he drops it while he is being examined at the hospital toward the end of the film, marking his awakening. Nowhere in the film are we more aware of physicality than during Pablo's final declaration. The description of his father's abuse includes references to being kicked, his hair being pulled, his skin being burned with cigarettes, and being forced to drink urine and to take laxatives, as well as being spat on.

In *Krámpack*, the boys' bodies serve as explicit references to their growing-up process: Nico (played by a real-life acrobat) wears muscle shirts and is often seen topless. He is a master of performing masculinity: when meeting the girls for a party he stresses the fact that he has just shaved and wears a formal suit. He is proud of his toned body and especially his pronounced Adam's apple, which he shows to Dani as proof of his grown-up status and sexual appeal, saying that girls notice it when he drinks at the bar, and adding that they love it because "a big Adam's apple signifies other things." In response, Dani points out that his feet have also grown, perhaps unconsciously drawing attention to his own phallic power. The mutual masturbation scenes of the film's title are noteworthy as they clearly define the heterosexual boy as the one in control and also the one who would adopt the "active" role sexually.[15] Dani has learned to send his hand to sleep by sitting on it before masturbating, so that it feels like someone else's hand. Nico breaks the palpable homoerotic tension by saying that he was thinking it was the hand of a famous female newscaster. In the next krámpack, Dani switches the light off for intimacy. What for Nico is a mechanical act of pleasure is for Dani an intimate act of love. The camera shows him from behind, with soft lighting drawing attention to his backside, and then he performs fellatio on his friend. References to his sexual role are more explicit in the third erotic scene between the two boys, which takes place just after Dani interrupts Nico's sexual adventure with Elena. After Nico confesses that he is fed up with the krámpacks and with spending so much time with Dani, Dani suggests they have penetrative sex and immediately adopts the receiving position (the act never materializes, as Nico reaches the orgasm before penetration). While the bodies of the two boys are equally exposed and presented as attractive, Nico, the heterosexual, is seen as the one in phallic, penetrative control and Dani, like Rai in *Barrio* or Pablo in *El Bola*, as the vulnerable passive other.[16]

CONCLUSION: TRACKING DESIRE

One of the most striking similarities between these three films is the prominent presence of the railroad tracks and the railway system, partly reminiscent of the classic *El espíritu de la colmena*, to which I referred at the beginning of this essay. Ironically, in *Barrio*, the tracks are also symbolic of the boys' stasis and inability to move beyond the city and to escape their tough realities. It is on a train that Manu and Javi embrace each other on learning about Rai's death, as if the rootedness evoked by the tracks were to blame for the tragedy. The tracks are also metaphorically linked to the family ties (especially in the case of Manu, because of his father's old job as train driver, and as Marsh has argued [171], the parallelism between his brother's punctured veins and the city's underground system). Similarly, in the first half of *El Bola*, Pablo is drawn to the railroad tracks, which in his case are symbolic of his fascination with death and destruction but also of escapism at a literal (the game) and metaphorical (the train) level; yet it is also at the tracks where he realizes that his friendship with Alfredo is much more valuable than the superficial relationships with his school peers, based on the competitive and suicidal games that are associated with the old macho style of his violent father, which his new friend is not prepared to accept. Pablo's final declaration to the police is crosscut with close-up shots of the tracks. The pellet is abandoned there and is finally smashed by the passing train, symbolically marking the end of his old, repressed self as "Pellet" and his new start as Pablo. Finally, in *Krámpack*, the tracks mark the separation between the city and the coast, with all the implied binarisms: winter and summer, families and friendship, heterosexuality and homosexuality, and so on. For both Dani and Nico, the station is the borderline between the reality of their everyday, separate lives and their idyllic time on holiday together. It is also at the station where they playfully wrestle and embrace, conciliating a modern style of masculine friendship with no hang-ups about sexual orientation.

I use the tracks as a convenient reminder of the three aspects studied in this essay—strong family ties, friendship, and the vulnerable body—but one which is also symbolic of the main themes of these films, as for these boys, the tracks also mark their coming-of-age when they eventually manage to reach the other side by facing the harsh realities of life. Despite the connotations of immobility, I would like to argue that the tracks can also be seen in their more literal meaning of forward movement and become a positive symbol of progression, as the boys in these stories (especially in *El Bola* and *Krámpack*) seem to leave traumas behind and welcome a more flexible model of masculinity.

NOTES

1. Baca Lagos points out that while youth represented only 24.4 percent of the total Spanish population in 1991, young people were featured in 67 percent of Spanish advertising and 59 percent of Spanish television programs (39–40). Issues of youth, adver-

tising, and consumption at a more global—and alarming—scale are analyzed in Alissa Quart's *Branded* (2002).

2. The emphasis of the *Revista* is largely sociological, although a recent issue (64) was devoted to Spanish youth cultures (March 2004). Authors such as Gil Calvo (1985) and Baca Lagos (1998) have also addressed issues of youth culture and its representation in the Spanish mass media.

3. On early Almodóvar and 1980s Spanish youth culture see Allinson and Triana-Toribio.

4. I have written elsewhere on both the novel and film *Historias del Kronen*, focusing mainly on issues of youth culture which I will not address in this article. See Fouz-Hernández (2000).

5. *Barrio* and *El Bola* had audiences of over 700,000, *Krámpack* just under 200,000 —very few Spanish films reach audiences over 1 million. Both *Barrio* and *El Bola* received Spanish Academy Awards—three and four respectively—as well as other awards in the prestigious San Sebastián film festival, while *Krámpack* received two awards at the Malaga Festival and various recognitions abroad.

6. Fernando León de Aranoa was born in 1968, Cesc Gay in 1967, and Achero Mañas in 1966. The classic and real generation gap that often exists between director and characters and also between the latter group and some of the more conservative critics is often an issue in this type of film. Famous examples include *Kids* (director Larry Clark was 52 when the film was released in 1995) and, in the Spanish context, *Historias del Kronen* (directed by the then 45-year-old Montxo Armendáriz).

7. The film was intentionally shot in many barrios of the Spanish capital as the director wanted to avoid associating the story with a specific area of Madrid (DVD director's commentary).

8. The news bulletins accentuate the family's misery by focusing on items about holidays on the coast or about the entry of Spain into the Euro-zone, issues far removed from their harsh reality. This is a characteristic element of the contemporary cultural representation of the Spanish family and serves both as a critique of this unsociable custom and as a convenient reminder of the social context, often related to underlying issues of the narrative.

9. Recent studies show that the tradition of extended families and duration of co-habitation with grandparents has decreased considerably in the last few years in Spain (Requena, 4–5).

10. On this behavior in schoolchildren see Skelton, 96–115.

11. Edley and Wetherell (100) make the first of these points in relation to male violence about their female partners.

12. For a recent study on the issue of violence in the Spanish contemporary family, see Femenia and Muñoz Guillén (2003).

13. Unaccomplished pleasure is a running theme in *Barrio*, symbolized by the cardboard mulatto girl—a substitute for the unreachable mulatto babysitter, the phone sex, the jet ski, and the constant contrast that is established between fantasy and reality.

14. In contrast, Alfredo's confidence is signaled by his refusal to accept the prospect of death.

15. In the words of the director, "Krámpack" is an untranslatable slang term that refers to an act of intimate friendship—not necessarily physical (Armengol).

16. I am aware that the old-fashioned active/passive hierarchy runs against post-modern conceptions of fluidity celebrated by queer movements. As Mercer has argued, the potentially active connotations of the "passive" sexual role should not be underestimated (286).

PART 5

COMING-OF-AGE QUEER

CHAPTER 15

GIRLS LOOKING AT GIRLS
LOOKING FOR GIRLS

The Visual Pleasures and Social Empowerment of Queer Teen Romance Flicks

SUSAN DRIVER

ELIN: Is it true you're a lesbian? If it's true, I understand 'cause guys are so gross. I'm also going to be one, I think . . .   *Show Me Love*

Queer girls have come to represent some of the most transformative sub-jects within contemporary independent film, giving rise to new forms of youth cinema. The emergence of queer girl characters driving romantic nar-ratives challenges normative ideals of heterosexual adolescent femininity while also opening up new ways of perceiving a desiring girl self-active within an intelligent process of becoming sexual. The emergence of diverse forms of visual storytelling that center on girls fantasizing about and pur-suing other girls compels new interpretative practices. Unlike more oblique strategies of reading queerly against the grain of heteronormative cultural texts, intimate portrayals of girls' amorous relations with each other draw viewers into vividly sensual worlds, compelling a process of reception that engages directly with the cultural significations of queer girl experiences. What I am calling "queer girl romance films" do not merely add sexual mi-nority subjects within an existing field of youth films; they offer chances to rethink the very assumptions of gender and sexuality that underpin how we come to make sense of girls. I argue that the emergence of girl-on-girl images of romance exceed and realign our expectations and understandings of coming-of-age film narratives. Not only do these films explore specific ex-periential differences of youth in psychosexually subtle and historically nu-anced contexts, but they creatively challenge hegemonic ideologies of what it means be a girl who falls in love, becomes sexually active, and grows up.

Shaking the cultural foundations of being young, female, and sexual at the turn of the new millennium, queer girls in film test the limits of analysis and reception of youth films today.

In this essay I trace the languages through which girls become visibly queer within romance film narratives. No single story line or visual representation structures the experiences of queer girls on the screen. I argue that it is precisely an attention to the everyday details of girls' struggles to know and act on their romantic and sexual longings that defines this subgenre as well as interpretive practices capable of following them. Like many teen genres, queer girl films involve movement along a boundary separating childhood from adulthood that pivots around first sexual experiences. Going beyond conventional mappings of a male heterosexual desiring gaze to consider the specificity of girls as active subjects of the gaze, my readings involve tricky negotiations between named and silent, the visible and the invisible, represented and unrepresentable relations. What these films teach us is that there are no transparent approaches to meaning when it comes to understanding young female subjects whose sexual identities are precisely what is in question. Existing in between the categories of adult identification, in a state of flux and transition to sexually aware and contested selfhood, queer youth present unique predicaments to the imaging and conceptualization of desiring subjects on the screen. The very enactment of girls within films who disrupt heteronormative relations needs to be explored in terms of the difficult ways desires appear and disappear, moving in and out of cultural recognition. The crux of queer girl subjectivities is precisely their refusals to fit neatly into ideological frameworks that produce fixed identifications and desires. At the level of textual framing, categorization, and interpretation, queer girls mark a crisis in representation. Yet this crisis does not result in an absence of meaning but rather in a rewriting of the scripts of young love to include intelligent, sexually passionate girls.

AMBIGUOUS SEXUAL SUBJECTS: THEORIZING QUEER GIRLS IN FILM

The emergence of independent queer girl romance films in the 1990s can be traced to the release of Rose Troche's *Go Fish* (1994), which promised quirky insider ways of seeing the lives of individuals and communities historically marginalized within mainstream cinema. Marking a turning point in which young lesbians are positioned at the center of fictional feature films, these and other films, such as Cheryl Dunye's *Watermelon Woman* (1997), contributed to a growing range of lesbian characters whose intimate relations appear for public viewing. While *Go Fish* and *Watermelon Woman* profile communities of youth in their early twenties, other films emerged that began to explore the nascent queer experiences of teen girls. With *Heavenly Creatures* (1994), *The Incredibly True Adventure of Two Girls in Love* (1995), *All Over Me* (1997), *Show Me Love* (1998), and *Lost and Delirious* (2001), adolescent girls are portrayed as strong central protagonists struggling to deal with social isolation, friendship crushes, coming out, suicide, and homophobia. These films convey troubling and thrilling realms of girls' experiences as they resist normative feminine ideals in daily school and family environments. Portraying ordinary struggles of teens to find belonging and fall in love, they represent girls in transitional spaces between childhood and adulthood who have yet to establish their sexual identities as they learn to express their feelings for girls, engaging with the complexity of girls whose erotic and social attention is fully turned to other girls.

An expanding range of queer girl films grapple with the visual storytelling of girl-on-girl lust, fantasy, and love. Yet tensions pervade the theorization of queer youth in film, between cultural marginalization and the tendency to normalize differences within teen narratives of romance. Timothy Shary (2002) writes that recent films such as Alex Sichel's *All Over Me* suggest an "integration of homosexual teen characters into plots that further normalize queer lifestyles and depict queerness as one of many qualities that youth may encounter on their path to adulthood" (246). Shary gestures toward an acceptance and integration of queer youth within film narratives in ways that encourage a more holistic view of their social lives rather than isolating their sexual differences in exclusionary ways. This is especially crucial when the class, racial, and ethnic dimensions of youth coming-of-age and coming-out narratives are fully acknowledged as integral to how youth define their sexuality. Youth are always so much more than any single dimension of experience, and many contemporary films have begun to explore this complexity by constructing subtle psychosocial characterizations. At the same time, it is important not to skim over the unique status of queer youth within visual media, the uniquely situated signs and shifts in perception through which youth communicate same-sex desires.

To begin a critical process of interpreting queer girls in film, both feminist and queer interpretive tools of analysis are needed. Yet feminist film theories of gender representation tend to conflict with queer theories of sexual heterogeneity, and both have been developed to concentrate on the cultural predicaments of adult subjects. Feminist approaches focus on women's identifications and pleasures as spectators, paying close attention to interactions between Woman as textual image and women as historical subjects, exploring formations of and resistance to ideologies of femininity. Queer approaches reveal the slippery contested ground of all gender/sexual categorization. Queer theories conscientiously pursue languages of desire in multiple directions, foregrounding and exceeding hetero/homo typologies. Use of performative theories of language becomes vital in struggling to overcome ossified definitions and descriptions, focusing on the interactive events of naming as a process through which sexuality emerges out of signifying movements rather than reflections of a prefixed reality. It is precisely through linguistically and visually creative possibilities to speak back that subjects are able to transform their marginalized and "shameful" queer identities into queer affirmations of difference. Eve Sedgwick characterizes queerness as a dialogical process rather than a fixed identity: "the emergence of the first person, of the singular, of the present, of the active, and of the indicative are all questions, rather than presumptions, for queer performativity" (1993, 4).

Focusing on youth sex/gender/sexuality, I call for new ways of utilizing feminist and queer concepts together with a sensitivity to representations of adolescent becoming. The challenge becomes analyzing the ideological constraints and meanings of growing up girl within a heteronormative society, while also watching how films exceed and disrupt normalizing expectations. For the purposes of understanding and naming films and the girls within them "queer," my aim is to develop a reflexive and open-ended process of theorizing particular film texts as well as broader social and cultural movements. Within many recent girl films, desire does not necessarily translate into clear-cut sexual identity, vividly demonstrated when Paulie expresses shock at being called a lesbian in *Lost and Delirious:*

PAULIE: You think I'm a lesbian?
MARY: You're a girl in love with a girl, aren't you?
PAULIE: No, I'm Paulie in love with Tori. And Tori is—she is in love with me, because she is mine and I am hers. And neither of us are lesbians.

Paulie's words resonate with youth resistance to labels that would fix their personal erotic experiences. In response, I use "queer" to signify those subjects who do not fit into neat static categories of gender and sexual identity, while also retaining a feminist focus on the specific emotional and social world of girls.

The indeterminacy of young selfhood, in the process of formation, calls forth a theoretical focus on instability and change. Yet in using queer theory there is a risk of generalizing the malleability of youth identity. Katherine

Driscoll writes that, because youth have become associated with ambiguous, in-between states of becoming,

> the poststructuralist theories of sexuality articulated around the label "queer theory" problematize how one might form or claim sexual identity and thus dominant understandings of adolescence as the formation of sexuality. . . . If adolescence locates (as yet) unfixed sexuality identities it can only with difficulty be assigned a gay or lesbian identity. (160)

Driscoll ends up invoking the queerness of all adolescent sexuality. This move is both tempting and troubling as it erases the struggles of particular queer youth as they articulate their desires and relations against cultural assumptions of sameness. While vague notions of sexual instability are continually attributed to girls as signs of their immaturity and innocence, it is much more difficult to find portrayals of strong, intelligent, and willfully desiring girls. I prefer to look specifically at those instances in film where young girls learn to express their queerness through situated and provisional words and acts. It is not a general indeterminacy that marks out queer youth in films but precisely their determination to pursue and experience same-sex love. At the same time, naming the sexual orientations of girls in films must not be taken for granted.

Much has been written about transgressive processes of reading films through the queer desires and identifications of spectators. Yet for the most part, these texts are adult centered and often invoke a sophisticated interpretive process in which queer desire is traced in the margins and subtexts of dominant narrative cinema. Queer youth tend to be left out of these discussions of film representation and reception. Watching and analyzing queer girls in film is a delicate endeavor for me as an adult queer viewer. Positions and conventions of film reception need to be questioned: What do queer girls look like on the screen? Who is looking at them? How are they looked at? Who do they look at? How do they look at other girls? In what ways can these looks be named and compared? By attempting to scrutinize and theorize queer girls, what kinds of limits do we impose? Is it my queer adult gaze that shapes the meanings of young girls on the screen? Am I queerly sexualizing their looks for pleasure, nostalgia, or control? As I watch films in which girls desire other girls, I am troubled by these questions, fearing that my search for knowledge might reify the differences I seek out. Becoming a responsive viewer involves following the subtle ways a girl's desire for another girl spurs narrative and visual meaning. From the start, a reflexive eye/I becomes crucial to a practice of reading across a disparate field of girl-girl romance films signifying small intimate moments rarely glimpsed in commercial cinema. In Mallen and Stephens' words: "looking becomes a complex play between characters and viewers . . . the act of looking that characters undertake also helps to make the viewer aware of the particular quality of their own gaze . . . to position the viewer in ways that focus attention on the specific nature of his/her gaze" (paragraph 5).

In this way my readings of queer girl films are emotionally invested and partial; they are shaped through textual analysis combined with the creative edges of my own desire for images of girl desire, which gains significance within the broader context of systemic invisibility and devaluation. I have chosen to work on three film texts which I argue provide exemplary instances of innovations involved in representing queer girls; at the same time, there is no escaping the pleasures these texts offer me as I look for signs of girls growing up queer. Linking each film with a set of theoretical problems, I focus in on the detailed visual and verbal narratives and character formations in specific film texts. Structural patterns tie into my subjective responses, which are refracted through the idiosyncrasy of my queer eye for queer girls. At times they conflict, contradict, overlap, and diverge. Whereas I focus on the silent expressions of queer girl crushes in *Show Me Love*, I go on to explore embodied gender-bending performances in *All Over Me* and defiant queer naming in *The Incredibly True Adventure of Two Girls in Love*. In each case, these films elicit the very question of what it is we desire in watching the desires of girls for girls. These films highlight distinct features of queer girl experience and representation, while also turning back onto our own need to see and understand them. At stake is learning how to read the shared elements across these films while focusing in on the textual, imaginary, and contextual details that enable nuanced narrative constructions of queer girls in film.

SHOW ME LOVE, *ALL OVER ME*, AND *THE INCREDIBLY TRUE ADVENTURE OF TWO GIRLS IN LOVE*: SHAMING WORDS, VISIBLE DESIRES, AND ACTIVE PLEASURES

Show Me Love, an independent Swedish film directed by Lukas Moodysson, recounts the everyday angst and frustrations of growing up in a rural environment where dreams of escape and excitement coexist alongside mundane longings for connection. The story follows Agnes, a pensive high school outcast who has lived in Åmål for almost two years without being able to make friends or feel a sense of belonging. Though Agnes is detached from her peers, she develops an agonizingly intense and shy crush on Elin, a pretty, sharp, and popular blond girl. Elin is sexy, is well liked by the "in crowd," and has an extraordinary physical self-confidence—"I'm so beautiful. I'm going to be Miss Sweden." Yet she is deeply unsatisfied by the world and the people that surround her: the boys are dull and predictable, gender roles are stultifying, adults sink into routine entertainments, and her classmates are caught up in cruel girl gossip. It is Elin and Agnes' persistent refusal to give in to the expectations of their family and friends that establishes their bond.

The opening scene of Agnes pouring her heart out over her computer keyboard sets the mood and direction of this romantic story. Agnes, lonely and isolated, closes the door to her bedroom, plays somber music, and writes desperate messages to herself:

My Secret Wish List
I don't want to have a party
Elin will see me
Elin will fall in love with me
I love Elin !!!!!!!

The secret longings of an adolescent wish list constitute the opening lines of *Show Me Love*, inscribed across Agnes' computer screen as she confesses her love of Elin alone, in the privacy of her room. Private spaces have multiple meanings for girls who are excluded from boy public cultures and also from the shared intimacies of girl-friend rituals. Agnes' room represents the solitary place of her romantic reveries. What becomes clear is that the enclosed space and silence that surround Agnes' awakening erotic attraction are filled with uncertain risk and knowledge. An uneasy space between her inner desires and lack of social recognition renders Agnes a remarkably vulnerable character.

Agnes' awkward secrecy is reinforced within a homophobic context in which her schoolmates attempt to shame her. Agnes is outed as a "lesbian" through harsh words of gossip before she has had a chance to even kiss a girl. The quick tongues of teen girls making fun of those who are different designates coming out as a locus of ridicule, stereotyping, and innuendo. Even Agnes' mother invades her privacy to find out the "truth" of the lesbian rumors. Being called a "lesbian" by others works to reify Agnes' subjectivity at a time in her life when being able to explore feelings and impulses is more important than taking on labels imposed by others. Elin lives on an edge of self-discovery and despair as she tries to kill herself after being outed in a humiliating game by the girl she adores. There is a protective silence in Agnes' refusal to name herself, revealing how vulnerable and simultaneously resilient she is in the face of those seeking to belittle her. If words are weapons of public shame, the gaze becomes a realm of subversive possibility for queer youth. *Show Me Love* allows the contradictions of Agnes' desiring presence to be represented through images of her watching eyes. From an abject position that places her in the background of school social life, we catch her looking at Elin. The camera pauses, offers a close-up, and stays still for a moment in which to catch visual signs of the aloneness and desire in Agnes' eyes. Seeing and being seen are crucial here—"Elin will see me"—a process that is painfully tentative and slow. Agnes' gaze becomes an active expressive force creating a queer scopic field of looking that fosters the development of a nonheterosexual romantic plot. *Show Me Love* conveys the desires of a girl for another girl through an oblique glance of fascination: the camera lingers over the tension between wanting and indecision, leaving room for viewers to identify with the emotional charge of Agnes' gaze. The status of the visual image over verbal expression becomes meaningful in the context of an adolescent who has not fully come out to herself and others. There is a weight to the quiet passion of Agnes' gaze that lets viewers inside the difficult emotional predicaments of queer youth coming-of-age.

Show Me Love does not simplify or glamorize the process through which Elin comes out to herself and others. Her fear, ambivalence, and confusion are integral to her realization that choosing Agnes will transform her life. But unlike many stereotypical narratives that leave gay and lesbian youth alone, scorned, and unhappy, this film offers a joyful and empowering image of togetherness to end the film. Playing with the metaphor of coming out, the girls are literally locked in a bathroom together as they confess their mutual love. This scene evokes another closed interior space in which the girls grapple with their desires. Tensions build as schoolmates and teachers bang on the door trying to get them to come out. When they finally emerge, Elin aggressively calls out, "This is my new girlfriend. . . . We're going to go and fuck." They storm past the crowd with smiling faces, moving defiantly outside and into the public world. *Show Me Love* represents the stasis of being alone and withdrawn along with the pull of erotic anticipation and action that drives this teen romance forward.

Show Me Love represents Agnes' process of coming out as a movement from interior secret spaces to shared intimacy, from the homophobic bigotry of small-town teen cultures, as well as from the socially isolated realm of her bedroom toward a rebellious public declaration of girl-on-girl romance. Throughout most of the film, Agnes' hidden desires are visually signified by positioning her within closed claustrophobic settings where she exists im-

In *All Over Me* (1997), Ellen (Tara Subkoff, left) knows that her friend Claude (Alison Folland) is attracted to her, but she does not know how to handle the situation.

mobile and alone. In contrast, the American film *All Over Me* represents a working-class queer girl on the brink of self-discovery who self-inhabits city spaces. This film, directed by Alex Sichel, follows 15-year-old Claude as she walks through an inner-city New York neighborhood with an unself-conscious sense of independence, making friends with other queer youth, working in a pizza parlor, and eventually going by herself to a local lesbian bar. *All Over Me* locates many of Claude's coming-of-age experiences within public street contexts. Using a realist fictional style, this film frames how queer youth enact subversive languages of visibility in the face of hegemonic public invisibility. Claude is neither physically isolated within the private space of her bedroom nor emotionally detached; she is engaged and open to her changing environment, dreaming of being a girl rock star in an all-girl band as she practices guitar with her best friend Ellen. At the same time, *All Over Me* offers a gritty portrayal of queer bashing, refusing to gloss over the daily risks and traumas that confront queer youth in public spaces. We see Claude struggle to take hold of her awareness of her sexual self as she shifts her social, cultural, and erotic alliances across public/private boundaries.

Queer differences are vividly elaborated through the cultural details of speech, body language, dress, and movements: the ways Claude walks down the street with a clumsy teenage masculine stride, takes up space with her roller skates on the sidewalk, and eats with an aggressive appetite. Claude and Ellen play sex together—humping each other in a distorted circus mirror—laughing as they imitate boy/girl roles in exaggerated heterosexual postures:

CLAUDE: Hi there.
ELLEN: Gee, you're real cute.
CLAUDE: So are you.
ELLEN: Great, let's fuck, fatso.
CLAUDE: All right.
ELLEN: I'm going to suck your big juicy cock.
CLAUDE: Suck me, suck me.
ELLEN: This is stupid.

Ellen cuts off this silly queer spectacle and walks away, leaving Claude in front of the mirror simultaneously aroused and abandoned. This scene offers a spontaneous outburst of girl teen mimicry, and a glimpse of Claude's delight in playing sex to a point where fiction and reality blur. A little later Ellen returns late at night to brag about her sex with her new boyfriend, Mark. Claude asks her to show her what it feels like and they passionately kiss. The film signifies Claude's aching pleasure and frustration in these ephemeral moments of erotic touch and talk, which mean much more to her than a friendship crush. A performative process of queer desire and identification resonates through the role-playing between Claude and Ellen which constructs differences and connections between them and shows up the instability of the sexual conventions they play out.

Refusing to remain stuck adoring a straight girl who gives her little in return, we watch as Claude begins to transform herself through the interplay of another girl's mutually recognizing desire. She makes pivotal decisions about ending friendships and forming new ones. Claude eventually hooks up with another queer girl, Lucy, who not only reciprocates desire but also teaches her the importance of showing her affection for girls in public, outside the walls of her bedroom. Claude finds in Lucy a responsive desire for her desire that confirms and enables her to realize a queer self. *All Over Me* represents Claude's coming out as gradual, partial, and relational. A transition occurs that bridges the romantic distance of adolescent crushes and the physical passion of girl-on-girl sex. We only catch brief moments, but they allow us to see the interplay of knowing and not knowing, hesitation and action, fear and reaction as Claude begins to let go and experience her desires with Lucy. As she opens up erotically, she must also confront her social marginalization in a heterosexist society and the violence that surrounds her. Coming out emerges with subtle intersubjective acts of mutual recognition that work to bridge Claude's embodied attractions with her social possibilities and responsibilities. *All Over Me* explores the uncertainties of coming out without foreclosing the show of affection here and now, since the film ends with Claude and Lucy kissing outside on the street, disclosing to the world their appearance as queer girls. This romantic ending takes the idea of queer public presence and acceptance further than *Show Me Love*, insisting on the empowerment of young girls to inhabit city spaces as fully as possible. *All Over Me* not only represents the coupling of two girls in love, but also glimpses a world of cultural belonging and participation criss-crossing everyday spaces of street, work, and family, as well as the ephemeral subcultural realms of queer girl movements.

Show Me Love and *All Over Me* are serious complex romantic dramas, representing the silence and solitary emotional struggles for recognition, unfolding long, slow moving images of girls experiencing their desire for girls for the first time. In a different vein, *The Incredibly True Adventure of Two Girls in Love* is a light romantic comedy that plays off the predictable twists and turns of a popular teen genre in which opposites fall in love against all odds. Directed by Maria Maggenti, this film breaks ground by refusing to focus on the "problems" of being a young lesbian, and instead allows a working-class tomboy named Randy to exist as an already out, proud, and politicized dyke from the start. Randy is repeatedly insulted as a "freak" and "diesel dyke" by the kids at school, yet she creatively resists the status of social outcast. While spending time alone, smoking and playing her guitar in her room, she is outgoing and engaged with her "normal lesbo family," her gay friend Frank, and her job at a gas station. When Randy develops a crush on Evie, a popular straight girl, we watch as she risks opening up her feelings and her queer world with a boldly direct honesty. In many ways this film replays standard themes of the smart pretty rich girl falling for the working-class outsider, stressing the gulf between them. Yet this theme gets repeated as a queer girl romance across race and class lines, working inside and outside conventional narrative structures, as the film broaches the specificity of girl-on-girl affections within hegemonic contexts of social division.

The Incredibly True Adventure playfully launches into Randy's sexual explorations from the first scene, where she lustfully kisses and grabs an older femme married woman in the bathroom of the garage where she works. This departs from the very gradual, indirect view of young lesbian romance provided by *Show Me Love* and *All Over Me*. This film begins with images of raw physical sexual action. Opening with a frenzied erotic encounter sets up a very distinct view of Randy as impulsively sexual: she is portrayed as a 17-year-old who actively pursues other women and puts her body on the line to feel pleasure. Her attentions quickly move toward a deeper, more engaging object of affection as she falls in love with Evie, who is someone she will come to both love and lust after. Randy's challenge is to bring her carnal passion into her new friendship with Evie and to allow herself to become in return a sexual object of a femme girl's desire. While friendship is key to this budding relationship, sexual allure remains a driving force of attraction between these girls. Here, love and sex converge in a gradual process of mutual discovery.

The Incredibly True Adventure elaborates Randy's socialization as a queer girl by situating her within a lesbian household. This pushes beyond a romance-centered teen narrative to include family and community formations of queer culture as integral to Randy's sense of self and belonging. Dialogue about coming out is spoken with personal recognition within her family:

RANDY: I came out to a girl at school today.

AUNT'S GIRLFRIEND: How'd it go?

AUNT: Well, she didn't run for the hills or anything.

RANDY: She's like this totally cute popular girl in my school.

AUNT: Well, be careful, you know how people can be, but it's good to come out. I'm proud of you.

RANDY: Why do you have to make everything into a federal discrimination case!

We witness a volatile back-and-forth conversation across generations of queer women, a rare scene in contemporary films exploring teen relations. This presents a very different set of family supports to deal with the daily realities of being harassed for coming out in a heteronormative society. Whereas *Show Me Love* and *All Over Me* represent an impasse between girls on the verge of coming out and their straight parents, *The Incredibly True Adventure* offers an alternative dynamic of queer family resistance. What stands out in Randy's family are the caring bonds of community that includes friends, ex-lovers, and lesbian partners. The unique atmosphere of this context is vividly shown when Evie comes over to Randy's home for dinner, taken aback by the vivacious, messy, noisy, and chaotic ritual of food preparation in a working-class lesbian household. This sharply contrasts with the sophisticated, neat, and controlled family environment Evie and her mother live in, where we watch them eat an elegant sushi meal over intellectualized discussions of parent-child separation. Communication across these class lines is mediated by race as Evie assumes that Randy's aunt does not like her because she is black, which Randy reinterprets as a dislike of Evie's heterosexual class privilege. Coming up against social inequalities that divide their families, these girls help guide each other through their respective worlds of experience as integral to forging their romance.

While Randy and Evie are from radically separate worlds, they are drawn together in a fictional narrative of teen sexual discovery and independence. Both defy the rules imposed by peers and adult authorities to follow their desires, and both risk social isolation along the way. What stands out in *The Incredibly True Adventure* is the girls' power to defy those prohibiting their union, their refusal to limit their erotic imaginations and actions to accommodate adults and peers. This film's innovative elements pivot around the development of girls' desires for each other, visualized as a mise-en-scène that foregrounds their sexual pleasure and sensual explorations. Constructing a fantasy space of queer girl erotic intimacy, the film sets up dreamy flowing images of them listening to music while touching, lying in the grass, collapsing ecstatically together on the floor, sucking, grabbing, and kissing each other's naked bodies with abandon. In these moments, *The Incredibly True Adventure* exceeds the heteronormative boundaries of teen romance films, glimpsing mobile and shifting carnal embodiments of two girls in love.

CONCLUSION: WATCHING GIRLS LOVING GIRLS

It is impossible to escape the fact that the textual analysis outlined in this essay is imbued with my desire to see cinematic images of teen girls desiring girls. Queer girl films thrill and provoke me! Coming to them as a cultural theorist, I try to be conscious of how my feelings and fantasies inform my ideas. These films are important to me as a queer adult craving stories through which to make sense of my adolescent past. I also feel strongly that they are crucial to younger generations of film viewers looking for a broad range of possibilities for identification and imaginative projection. By making the claim that these films are culturally transformative, I have selected and highlighted certain parts that help build an argument centered on the representational specificity of queer girl experiences. I am deeply aware of how little cultural attention is paid to queer youth and how dominant heterosexual ideologies pervade popular and critical interest in youth. This leads me to argue that reading queer girl films for their nuanced differences is a reflexive and critical interpretive activity. In this sense the personal edges of my reading are also political, an approach that consciously values subjects that have been historically erased and marginalized from public view. Jean Bruce writes that "a queer reading against the grain, to steal pleasure, is also an implicit politics of interpretation. This is one place where the politics of identity and the aesthetics of resistance coincide in textual analysis" (288). Films constituting the lives of queer youth in fictional narratives are politically meaningful insofar as they enable ways of seeing and imagining young romance beyond the heteronormative gaze and narrative structures while borrowing and resignifying elements from teen film genres. The point is not to formalize a new subgenre but to open up a dialogue about the representational practices that enable viewers to identify and interpret these stories in multiple ways, to develop languages through which queer girls are engaged with as culturally visible and viable subjects.

The rich variety of stories and images constructed within these films attests to a creative field of queer girl cinema emerging today, calling forth reflexively engaged viewer responses. The significance of these specific romance films lies in their detailed perspectives centered on the psychic, intersubjective, and cultural work involved in queerly coming-of-age as girls. *Show Me Love, All Over Me,* and *The Incredibly True Adventure of Two Girls in Love* help viewers see that becoming queer as an adolescent involves self-knowledge and the ability to communicate and act in the face of widespread denial and hostility. In other words, queerness is portrayed as an active verb, a doing, a growing, and a maturing into agency. The strength of these films lies in their willingness to profile the emergence of queer girl subjectivity in diverse relational contexts. It is not a rational progression toward moral normative maturity that structures these films, but rather a dynamic interplay of self and other, body and mind, silence and language. Performative contours of girls' identities and desires are elaborated through daily enactments, what they say and wear, and the music and cultural icons they enjoy, as well as how they move and interact with those around them. The characters are visually and verbally produced as queer girls in and through their embodied relations. By framing the sexual identifications of girls as an ongoing accomplishment that is contingent and mobile, while also being grounded in their specific stories, these films overcome the closure of heterosexist endings. While each film demonstrates that the path toward the self and social recognition of queer adolescence are not reducible to a static formula, they trace difficult challenges as each character comes to terms with her sexual difference. Coming out and coming-of-age is represented as a creative process involving deep feeling, emotional intelligence, and social insight.

The transformative crux of *Show Me Love, All Over Me,* and *The Incred-*

ibly True Adventure is the chance they offer to see smart girls who are determined to find love and become sexually active with other girls. This offers another take on "girl power" premised on the strength of girls to defy gender and sexual norms of beauty and desirability and seek out alternatives. Their power is portrayed as vulnerable and relational, breaking with the commodified presentations of the hyperglamorous sexuality of heterosexual girl power icons. Images of ordinary girls embracing, kissing, and fucking girls provide key visual moments through which we glimpse embodied desires, getting a close-up view of queer girl physical pleasures. The protagonists' desires are also the driving impetus of narrative development, making things happen and moving the story along. Through the force of their desires, these girls are compelled to make choices and act in ways that change the course of their social lives, foregoing conformity for risky pursuits. Yet there is no causal or predictable outcome to the plots of these films. While in some sense the girls become heroic individuals overcoming obstacles to get the girl they want, they are also shown hesitating in the ambiguity of adolescent uncertainties. There is a striking vulnerability in the persistence of these girls' erotic longings that combines quiet caution and visible determination. Yet all these films provide narrative endings that involve a happy queer coupling of girls, and they come together if only briefly to affirm the possibility of fulfillment. This queers conventional hetero-endings of teen romances, as we are left to imagine the futures of these girls as queer desiring subjects. It is not the guarantee of a type of romance that matters here but ephemeral images of love actualized between girls that provides hope and promotes change.

■ ■

CHAPTER 16

YOUTH, SEXUALITY, AND THE NATION

Beautiful Thing *and* Show Me Love

SCOTT HENDERSON

Alexander Doty notes the possibility of queer spectatorship of mainstream texts in his identification of "queer moments" in texts.[1] In conjunction with this idea, it might be possible to conceive of queer texts that rely on mainstream constructions in relation to issues of queer, or more specifically queer youth, identities. As Doty's argument suggests, many mainstream "straight" texts remain open to possible "queer readings," an aspect that, according to Doty, inheres in the text itself rather then being constructed by the audience. Within the parameters of this study, the construction of the filmic text, and particularly the ways in which agency is constructed within that text, is of paramount importance. While both of the films to be discussed here foreground gay and lesbian characters, my concern is not with the articulation of sexual identity but rather how each film employs gay and lesbian agency as a means of addressing wider social concerns, particularly in response to the expectations of the dominant culture. Doty's explanation of his terminology raises similar concerns: "when I use the terms 'queer' or 'queerness' as adjectives or nouns, I do so to suggest a range of nonstraight expression in, or in response to, mass culture."[2] Similarly, neither of the films discussed here need be considered as gay and/or lesbian texts, but instead as youth films which employ a gay or lesbian gaze and foreground moments of "queer positions" of spectatorship as a response to mass culture constructions of youth. The need to establish agency which breaks from that of the dominant culture provides impetus for the perspective that these films provide.

Here I will analyze two such films, each emerging from separate national cinema traditions—the Swedish film *Show Me Love* (a.k.a. *Fucking Åmål,* Lukas Moodysson, 1998) and the British film *Beautiful Thing* (Hettie Mac-

Donald, 1996). Each of these films uses standard teen film conventions of escape from an oppressive family and social life to explore not only youth anxieties but also anxieties around sexual identities in contemporary settings. The aim of this analysis is to examine how each of these films, in negotiating boundaries of national and sexual identity, composes its own construction of "otherness" as the main characters interact with and respond to mainstream culture.

In accordance with Chris Straayer's arguments identifying a lesbian gaze,[3] but extrapolating these findings to a queer gaze more widely, it can be argued that texts such as those identified above incorporate their gay and lesbian protagonists as a means of addressing other issues, particularly those relating to a rejection of status quo representations. In both films, the main characters' seeming entrapment within restrictive families and/or communities makes the idea of "getting out" synonymous with "coming out." The films do address other youth culture interests, but significantly employ aspects of gay and lesbian representation in articulating their concerns. This identification of queer spectatorship and representation and its role in addressing wider cultural issues is the primary focus of this chapter. A careful analysis of each film will show how they represent the subjectivities of their young lesbian or gay protagonists within the context of their respective national cinemas.

Doty's notion of queer moments suggests that "'queerness' as a mass culture reception practice is shared by all sorts of people in varying degrees of consistency and intensity."[4] In other words, he suggests that texts can create queer subject positions to which all spectators may relate and respond. Doty's own definition of this space and his choice of terms overlaps with issues that have been raised around representations of youth. Says Doty, "I am using the term 'queer' to mark a flexible space for the expression of non- (anti-, contra-) straight cultural production and reception."[5] While most youth films do not expressly deal with openly nonstraight representations, their concerns with issues of sexual identity and expression and their challenge to mainstream aspects of "cultural production" align them with fundamental elements of Doty's definition. The films discussed here illustrate the "queer" possibilities in youth narratives and their relationship to the mainstream. As Doty himself says, "Queer positions, queer readings, and queer pleasures are part of a reception space that stands simultaneously beside and within that created by heterosexual and straight positions."[6] Much the same can be said of youth positions and representations, which so often are constructed as both outside and inside dominant cultural positions.

While many youth films have dealt with young people's sexual anxieties, particularly around issues of coming-of-age, very few have dealt with non-straight youth. Some teen films have addressed the concerns of homosexual youth, but these tend to be independent productions subject to limited theatrical release, and often very difficult to obtain on video or DVD.[7] Even films with more mainstream possibility and major studio support would seem to run into roadblocks. Timothy Shary describes the case of *Coming Soon* (Colette Burson, 1999), in which one of the three main characters realizes she is a lesbian. Shary points out that in the United States the film was given an NC-17 rating, making it very difficult to distribute. And as Shary notes, this seems "due to the film's extolling of young women's sexual satisfaction."[8] Shary contrasts this with the R-rated *American Pie* (Paul Weitz, 1999), which focuses on male sexuality. Though *American Pie* does not overtly address homosexuality, it would seem to be a topic which creates fear, primarily for the father of the main character, Jim. Throughout the film are scenes of father-and-son talks that demonstrate the father's anxiety. At the film's conclusion, when the father happens upon Jim viewing a live Internet feed of a striptease being offered by his female, overseas love interest, the contented father dances down the hall, calling out to his offscreen wife. Any fears regarding his son's sexual orientation have seemingly been laid to rest.

So within the mainstream teen film, representations of homosexuality have been effectively marginalized, as they tend to be in mainstream cinema more widely. Yvonne Tasker has addressed the critical debates surrounding lesbian representations within the mainstream, noting that popular representations of lesbians and lesbian desire have been negatively received. Tasker suggests that these films "are simultaneously deemed interesting and yet found wanting in quite complex ways," and that while "women, feminist or not, have flocked to see them . . . various feminist critics have contemptuously dismissed popular films such as *Lianna*, *Black Widow*, and *Desert Hearts*."[9] Tasker alludes to significant debates over how gay and lesbian experience should be represented. The formal properties of art cinema, experimental film, and documentary have often been seen as key shifts away from the dominant structures of the mainstream, popular cinema. Yet, as Julianne Pidduck has noted, "many lesbian viewers have long craved the retelling of familiar stories to accommodate lesbian desire, courtship and sexuality."[10] Still, gay and lesbian perspectives have more readily been identified in other film forms, such as documentary or experimental works. In terms of youth representations, the most frequently addressed may be the pixel vision video works of Sadie Benning. Benning's works, described as autobiographical, give voice to a lesbian perspective. Christie Milliken stresses the development of a specific subjectivity in their performativity. She notes that "Benning is clearly part of a younger generation of lesbians characterized by a move-ment from an emphasis on identity to an emphasis on performance."[11] This performative power is crucial in allowing for the emergence of a "queer" voice, as opposed to merely offering gay or lesbian representations. While Benning's films may remain classified and marginalized as documentaries, experimental works, or Milliken's term, video essays, the possibilities for a queer subjectivity that they create point to the way in which these voices can be used to break from dominant representations. It may be that in non-Hollywood systems, the representations of queer perspectives align more effectively with broader national cinema concerns in response to Hollywood and its dominant discourses. What is significant in the films I am looking at here is that they do offer gay and lesbian narratives, but do so within the tra-ditions of their national cinemas, rather than being from the margins. Gay and lesbian "looks" are offered in these films to open up questions surround-ing the hegemony over youth representation, and it is through the opening up of these questions that national cinema discourses are able to emerge.

Beautiful Thing opens by establishing a sense of social and cultural alien-ation as the film's protagonist, Jamie Gangel (Glen Berry), runs away from school and toward his home in the concrete wastelands of South East Lon-don. Overhead shots emphasize his position as small and seemingly insig-nificant against this cold landscape, establishing a mood which is in align-ment with numerous teen films where alienation is a central theme. At the same time a rainbow is seen, representing the possibilities of beauty to be uncovered or discovered "somewhere over the rainbow." As in Dorothy's case in The Wizard of Oz, Jamie discovers that his "escape" leads to a re-evaluation of the world in which he already lives. The film has much in com-mon with several other class-focused British films of the 1980s and the 1990s, including another film concerned with articulations of young gay identity, Stephen Frears' My Beautiful Laundrette (1985). Characters are trapped in an oppressive social environment in which social mobility is limited. In Beautiful Thing's concrete and breeze block projects, social and gender roles seem well defined; boys are expected to excel at football and fighting while girls are defined by their sexuality. The film's frequent intersections between concerns typical of youth films and those typical of contemporary British cinema relate to the main character's concerns over sexual identity. As such the film might be argued to be as concerned with issues of class and iden-tity as it is with issues of growing up gay, using the gay story line as a further means of underlining and representing social isolation.

Jamie becomes attracted to his next door neighbor Ste Pearce (Scott Neal), who is frequently abused by his alcoholic father and violent older brother.

This playful Australian print ad for *Beautiful Thing* (1996) features its young gay couple in a way that U.S. films about queer youth tend to avoid.

Raised in this environment of overblown masculinity, Ste is initially reluctant to return Jamie's affection and is particularly wary of how others will view his relationship. This sense of social entrapment is echoed in the film's visual style, where the world of the estates is oppressive and restrictive. These ties to locale are significant in aligning *Beautiful Thing* with other recent working-class films in Britain. As Julia Hallam has noted, "these films all foreground a sense of place in their use of location shooting and vernacular dialogue."[12] This place is made all the more significant in *Beautiful Thing*, for it not only works to mark class, but also serves as a means of further repressing sexual identity, particularly the alignment of masculinity and working-class culture echoed in Ste's family. The two boys find escape, and a sense of belonging, in a gay pub; distance from the estate is emphasized by a lengthy (but conveniently direct) bus ride and also through gay lifestyle magazines which seem to depict gay culture as "out there" rather than in their immediate environment.

All of the main characters in the film are portrayed as desiring escape from the identities they have been expected to assume. Leah's desires to become Mama Cass are emblematic of this. Cass' whiteness is in contrast to Leah's blackness, made evident in one scene where Leah coats her face in white beauty cream in her attempt to become more like Cass. While not categorically a youth, Jamie's mother, Sandra, who evidently had Jamie at a relatively young age, and who retains a youthful, hippie boyfriend, is also marked as an outsider; her thwarted efforts to become a pub manager illustrate the barriers confronting her. The manager of the local pub where she works shares a sexist joke with her, but when Sandra repeats it at her own managerial interview, it offends her interviewers. It is clear that Sandra, and the world in which she lives and works, is far removed from that to which she aspires. The humor, seemingly acceptable as part of the cultural landscape of the estate, is as out of place as Sandra seems to be during the interview, and it undermines her attempts to seemingly "grow up" and grow out of her surroundings.

Beyond cultural definitions of youth also exist those of nation. While there is much to align *Beautiful Thing* with a wide range of British films of the 1980s and '90s, particularly in its explorations of working-class, or underclass, existence, the sexual orientation of its protagonists marks the film as more of an exception. This links to questions of how one might define a national cinema, and where such alternative, marginalized voices may be positioned. Justine Ashby, as Andrew Higson notes, shows how the British woman's film of the '80s offers an "escape from the claustrophobic confines of Britishness by entering a liminal space elsewhere, beyond the boundaries of nation."[13] The opening of *Beautiful Thing* alerts us to the liminal space in which these characters exist. Already on the margins of society socioeconomically, the characters are further marginalized within this landscape. For Jamie the marginalizing force is sexual orientation, for Leah it is both race and gender, and for Sandra it is class and single parenthood.

Beautiful Thing echoes earlier British cinema, such as the Ealing films, which Higson suggests "explore a liminal space on the margins of the nation in order to grasp its apparent center."[14] Similarly "kitchen sink" films such as *Saturday Night and Sunday Morning* (Karel Reisz, 1960) and *My Beautiful Laundrette*, according to Higson, "return to similarly liminal spaces on the metaphorical edge of the nation."[15] But such films imply a relationship with the "center," even if it is one of alienation, and as Higson states in relation to Ealing, these films do wish to "grasp its apparent center." The "happy" ending of the communal dance in *Beautiful Thing* may mark a rejection, or at least a reorientation of that center. When Jamie and Ste venture into the city, it is to visit a gay pub, perhaps an indication that the center is more heterogeneous while it is the margins that still cling to the older, dominant-values mainstream culture. For those on the economic margins, the sexist jokes, homophobia, racism, and strict defining of gender roles become less a grasping of an "apparent center" than a grasping at straws to maintain some sense of connection to a center which no longer exists.

The liminal space occupied by characters such as Jamie or Leah within the already liminal space of the estate actually functions to align them with shifting ideas of what constitutes nation. Traditional, established values are outmoded in relation to the diversity and fragmentation which now exists at the center. Such a reading of the film is consonant with Higson's notion of a postnational cinema. The ideas of a stable, national community are replaced by a heterogeneity—a diversity of perspectives and ideals. Yet, as *Beautiful Thing* ultimately shows, the acceptance of this diversity reinvigorates rather than destroys community. The cold, concrete atmosphere of the estate is given new life and vibrancy in the dance at the film's conclusion. Ultimately *Beautiful Thing* uses its gay plotline as part of its rearticulation of the national. But rather than address the anxieties of the underclass, the film addresses how such marginalized groups are often "stuck," clinging to outmoded ideals. They remain liminal by staying with ideas of nation that are no longer in keeping with the heterogeneity of the center. In doing so, the film represents the possibilities for a national cinema envisioned by John Hill: that is, to "re-imagine the nation, or rather nations within Britain, and also to address the specificities of a national culture in a way that does not presume a homogeneous and 'pure' national identity."[16] *Beautiful Thing* may even be pushing this further, as it not only works to "re-imagine the nation" but also to critique how traditional notions of national identity present a conservative roadblock to the development of contemporary communities. By allowing for the articulation of otherwise marginalized voices, the film establishes a new sense of cultural identity within postcolonial Britain. In doing so the film is able to respond to concerns around identity and nation, which is also a function of Moodysson's *Show Me Love* in relation to Sweden.

A significant aspect of *Show Me Love* is its adaptation of the standard youth film, particularly that of the high school films popular in American cinema. Though transposed to Sweden, the film incorporates the same settings, styles, and structures as those found in numerous Hollywood youth films. The socially outcast main character, Agnes (Rebecka Liljeberg), is attracted to the popular Elin (Alexandra Dahlstrom), and the two are eventually drawn together. This takes place against familiar teen film locales and scenarios, such as school, home, and teen parties, and the action is accompanied by a sound track of popular songs, including the title track, sung in English by Swedish teen pop star Robyn. The mass culture construction of a the teen star, including a reference to a Robyn-endorsed brand of perfume, is

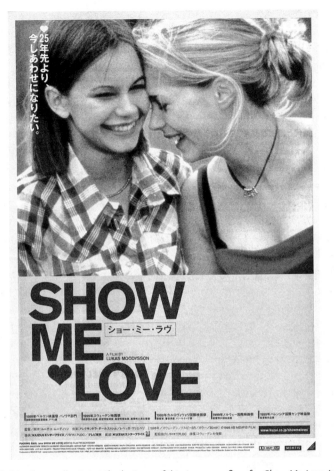

As revealed by the small print at the bottom of this Japanese flyer for *Show Me Love* (1998), the film's original title, *Fucking Åmål*, was often elided outside of Europe.

crucial to the film's critique of the way in which the teens of this film have their gender roles constructed by the mass media. Although shot in a style akin to Dogme 95, the film employs recognizable cinematic codes and structures so that the story is familiar despite the shifting of subject positions and setting. The main distinction between this film and the sorts of films it borrows from is in the sexuality of the two main characters.

Show Me Love offers a lesbian narrative as a means of critiquing dominant culture representations rather than offering itself as a lesbian film. In accordance with Straayer's arguments, *Show Me Love* provides examples of the "lesbian look," one that Straayer suggests "requires exchange," unlike the dominant male gaze that looks upon the female as object of desire.[17] In Straayer's explanation of the lesbian gaze, the unidirectional gaze is done away with in favor of shots that demonstrate an equal exchange of looks or a two-shot in which both characters are seen. In Straayer's examples these representations are overshadowed by the films' rearticulations of a dominant heterosexuality. This is not the case in *Show Me Love*, as instead the lesbian gaze is usurped as part of a wider critique of mass culture's gender and social roles for youth. Elin's desires to escape the confinement of small-town life and its cultural expectations are realized in her discovery of her own subjectivity and her declaration of her desires for Agnes. Agnes and Elin do present themselves as a couple at the end, and in contrast to Straayer's examples of *Entre Nous* (Diane Kurys, 1983) and *Voyage en Douce* (Michele Deville, 1980), they are assertive about their sexuality. Straayer points out that neither of the films she discusses foregrounds its female protagonists' relationships as lesbian, but that both films are "open to lesbian readings."[18] She suggests that "female bonding" provides possibilities in films for potential "lesbian appropriation." However, she argues that this is often "acknowledged by internal efforts to forbid such conclusions."[19] *Show Me Love* aligns its female bonding more overtly with a lesbian story line in the relationship between Elin and Agnes, but despite this it may be read as a film which actually appropriates lesbian representation to address wider concerns. *Show Me Love* remains a film written and directed by a male, Lukas Moodysson, and its thematic concerns deal more with the alienation that youth may feel in a small-town setting in the context of a global culture. Hence, it is arguably less a lesbian film than a film that employs lesbian desire, and a filmic means of expressing this desire, as part of its critique of the dominant culture.

One of the striking elements of *Show Me Love* is the dominance of familiar brand names, trademarks, icons and other marks of mass culture. Unlike films where product placement is paramount, these elements are not foregrounded but rather seem to permeate the environment in which the protagonists exist. Moodysson, in his mise-en-scène, is indicating how mass culture images function to structure youth's lives. One of these repeated elements is that of the images of hockey stars and their effects on the males of the film. On a number of occasions posters of hockey players are seen on the walls of the young men's bedrooms, suggesting the influence these masculine images might have on their conception of gender roles. To underline this point, Moodysson includes a scene at a hockey practice where the coach derides his players with phrases such as "mommy's boys," thus reinforcing dominant cultural expectations around gender. It is not then surprising that within this environment Markus (Stefan Horberg) and Johan (Mathias Rust),

two central male characters, would emerge with shallow, uninformed opinions about women. When confronted by his girlfriend—Elin's sister Jessica
(Erica Carlson)—as to why he has fought another male while they are loitering in front of a store, Markus is unsure, referring to it as something he just
had to do, reinforcing how these characters are compelled to adhere to social expectations of gender. Johan is shown as being so weak that he cannot
voice his own opinions when challenged on his views by Elin; instead he can
only weakly echo Markus' sexist posturing. One scene provides an ironic in-
version in the form of a comparison of cellular phones, where having the
smaller and thinner phone, and hence better technology, is seen as a mark
of one's manhood.

Show Me Love depicts a group of young people in a relatively remote city
whose lives are dominated by the largely foreign, mass culture images they
are offered. A frequent point of complaint for Elin is the contrast between
what is available in Åmål in contrast with larger urban centers. She bemoans
the fact that according to a popular magazine, raves are "out" before they
have ever reached Åmål. At one point, as Elin and her mother are watching
the televised national lottery, they (and we) are confronted with advertising
images of the idealized family as potential winners. It is clear that the images
the mass culture sells are out of reach for the inhabitants of Åmål—a fact
that the adults of the film seem resigned to, but from which at least the two
lead protagonists long to escape. Their friends, in contrast, accept their fate
and the limitations that it offers them. Opportunities for these youth to determine and to express their own identities are limited.

As a response to these mass culture constructions, the film uses the relationship between Agnes and Elin as a means of countering the traditional
representation of youth and romance offered in teen films. The film borrows
what might loosely be described as a "John Hughes" aesthetic in terms of its
use of setting, characters, issues, and reliance on sound track. While Hughes'
films so often validate a dominant, heterosexual discourse, *Show Me Love*
employs many of the same generic aspects in working to counter that dominant voice. As with many teen films, music plays a large role, especially the
use of Foreigner's "I Want to Know What Love Is" in the scene where the two
girls exchange their first meaningful kiss, and in the use of the title track.

As Straayer notes, the "Hollywood romance formula of love at first sight
relies on a slippage between sexuality and love."[20] As argued by other feminist theorists, the sexual desires represented by the voyeuristic pleasure of
looking become coded culturally as "love," thus recuperating them in a socially acceptable and less threatening manner. This is even more significant
when women look, as classical texts deny female subjectivity based upon

desire. So the normal pattern is one where sexual desire is enough to motivate love, but by the film's end love replaces sex. The two song titles suggest the possibility of the same transformation in the relationship between Elin and Agnes, thus negating the threat that might be represented by an expression of female desire. But this, it turns out, is not the case in *Show Me Love*. Rather than allowing her desires to be transformed solely into love, Elin announces to her schoolmates, as she and Agnes emerge from the bathroom, "This is my new girlfriend. . . . We're going to go and fuck." Her feelings are combined with her sexual desires rather than being culturally constructed as the typical teen film might imply. Her openly expressed desire for both bonding and sexuality, "loving" and "fucking," is in contrast with her earlier reactions to sex with Johan, which were based solely on saying what was expected of her rather than revealing her true feelings. The title "Show Me Love" may thus equate with "show me subjectivity," or let me act rather than be acted upon. In relation to Elin it may also function as somewhat of a challenge. As suggested in the film, she has been the object of desire for a number of boys, but as is evidenced by her frustrations, she remains unsatisfied by their attention. Following Elin's sexual encounter with Johan, she admits to her sister that while she said nice things to Johan, she remained unimpressed and unfulfilled. By contrast, Agnes' desire, and the depth of it as indicated through her diary entries, may be a means of showing Elin "love," so that she will "know what love is."

One of the ways in which the film addresses these concerns is through its shifting subjectivity. The film begins by focusing on Agnes—her perspective and her desire for Elin. Her feelings parallel those of Johan: in one scene we see both Agnes and Johan admiring and then clipping the same picture of Elin from a school yearbook. Elin is clearly cast as an object of each gaze, and at this point we see that Agnes' "lesbian" gaze is equated with the male gaze. The fulfillment of her desires actually comes when that alignment with the male gaze is broken, and we get, as Straayer notes, an "exchange" of looks. Again, Straayer states that "the lesbian look requires exchange. It looks for a returning look, not a receiving look. It sets up two-directional sexual activity."[21] Elin moves in the film from being an object of desire to someone whose subjectivity is activated so that eventually she is able to provide the necessary "returning look" in developing her relationship with Agnes.

Elin eventually becomes her own viewer as the film progresses. As Straayer notes, drawing on Doane's notion that traditional texts structure women's position in two possible ways: "the masochism of overidentification," as is seen in Elin's exaggerated, and false, attempts at conformity in pursuing Johan, or "the narcissism entailed in becoming one's own object of desire."[22] In Doane this latter aspect is seen as part of the mass culture construction of women, wanting to be as beautiful and desirable as the female film stars they see on screen, and the ways in which mass culture encourages such identification. This is something that Elin faces in her relationship with Jessica, with whom discussions revolve around issues of appearance. One such conversation relates to Elin's desires to become a future Miss Sweden, an aspiration Jessica derides, as she believes Elin is too short. During this conversation we see the girls resort to using an elevator's mirror as a means of checking their appearance, since it turns out that Elin has broken the household mirror in a fit of frustration over her image. This coincides with Lacanian notions of the mirror stage, for Elin's breaking of the mirror prevents her moving into the symbolic, and hence she is not codified by the social "norms." Furthermore, her unwillingness to move beyond this "mirror stage" may symbolize Elin's refusal to grow up and grow into the sorts of social conformity against which she rebels. Her relationship with Agnes permits her to "grow up" in a manner outside of the dominant social discourse. This then overlaps with her stated career goals of becoming either a model or a psychoanalyst—either the object of desire or the taking of a subjective role. This split is evident in the hitchhiking scene, where Elin, in essence, becomes her own object of desire as she kisses Agnes. We do not see the two in a typical shot/reverse shot, but rather in a two-shot as they kiss in the backseat of a car. Elin's comment of "look at us, we're so fucking cool" becomes significant here, as she encourages herself and Agnes to look at themselves, to assume a position of subjectivity. When they enter the car, a Saab family sedan driven by a middle-aged, patriarchal father figure, the camera shows the subjective position of the driver, looking down Elin's shirt at her breasts. The kiss between the girls disrupts this dominant gaze. The male driver is unable to get his car started, and upon seeing the girls kiss, questions whether or not he is on *Candid Camera*, a mark of his loss of control over subjectivity.

Elin's newfound subjectivity has been activated as a result of Agnes' looking and desire. In the segment following the encounter in the car, we are fooled as viewers by a scene that at first seems to reflect Agnes' point of view. The scene at first seems to be a next-day follow-up to the kiss in the car, but is instead, we realize, a dream sequence. It takes place in the school cafeteria, and its narrative corresponds with Agnes' written diary fantasies. However, we find out that the dream in fact has been Elin's, motivated by her desires for Agnes. This is revealed when Jessica wakes Elin. In response to her sister's questions about the dream, Elin opts for conformity, implying that the dream was about a heterosexual love interest. Elin repeatedly expresses her desire to escape from the conformity expected in Åmål, a conformity even Jessica acknowledges when she notes that her relationship with Markus is not borne of desire but rather out of a sense of social expectation. Throughout the film we see Elin and Jessica avoid stepping on sewer drains marked with an A, as cultural myths suggest that stepping on such drains will unleash a scourge of a-related afflictions, such as AIDS, anorexia, acne, and anal sex. Finally, near the end of the film, Elin finds the courage to point out the absurdity of such myths, noting the negative attributes that could just as easily be associated with drains marked with a C.

Nonetheless, because of her attempts to conform to expectations, Elin ends up in a relationship with Johan as a means of preventing Jessica from finding out about her desires for Agnes. From Elin's perspective, the relationship between her and Johan is not one of passion, or true feelings, but one of social obligation. The sex we see is without passion, and Johan's culturally anticipated expectations are undermined by the lack of authenticity in Elin's reactions. Instead, sex with Johan seems to stand in for the sex with Agnes that she is not yet able to have. Following the kiss between Agnes and Elin, the film cuts back and forth between their responses and desires, and Agnes' numerous rebuffed attempts to contact Elin. Across this void, Moodysson's clever use of crosscutting creates an exchange of glances, culminating with Elin almost telling her mother about her desires. Instead, Elin criticizes her mother for pointlessly following the dreams of the lottery; we then see Agnes begin to masturbate while looking at the yearbook picture of Elin. Agnes' response to her desire is action, but Elin's links to conformity do not permit her to openly speak of her desire; rather, she rechannels that energy into the critique of her mother's conformity. Following the shot of Agnes, we see an image of Elin defacing pictures in a fashion magazine, in effect destroying the gendered expectations that have been placed on her. This visual building of their relationship is then disrupted by Jessica, who insists that Elin meet with Johan, a relationship which then further disrupts the possibility for contact between the two girls.

Straayer points out that mainstream cinema, and the theories related to it, are too limited in how they address gay spectatorship, for they assume certain existent subject positions. Hence, it is stressed that lesbian or queer desire is expressed via a masculine gaze and a regression on the part of women to align themselves with that dominant subjectivity. Straayer's analysis, and my analysis of *Show Me Love*, suggest that there may be means of opening up other kinds of spectatorship or subjectivity. For *Show Me Love* this works in aid of a larger goal of undermining the mass culture codes that so often work to determine gender. The relationship between Elin and

Johan goes some way toward redressing this viewpoint as it undermines the heterosexual gaze by demonstrating the ultimate futility of Johan's efforts. His gaze, and his desires for Elin, are not the gaze or desires that motivate the narrative; rather, we are encouraged to identify with the exchange of looks between Elin and Agnes. This exchange opens up the possibility of other kinds of spectatorship within the text and thus of the possibility of breaking from the mass-mediated culture which provides the social norms for a city like Åmål.

The films addressed here can be seen as employing "queer" subjectivity as a means of deviating from the norms of youth representation. In an era of increased globalization, and with the concurrent domination of Hollywood-style images of youth, such deviations function beyond solely representing sexual difference. As Shary has pointed out, "Since most movie studios are now owned by a handful of corporations that also own vast Internet and television outlets, the industry's appeal to youth may have formed into a more diffuse effort to maintain constant media consumption rather than any media-specific loyalty."[23] The ability for films from other national cinema traditions to break from such monopolistic depictions is clearly significant. Nationally specific concerns and popular culture are exemplified in both films discussed here. By breaking from the "norms" surrounding youth representation, the films have been able to articulate wider concerns surrounding cultural appropriation. The hegemonic discourses of globalization are challenged as the norms of youth depiction are discarded, and a "queer" subjectivity is permitted to emerge. The central characters in both of these films long to escape from the social forces that dominate their lives. Likewise, the films themselves seem to escape from the dominant forces surrounding youth representation in cinema and in doing so articulate a space for their national voices to be heard.

NOTES

1. Alexander Doty, *Making Things Perfectly Queer: Interpreting Mass Culture* (Minneapolis: University of Minnesota Press, 1993).

2. Doty, xvi.

3. Chris Straayer, "The Hypothetical Lesbian Heroine in Narrative Feature Film," in *Out In Culture: Gay, Lesbian and Queer Essays on Popular Culture*, ed. Corey K. Creekmur and Alexander Doty (Durham: Duke University Press, 1995), 44–59.

4. Doty, 2.

5. Doty, 3.

6. Doty, 15.

7. Among the more recent nonmainstream teen films that have featured homo-

sexual protagonists are *The Incredibly True Adventure of Two Girls in Love* (Maria Maggenti, 1995), *All Over Me* (Alex Sichel, 1997), *Totally Fucked Up* (Gregg Araki, 1993), *Edge of Seventeen* (David Moreton, 1998), and *But I'm a Cheerleader* (Jamie Babbit, 1999).

8. Timothy Shary, "Teen Films: The Cinematic Image of Youth," in *Film Genre Reader III*, ed. Barry Keith Grant (Austin: University of Texas Press, 2003), 507.

9. Yvonne Tasker, "Pussy Galore: Lesbian Images and Lesbian Desire in the Popular Cinema," in *The Good, The Bad and The Gorgeous: Popular Culture's Romance with Lesbianism*, ed. Diane Hamer and Belinda Budge (London: Pandora, 1994), 172.

10. Julianne Pidduck, "After 1980: Margins and Mainstreams," in *Now You See It: Studies on Lesbian and Gay Film*, ed. Richard Dyer and Julianne Pidduck, 2nd ed. (London: Routledge, 2003), 286.

11. Christie Milliken, "The Pixel Visions of Sadie Benning," in *Sugar, Spice, and Everything Nice: Cinemas of Girlhood*, ed. Frances Gateward and Murray Pomerance (Detroit: Wayne State University Press, 2002), 287.

12. Julia Hallam, "Film, Class and National Identity: Re-imagining Communities in the Age of Devolution," in *British Cinema, Past and Present*, ed. Justine Ashby and Andrew Higson (London: Routledge, 2000), 266.

13. Andrew Higson, "The Instability of the National," in Ashby and Higson, 45.

14. Higson, 45.

15. Higson, 45.

16. John Hill, "British Cinema as National Cinema: Production, Audience and Representation," in *The British Cinema Book*, ed. Robert Murphy (London: British Film Institute, 1997), 252.

17. Straayer, 45.

18. Straayer, 48.

19. Straayer, 52.

20. Straayer, 45.

21. Straayer, 45.

22. Mary Ann Doane, "Film and Masquerade: Theorizing the Female Spectator," in *Femmes Fatales: Feminism, Film Theory, Psychoanalysis* (New York: Routledge, 1991), 31–32, as quoted in Straayer, 47.

23. Shary, 511.

■ ■

CHAPTER 17

DIFFERENT FROM THE OTHER(S)

German Youth and the Threat of Homosexual Seduction

STEPHEN TROPIANO

In his autobiographical film *Taxi Zum Klo* (*Taxi to the Toilet*, 1980), German actor/director Frank Ripploh offers a candid, personal account of his double life as a closeted gay schoolteacher with a passion for cruising the streets of West Berlin. Through his blend of absurd humor and the explicit, unapologetic depiction of his many anonymous sexual encounters, Ripploh critiques the values that "straight" society imposes on both his public and private life.

In one amusing and insightful sequence, Ripploh sits at his kitchen table tutoring one of his pupils, a young boy named Holger. Meanwhile, in the next room, Ripploh's lover, Bernd, and their friend, Wally, a transvestite, watch an educational film Ripploh brought home from school. The film, *Christian und sein Briefmarkenfreund* (*Christian and His Stamp Collector Friend*), is an actual short produced by the West German education system that was still being shown in schools to warn young boys about child molesters. The story focuses on 10-year-old Christian, who visits his adult friend, Herr Buckard, to see his stamp collection. The gentleman generously offers the lad one of his rare stamps, which he graciously accepts. But Christian soon discovers what his "stamp collector friend" expects in return when he starts to fondle him. As the panic-stricken boy heads out the door, Buckard warns him not to tell anyone or they will both be imprisoned. But when Christian arrives home, he tells his mother what happened.

Bernd and Wally are both offended by the film and the implication that Buckard is a homosexual. Wally insists there is no correlation between consensual adult male sexual relations and child molestation. "Do you think that's [Buckard fondling Christian] right?" Wally asks. "I don't think that's right. I mean, when we adults do that, it's something different." Meanwhile, in the kitchen, a restless Holger would rather play "horsy" with Ripploh than do his homework. The boy offers his teacher one of his toy soldiers (mirroring Buckard giving the stamp to Christian) and then jumps into his lap. Ripploh promptly picks up Holger, puts him back in his chair, and insists they get back to work.

By crosscutting between *Christian* and the tutoring session, Ripploh draws an obvious comparison between Buckard and himself, who, despite the boy's innocent flirtations, displays no sexual interest in his pupil. The sequence completely shatters the homosexual seduction myth, which constructs adult gay men as lechers who, unable to control their sexual desires, prey on innocent youth, thereby transforming them into homosexuals. As Simon Watney explains, the adult male homosexual's pursuit of a young boy is one of the major "streams of images" which constitute the "long shadow of 'the homosexual'": "the spectacle of erotic seduction, in which an 'innocent,' 'vulnerable' youth is fantasized as an unwilling partner to acts which, nonetheless, have the power to transform his (or her) entire being."[1]

The myth (henceforth referred to as the "seduction myth") is based on an ahistorical and acultural interpretation of the sexual practices of the ancient Greeks. As Dover, Halperin, Foucault, and other historians have demonstrated, homosexual relations in ancient Athens (c. fifth century BC) were an institutionalized practice that operated in accordance with the patriarchal power structure of the state.[2] As the most powerful members of Athenian society, adult male citizens could hold office, participate in the state assembly, and have sex with any member of a subordinate group who was inferior in social and political status (namely females, boys, foreigners, and slaves). The intergenerational relationship between an adult male citizen (the *erastes*, which means "lover") who pursued and seduced a male youth (the *eromenos*, the "one who is loved") was pedagogical in nature and consensual. An individual's social status also determined the role one assumed in sexual relations. Consequently, the adult *erastes* would always assume the "active" position, while the *eromenos* was always "passive."

Although they are often equated, there is no correlation between the *sanctioned* pursuit and seduction of an *eromenos* by his *erastes* in ancient Greece and what are today commonly referred to as pederasty and pedophilia. Still, labels like "pederast," "pedophile," and "child molester" have been and continue to be used interchangeably with "homosexual." This association is by no means accidental, but rather "stems from the way in which homosexuality has been theorized since the late nineteenth century, when the word largely replaced other terms and produced the idea of a single, coherent, uniform type of human being—'the homosexual.'"[3] In fact, the equation of homosexuality with pedophilia explains why sodomy laws have often carried harsher penalties for the "active" partner, who, assuming the dominant position in the sexual act, poses the greater threat to a passive youth. It is also the reason why, in some cultures, the age of consent for sexual relations between two males is higher than it is for relations between a man and a woman or between two women.[4]

"JUSTICE THROUGH KNOWLEDGE": PARAGRAPH 175 AND THE HOMOSEXUAL SEDUCTION MYTH

From the late nineteenth century through the late 1960s, sodomy laws in Germany and postwar East and West Germany constructed the male homosexual as a monstrous figure who poses a threat to the patriarchal power of the state and the welfare and morality of its youth. In 1871, the newly formed German state adopted Prussia's anti-sodomy law, which became Paragraph 175 of the Reich Criminal Code. The law declared that an "unnatural sexual offense, which is committed by two people of the male sex or by people with animals, is to be punished by incarceration; the verdict may also include the loss of *bürgerlich Ehrenrechte* [civil rights]."[5]

In response to the adoption of Paragraph 175, the first homosexual emancipation organization, the Wissenschaftlich-humanitäres Komitee [Scientific-Humanitarian Committee], was cofounded by homosexual physician and scientist Dr. Magnus Hirschfeld, publisher Max Spohr, and ministry official Erich Oberg.[6] The committee's motto—"*Per scientiam ad justitiam*" [Justice through knowledge]—summarized its central mission: to repeal Paragraph 175 of the Reich Criminal Code.

In 1897, the committee circulated a three-page petition directed to "the Legislative Bodies of the German Empire" calling for a revision of Paragraph 175. The committee recommended that homosexual sex be punished only in cases involving "the use of force, or arousing 'public annoyance,' or when performed between an adult and a minor under the age of 16."[7] The petition included 900 signatures from the "opinion makers of Wilhelmine Germany—prominent scientists, lawyers, educators, writers, highly placed civil servants, church functionaries, and the like."[8] Over time, the list of notable signers included Dr. Richard von Krafft-Ebing, Martin Buber, Albert Einstein, Heinrich Mann, Thomas Mann, and Rainer Maria Rilke.[9]

When the Reichstag turned down their petition, Hirschfeld launched an educational campaign that aimed to educate lawmakers and the general public about homosexuality. The committee came closer to achieving their goal when a Communist member of the Reichstag Committee for Penal Code Reform proposed to remove Paragraph 175 from the Code. On October 16, 1929, the committee approved the motion by a vote of 15 to 13.[10] Unfortunately, the legislation never reached the Reichstag for a final vote.

Before seizing power in 1933, the National Socialist Party made their position on homosexuality clear in an official statement released in 1928 opposing the proposed repeal of Paragraph 175:

> Anyone who thinks of homosexual love is our enemy. We reject anything which emasculates our people and makes it a plaything for our enemies, for we know that life is a fight and it's madness to think that men will ever embrace fraternally. Natural history teaches us the opposite. Might makes right. And the stronger will always win over the weak. . . . We therefore reject any form of lewdness, especially homosexuality, because it robs us of our last chance to free the people from the bond which now enslaves it.[11]

The protection of the German state would later serve as the foundation of the new antihomosexual statutes added to the Penal Code in 1935. The statute that made homosexuality a crime, Paragraph 175, was expanded to encompass a wider range of homosexual behavior as well as to impose greater restrictions on specific situations involving youth. The newly revised law, which officially took effect on September 1, 1935, read as follows:

Paragraph 175
1. A man who commits a sexual offense with another man or allows himself to be sexually abused is punished with incarceration.
2. If one of the persons involved was not yet 21 years old at the time of the act, the court can refrain from punishment in particularly minor cases.

Paragraph 175a
The following is punishable by a prison term of up to 10 years; in the case of mitigating circumstances, by a jail term of no less than 3 months:

1. A man who coerces another man with violence or the threat of present danger to life and limb either to commit a sexual offense with him or to submit himself to be sexually abused by him.
2. A man who through abuse of professional, work or other relationships of power and subordination orders another man to either commit a sexual offense with him or to submit himself to be sexually abused by him.

3. A man over 21 years of age who seduces a male under the age of 21 either to commit a sexual offense with him or to submit himself to be sexually abused by him.
4. A man who prostitutes himself with or lets himself be abused or offers himself for such purposes.

The penalty for homosexual acts between adult males was now harsher, though the courts were allowed to consider offenses involving an individual under 21 (under Section 2 of Paragraph 175) as a mitigating circumstance. This is not to suggest that the National Socialist government was condoning intergenerational homosexuality, for Section 3 of Paragraph 175 explicitly prohibited sexual acts between an adult and a youth, though the penalty was more severe when the offense involved two adults. The homosexual seduction of minors was also included in Paragraph 174 ("sex offences with dependents") and Paragraph 176 of the German Penal Code. Paragraph 176, in particular, involves vice with children under the age of 14:

A penitentiary sentence of up to ten years will be imposed on anyone who . . . undertakes indecent acts with a person under fourteen years of age or lures such persons to carry out or tolerate indecent acts. If mitigating circumstances are present, a prison sentence of no less than six months will ensue.[12]

In addition to the revised laws, Heinrich Himmler, head of the Schutzstaffel (SS), restructured the Criminal Police Force and established a headquarters in Berlin that offered local police forces throughout Germany assistance with prosecuting homosexual offenses. The police reported legal proceedings for anyone suspected of sexual-related offenses (Paragraphs 174–176) or "blackmail on grounds of homosexuality" (Paragraph 253) to the Reich Office for the Combating of Homosexuality and Abortion, particularly if he or she was a Jew, a civil servant, or in a leadership position.[13] The 1937 guidelines issued by the Criminal Police for combating homosexuality and abortion emphasized the serious threat homosexuals posed to German youth:

Especially dangerous are homosexuals who feel attracted to the youth. By their arts of seduction they are constantly winning over and contaminating young people. . . . Someone who is known as a corrupter of youth is to be mercilessly removed from human society. It should not be thought that he has done it only once. . . . And the likelihood of a subsequent offense is too great that, in the interests of the state, it appears necessary to put him for a long time in a place of confinement.[14]

Before the revised Paragraph 175 went into effect, homosexuals were being imprisoned in a concentration camp in Fuhlsbüttel. Although the number of homosexuals incarcerated in the death camps is difficult to ascertain due to limited existing records, it is estimated that 10,000 homosexuals were imprisoned in over 11 camps.[15] Historical records and memoirs of camp survivors indicate that the men and women who wore the "pink triangles"—the prison markings signifying their homosexual status—were, in some camps, at the bottom of the prison hierarchy.[16] Many homosexuals were coerced into castration or were used as guinea pigs for experiments involving typhus fever and hormones.[17]

Although nothing in pre– or post–World War II German history would mirror the atrocities committed by the Nazis between 1933 and 1945, the liberation of Germany at the end of the war did not mean freedom for homosexuals living in East Germany or the Federal Republic of West Germany. Homosexuality remained illegal in both countries, and homosexuals would not receive formal recognition as Holocaust victims until 1985.[18] Paragraph 175 was retained as part of the Penal Code, and the seduction myth would continue to serve as the rationale for the criminalization of homosexuals. In the Federal Republic, the number of prosecutions under Paragraph 175 increased from 1953 to 1965 as former concentration camp victims who did not renounce their homosexuality received sentences lasting up to six years.[19]

The first opportunity for the repeal of Paragraph 175 did not occur until May of 1957, when the Bundesverfassungsgericht (West German Federal Constitutional Court) heard an appeals case involving a merchant, Oskar K., and a cook, Günter R., who were sentenced in 1952 and 1953, respectively, to jail terms under Paragraph 175. Oskar K. received one year and eight months for violating Paragraph 175 and Paragraph 175a No. 3 (seducing a male under 21 or committing a sexual offense with him). Günter R. was sentenced to one year in jail under Paragraph 175a No. 3 plus one crime of accessory under the same law and misdemeanor for the crime of sexual offense (under Paragraph 175). Their convictions were challenged on three grounds: (1) both men were convicted under a law that had been revised by National Socialists and embodied the principles of Rassenlehre [National Socialist racial teaching]; (2) Paragraph 175 violated the Grundgesetz [Basic Law] of the West German Constitution, which insured that every individual had the right to develop his or her personality freely; (3) Paragraph 175 was unconstitutional because it discriminated against male homosexuals while lesbians were exempt, thus violating Paragraph 2 of Article 3 of the Basic Law, which states that "men and women have the same rights" and that "no one may be disadvantaged or advantaged on account of his sex."[20]

The court ruled that the three objections were without merit. Although

Paragraph 175 had been revised under Nazi rule, the court argued that the present government did allow laws issued under the National Socialists. More importantly,

> not all laws that were issued by the National Socialist government can be treated as legally void without considering their content and posing the question of whether they are still recognized as having legal validity by those whom they affect.[21]

The record also stated that there was "virtual unanimity" in the western occupied zones that Paragraph 175 and Paragraph 175a "were not 'laws shaped by National Socialism' to such a degree that they should be denied force in a free democratic state . . ."[22] In response to the claims that antihomosexual legislation violated the Basic Law, the court ruled there were fundamental "biological" and "functional" differences between men and women, which could justify the different treatment of the sexes in terms of homosexuality. Through extensive testimony from over a dozen "expert" witnesses, the court established that male homosexuality posed more of a threat to society than lesbianism because male homosexuals were more likely to seduce, have a greater sexual drive, and change partners more frequently. Consequently, the constitutional appeal of Günter R. was rejected, while the appeal of Oskar K. was irrelevant due to his death.

The transcript of the 1957 court case remains an important testament to the antihomosexual attitudes of postwar Germany. Despite the intolerance endured by homosexuals since the turn of the century, the dominant German construction of homosexuals as "seducers of youth" would remain intact. The German high court revitalized the fear propagated by the National Socialists that homosexuals posed a social danger to the welfare of the German people. This fear is the subject of the only gay-themed film produced in Germany in the 1950s, *Anders als du und ich*.

ANDERS ALS DU UND ICH

In *Anders als du und ich* (*Different from You and Me*, 1957), which was released in the United States in 1959 under the title *The Third Sex*, a West German couple struggle to prevent their son from turning into a homosexual. The film was directed by Veit Harlan, a former stage actor who, under the supervision of Joseph Goebbels, emerged as one of Nazi Germany's leading filmmakers. Harlan's most famous work was an anti-Semitic version of Lion Feuchtwanger's 1925 pro-Jewish novel *Jud Süss* [*Jew Süss*], in which the title character, Süss Oppenheimer, is portrayed as an evil Jewish tax collec-

A notorious film dealing with teenage homosexuality, *Anders als du und ich* (1957) shows Klaus (Christian Wolff) under the gaze of Dr. Boris Winkler (Friedrich Joloff).

tor who uses his position to gain power for himself and the Jewish community. Tried, but never convicted of war crimes, Harlan returned to directing in 1950 and continued to work in Germany until his death in 1964.

In *The Third Sex*, Werner Teichmann (Paul Dahlke), a bank director, and his wife, Christa (Paula Wessely), are concerned that their teenage son, Klaus (Christian Wolff), is spending too much time with his best friend, Manfred (Günter Theil). Klaus and Manfred share a mutual interest in modernist literature, music, and art, which is fostered by their friendship with a homosexual art dealer, Dr. Boris Winkler (Friedrich Joloff). With the help of his brother-in-law Max (Hans Nielsen), Werner confronts Dr. Winkler about his relationship with his son and files charges against him for corrupting a minor. Meanwhile, Christa consults their family doctor, who suggests that a heterosexual experience would perhaps lead her son down the path to normalcy. Christa makes a subtle hint to their live-in housekeeper, Gerda (Ingrid Stenn), saying that she would reward her with a bracelet if she would sleep with her son. While the Teichmanns are away, Gerda seduces Klaus and the couple fall madly in love. When Manfred learns about Klaus and Gerda, he tells Dr. Winkler, who uses the information against the Teichmanns. Christa is charged with procurement, and although the judge understands that she was acting in her son's best interest, he must still give her the minimum six-month sentence.

Based on an actual court case, the film sought to educate parents about the warning signs of homosexuality. Although director Harlan and screenwriter Dr. Felix Lutzkendorf, who based his script on a story by Robert Pilchowski, expressed an occasional pang of sympathy for those who are on the sexual margins of German society, the film rejects homosexuality as a healthy, acceptable alternative lifestyle.

The Teichmanns are initially concerned about their son when he demonstrates an "unusual" fondness for his friend Manfred, whom Klaus protects from their cruel classmates. In return, Manfred introduces Klaus to modernist music and poetry and encourages him to show his abstract paintings to his mentor and benefactor, Dr. Winkler. In a scene that could be straight out of *Christian and His Stamp Collector Friend*, Dr. Winkler waits for Klaus in the schoolyard after school. He introduces himself to Klaus, looks him over from top to bottom, and asks to see his paintings. He even offers him a ride in his car, but Klaus declines and later confesses to Manfred that Dr. Winkler makes him feel uncomfortable.

Neither Dr. Winkler's attraction to Klaus nor Manfred's obvious infatuation with his friend is fully articulated. Homosexual desire is instead displaced onto a discourse of modernist culture in the form of Klaus' abstract paintings, Manfred's prose, and the atonal music played on Dr. Winkler's electronic synthesizer, which the good doctor describes as "music that has a relationship to our daily lives, rather than sheer romanticism." Winkler is impressed by Klaus' paintings, which the young artist describes as a combination of Picasso and Kandinsky. He encourages Klaus to paint his own vision, which he assures him will emanate from his "inner eye." "No one ever explained it to me before," confesses a dazed Klaus, who appears to be under the spell of Winkler's hypnotic stare.

The film's antimodernist position and the equation of modernism with homosexuality echoes the vicious campaign launched by the National Socialists against modernist art, which they regarded as degenerate and anti-German. Only then, in the Adenauer era, homosexuality was not so much anti-German as it was anticapitalist. Consequently, Werner's discussion with Klaus over his friendship with Manfred turns into a debate between culture and capitalism. Klaus accuses his father of caring only about money, while Werner reminds him that it is the bank that provides the cash that allows him to enjoy the "beauties" of life. Underlying their discussion of the value of culture is the issue of Klaus' homosexuality:

WERNER: Klaus, I'm concerned about you.
KLAUS: You're worried because you don't understand.

WERNER: What is there to understand? We've all had friendships but it was never the way it is between you and Manfred.

KLAUS: You really want me to explain. For you, business is all. Painting and poetry mean nothing. You live the bank until you go to sleep. And that's it, father.

WERNER: Very astute. Only the bank offers you the chance to find the beauties you seek from life because of where the cash is from. That's how this culture your father can't understand is provided. . . . I talked with your mother and now I feel that the hour has come. In fact, I feel, Klaus, that it may be too late. You have been living in a dream. And I think that this Manfred thing ought to finish now. It's better for you and for him.

Werner Teichmann serves as the film's mouthpiece for the procapitalist values of the Adenauer era. More importantly, *The Third Sex* reiterates the association the Nazis made between homosexuality as a sexual perversion and modernism as a decadent aberration of German culture in order to position homosexuality as antithetical to the capitalist ideology of the Federal Republic. Thus, as the narrative proceeds, Teichmann has two interrelated goals: transform his son into a heterosexual and wake him up to the capitalist realities of postwar Germany.

Werner's goals can only be attained by reclaiming his patriarchal role of the father from Dr. Winkler. When Teichmann confronts Winkler over the doctor's self-proclaimed role as his son's "instructor," homosexuality is once again displaced onto the modernism versus capitalism debate:

WINKLER: These young men, you see, they come here to me because they discover something here their fathers cannot give them—spiritual understanding—a kind of mental and artistic vision. It often prepares them for a career.

WERNER: As he is my son, I will instruct him now.

WINKLER: You'd find it better, for instance, if he ran with loose women, people of that sort, like so many of the others?

WERNER: Doctor, between those extremes, there is a normal world with normal people. I grew up in it and I am glad to say that I am happy in it.

WINKLER: Oh yes, naturally, the world of—

WERNER: Please say what you mean—you mean a commonplace world.

WINKLER: If it comes to that, I guess. You see, I feel that it's a world in which the intellectual, the modern man, is choking.

The danger homosexuality poses to Germany's youth thus becomes rewritten as a struggle between traditional and modern values. To insure that his son will follow in his footsteps and become part of the patriarchal order, Werner must rescue his son from the clutches of Dr. Winkler.

The film makes some attempt to acknowledge that homosexuals do exist, if only on the margins of society. In their search to locate Dr. Winkler, Werner and his brother-in-law Max visit a homosexual bar where they watch a drag show. Werner is in shock when he realizes that women sitting around him and performing on stage are actually men. Max seems to be suspiciously comfortable and knowledgeable about gay life. "The world is full of shadows," Max explains to Werner, "but the shadows are a world too." The film also supports Magnus Hirschfeld's theory that homosexuality is inborn; homosexuals constitute a third, intermediate sex that possesses the combined traits of a heterosexual male and a heterosexual female. Although Hirschfeld is never directly mentioned, his theory is the basis for the film's English title, and it informs a fictional study that Crista has consulted in order to gain a better understanding of Klaus' relationship with Manfred. The film suggests that homosexuality is genetic when Manfred's mother reveals to Werner and Max that her husband and son are similar. "My husband was a dancer at the opera years ago," she explains. "I know just what Manfred is like. It's sometimes better to face it."[23]

While Manfred's homosexuality is irreversible, there's hope for Klaus, whose heterosexuality is confirmed by his sexual encounter with Gerda. In the process, there is a shift in the oedipal configuration of the narrative as Dr. Winkler and Manfred are replaced by the more desirable Gerda. The story supports the myth that all a homosexual needs is one experience with a woman in order to be cured. It also displaces the "fault" of Klaus' two father figures—the homosexual and the uncompassionate Werner—onto the mother, who believed she was only acting out of love for her son ("It would be a magic cure . . . to love someone"). In fact, Crista admits she gladly accepts her sentence because it is worth spending six months in prison to insure her son's future as a heterosexual.

The tale of Klaus Teichmann, whose heterosexuality was redeemed thanks to a mother's love, exemplifies how little the attitudes surrounding homosexuality had progressed in West Germany. The seduction myth and the homophobia, stereotypes, and misinformation, which Hirschfeld and his contemporaries sought to dispel, continued to be at the core of the government's social and legal construction of homosexuality in the postwar era. In 1962, the Christian Democrat government presented a revised version of Paragraph 175 (known as E62) that would abolish only the additions made by the National Socialists. As Martin Dannecker observes, liberals found the revisions disturbing because the rationale provided by the government for the maintenance of Paragraph 175 "echoed in form and content the fascist propaganda calling for the extermination of homosexuals."[24] Dannecker compares the arguments made for E62 and the rationale for the elimination of homosexuals offered by Klare in *Homosexual Penal Law*, the 1937 publication commissioned by Himmler outlining the antihomosexual views of the National Socialists.

Both E62 and Klare argued that the criminalization of homosexuality (in Klare's case, incarceration and extermination) was essential for the protection of German youth as well as the maintenance of the strength of the German state. Klare warned about the

> terrifying increase in homosexual activity, especially among the young, which could not but present a danger for people, state and race, unless it was halted by the ruthless vigor and determination of the law.[25]

Similarly, E62 argued that the

> purity and health of sexual life is a precondition of extraordinary importance for the stability of the people and the preservation of the natural order of life, and our growing young people in particular require express protection from moral danger.[26]

Consequently, the fall of civilizations can also be attributed to the spread of homosexuality through seduction. As Klare put it:

> History teaches us that a state is committed to decay if it does not counter the spread of homosexual practices with decisive counter-measures.[27]

And E62:

> Wherever homosexual vice has taken hold and become widespread, the consequence has always been the degeneration of the people and the decay of its moral powers.[28]

The basic belief that homosexuality would be on the rise if it were legalized was still intact, despite the absence of evidence that homosexuality was on the rise in countries where it had been legalized (e.g., Italy, Denmark, and France).[29] According to Dannecker, homosexuality was viewed through the lens of fear regarding the consequences of repealing Paragraph 175:

> By reducing the debate to the law and its consequences, not only was the life situation of homosexuals reduced to the aspect of criminaliza-

tion, but this also contributed to repression from consciousness the general homophobic structures in West Germany. Because discrimination and antipathy were only discussed in terms of the criminal law, the impression was given that the problem would be ended once the law was changed. . . . What was problematic and in need of change in the social position of homosexuals was reduced to the single issue of criminality. Ultimately, this abstraction from the overall context of homosexual life led to the widespread idea that the absence of discriminatory legislation was identical with positive tolerance.[30]

As drafted in 1962, E62 was never enacted, but would serve as the first in a series of revisions of the penalties for sex crimes that would continue for the next six years. Finally, in May of 1969, the penalties for sodomy between consenting adults and adultery were eliminated from the penal code of West Germany. The new bill begins with a quote from Seneca: "Only this proves wisdom—to punish not because a crime occurred yesterday but rather that it will not occur tomorrow." The motivation for the repeal of Paragraph 175, which went into effect on September 1, 1969, was explained in a brochure entitled "Progress in Penal Law, Demand of Our Time," by Gustav Heinemann, West Germany's president-elect and former justice minister. Heinemann explained that "a penal code which brands people as criminals because of abnormal sexual qualities encourages hypocrisy, snooping and blackmail. Thus it must be welcomed that the Bundestag has been called to abolish offenses such as homosexuality."[31]

Although the law decriminalized consensual homosexual relations between adults, it retained strict penalties for minors who engage in consensual or forced relations with an adult. Under the new code, the active partner had to be over the age of 18, while the restrictive age for the passive partner was over 21. The definition of homosexual relations in active/passive terms and, more importantly, the three-year age difference between the active and passive partners demonstrates how the German Penal Code continued to "protect" the youth of Germany.

As *The Third Sex* illustrates, the anti-gay myths perpetuated by the Third Reich remained long after the Nazi flags and banners were taken down. It was only after the gay rights movement was in full force in West Germany in the early 1970s that a new generation of filmmakers emerged, which included Wolfgang Petersen (*Die Konsequenz* [*The Consequence*], 1978); Rainer Werner Fassbinder (*Faustrecht der Freiheit* [*Fox and His Friends*], 1975, and *Querelle*, 1982); Lothar Lambert (*Nachtvorstellungen* [*Late Show*], 1977); and Rosa von Praunheim (*Nicht der Homosexuelle ist pervers, sondern die Situation, in der er lebt* [*It Is Not the Homosexual Who Is Perverse,*

But the Situation in Which He Lives], 1970). These filmmakers would at last begin to deconstruct the false myths surrounding homosexuality, homosexuals, and gay male relationships.

NOTES

1. Simon Watney, *Policing Desire* (Minneapolis: University of Minnesota Press, 1987), 23.

2. K. J. Dover, *Greek Homosexuality* (Cambridge, MA: Harvard University Press, 1989); David M. Halperin, *One Hundred Years of Homosexuality* (New York: Routledge, 1990); Michel Foucault, *The History of Sexuality: An Introduction*, vol. 1, trans. Robert Hurley (New York: Vintage, 1980).

3. Watney, 23.

4. For example, up until 2001, the age of consent for gay men in England was considerably higher (20) than for lesbians and heterosexuals (16 in England, Wales, and Scotland; 17 in Northern Ireland). The list of countries that have had a higher age for gay males include Antiqua (Barbuda), Bermuda, the Bahamas, and Lithuania. See www.ageofconsent.com.

5. As quoted in Robert Moeller, *Sex, Society and the Law in Postwar West Germany: Homosexuality and the Federal Constitutional Court* (Berkeley: Center for German and European Studies, 1993), 29.

6. James Steakley, *The Homosexual Emancipation Movement* (New York: Arno Press, 1975), 62 (6n). Steakley suggests that there was a fourth founder, Leopold von Meerescheidt-Hullesem, who handled homosexual matters for the Berlin police.

7. John Lauritsen and David Thorstad, *The Early Homosexual Rights Movement* (New York: Times Change Press, 1974), 11.

8. Steakley, 30.

9. Lauritsen and Thorstad, 14.

10. Steakley, 85.

11. Rudolf Klare, *Homosexualität und Strafrecht* [Homosexuality and Penal Law] (Hamburg: Hanseatische Verlagsanstalt, 1937), 114, as quoted in Steakley, 84.

12. *Sonderrichtlinien: Die Bekämpfung gleichgeschlechtlicher Verfehlungen im Rahmen der Jugenderziehung* [Special Guidelines: Combating Same-Sex Transgressions in the Framework of Youth Training] (1943), 7. I am indebted to James Steakley for providing me with this information.

13. Gunter Grau, *Hidden Holocaust?* trans. Patrick Camiller (London: Cassell, 1995), 86–87. For documents relating to the nationwide registration of homosexuals, see Grau, 89–103.

14. As quoted in Grau, 96.

15. Rüdiger Lautmann, "The Pink Triangle: The Persecution of Homosexual Males in Concentration Camps in Nazi Germany," *Historical Perspectives on Homosexuality*, ed. Salvatore J. Licata and Robert P. Peterson (New York: Haworth Press, 1980), 146.

16. Lautmann, 157.

17. Grau, 246–249, 281–282.

18. Barry D. Adam, *Rise of a Gay and Lesbian Movement* (Boston: Twayne, 1987), 65.

19. Adam, 65. One such "repeat offender" was Karl Gorath, who was turned in to the Gestapo by a jealous lover and sent to a concentration camp, where he managed to survive by switching his pink triangle for a red one (the symbol for political prisoners). When the Americans liberated Germany in 1945, Gorath was released, but was sentenced soon after to four years in prison for violating Paragraph 175. Klaus Müller, "Introduction," in *The Men with the Pink Triangle*, ed. Heinz Heger, trans. David Fernbach (Boston: Alyson Publications, 1994), 14. Gorath is one of the gay concentration camp survivors whose life is commemorated in the United States Holocaust Memorial Museum in Washington, DC. See Müller, 15.

20. Moeller, 1–2.

21. Moeller, 58–59.

22. Moeller, 61.

23. Apparently the film's U.S. distributor, D & F, was not able to face it. Released under the title *The Third Sex*, the film's trailer makes no mention of its homosexual content. Instead, it focuses on Klaus and Gerda and how their "shocking relationship" and "illicit love" lead to "the most lurid trial in history." The trailer is included on *Homo Promo* (2004, Strand Releasing), a DVD curated by Jenni Olson that features trailers from gay- and lesbian-themed films released between 1953 and 1977.

24. Martin Dannecker, *Theories of Homosexuality*, trans. David Fernbach (London: Gay Men's Press, 1981), 15.

25. Klare, 11, as quoted in Dannecker, 18.

26. *Bundestagsdrucksache IV 650, 4 October 1962—Regierungsentwurf eines Strafgesetzbuches E 1962* [Bundestagsdrucksache IV 650, 4 October 1962—Government draft of the Penal Code E 1962], quoted from *Plädoyer fur die Abschaffung des ¶175* [Plea for the Abolition of Paragraph 175] (Frankfurt: Suhrkamp, 1966), as quoted in Dannecker, 18.

27. Klare, 12, as quoted in Dannecker, 18.

28. *Plädoyer*, 142, as quoted in Dannecker, 18.

29. "*Homosexualität* [Homosexuality]," *Der Spiegel*, no. 20 (May 1969): 68.

30. Dannecker, 19.

31. "Homosexuality Laws East by West Germany," *Los Angeles Times*, May 11, 1969.

▧ ▧

FILMOGRAPHY OF GLOBAL YOUTH FILMS BY NATION

This filmography consists of all the non-U.S. feature films about youth listed in this book, as well as over 700 other titles culled from many different indexes and databases. The list is as exhaustive as possible, although it is not complete due to the numerous international films that have not found their way into wide release and/or have not been properly catalogued. All of the films below feature a significant role or roles for people in their adolescence or puberty; in terms of years, that generally means characters aged 12 to 20.

The title of each film is listed in its native language first, with its English or international title listed second, unless the film is primarily known by its English title, in which case the native title comes second. Films that had a popular non-English title are often listed without translation.

The nationality of each film was sometimes difficult to determine, since certain catalogues list films' nationalities according to the location of their production companies. In this case, nationality has been determined almost exclusively by where the film was made and in what language. In some cases, films are multilingual and/or employ multiple nation locations, in which case the national identity that is most predominant within the film itself is listed. In the case of nations that have changed names in the past century, or have been divided (such as Yugoslavia, the Soviet Union, Germany, etc.), please refer to the name of the nation at the time of the film's release.

The year for each film is generally the year the film was theatrically released in its native country. In rare cases where films did not achieve theatrical release, their debut on video is listed. Films intended for television broadcast are not listed, nor are films under one hour in length, nor documentaries.

AFGHANISTAN
Osama (2003)

ANGOLA
O Herói/The Hero (2004)

ARGENTINA
Breve cielo/Brief Heaven (1969)
Buenos Aires Vice Versa (1996)
Caja negra/Black Box (2002)
La Casa del ángel/The House of the Angel (1957)
La Ciénaga/The Swamp (2001)
Crónica de un niño solo/Chronicle of a Boy Alone (1965)
Dar la cara/Responsibility (1962)
Escrito en el agua/Ever Changing Waters (1998)
Fin de fiesta/The Party Is Over (1960)
El Jefe/The Boss (1958)
La Mano en la trampa/The Hand in the Trap (1961)
Martín (Hache) (1997)
El Nadador inmóvil (2000)
Nadar solo (2003)
La Niña santa/The Holy Girl (2004)
No sabe, no contesta (2002)
Picado fino (1996)
Pizza birra faso (1997)
El Polaquito (2003)
Rapado (1992)
Vagón fumador/Smokers Only (2001)

AUSTRALIA
Age of Consent (1969)
Alison's Birthday (1979)
An Angel at My Table (1990)
Australian Rules (2002)
Beneath Clouds (2002)
Blue Fin (1978)
BMX Bandits (1983)
Deck Dogz (2005)
The Delinquents (1989)
The Devil's Playground (1976)
The F. J. Holden (1977)
Flirting (1991)
The Fourth Wish (1976)
The Fringe Dwellers (1986)
The Getting of Wisdom (1978)
Hating Alison Ashley (2005)
Head On (1998)

The Heartbreak Kid (1993)
High Tide (1987)
Initiation (1987)
Looking for Alibrandi (2000)
The Mango Tree (1977)
Max: A Cautionary Tale (2003)
The Nostradamus Kid (1993)
Peaches (2004)
Picnic At Hanging Rock (1975)
The Pirate Movie (1982)
Puberty Blues (1981)
Rabbit-Proof Fence (2002)
The Rage in Placid Lake (2003)
See Jack Run (1991)
Selkie (2000)
Shame (1987)
Shine (1995)
Somersault (2004)
Violet's Visit (1995)
Walkabout (1971)
Windrider (1986)
The Year My Voice Broke (1987)
Yolngu Boy (2001)

AUSTRIA
Asphalt (1951)
Atemnot (1984)
Auf Wolke Nr. 7 (2004)
Beastie Girl (1998)
Benny's Video (1992)
Flucht ins Schilf/Brutality (1953)
Geständnis einer Sechzehnjährigen (1960)
Die Halbzarte/Eva (1958)
Himmel oder Hölle/Heaven or Hell (1990)
Hurensohn (2004)
Ich gelobe/I Promise (1994)
In Heaven (1998)
Lauf, Hase, lauf (1979)
Lovely Rita (2001)
Malaria/Cafe Malaria (1982)
Mein Stern/Be My Star (2001)
Praterbuben/Boys of the Prater (1946)
Slidin': Alles bunt und wunderbar/Slidin': All Bright and Wonderful (1998)
Tempo (1996)
Ternitz, Tennessee (2000)
Twinni (2003)
Unter Achtzehn/Unter 18 (1957)

Untersuchung an Mädeln/Girls under Investigation (1999)
Verdammt die jungen Sünder nicht/Morgen beginnt das Leben (1961)
Die Verwundbaren/Engel der Lust (1967)
Warum sind sie gegen uns? (1958)
Was kostet der Sieg? (1981)
Wegen Verführung Minderjähriger (1960)

BELARUS (*SEE ALSO* SOVIET UNION)
Moi Ivan, toi Abraham/Me Ivan, You Abraham (1993)

BELGIUM
Iedereen beroemd!/Everybody's Famous! (2000)
Meisje (2002)
Rosie (1998)

BOLIVIA
Dependencia sexual/Sexual Dependency (2003)

BRAZIL
Amor bandido (1979)
Bicho de Sete Cabeças (2001)
Cama de Gato/Cat's Cradle (2002)
Cidade de Deus/City of God (2002)
Com Licença, Eu Vou à Luta (1986)
Contos Eróticos/Erotic Stories (1977)
Houve Uma Vez Dois Verões/Two Summers (2003)
Pixote: A Lei do Mais Fraco (1981)

BULGARIA
Az Grafinyata/The Countess (1989)
Mila ot Mars/Mila From Mars (2004)
Spomen za bliznachkata/Memory of the Twin Sister (1976)
Vsichko e lyubov/All Is Love (1979)

CANADA
Aliens in the Wild Wild West (1999)
The Bay Boy (1984)
The Boys Club (1997)
Le Collectionneur (2002)
Come Together (2001)
Crazy Moon (1986)
Dancing on the Moon (1997)
Dead End (1998)
Deeply (2000)
Detention (2003)
Emporte-moi/Set Me Free (1999)

L'Enfant d'eau/Water Child (1995)
Falling Angels (2003)
Ginger Snaps (2000)
Ginger Snaps: Unleashed (2004)
Hello Mary Lou: Prom Night II/The Haunting of Hamilton High (1987)
Hurt (2003)
Ill Fated (2004)
L'Île de sable (1999)
Innocent (2005)
Kitchen Party (1997)
Lapse of Memory (1992)
Laserhawk (1997)
Les Liens du sang/Blood Relatives (1978)
Lilies—Les feluettes (1996)
The Little Girl Who Lives Down the Lane (1976)
Lost and Delirious/La Rage au coeur (2001)
Marine Life (2000)
Meatballs (1979)
Meatballs III: Summer Job (1987)
Mon oncle Antoine/My Uncle Antoine (1971)
My American Cousin (1985)
New Waterford Girl (1999)
The Outside Chance of Maximillian Glick (1988)
A Passage to Ottawa (2001)
Pick-up Summer/Pinball Summer (1980)
Porky's (1982)
Prom Night (1980)
Prom Night III: The Last Kiss (1989)
Red Hot (1993)
Rollercoaster (1999)
The Sweet Hereafter (1997)
Sweet Substitute (1964)
Teen Knight (1998)
Toby McTeague (1986)
Try Seventeen/All I Want (2002)
The Virgin Queen of St. Francis High (1987)
The Wars (1983)
Wild Horse Hank (1979)

CHAD
Abouna (2002)

CHILE
Johnny cien pesos (1993)
Julio comienza en julio/Julio Begins in July (1977)

CHINA

Balzac et la petite tailleuse chinoise/Balzac and the Little Chinese Seamstress (2002)
Beijing zazhong/Beijing Bastards (1993)
Da chuan qi/Out of Breath (1988)
Fenghuang de daijia/Obsession (1988)
A Girl from Hunan/Xiangnu xiaoxiao (1986)
Guo nian hui jia/Seventeen Years (1999)
Nashan naren nagou/Postmen in the Mountains (1999)
Qingchun/Youth (1977)
Qingchun wansui/Forever Young (1983)
Ren sheng/Life (1984)
Ren xiao yao/Unknown Pleasures (2002)
Ruoma de shiqishui/When Ruoma Was Seventeen (2002)
Samsara/Lun hui (1988)
Sha Ou/Drive to Win (1980)
Shiqi sui de dan che/Beijing Bicycle (2001)
Su xing/Awakening (1980)
Wan zhu/Masters of Mischief (1988)
Yaogun qingnian/Rock Kids (1988)
Yiban shi huoyan, yiban shi haishui/Half Flame, Half Brine (1988)

COLOMBIA

Maria Full of Grace (2004)
Rodrigo D: No futuro/Rodrigo D: No Future (1990)
Vendedora de rosas/The Rose Seller (1998)

CUBA

Amor vertical (1997)
El Brigadista/The Teacher (1977)
Hello Hemingway (1990)
Madagascar (1994)
Nada (2001)
Tesoro (1987)

CZECHOSLOVAKIA

Obecná skola/The Elementary School (1989)
Sedmikrasky/Daisies (1966)

CZECH REPUBLIC

Mandragora (1997)
Pelísky/Cosy Dens (1999)

DENMARK

Daddy, Darling/Katja—Vom Mädchen zur Frau (1968)
Drengene Fra Sankt Petri/The Boys from St. Petri (1991)
Du er ikke alene/You Are Not Alone (1978)

Kundskabens træ/Tree of Knowledge (1981)
Skønheden og udyret/Beauty and the Beast (1983)
Det Store flip (1997)
Twist and Shout/Tro, håb og kærlighed (1984)
Venner for altid/Friends Forever (1987)

EAST GERMANY (*SEE ALSO* GERMANY)
Berlin-Eeke Schönhauser (1957)
Coming Out (1989)
Heißer Sommer/Hot Summer (1968)
Sieben Sommersprossen/Seven Freckles (1978)
Verbotene Liebe/Forbidden Love (1989)

EGYPT
Al-Abwab al-moghlaka/The Closed Doors (1999)
Asrar el-banaat/A Girl's Secret (2001)
Mothakerat morahkah (2001)

ESTONIA (*SEE ALSO* SOVIET UNION)
Ma olen väsinud vihkamast/Too Tired to Hate (1995)
Sigade revolutsioon/Revolution of Pigs (2004)

FINLAND
Kesäkapina/Summer Revolt (1970)
Kissan kuolema (1994)
Poika ja ilves/Tommy and the Wildcat (1998)
Pojat/The Boys (1962)
Punahilkka (1968)
Sairaan kaunis maailma (1997)
Täältä tullaan, elämä! (1980)
Veturimiehet heiluttaa/Goodbye, Trainmen (1992)

FRANCE
À la place du coeur/Where the Heart Is (1998)
À nos amours (1983)
À nous les petites Anglaises/Let's Get Those English Girls (1976)
À toute vitesse/Full Speed (1996)
L'Amant/The Lover (1992)
L'Amour (1990)
L'Année des méduses/Year of the Jellyfish (1984)
Les Années campagne/The Country Years (1992)
L'Argent de poche/Small Change (1976)
Artemisia (1997)
Au revoir les enfants/Goodbye Children (1987)
La Barbare/The Savage (1989)
Bar des rails/Railway Bar (1991)
Beau-père (1981)

Bilitis (1977)
La Boum/The Party (1980)
La Boum 2 (1982)
Brève traversée/Brief Crossing (2001)
Brodeuses/A Common Thread (2004)
Bronx-Barbès (2000)
C'est la tangente que je préfère/Love, Math and Sex (1997)
Les Choristes/The Chorus (2004)
Les Collégiennes/The Twilight Girls (1957)
Comme une image/Look at Me (2004)
Les Diables/The Devils (2002)
Diabolo menthe/Peppermint Soda (1977)
Les Dimanches de Ville d'Avray/Sundays and Cybele (1962)
Dormez, je le veux! (1998)
Douches froides (2005)
The Dreamers/Les Innocents (2003)
Du poil sous les roses/Hair Under the Roses (2000)
L'Effrontée/Charlotte and Lulu (1985)
Les Égarés/Strayed (2003)
18 ans après (2003)
L'Enfant sauvage/The Wild Child (1970)
Les Enfants terribles (1950)
L'Ennui (1998)
L'Esquive (2004)
Fat Girl (2001)
Les Filles ne savent pas nager/Girls Can't Swim (2000)
Games of Love and Chance (2004)
Le Gendarme de St. Tropez (1964)
Le Genou de Claire/Claire's Knee (1970)
Girls (1980)
La Haine/Hate (1995)
Jeux d'artifices (1987)
Kung-Fu master/Le Petit amour (1987)
Lacombe Lucien (1974)
Laura, les ombres de l'été/Laura, Shadows of a Summer (1979)
Lila Says/Lila dit ça (2004)
A Little Romance (1979)
The Little Thief/La Petite voleuse (1988)
Ma mère (2004)
Marie Baie des Anges/Marie from the Bay of Angels (1997)
Mauvaises fréquentations/Bad Company (1999)
Ma vraie vie à Rouen/My Life on Ice (2002)
Mes petites amoureuses (1974)
Un moment d'égarement/One Wild Moment (1977)
Mouchette (1967)
Nénette et Boni (1996)
Pauline à la plage/Pauline at the Beach (1983)

Le Péril jeune (1994)
La Petite sirène/The Little Mermaid (1980)
Premiers désirs/First Desires (1983)
Presque rien/Come Undone (2000)
Les Quatre cents coups/The 400 Blows (1959)
Red Kiss/Rouge baiser (1985)
Les Roseaux sauvages/The Wild Reeds (1994)
Série noire (1979)
Sexy Boys (2001)
60 millions d'ennemis (1998)
Sonatine (1984)
Le Souffle au coeur/Murmur of the Heart (1971)
Swimming Pool (2003)
Tendres cousines/Cousins in Love (1980)
Therese und Isabell/Therese and Isabelle (1968)
36 fillette (1988)
Trop de bonheur/Too Much Happiness (1994)
Les Turlupins/The Rascals (1980)
Une vraie jeune fille/A Real Young Girl (1976)
La Vie devant soi/Madame Rosa (1977)
Les Zozos (1973)

GEORGIA (*SEE ALSO* SOVIET UNION)
27 Missing Kisses (2000)

GERMANY (*SEE ALSO* EAST GERMANY; WEST GERMANY)
Crazy (2000)
Elefantenherz (2002)
Harte Jungs/Just the Two of Us (2000)
Helden wie wir/Heroes Like Us (1999)
Hitlerjunge Quex: Ein Film vom Opfergeist der deutschen Jugend/Hitler Youth Quex (1933)
Irgendwo in Berlin/Somewhere in Berlin (1946)
Jenseits der Stille/Beyond Silence (1996)
Kaspar Hauser (1993)
Die Klasse von /'99 — Schule war gestern, Leben ist jetzt (2003)
Knallhart (2006)
Knallharte Jungs (2002)
Lola + Bilidikid/Lola and Billy the Kid (1999)
Mädchen in Uniform (1931)
Mädchen, Mädchen/Girls On Top (2001)
Maries Lied: Ich war, ich weiß nicht wo (1994)
Mein Bruder, der Vampir/My Brother the Vampire (2001)
Nach Fünf im Urwald/After Five in the Forest Primeval (1995)
Nichts bereuen/No Regrets (2001)
Oi! Warning (1999)
Sommersturm/Summer Storm (2004)

Sonnenallee (1999)
Sophiiiie! (2002)
Swimming Pool—Der Tod feiert mit/The Pool (2001)
. . . und über uns der Himmel/The Sky Above Us (1947)
Verschwende Deine Jugend/Play it Loud (2003)

GREECE

Agoria stin porneia (1985)
Apo tin akri tis polis/From the Edge of the City (1998)
I Epikindini (mia diamartiria) (1983)
Fylakes anilikon (1982)
Peppermint (1999)
Telos epochis/End of an Era (1994)
Topio stin omichli/Landscape in the Mist (1988)

HONG KONG

A Fei zheng zhuan/Days of Being Wild (1991)
Che goh ang ang chan baau cha/PaPa Loves You (2004)
Di yi lei xing wei xian/Don't Play with Fire (1980)
Jo Sok/2 Young (2005)
Mo yan ka sai/Spacked Out (2000)
Xiu Xiu: The Sent-Down Girl (1998)
Zhen xin hua/The Truth About Jane and Sam (1999)

HUNGARY

Amerikai rapszódia/An American Rhapsody (2001)
Apám beájulna (2003)
Csapd le csacsi (1990)
Gyerekgyilkosságok/Child Murders (1993)
I ♥ Budapest (2001)
Kísértések/Temptations (2002)
Megáll az idö/Time Stands Still (1982)
Moszkva tér/Moscow Square (2001)
Naplo gyermekeimnek/Diary for My Children (1984)
Sorstalanság/Fateless (2005)
Sose halunk meg/We Never Die (1993)
Sunshine (1999)
Szerelmes szívek (1991)

ICELAND

Nói albínói/Nói (2003)

INDIA

Aparajito/The Unvanquished (1957)
Durga (1939)
Fiza (2000)
Haasil (2003)

Main Solah Baras Ki (1998)
Mammo (1994)
19 Revolutions (2004)
Papa Kahte Hain (1996)
The River (1951)
Salaam Bombay! (1988)

INDONESIA
Aku ingin menciummu sekali saja/Bird-Man Tale (2002)
Biarkan bintang menari (2003)
Daun di atas bantal/Leaf on a Pillow (1998)

IRAN
Aab, baad, khaak/Water, Wind, Dust (1989)
Abjad/The First Letter (2003)
Baran (2001)
Lakposhtha hâm parvaz mikonand/Turtles Can Fly (2004)
Masaebe shirin/Sweet Agony (1999)
Pedar/The Father (1996)
Sib/The Apple (1998)
Zir-e poost-e shahr/Under the City's Skin (2001)

IRELAND
The Last of the High Kings/Summer Fling (1996)
The Miracle (1991)
Skegs & Skangers (2002)

ISRAEL
Eskimo Limon/Lemon Popsicle (1978)
Etz Hadomim Tafus/Under the Domim Tree (1994)
Ha-Kochavim Shel Shlomi/Bonjour Monsieur Shlomi (2003)
Ingil (2001)
Noa Bat 17/Noa at 17 (1982)
Pitzai Bogrut 80/Growing Pains (1979)
Shifshuf Naim/Hot Bubblegum (1981)
Tza'ad Katan/One Small Step for Man (2003)

ITALY
Amarcord (1973)
Appassionata (1974)
Aprimi il cuore/Open My Heart (2004)
Beatrice Cenci (1969)
Bersaglio mobile/Death on the Run (1967)
Caterina in the Big City/Caterina va in città (2003)
Certi bambini/A Children's Story (2004)
Le Chiavi di casa/The Keys to the House (2004)
Desideria: La vita interiore/Desire, The Interior Life (1980)

Dillo con parole mie/Ginger and Cinnamon (2003)
La Discesa di Aclà a Floristella/Acla's Descent Into Floristella (1992)
Le farò da padre (1974)
*Infanzia, vocazione e prime esperienze di Giacomo Casanova, veneziano/
   Giacomo Casanova: Childhood and Adolescence* (1969)
L'Isola di Arturo/Arturo's Island (1962)
Il Ladro di bambini/The Stolen Children (1992)
La Luna (1979)
La Lupa/She Wolf (1952)
Malabimba/Possession of a Teenager (1979)
Maladolescenza/Spielen wir Liebe (1977)
Malèna (2000)
Mamma Roma (1962)
Il Mare/The Sea (1962)
The Mark (2003)
Morte a Venezia/Death in Venice (1971)
Nuovo cinema Paradiso/Cinema Paradiso (1989)
Ovosodo/Hardboiled Egg (1997)
Padre padrone/My Father My Master (1977)
Piso pisello/Sweet Pea (1982)
Il Posto/The Sound of Trumpets (1961)
Salò o le 120 giornate di Sodoma/Salo, or The 120 Days of Sodom (1976)
Sciuscià/Shoeshine (1946)
La Settima donna/The Last House On the Beach (1978)
Stealing Beauty/Io ballo da sola (1996)
Two Women/La Ciociaria (1960)
Un Urlo nelle tenebre/Cries and Shadows (1975)

JAPAN
L'Amant (2004)
Batoru rowaiaru/Battle Royale (2000)
Chi o suu bara/Evil of Dracula (1974)
Cruel Story of Youth/Seishun zankoku monogatari (1960)
Daremo shiranai/Nobody Knows (2004)
Dokuritsu shonen gasshoudan/Boy's Choir (2000)
Gokudô sengokushi: Fudô/Fudoh: The New Generation (1996)
Jinruigaku nyumon: Erogotshi yori/The Pornographers (1966)
Jisatsu saakuru/Suicide Club (2002)
Kazoku gêmu/The Family Game (1983)
Kenka erejii/Fighting Elegy (1966)
Kono Mado wa Kimi no Mono/This Window Is Yours (1994)
Nagisa no Shindobaddo/Like Grains of Sand (1995)
Nogiku no haka/The Wild Daisy (1981)
Nora-neko rokku: Sekkusu hanta/Stray Cat Rock: Sex Hunter (1970)
Riri Shushu no subete/All About Lily Chou-Chou (2001)
Sakura no sono/The Cherry Orchard (1990)
*Sekai no chûshin de, ai wo sakebu/Crying Out Love in the Center of the
   World* (2004)

Shimotsuma monogatari/Kamikaze Girls (2004)
Shiosai/The Surf (1954)
Shiosai/The Sound of the Waves (1964)
Shiosai/The Sound of the Waves (1975)
Tenkosei/Exchange Students (1982)

KAZAKHSTAN (*SEE ALSO* SOVIET UNION)
Posledniye kanikuly/Last Holiday (1996)
Shiza/Schizo (2004)

MEXICO
Amar te duele (2002)
Amores perros/Love's a Bitch (2000)
Angel del fuego/Angel of Fire (1991)
Anoche soñé contigo/Dreaming About You (1992)
Atlético San Pancho/Never Too Young to Dream (2001)
Bandidos/Bandits (1991)
Los Caifanes/The Outsiders (1967)
Canoa (1975)
El Cometa/The Comet (1999)
¿Cómo ves? (1985)
El Crimen Del Padre Amaro/The Crime of Father Amaro (2002)
De la calle/Streeters (2001)
Un Dulce olor a muerte/A Sweet Scent of Death (1999)
Elisa antes del fin del mundo/Elisa Before the End of the World (1997)
Un Embrujo (1998)
Eréndira (1983)
Espinas (2005)
Fiebre de amor (1985)
Un Hilito de sangre/A Trickle of Blood (1995)
La Joven/The Young One (1960)
Los Jóvenes/Young People (1960)
Matinée (1977)
Los Olvidados (1950)
Perfume de violetas, nadie te oye/Violet Perfume: Nobody Hears You (2001)
La Primera noche/The First Night (1998)
Pueblo de madera (1990)
Ratas de la ciudad (1986)
La Segunda noche (1999)
Temporada de patos/Duck Season (2004)
Ya nunca más (1984)
Y tu mamá también/And Your Mother Too (2001)

MOROCCO
Ali Zaoua, prince de la rue/Ali Zoua: Prince of the Streets (2000)
Le Grand voyage (2004)

NETHERLANDS
Because of the Cats/The Rape (1973)
Voor een verloren soldaat/For a Lost Soldier (1992)

NEW ZEALAND
Alex (1993)
Heavenly Creatures (1994)
In My Father's Den (2004)
Once Were Warriors (1994)
Orphans and Angels (2003)
Rain (2001)
The Scarecrow/Klynham Summer (1982)
Vigil (1984)
Whale Rider (2002)

NICARAGUA
Alsino y el condor/Alsino and the Condor (1982)

NORWAY
Bare Bea (2004)
Frida—med hjertet i hånden/Frida—Straight from the Heart (1991)
Is-slottet/Ice Palace (1987)
När alla vet/Sebastian (1995)
Ofelas/Pathfinder (1987)
Ti kniver i hjertet/Cross My Heart and Hope to Die (1994)
Tommy's Inferno (2005)

PERU
No se lo digas a nadie/Don't Tell Anyone (1998)

PHILIPPINES
Gumapang ka sa lusak/Dirty Affair (1990)
Macho Dancer (1988)

POLAND
Biale malzenstwo (1992)
Czesc Tereska/Hi Tereska (2001)
Europa Europa (1990)
Kolejnosc uczuc/Sequence of Feelings (1992)
Limuzyna Daimler-Benz/The Consul (1982)
Pokolenie/A Generation (1955)
Wsród nocnej ciszy/Quiet Is the Night (1978)
Yesterday (1985)
Zmory/Nightmares (1979)

ROMANIA
The Shrunken City (1998)
Teen Sorcery (1999)

RUSSIA (*SEE ALSO* SOVIET UNION)
Vozvrashcheniye/The Return (2003)

SINGAPORE
15 (2003)
Street Angels (1999)

SLOVENIA (*SEE ALSO* YUGOSLAVIA)
Barabe!/Rascals! (2001)

SOUTH KOREA
*Bom yeoreum gaeul gyeoul geurigo bom/Spring, Summer, Fall, Winter . . .
 and Spring* (2003)
Noksaek uija/Green Chair (2005)
Samaria/Samaritan Girl (2004)
Suchwiin bulmyeong/Address Unknown (2001)
Sureongseo geonjin naeddal/My Daughter Rescued from a Swamp (1984)
13se sonyeon/At 13 Years Old (1974)
Uribanul chasubnida/Searching for Our Class (1990)
Whasango/Volcano High (2001)
Yeopgijeogin geunyeo/My Sassy Girl (2001)

SOVIET UNION (*SEE ALSO* BELARUS;
 ESTONIA; GEORGIA; KAZAKHSTAN; RUSSIA)
Avariya—doch menta/Crash—Cop's Daughter (1989)
Bakenbardy/Sideburns (1990)
Come and See/Idi i smotri (1985)
Do svidaniya, malchiki!/Goodbye, Boys (1964)
Ivanovo detstvo/Ivan's Childhood (1962)
Malenkaya Vera/Little Vera (1988)
S.E.R.—Svoboda eto rai/Freedom Is Paradise (1989)

SPAIN
Barrio/Neighborhood (1998)
Bear's Kiss (2002)
El Bola/Pellet (2000)
La Buena vida/The Good Life (1996)
Colegas/Pals (1982)
Como un relámpago (1996)
Del rosa al amarillo/From Pink to Yellow (1963)
Eres mi héroe/My Hero (2003)
La Fiesta (2003)
Fin de curso (2005)
Food of Love/Menja d'amor (2002)
Krámpack/Nico and Dani (2000)
Malena es un nombre de tango (1996)
La Mansión de los Cthulhu/Cthulhu Mansion (1990)
Menos es más/Less Is More (2000)

¿Qué he hecho yo para merecer esto?/What Have I Done to Deserve This?
(1984)
La Residencia/The House That Screamed (1969)
7 vírgenes (2005)
El Viaje de Carol/Carol's Journey (2002)

SWEDEN
Familjehemligheter/Family Secrets (2001)
Fjorton suger (2004)
Fucking Åmål/Show Me Love (1998)
Hets/Torment (1944)
Hon dansade en sommar/One Summer of Happiness (1951)
Ingen kan älska som vi/Only We Can Love Like This (1988)
Lilja 4-ever/Lilya 4-ever (2002)
Lust och fägring stor/All Things Fair (1995)
Mitt liv som hund/My Life as a Dog (1985)
Den Osynlige/The Invisible (2002)
Populärmusik från Vittula (2004)
P.S. sista sommaren (1988)
Sandor slash Ida (2005)
Sanning eller konsekvens/Truth or Dare (1997)
Sökarna (1993)
Vinterviken/Winter Bay (1996)

TAIWAN
Ch'ing shaonien na cha/Rebels of the Neon God (1992)
Fengkuei-lai-te jen/All the Youthful Days (1983)
Heian zhi guang/Darkness and Light (1999)
Lanse da men/Blue Gate Crossing (2002)
Shi qi sui de tian kong/Formula 17 (2004)
Tong nien wang shi/A Time to Live and a Time to Die (1985)

THAILAND
999-9999 (2002)
Dek hor (2006)
Pee chong air (2004)
Sia dai (1996)

TUNISIA
Asfour Stah/Halfaouine: Child of the Terraces (1990)
Un été à La Goulette/Halk-el-wad (1996)
Satin rouge/Red Satin (2002)

TURKEY
Gençlik Köprüsü/The Bridge of Youth (1975)
Kizim Ayse/My Daughter Ayse (1974)
Memleketim/My Homeland (1974)

Oglum Osman/My Son Osman (1973)
Yalnız Değilsiniz/You Are Not Alone! (1990)
Zehra (1972)

UNITED KINGDOM

AKA (2002)
Assault (1971)
Baby Love (1968)
Beat Girl (1960)
Beautiful Thing (1996)
Bend It Like Beckham (2002)
Billy Elliot (2000)
The Black Rose (1950)
The Browning Version (1951)
The Browning Version (1994)
Buddy's Song (1990)
The Cement Garden (1993)
The Chalk Garden (1964)
The Class of Miss MacMichael (1978)
A Clockwork Orange (1971)
The Company of Wolves (1984)
Cosh Boy (1952)
Dead Cool (2004)
Demons of the Mind (1972)
East Is East (1999)
Every Day's a Holiday (1965)
Expresso Bongo (1960)
Friends (1971)
Gadael Lenin/Leaving Lenin (1993)
The Ghost of Greville Lodge (2000)
Girl with a Pearl Earring (2003)
The Greengage Summer/Loss of Innocence (1961)
Gregory's Girl (1981)
The Hanging Garden (1997)
Here We Go Round the Mulberry Bush (1967)
The Hole (2001)
If . . . (1968)
I'll Be There (2003)
Kes (1969)
Kevin & Perry Go Large (2000)
King, Queen, Knave (1972)
Let Him Have It (1991)
Let's Kill Uncle (1966)
The Loneliness of the Long Distance Runner (1962)
Lord of the Flies (1963)
Madame Sousatzka (1988)
Me Without You (2001)

Millions (2004)
Mumsy, Nanny, Sonny and Girly (1969)
My Brother Tom (2001)
My Life So Far (1999)
My Summer of Love (2004)
New Year's Day (2001)
Paradise Grove (2003)
Paul and Michelle (1974)
Personal Affair (1953)
Please Turn Over (1959)
The Prime of Miss Jean Brodie (1969)
Quadrophenia (1979)
Reach for Glory (1962)
Scum (1979)
Small Faces (1996)
Sweet Sixteen (2002)
A Taste of Honey (1961)
The Testimony of Taliesin Jones (2000)
There's Only One Jimmy Grimble (2000)
The Third Secret (1964)
To Sir, with Love (1967)
Total Eclipse (1995)
Twins of Evil (1971)
Virtual Sexuality (1999)
The War Zone (1999)
Wish You Were Here (1987)
Wondrous Oblivion (2003)
The Young Americans (1993)
The Young Poisoner's Handbook (1995)

URUGUAY
Estrella del sur (2002)
25 Watts (2001)

UZBEKISTAN (*SEE ALSO* SOVIET UNION)
Malchiki v Nebe/Boys in the Sky (2002)

VENEZUELA
Mestizo (1988)
Oro diablo/Devil Gold (2000)
Sicario (1994)

WEST GERMANY (*SEE ALSO* GERMANY)
Anders als du und ich/The Third Sex (1957)
Chinesisches Roulette/Chinese Roulette (1976)
Christiane F.—Wir Kinder vom Bahnhof Zoo/We Children from Bahnhof Zoo (1981)

Die Erben/The Inheritors (1982)
Die Halbstarken/Teenage Wolfpack (1956)
Endstation Liebe/Last Stop Love (1958)
Im Himmel ist die Hölle los (1984)
Leidenschaftliche Blümchen/Boarding School (1978)
Nordsee ist Mordsee/North Sea Is Dead Sea (1976)
Schulmädchen-Report: Was Eltern nicht für möglich halten (1970)
Schulmädchen-Report 2: Was Eltern den Schlaf raubt (1971)
Schulmädchen-Report 3: Was Eltern nicht mal ahnen (1972)
Taxi Zum Klo/Taxi to the Toilet (1980)
Was Schulmädchen verschweigen/Secrets of Sweet Sixteen (1973)

YUGOSLAVIA (SEE ALSO SLOVENIA)
Bubasinter (1971)
Hey Babu Riba (1986)
Sjecas li se, Dolly Bell/Do You Remember Dolly Bell? (1981)
Time of the Gypsies/Dom za vesanje (1988)
Tito and Me/Tito i ja (1992)

ZIMBABWE
Everyone's Child (1996)

■ ■

FILMOGRAPHY OF GLOBAL YOUTH
FILMS BY THEME

This filmography consists of 21 common themes within global youth cinema and films that are relevant to those themes. Please note that this list is selective and in many cases subjective (since attempting to qualify or quantify such categories as "abuse" or "religion" is difficult indeed). Films are only listed here if the editors or contributors knew of their specific themes, and thus many films from Appendix A are not listed, while some films are listed in more than one category.

ABUSE
Amores perros (2000)
El Bola/Pellet (2000)
Demons of the Mind (1972)
La Discesa di Aclà a Floristella/Acla's Descent Into Floristella (1992)
Hets/Torment (1944)
Mouchette (1967)
Once Were Warriors (1994)
Osama (2003)
Padre padrone/My Father My Master (1977)
Salò o le 120 giornate di Sodoma/Salo, or The 120 Days of Sodom (1976)
Sib/The Apple (1998)
Yeopgijeogin geunyeo/My Sassy Girl (2001)

ARTISTIC TALENT
Billy Elliot (2000)
Les Choristes/The Chorus (2004)
Les Diables/The Devils (2002)
Madame Sousatzka (1988)
Memleketim/My Homeland (1974)

Rodrigo D: No futuro/Rodrigo D: No Future (1990)
Shine (1995)

CULTURAL/NATIONAL IDENTITY
Baran (2001)
Beneath Clouds (2002)
Da chuan qi/Out of Breath (1988)
East Is East (1999)
Europa Europa (1990)
The Fringe Dwellers (1986)
Gençlik Köprüsü/The Bridge of Youth (1975)
Le Grand voyage (2004)
Die Halbstarken/Teenage Wolfpack (1956)
I ♥ Budapest (2001)
Megáll az idö/Time Stands Still (1982)
Memleketim/My Homeland (1974)
Once Were Warriors (1994)
Les Roseaux sauvages/The Wild Reeds (1994)
Sonnenallee (1999)
Su xing/Awakening (1980)
Time of the Gypsies/Dom za vesanje (1988)
Tito and Me/Tito i ja (1992)
Topio stin omichli/Landscape in the Mist (1988)
La Vie devant soi/Madame Rosa (1977)
Walkabout (1971)
Wan zhu/Masters of Mischief (1988)
Whale Rider (2002)
Yalnız Değilsiniz/You Are Not Alone! (1990)
Yaogun qingnian/Rock Kids (1988)

DELINQUENCY
Cama de Gato/Cat's Cradle (2002)
Certi bambini/A Children's Story (2004)
Cidade de Deus/City of God (2002)
A Clockwork Orange (1971)
Di yi lei xing wei xian/Don't Play with Fire (1980)
Fylakes anilikon (1982)
La Haine/Hate (1995)
Die Halbstarken/Teenage Wolfpack (1956)
The Little Thief/La Petite voleuse (1988)
The Loneliness of the Long Distance Runner (1962)
Mo yan ka sai/Spacked Out (2000)
Pixote: A Lei do Mais Fraco (1981)
Los Olvidados (1950)
Les Quatre cents coups/The 400 Blows (1959)
Rosie (1998)
Sia dai (1996)

DRUGS
Bicho de Sete Cabeças (2001)
Christiane F.—ir Kinder vom Bahnhof Zoo/We Children from Bahnhof Zoo (1981)
Cidade de Deus/City of God (2002)
La Luna (1979)
Mo yan ka sai/Spacked Out (2000)
Orphans and Angels (2003)
Sairaan kaunis maailma (1997)
Sweet Sixteen (2002)
Temporada de patos/Duck Season (2004)

FAMILY PROBLEMS
À nos amours (1983)
Al-Abwab al-moghlaka/The Closed Doors (1999)
Barrio/Neighborhood (1998)
Chinesisches Roulette/Chinese Roulette (1976)
La Ciénaga/The Swamp (2001)
Falling Angels (2003)
Fiza (2000)
Heavenly Creatures (1994)
High Tide (1987)
Kazoku gêmu/The Family Game (1983)
Mitt liv som hund/My Life as a Dog (1985)
Mon oncle Antoine/My Uncle Antoine (1971)
Mouchette (1967)
Pelísky/Cosy Dens (1999)
Les Quatre cents coups/The 400 Blows (1959)
Shine (1995)
Sweet Sixteen (2002)
Vigil (1984)
Violet's Visit (1995)
Wan zhu/Masters of Mischief (1988)
Whale Rider (2002)
The Young Poisoner's Handbook (1995)

GENDER SWITCHING
Baran (2001)
Lola + Bilidikid/Lola and Billy the Kid (1999)
Mitt liv som hund/My Life as a Dog (1985)
Osama (2003)
Pixote: A Lei do Mais Fraco (1981)
Tenkosei/Exchange Students (1982)
Virtual Sexuality (1999)

HETEROSEXUAL RELATIONS
À nos amours (1983)
L'Amant/The Lover (1992)

The Delinquents (1989)
Dependencia sexual/Sexual Dependency (2003)
The Dreamers/Les Innocents (2003)
Eskimo Limon/Lemon Popsicle (1978)
Gregory's Girl (1981)
The Heartbreak Kid (1993)
Mädchen, Mädchen/Girls On Top (2001)
Malabimba/Possession of a Teenager (1979)
Malenkaya Vera/Little Vera (1988)
Porky's (1982)
Puberty Blues (1981)
Sexy Boys (2001)
Shifshuf Naim/Hot Bubblegum (1981)
Sieben Sommersprossen/Seven Freckles (1978)
Somersault (2004)
Swimming Pool (2003)
Tendres cousines/Cousins in Love (1980)
Y tu mamá también/And Your Mother Too (2001)

HOMOSEXUAL/BISEXUAL RELATIONS
Anders als du und ich/The Third Sex (1957)
À toute vitesse/Full Speed (1996)
Beautiful Thing (1996)
Bilitis (1977)
Dependencia sexual/Sexual Dependency (2003)
Fucking Åmål/Show Me Love (1998)
Head On (1998)
Krámpack/Nico and Dani (2000)
Lilies—Les feluettes (1996)
Lola + Bilidikid/Lola and Billy the Kid (1999)
Lost and Delirious/La Rage au coeur (2001)
Mädchen in Uniform (1931)
My Summer of Love (2004)
Nagisa no Shindobaddo/Like Grains of Sand (1995)
No se lo digas a nadie/Don't Tell Anyone (1998)
Les Roseaux sauvages/The Wild Reeds (1994)
Shi qi sui de tian kong/Formula 17 (2004)
Sommersturm/Summer Storm (2004)
Therese und Isabell/Therese and Isabelle (1968)
Total Eclipse (1995)
Y tu mamá también (2001)

INCEST
Beau-père (1981)
The Cement Garden (1993)
Demons of the Mind (1972)
La Luna (1979)
Malabimba/Possession of a Teenager (1979)

Ma mère (2004)
Le Souffle au coeur/Murmur of the Heart (1971)
The Sweet Hereafter (1997)
Tendres cousines/Cousins in Love (1980)
The War Zone (1999)

MENTAL DISORDERS
Bicho de Sete Cabeças (2001)
Crazy Moon (1986)
Les Diables/The Devils (2002)
L'Enfant sauvage/The Wild Child (1970)
Kaspar Hauser (1993)

MURDER
Batoru rowaiaru/Battle Royale (2000)
Gençlik Köprüsü/The Bridge of Youth (1975)
Heavenly Creatures (1994)
The Little Girl Who Lives Down the Lane (1976)
The Young Poisoner's Handbook (1995)

PEDOPHILIA
The Devil's Playground (1976)
La Discesa di Aclà a Floristella/Acla's Descent Into Floristella (1992)
La Joven/The Young One (1960)
Lust och fägring stor/All Things Fair (1995)
Morte a Venezia/Death in Venice (1971)
La Niña santa/The Holy Girl (2004)
Salò o le 120 giornate di Sodoma/Salo, or The 120 Days of Sodom (1976)
Was Schulmädchen verschweigen/Secrets of Sweet Sixteen (1973)

PREGNANCY
À la place du coeur/Where the Heart Is (1998)
Asrar el-banaat/A Girl's Secret (2001)
Brodeuses/A Common Thread (2004)
Friends (1971)
Hey Babu Riba (1986)
Malenkaya Vera/Little Vera (1988)
Mila ot Mars/Mila From Mars (2004)
Nénette et Boni (1996)
Picado fino (1996)
Sophiiiie! (2002)
A Taste of Honey (1961)
Wish You Were Here (1987)

PROSTITUTION
Christiane F.—Wir Kinder vom Bahnhof Zoo/We Children from Bahnhof Zoo (1981)

Le Collectionneur (2002)
Eréndira (1983)
Il Ladro di bambini/The Stolen Children (1992)
Lilja 4-ever/Lilya 4-ever (2002)
Mandragora (1997)
Mauvaises fréquentations/Bad Company (1999)
El Polaquito (2003)
Xiu Xiu: The Sent-Down Girl (1998)

RACISM
À la place du coeur/Where the Heart Is (1998)
Au revoir les enfants/Goodbye Children (1987)
Australian Rules (2002)
Beneath Clouds (2002)
La Haine/Hate (1995)
La Joven/The Young One (1960)
Rabbit-Proof Fence (2002)

RAPE
Assault (1971)
Because of the Cats/The Rape (1973)
A Clockwork Orange (1971)
De la calle/Streeters (2001)
Fenghuang de daijia/Obsession (1988)
La Settima donna/The Last House On the Beach (1978)
Shame (1987)
Topio stin omichli/Landscape in the Mist (1988)
Two Women/La Ciociaria (1960)

RELIGION
Al-Abwab al-moghlaka/The Closed Doors (1999)
El Crimen Del Padre Amaro/The Crime of Father Amaro (2002)
East is East (1999)
Fiza (2000)
Le Grand voyage (2004)
Malabimba/Possession of a Teenager (1979)
La Niña santa/The Holy Girl (2004)
The Nostradamus Kid (1993)
The Outside Chance of Maximillian Glick (1988)
Yalnız Değilsiniz/You Are Not Alone! (1990)

SCHOOLING
Au revoir les enfants/Goodbye Children (1987)
The Browning Version (1951)
The Browning Version (1994)
Diabolo menthe/Peppermint Soda (1977)
The Getting of Wisdom (1978)

Hets/Torment (1944)
If . . . (1968)
Kazoku gêmu/The Family Game (1983)
Leidenschaftliche Blümchen/Boarding School (1978)
Lost and Delirious/La Rage au coeur (2001)
Megáll az idö/Time Stands Still (1982)
Obecná skola/The Elementary School (1989)
The Prime of Miss Jean Brodie (1969)
Therese und Isabell/Therese and Isabelle (1968)
To Sir, with Love (1967)
Whasango/Volcano High (2001)

SPORTS
Alex (1993)
Australian Rules (2002)
Bend It Like Beckham (2002)
Deck Dogz (2005)
High Tide (1987)
The Loneliness of the Long Distance Runner (1962)
Puberty Blues (1981)
Sommersturm/Summer Storm (2004)
Whasango/Volcano High (2001)

WAR
Alsino y el condor/Alsino and the Condor (1982)
Come and See/Idi i smotri (1985)
Drengene Fra Sankt Petri/The Boys from St. Petri (1991)
Les Égarés/Strayed (2003)
Europa Europa (1990)
Ivan's Childhood/Ivanovo detstvo (1962)
Lacombe Lucien (1974)
Pokolenie/A Generation (1955)
Sorstalanság/Fateless (2005)
Voor een verloren soldaat/For a Lost Soldier (1992)

BIBLIOGRAPHY

Adam, Barry D. *Rise of a Gay and Lesbian Movement.* Boston: Twayne, 1987.
Addison, Erin. "Saving Other Women from Other Men: Disney's *Aladdin.*" *Camera Obscura* 31 (1993): 5–25.
Akbar, M. J. *Kashmir: Behind the Vale.* Delhi: Roli Books, 2002.
Alfonsi, Laurence. *Lectures asiatiques de l'oeuvre de François Truffaut.* Paris: Harmattan, 2000.
Alibhai-Brown, Yasmin. "In the English Arts, a Merry Racial Blend." *New York Times,* July 21, 2002, sec. 2, 1.
Allinson, Mark. "The Construction of Youth in Spain in the 1980s and 1990s." In *Contemporary Spanish Cultural Studies,* ed. Barry Jordan and Rikki Morgan Tamosunas. London and New York: Arnold, 2000, 265–273.
Altman, Rick. *The American Film Musical.* Bloomington: Indiana University Press, 1987.
———. *Film/Genre.* London: British Film Institute, 1999.
Amnesty International. "Dossiê Rio de Janeiro: Candelária e Vigário Geral 10 anos depois." London, Sept. 28, 2003. Originally published in *Jornal Zero Hora, Porto Alegre,* "Tribunas do Tráfico," June 17, 2002.
Anonymous. "Whale Rider." *People,* June 16, 2003, 42.
Ansen, David. "Girl Power, Kiwi Style." *Newsweek,* June 9, 2003, 59.
Armengol, Joseph M. "*Krámpack* o La Iniciació a la Masculinitat." Unpublished conference paper presented at the Primera Convenció Catalana sobre Masculinitats, Diversitat i Diferència Conference, Barcelona, March 2003.
Armstrong, Philip. "Whale Rider." Lecture, School of Culture, Literature and Society, University of Canterbury, Christchurch. May 27, 2004.
Baca Lagos, Vicente. *Imágenes de los jóvenes en los medios de comunicación de masas.* Madrid: Instituto de la Juventud, 1998.
Baldi, Alfredo. *Lo sguardo punito.* Rome: Bulzoni, 1994.
Baltake, Joe. "*Bend It Like Beckham* Heroine Challenges Traditions." *Sacra-*

mento Bee. Rpt. Scripps Howard News Service, March 18, 2003, sec. Entertainment.

Barazanji, Nimat Hafiz. "Education." In *Oxford Encyclopedia of the Modern Islamic World,* ed. John Esposito. Vol. 1. Oxford: Oxford University Press, 2001, 406–411.

Barmé, Geremie. *In the Red: On Contemporary Chinese Culture.* New York: Columbia University Press, 1999.

Benjamin, Walter. "The Storyteller." In *Illuminations,* ed. Hannah Arendt. New York: Schocken, 1968, 83–109.

———. "Estéticas da violência e cultura nacional." In *A Missão e o grande show,* ed. Ângela Maria Dias. Rio de Janeiro: Tempo Brasileiro, 1999, 101–127.

Bentes, Ivana. "Estéticas da violência no cinema." *Interseções. Revista de Estudos Interdisciplinares* 5, no. 1 (2003): 224–237.

Bentes, Ivana, and M. Herschmann. "O espetáculo do contra-discurso." *Folha de São Paulo* Caderno *Mais,* Aug. 18, 2002, 10–11.

Bernard, Jami. "Teen Kicker's in a Twist over Folks' Tradition." *Daily News,* March 12, 2003, 35.

Bhabha, Homi. *The Location of Culture.* London: Routledge, 1994.

Biskind, Peter. *Seeing Is Believing: How Hollywood Taught Us to Stop Worrying and Love the Fifties.* New York: Pantheon, 1983.

Blouin, Patrice. "Plume d'éléphant." *Cahiers du cinema* 583 (Oct. 2003): 13–15.

Bonasso, Miguel. "De los 'Desaparecidos' a los 'Chicos de la Guerra.'" *Nueva Sociedad* 76 (1985): 52–61.

Boudreau, Brenda. "The Battleground of the Adolescent Girl's Body." In *The Girl: Constructions of the Girl in Contemporary Fiction by Women,* ed. Ruth O. Saxton. New York: St. Martin's Press, 1998, 43–56.

Broderick, Mick. "Is This the Sum of All Fears? Nuclear Imagery in Post–Cold War Cinema." In *Atomic Culture,* ed. Scott C. Zeman and Michael A. Amundson. Boulder: University of Colorado Press, 2004, 125–147.

———. *Nuclear Movies.* Jefferson, NC: McFarland, 1991.

Bruce, Jean. "Querying/Queering the Nation." In *Gendering the Nation: Canadian Women's Cinema,* ed. Kay Armatage. Toronto: University of Toronto Press, 1999, 278–298.

Buescher, Derek T., and Kent A. Ono. "Civilized Colonialism: *Pocahontas* as Neocolonial Rhetoric." *Women's Studies in Communication* 19, no. 2 (1996): 127–153.

Butler, Robert W. "*Whale Rider* Will Take Our Breath Away: Young Actress's Performance Stirs Amazing Story." *Kansas City Star,* June 27, 2003, sec. Preview, 7.

Calder, Peter. "Caro's *Whale* Breaches Int'l Arena." *Variety,* Dec. 16–22, 2002, B2.

Callegaro, Adriana, and Miriam Goldstein. "Cine Argentino, 1998–2000: Universo juvenil y mundo urbano." *Revista de cine* 1 (2001): 59–62.

Canclini, Néstor. *Consumidores e cidadãos.* Rio de Janeiro: UFRJ, 1997.

Candido, Antonio. "A dialética da malandragem." *Revista do Instituto de Estudos Brasileiros,* no. 8 (1970): 76–89.

Caro, Mark. "*Whale Rider's* Heroine Wins Tribe, Hearts." *Chicago Tribune*, June 20, 2003, sec. Movies, 1.

Carpignano, Paolo, Robin Andersen, Stanley Aronowitz, and William Di-Fazio. "Chatter in the Age of Electronic Reproduction: Talk Television and the 'Public Mind.'" In *The Phantom Public Sphere*, ed. Bruce Robbins. Minneapolis: University of Minnesota Press, 1993, 93–120.

Chapman, Robert. "Fiction and the Social Pattern." In *Essays on New Zealand Literature*, ed. Wystan Curnow. Auckland: Heinemann Educational Books, 1973, 71–98.

Chordas, Nick. "Odd Girl Out: 11-Year-Old Newcomer Provides Example of a Strong Female Who Triumphs." *Columbus Dispatch*, June 27, 2003, 10G.

Cicourel, Aaron V., and John I. Kitsuse. *The Educational Decision Makers*. Indianapolis: Bobbs-Merrill, 1963.

CIS [Centro de Investigaciones Sociológicas]. *Los jóvenes de hoy*. Bulletin 19. Madrid, Spain.

Clark, Janine A. *Islam, Charity, and Activism*. Bloomington: Indiana University Press, 2004.

Clark, Paul. "Chinese Cinema in 1989." In *The Ninth Hawai'i International Film Festival*. Honolulu: East-West Centre, 1989.

Cohen, Stanley. *Folk Devils and Moral Panics: The Creation of the Mods and Rockers*. St. Albans, England: Paladin, 1973.

Considine, David M. *The Cinema of Adolescence*. Jefferson, NC: McFarland, 1985.

Couto, José Geraldo. "Cidade de Deus questiona produção nacional." *Folha de São Paulo Folha Ilustrada*, Sept. 7, 2002, 6.

Critser, Greg. *Fat Land: How Americans Became the Fattest People in the World*. Boston: Houghton Mifflin, 2003.

Cruz, Clarissa. "Girl Power: Thanks to Box Office Bonanzas like *Legally Blonde*, Summer Isn't Just for Boys Anymore." *Entertainment Weekly*, July 11, 2003, 39–40.

DaMatta, Roberto. *Carnavais, malandros e heróis*. Rio de Janeiro: Zahar, 1978.

Dannecker, Martin. *Theories of Homosexuality*, trans. David Fernbach. London: Gay Men's Press, 1981.

Davis, Mike. *Ecology of Fear: Los Angeles and the Imagination of Disaster*. New York: Vintage, 1999.

Dawtrey, Adam. "Bollywood Flavor Curries Brit Favor: Pix with Indian Themes Add Spice at Blighty Wickets." *Variety*, April 8–14, 2002, 14.

Decharneux, Raymond. "Le cinéma et la délinquance juvenile." *Revue de Droit Pénal et de Criminologie* 4 (Jan. 1957): 747–804.

de Haas, Helmuth. "Wenn ich erst einmal, oben' bin . . ." *Die Welt*, Sept. 29, 1956, n.p.

D'Lugo, Marvin. "La teta i la lluna: The Form of Transnational Cinema in Spain." In *Refiguring Spain: Cinema/Media/Representation*, ed. Marsha Kinder. Durham and London: Duke University Press, 1997, 196–214.

Doherty, Thomas. *Teenagers and Teenpics: The Juvenilization of American Movies in the 1950s*. Boston: Unwin Hyman, 1988; revised and expanded ed. Temple University Press, 2002.

Doty, Alexander. *Making Things Perfectly Queer: Interpreting Mass Culture.* Minneapolis: University of Minnesota Press, 1993.

Dover, K. J. *Greek Homosexuality.* Cambridge, MA: Harvard University Press, 1989.

Downing, John. "Full of Eastern Promise? Central and Eastern European Media after 1989." In *Electronic Empires: Global Media and Local Resistance,* ed. Dayan Kishan Thussu. London: Arnold, 1998: 47–62.

Driscoll, Katherine. *Girls: Feminine Adolescence in Popular Culture and Cultural Theory.* New York: Columbia University Press, 2002.

Durham, Meenakshi Gigi. "The Girling of America: Critical Reflections on Gender and Popular Communication." *Popular Communication* 1, no. 1 (2003): 23–31.

Dwyer, Rachel. *All You Want Is Money, All You Need Is Love: Sexuality and Romance in Modern India.* London: Cassell, 2000.

Dyer, Richard. "The Colour of Entertainment." In *Musicals: Hollywood and Beyond,* ed. Bill Marshall and Robynn Stilwell. Exeter: Intellect Books, 2000, 23–30.

———. "Entertainment and Utopia." *Movie* 24 (Spring 1977): 2–13. Reprinted in *Hollywood Musicals: The Film Reader,* ed. Steven Cohan. London: Routledge, 2002, 19–30.

———. *Heavenly Bodies.* London: Macmillan, 1992.

———. *The Matter of Images: Essays on Representations.* London and New York: Routledge, 1993.

Dyer, Richard, with Julianne Pidduck. *Now You See It: Studies on Lesbian and Gay Film.* 2nd ed. London: Routledge, 2003.

Easlea, Brian. *Fathering the Unthinkable: Masculinity, Scientists and the Nuclear Arms Race.* London: Pluto Press, 1983.

Ebert, Roger. "Soccer-Minded *Beckham* Achieves Its Goal." *Chicago Sun Times,* March 12, 2003, 51.

———. "*Whale* of a Film Wins Top Prize." *Chicago Sun Times,* Sept. 16, 2002, 33.

———. "Witherspoon's Ditzy *Blonde* Has Wrong Look for Beltway." *Chicago Sun Times,* July 2, 2003, 51.

Edelstein, David. "Kicking, but not Alive." *Slate,* March 14, 2003, sec. Movies.

Edley, Nigel, and Margaret Wetherell. "Masculinity, Power and Identity." In *Understanding Masculinities: Social Relations and Cultural Arenas,* ed. Máirtín Mac an Ghaill. Buckingham and Bristol, PA: Open University Press, 1996, 97–113.

Eisenhower, Dwight D. *Public Papers of the Presidents, 1960,* pp. 1035–1040. http://coursesa.matrix.msu.edu/~hst306/documents/indust.html.

Eisenstein, Zillah. "Eastern European Male Democracies: A Problem of Unequal Equality." In *Gender Politics and Post-Communism,* ed. Nanette Funk and Magda Mueller. New York: Routledge, 1993, 303–330.

Epstein, Jonathon S. "Introduction: Generation X, Youth Culture, and Identity." In *Youth Culture: Identity in a Postmodern World,* ed. Jonathon S. Epstein. Oxford: Blackwell, 1998, 1–23.

Evans, Joyce A. *Celluloid Mushroom Clouds: Hollywood and the Atomic Bomb.* Boulder: Westview, 1998.

Fabian, Katalin. "Unexpressionism? Challenges to the Formation of Women's Groups in Hungary." *Canadian Woman Studies* 16 (1991): 80–89.

Fawal, Ibrahim. *Youssef Chahine.* London: British Film Institute, 2001.

Felix, Jürgen. "Rebellische Jugend. Die Halbstarken'-Filme: Vorbilder und Nachbildungen." *Positionen deutscher Filmgeschichte. 100 Jahre Kinematographie: Strukturen, Diskurse, Kontexte,* ed. Michael Schaudig. Munich: Diskurs-Film-Verlag, 1996, 309–328.

Femenia, Alicia Montserrat, and M. Teresa Muñoz Guillén. "Violencia y Familia." *Revista de estudios de juventud* 62 (2003): 51–58.

Feuer, Jane. *The Hollywood Musical.* Bloomington: Indiana University Press, 1993.

Fisher, Jean. "Wild Style." *Artforum International* 22 (April 1984): 84–85.

Foucault, Michel. *The History of Sexuality: An Introduction.* Vol. 1. Trans. Robert Hurley. New York: Vintage, 1980.

Fouz-Hernández, Santiago. "¿*Generación X*? Spanish Urban Youth Culture at the end of the Century in Mañas's/Armendáriz's *Historias del Kronen.*" *Romance Studies* 18, no. 1 (2000): 83–98.

———. "School Is Out: The British 'Coming Out' Films of the 1990s." *New Cinemas: Journal of Contemporary Film* 1, no. 3 (2003): 149–164.

Freud, Sigmund. "The Uncanny." In *The Standard Edition of the Complete Psychological Works of Sigmund Freud,* ed. and trans. James Strachey and Anna Freud. Vol. 17. London: Hogarth Press, 1955, 219–256.

Friedenberg, Edgar Z. *Coming of Age in America: Growth and Acquiescence.* New York: Vintage, 1965.

García Borrero, Juan Antonio. *La edad de herejía: Ensayos sobre el cine cubano, su crítica y su público.* Santiago de Cuba: Editorial Oriente, 2002.

García Domínguez, María Isabel. "La juventud cubana en una época de crisis y reestructuración." In *Cuba, período especial,* ed. José A. Moreno. Havana: Editorial de Ciencias Sociales, 1998, 222–247.

Garga, Bhagwan Das. *So Many Cinemas: The Motion Picture in India.* Mumbai: Eminence Designs, 1996.

Gateward, Frances, and Murray Pomerance. "Introduction." *Sugar, Spice, and Everything Nice: Cinemas of Girlhood.* Detroit: Wayne State University Press, 2002, 13–21.

Gessen, Masha. "Sex in the Media and the Birth of Sex Media in Russia." In *Postcommunism and the Body Politic,* ed. Ellen E. Berry. New York: New York University Press, 1995, 197–228.

Gilbert, James. *A Circle of Outrage. America's Reaction to the Juvenile Delinquent in the 1950s.* New York: Oxford University Press, 1986.

Gil Calvo, Enrique. *Los depredadores audiovisuales: Juventud urbana y cultura de masas.* Madrid: Tecnos, 1985.

Gillain, Anne, ed. *Le cinéma selon François Truffaut.* Paris: Flammarion, 1988.

Gillespie, Eleanor Ringel. "Girl Battles Exotic Culture's Bias." *Cox News Service,* June 25, 2003, sec. Entertainment, Television and Culture.

Gire, Dann. "Charismatic New Star Helps Make *Rider* a Treasure." *Chicago Daily Herald,* June 20, 2003, 43.

Giroux, Henry. *Fugitive Cultures: Race, Violence and Youth.* New York: Routledge, 1996.

Gleiberman, Owen. "Goal Rush: In the Exuberant Sports Comedy *Bend It Like Beckham,* a Girl Defies Her Punjabi Family to Score at Soccer." *Entertainment Weekly,* March 21, 2003, 85.

Gökalp, Ziya. *Türkçülü ün Esasları.* Istanbul: Inkılap ve Aka, 1978.

Gokulsing, K. Moti, and Wimal Dissanayake. *Indian Popular Cinema: A Narrative of Cultural Change.* Stoke-on-Trent, U.K.: Trentham, 1998.

Gómez, Luis. "La política cubana de juventud en los 90." *Cuba: Jóvenes en los 90.* Havana: Editoria Abril, 1999, 110–130.

Goven, Joanna. "Gender Politics in Hungary: Autonomy and Antifeminism." In *Gender Politics and Post-Communism,* ed. Nanette Funk and Magda Mueller. New York: Routledge, 1993, 224–240.

Grant, Barry Keith. *Voyages of Discovery: The Cinema of Frederick Wiseman.* Urbana: University of Illinois Press, 1992.

Grau, Gunter. *Hidden Holocaust?* trans. Patrick Camiller. London: Cassell, 1995.

Gray, Mary L. *In Your Face: Stories from the Lives of Queer Youth.* New York: Haworth Press, 1999.

Grob, Norbert. "'Es gibt keine bessere Kulisse als die Straße . . .' Berlin-Filme von Gerhard Oswald und Georg Tressler in den fünfziger Jahren." *Zwischen Gestern und Morgen, Westdeutscher Nachkriegsfilm 1946–1962.* Frankfurt am Main: Deutsches Filmmuseum, 1989, 206–222.

Grossberg, Lawrence. "The Political Status of Youth and Youth Culture." In *Adolescents and Their Music: If It's Too Loud, You're Too Old,* ed. Jonathon S. Epstein. New York: Garland, 1994.

Grotum, Thomas. *Die Halbstarken. Zur Geschichte einer Jugendkultur der 50er Jahre.* Frankfurt am Main: Campus Verlag, 1994.

Guelerman, Sergio. "Escuela, juventud y genocidio: Una interpretación posible." In *Memorias en presente, identidad y transmisión en la Argentina posgenocidio,* ed. Sergio J. Guelerman. Buenos Aires: Grupo Editorial Norma, 2001.

Gusterson, Hugh. *Nuclear Rites: A Weapons Laboratory at the End of the Cold War.* Berkeley: University of California Press, 1996.

Hall, Stuart, and Tony Jefferson, eds. *Resistance through Rituals: Youth Subcultures and Post-War Britain.* 1976; New York: Routledge, 1998.

Hallam, Julia. "Film, Class and National Identity: Re-Imagining Communities in the Age of Devolution." In *British Cinema, Past and Present,* ed. Justine Ashby and Andrew Higson. London: Routledge, 2000, 261–273.

Halman, Talat Sait. *Contemporary Turkish Literature.* Rutherford: Fairleigh Dickenson University Press, 1982.

Halperin, David M. *One Hundred Years of Homosexuality.* New York: Routledge, 1990.

Hammond, Dorothy, and Alta Jablow. "Gilgamesh and the Sundance Kid: The Myth of Male Friendship." In *The Making of Masculinities: The New*

Men's Studies, ed. Harry Brod. Boston, London, Sydney, and Wellington: Allen and Unwin, 1987, 241–258.

Harris, Anita. *Future Girl: Young Women in the Twenty-First Century*. New York: Routledge, 2004.

Hartai, László. "Vettem egy Maxot" [I Bought a Max]. In *Mozgókép és Médiaoktatás*. http://www.c3.hu/'mediaokt/input. Accessed on May 28, 2004.

Hausknecht, Gina. "Self-Possession, Dolls, Beatlemania, Loss: Telling the Girl's Own Story." *The Girl: Constructions of the Girl in Contemporary Fiction by Women*, ed. Ruth O. Saxton. New York: St. Martin's Press, 1998, 21–42.

Hay, James. "Dancing and Deconstructing the American Dream." *Quarterly Review of Film Studies* 10, no. 2 (Spring 1985): 97–117.

Hebdige, Dick. *Hiding in the Light*. London: Methuen, 1993.

Henriksen, Margot A. *Dr. Strangelove's America: Society and Culture in the Atomic Age*. Los Angeles: University of California Press, 1998.

Higson, Andrew. "The Instability of the National." In *British Cinema, Past and Present*, ed. Justine Ashby and Andrew Higson. London: Routledge, 2000, 35–48.

Hill, John. "British Cinema as National Cinema: Production, Audience and Representation." In *The British Cinema Book*, ed. Robert Murphy. London: British Film Institute, 1997, 242–262.

Hoffmann, E. T. A. "The Sandman." In *Tales of Hoffmann*, trans. R. J. Hollingdale. London: Penguin Books, 1982, 85–125.

Hohenadel, Kristin. "For the Youth of France, 'un Teen Movie' of Their Own." *New York Times*, Feb. 3, 2002, Arts Section, 1, 21.

Hornaday, Ann. "*Whale Rider:* This Girl, She Goes!" *Washington Post*, June 20, 2003, C5.

Horst, Sabine, and Constanze Kleis, eds. *Göttliche Kerle: Männer—Sex—Kino*. Berlin: Bertz, 2002.

Horton, Andrew. "Going Down and Out in Prague and Prerov: Wiktor Grodecki's *Mandragora*." *Kinoeye*. http://www.ce-review.org/kinoeye/kinoeye15old2.html. Accessed on May 17, 2004.

Houle, Michel, and Alain Julien. *Dictionnaire du cinéma québécois*, Montréal: Fides, 1978.

Houston, Penelope. "Rebels without Causes." *Sight and Sound* 25 (Spring 1945): 178–181.

Ihimaera, Witi Tame. *Whale Rider*. 1st U.S. ed. Orlando: Harcourt, 2003. Originally published 1987.

Irwin, Kathie. "Towards Theories of Maori Feminism." In *Feminist Voices: Women's Studies Texts for Aotearoa/New Zealand*, ed. Rosemary Du Plessis. Auckland: Oxford University Press, 1992, 1–21.

Jabbaz, Marcela, and Claudia Lozano. "Memorias de la dictadura y transmisión generacional: Representaciones y controversias." In *Memorias en presente: Identidad y transmisión en la Argentina posgenocidio*, ed. Sergio J. Guelerman. Buenos Aires: Grupo Editorial Norma, 2001, 89–109.

Jacobson, Harlan. "Charles Ahearn interviewed by Harlan Jacobson." *Film Comment* 19, no. 3 (May/June 1983): 64–66.

Jaehne, Karen. "Charles Ahearn: Wild Style." *Film Quarterly* 37, no. 4 (Summer 1984): 2–5.

Jameson, Frederic. "The Cultural Logic of Late Capitalism." In *Postmodernism, or The Cultural Logic of Late Capitalism*. Durham: Duke University Press, 1991, 1–54.

Jenkins, Henry. "Introduction: Childhood Innocence and Other Modern Myths." In *The Children's Culture Reader*, ed. Henry Jenkins. New York: New York University Press, 1988, 1–40.

Jiashan, Mi. "Discussing *The Troubleshooters*," *Chinese Education and Society* 31, no. 1 (Jan./Feb. 1998): 8–14.

Jiaxuan, Zhang. "Review of *The Big Parade*." *Film Quarterly* 43, no. 1 (Fall 1989): 57–59.

Jingming, Yan. "Wanzhu yu dushi de chongtu: Wang Shuo xiaoshuo de jiazhi xuanze" [The Masters of Mischief and Their Conflicts with the City: The Choice of Values in Wang Shuo's Writings]. *Wenxue pinglun* [Literature Criticism], no. 6 (1989): 87–91.

Jinhua, Dai. "Invisible Writing: The Politics of Chinese Mass Culture in the 1990s." *Modern Chinese Literature and Culture* 11, no. 1 (Spring 1999): 31–60.

Kaiser, Susana. "*Escarches:* Demonstrations, Communication and Political Memory in Post-Dictatorial Argentina." *Media, Culture and Society* 24 (2002): 499–516.

Karan, Donna. "What's Up Front—This Month's Phone Call—Teen Acting Prodigy Keisha Castle-Hughes Dishes with Donna Karan." *Interview*, April 2004, 90, 94–95.

Kaufman, Alejandro. "Memoria, horror, historia." In *Memorias en presente: Identidad y transmission en la Argentina posgenocidio*, ed. Sergio Guelerman. Buenos Aires: Grupo Editorial Norma, 2001, 15–28.

Kearney, Mary Celeste. "Girlfriends and Girl Power: Female Adolescence in Contemporary U.S. Cinema." In *Sugar, Spice, and Everything Nice: Cinemas of Girlhood*, ed. Frances Gateward and Murray Pomerance. Detroit: Wayne State University Press, 2002, 125–142.

Kehr, Dave. "Outsider Dives into Maori Myth" [Rev. of *Whale Rider*]. *New York Times* (Late Edition, East Coast), June 6, 2003, E1: 23.

Kenny, Glenn. "*Whale Rider*." *Premiere*, June 10, 2003, 22.

Kimmel, Michael, and Amy Aronson, eds. *Men and Masculinities: A Social, Cultural, and Historical Encyclopedia*. Santa Barbara: ABC-Clio, 2004.

Kinder, Marsha. *Blood Cinema: The Reconstruction of National Identity in Spain*. Berkeley and London: University of California Press, 1993.

Kirkham, Pat, and Janet Thumin, eds. *You Tarzan: Masculinity, Movies and Men*. London: Lawrence and Wishart, 1993.

Kısakürek, Necip Fazıl. *Batı Tefekkürü ve Islam Tasavvufu* [Western Thinking and Islamic Mysticism]. Istanbul: Büyük Dou, 1992.

Klare, Rudolf. *Homosexualität und Strafrecht* [Homosexuality and Penal Law]. Hamburg: Hanseatische Verlagsanstalt, 1937.

Kleinschrodt, Michael H. "New Zealand's *Whale Rider* Is a Compelling Family Film." *Times-Picayune*, June 27, 2003, sec. Lagniappe, 5.

Kristeva, Julia. *Strangers to Ourselves*, trans. Leon S. Roudiez. New York: Columbia University Press, 1991.

Kurihara, Sadako. "The Literature of Auschwitz and Hiroshima: Thoughts on Reading Lawrence Langer's *The Holocaust and the Literary Imagination*, Translated and Introduced by Richard H. Minear." *Holocaust and Genocide Studies* (Spring 1993): 91–96.

LaSalle, Mick. "A Born Leader, but not a Boy: A Maori Girl Must Cope with an Elder's Disdain in Simple *Whale Rider*." *San Francisco Chronicle*, June 20, 2003, D4.

Lauritsen, John, and David Thorstad. *The Early Homosexual Rights Movement*. New York: Times Change Press, 1974.

Lautmann, Rüdiger. "The Pink Triangle: The Persecution of Homosexual Males in Concentration Camps in Nazi Germany." In *Historical Perspectives on Homosexuality*, ed. Salvatore J. Licata and Robert P. Peterson. New York: Haworth Press, 1980, 136–166.

Lewis, Jon. *Hollywood v. Hard Core*. New York: New York University Press, 2000.

———. *The Road to Romance and Ruin: Teen Films and Youth Culture*. New York: Routledge, 1992.

Lifton, Robert. "The Prevention of Nuclear War." In *The Psychology of Nuclear Conflict*, ed. Ian Fenton. London: Conventure Ltd., 1986, 77–89.

Lifton, Robert, and Richard Falk. *Indefensible Weapons: The Political and Psychological Case against Nuclearism*. New York: Basic Books, 1982.

Lindenfeld, Laura Ann. "Feasting Our Eyes: Food Films, Gender, and U.S. American Identity." PhD dissertation. University of California, Davis, 2003.

Lins, Paulo. "Carta aberta." www.vivafavela.com.br and www.cienam.art.br/variedades-textos.asp?cod=20.

———. *Cidade de Deus*. 1st ed. São Paulo: Cia. das Letras, 1997.

Lorenzano, Sandra. "Contrabando de la memoria." In *Escrituras de sobrevivencia: Narrativa y dictadura*. Mexico City: Universidad Autónoma de México, 2001.

Luger, Kurt. *Die konsumierte Rebellion: Geschichte der Jugendkultur 1945–1990*. Vienna: Österreichischer Kunst und Kulturverlag, 1991.

Lung-kee, Sun. *Zhongguo wenhua de "shengceng jiegou"* [The "Deep Structure" of Chinese Culture]. Hong Kong: Jixianshe, 1983.

Macdonald, Moira. "Female Empowerment Is Theme of Lauded, Lyrical *Whale Rider*." *Seattle Times*, May 31, 2003, E2.

———. "Maori Tale, Voted SIFF's Best, Mixes the Mystical with Girl Power." *Seattle Times*, June 20, 2003, H22.

Mack, John. "The Threat of Nuclear War in Clinical Work: Dynamic and Theoretical Considerations." In *Psychoanalysis and the Nuclear Threat: Clinical and Theoretical Studies*, ed. Howard B. Levine, Daniel Jacobs, and Lowell J. Rubin. Hillsdale, NJ: Analytic Press, 1988, 43–80.

Mallen, Kerry, and John Stephens. "Love's Coming (Out): Sexualizing the Space of Desire." *Media/Culture Journal* 5, no. 6 (2002). www.media-culture.org.au.

Malti-Douglas, Fedwa. *Men, Women, and God(s): Nawal El Saadawi and Arab Feminist Poetics*. Berkeley: University of California Press, 1995.

Maltin, Leonard. *Leonard Maltin's 2004 Movie and Video Guide*. New York: Signet, 2003.

Mannur, Anita. "Culinary Fictions: Immigrant Foodways and Race in Indian American Literature." In *Asian American Studies after Critical Mass*, ed. Kent A. Ono. Malden, MA: Blackwell, 2005, 56–70.

Marcel, Mario. "La Generación Pendiente." *Nueva Sociedad* 76 (1985): 43–51.

Marsh, Steven. "Tracks, Traces and Common Places: Fernando León de Aranoa's *Barrio* (1998) and the Layered Landscape of Everyday Life in Contemporary Madrid." *New Cinemas* 1, no. 3 (2003): 165–177.

Martin, Helen, and Sam Edwards. *New Zealand Film: 1912–1996*. Oxford: Oxford University Press, 1997.

Martínez Mora, Carlos. "Thinking about youth," *CEPAL Review* 29 (1986): 153–170.

Martín Morán, Ana. "La ciénaga." In *The Cinema of Latin America*, ed. Alberto Elena and Mariana Díaz López. London: Wallflower, 2003, 250–271.

Martorell, Elvira. "Recuerdos del presente: Memoria e identidad. Una reflexión en torno a HIJOS." In *Memorias en presente: Identidad y transmission en la Argentina posgenocidio*, ed. Sergio Guelerman. Buenos Aires: Grupo Editorial Norma, 2001, 127–147.

Massood, Paula. "Mapping the Hood: The Genealogy of City Space in *Boyz N the Hood* and *Menace II Society*." *Cinema Journal* 35, no. 2 (Winter 1996): 85–97.

Matthews, James D. *Censored!* London: Chatto, 1994.

Mátyás, Péter. "Fiúk a rács mögött" [Boys behind Bars]. *Filmkultúra.* http://www.filmkultura.hu/2002/articles/films/torzok/hu.html. Accessed on May 9, 2004.

McRobbie, Angela. *Feminism and Youth Culture*. Boston: Unwin Hyman, 1991.

Mead, Margaret. *Culture and Commitment: The New Relationships between the Generations in the 1970s*. New York: Columbia University Press, 1978.

Melly, George. *Revolt into Style: The Pop Arts in the '50s and '60s*. Oxford: Oxford University Press, 1970.

Mercer, John. "Homosexual Prototypes: Repetition and the Construction of the Generic in the Iconography of Gay Pornography." *Paragraph* 26, no. 1 (2003): 280–290.

Messner, Michael. "The Meaning of Success: The Athletic Experience and the Development of Male Identity." In *The Making of Masculinities: The New Men's Studies*, ed. Harry Brod. Boston: Allen and Unwin, 1987, 193–209.

Milliken, Christie. "The Pixel Visions of Sadie Benning." In *Sugar, Spice and Everything Nice: Cinemas of Girlhood*, ed. Frances Gateward and Murray Pomerance. Detroit: Wayne State University Press, 2002, 285–302.

Mills, Nancy. "Actress Scores a Foothold in Film with Soccer Bent." *Daily News*, March 11, 2003, 40.

Mitchell, Elvis. "A Girl Born to Lead, Fighting the Odds." *New York Times,* June 6, 2003, E14.

Moeller, Robert. *Sex, Society and the Law in Postwar West Germany: Homosexuality and the Federal Constitutional Court.* Berkeley: Center for German and European Studies, 1993.

Molloy, Maureen. "Death and the Maiden: The Feminine and the Nation in Recent New Zealand Films." *Signs* 25, no. 1 (1999): 153–170.

Monteagudo, Luciano. "Lucretia Martel: Susurrus a la hora de la siesta." In *Nuevo cine argentino: Temas, autores, estilos de una renovación.* Buenos Aires: Ediciones Tatanka/FIPRESCI, 2002, 64–84.

Monterde, José Enrique. *Veinte años de cine español (1973–1992): Un cine bajo la paradoja.* Barcelona: Ediciones Paidós, 1993.

Moore, Ryan. "'. . . And Tomorrow Is Just Another Crazy Scam': Postmodernity, Youth, and the Downward Mobility of the Middle Class." In *Generations of Youth: Youth Culture and History in Twentieth-Century America,* ed. Joe Austin and Michael Nevin Willard. New York: New York University Press, 1998, 253–271.

Morgenstern, Joe. "Enchanting *Whale Rider* Spins Tough-Minded Gold Out of Everyday Magic: Girl's Quest for Glory Comes Up a Big Winner." *Wall Street Journal,* June 6, 2003, W1.

Mujun, Shao. "Why Did a Wang Shuo Cinema Craze Occur." *China Screen,* no. 4 (1989): 23–31.

Müller, Klaus. "Introduction." In *The Men with the Pink Triangle,* ed. Heinz Heger, trans. David Fernbach. Boston: Alyson Publications, 1994, 7–16.

Mulvey, Laura. "Visual Pleasure and Narrative Cinema." *Screen* 16, no. 3 (1975): 6–18.

Munoz, Lorenza. "A Girl Shall Lead Them." *Los Angeles Times,* May 6, 2003, E3.

Murray, Scott, ed. *Australian Film 1978–1994.* Melbourne: Oxford University Press, 1995.

Nam, Vicki. *Yell-Oh Girls! Emerging Voices Explore Culture, Identity, and Growing Up Asian American.* New York: Quill, 2001.

Nava, Mica. "Modernity's Disavowal: Women, the City and the Department Store." In *The Shopping Experience,* ed. Pasi Falk and Colin Campell. London: Sage Publications, 1997, 56–87.

Nerkowski, Wojtek. "Finding the Truth." Interview with Robert Glinski. *The Warsaw Voice.* http://www2.warsawvoice.pl/old/v708/News04.html. Accessed on May 9, 2004.

Neubauer, John. *The Fin-de-Siècle Culture of Adolescence.* New Haven: Yale University Press, 1992.

Newman, Kim. *Millennium Movies: End of the World Cinema.* London: Titan, 1999.

Noorani, Abdul Gafoor, ed. *The Babri Masjid Question, 1528–2003.* 2 vols. New Delhi: Tulika, 2003.

Nuckols, Ben. "At the Movies: *Whale Rider.*" *Associated Press,* June 4, 2003, sec. Entertainment News.

Null, Christopher. "I ♥ *Budapest.*" http://www.filmcritic.com. Accessed on June 12, 2004.

Occhipinti, Laurie. "Two Steps Back? Anti-Feminism in Eastern Europe." *Anthropology Today* 12, no. 6 (1996): 13–18.

Olczyk, Eliza, and Anna Twardowska. "Women and the Media." *Polish Women in the '90s.* http://free.ngo.pl/temida/media.htm. Accessed on March 2, 2004.

Oneida Pérez, Martha, Armando Perryman, Nilza González, Leydi González, and Mayra Abréu. "Identidad nacional, organizaciones culturales, y tiempo libre." In *Cuba: Jóvenes en los 90.* Havana: Editoria Abril, 1999, 254–274.

Paranagua, Paulo Antonio. "Cuban Cinema's Political Challenges." In *New Latin American Cinema. Volume Two: Studies of National Cinemas,* ed. Michael T. Martín. Detroit: Wayne State University Press, 1997, 401–424.

Parens, Henri. "Psychoanalytic Explorations of the Impact of the Threat of Nuclear Disaster on the Young." In *Psychoanalysis and the Nuclear Threat: Clinical and Theoretical Studies,* ed. Howard B. Levine, Daniel Jacobs, and Lowell J. Rubin. Hillsdale, NJ: Analytic Press, 1988, 1–17.

Pearlman, Cindy. "Young Star Hits the Road to Tell *Whale* Tale." *Chicago Sun-Times,* June 22, 2003, sec. Show, 7.

Peña, Fernando Martín, Paula Felix-Didier, and Ezequiel Luka. Interview with Lucretia Martel. In *60/90 Generaciones: Cine argentino independiente,* ed. Fernando Martín Peña. Buenos Aires: MALBA, 2003, 110–130.

Penezic, Vida. "Women in Yugoslavia." In *Postcommunism and the Body Politic,* ed. Ellen E. Berry. New York: New York University Press, 1995, 57–77.

Perrine, Toni A. *Film and the Nuclear Age: Representing Cultural Anxiety.* New York: Garland, 1997.

Pickle, Betsy. "Young Actress Shines in Elegant *Whale Rider.*" *Scripps Howard News Service,* June 26, 2003, sec. Entertainment.

Pidduck, Julianne. "After 1980: Margins and Mainstreams." In *Now You See It: Studies on Lesbian and Gay Film,* ed. Richard Dyer and Julianne Pidduck. 2nd ed. London: Routledge, 2003, 265–294.

Pike, Andrew, and Ross Cooper. *Australian Film 1900-1977.* Melbourne: Oxford University Press, 1978.

Pipher, Mary Bray. *Reviving Ophelia: Saving the Selves of Adolescent Girls.* New York: Ballantine, 1995.

Podalsky, Laura. "Affecting Legacies: Historical Memory and Contemporary Structures of Feeling in *Madagascar* and *Amores perros.*" *Screen* 44, no. 3 (Autumn 2003): 277–294.

Preckel, Claudia (a). "Masjid, Muscles, Machine Guns: Kashmir Mujahidun in Bollywood Cinema." Unpublished paper presented at the annual meeting of Indologists at the University of Leiden (The Netherlands), April 12, 2003.

——— (b). "'My Name Is Anthony Gonsalves'—Amitabh Baccan in Amar Akbar Anthony (1977)." In *Heroes and Heritage,* ed. Theo Damsteegt. Leiden: CNWS Publications, 2003, 206–226.

Projansky, Sarah. "The Postfeminist Context: Popular Redefinitions of Feminism, 1980–Present." *Watching Rape: Film and Television in Postfeminist Culture.* New York: New York University Press, 2001, 66–89.

Quart, Alissa. *Branded: The Buying and Selling of Teenagers.* Cambridge, MA: Perseus, 2002.

Quintín. "De una generación a otra: ¿Hay una línea divisoria?" In *Nuevo cine argentino: Temas, autores, estilos de una renovación.* Buenos Aires: Ediciones Tatanka/FIPRESCI, 2002, 105–125.

Rada, Uwe. "Zwischen Kino und Wirklichkeit." *Die Tageszeitung.* Feb. 18, 2002. http://www.taz.de/pt/2002/04/18/a0201.nf/text. Accessed on February 18, 2004.

Rainer, Peter. "My Big Fat Brit Life: An Unflappable Soccer Teen Fields *Bend It Like Beckham*'s Generational Anxieties." *New York,* March 17, 2003, 47.

Rajadhyaksha, Ashish, and Paul Willemen. *Encyclopaedia of Indian Cinema.* New rev. ed. London: British Film Institute, 1999.

Reich, Charles A. *The Greening of America.* New York: Random House, 1970.

Renoir Cinemas 2000 [unattributed]. *Krámpack* (Guide 668).

Requena, Miguel. "Juventud y dependencia familiar en España." *Revista de estudios de juventud* 58 (2002): 1–13.

Ribeiro, Paulo Jorge. "Alguns impasses da crítica cultural contemporânea: *Cidade de Deus.*" *Interseções. Revista de Estudos Interdisciplinares* 5, no. 1 (2003): 57–60.

Richard, Nelly. "La cita de la violencia: Convulsiones del sentido y rutinas oficiales." In *Residuos y metáforas (ensayos de crítica cultural sobre el Chile de la Transición).* Santiago: Editorial Cuarto Propio, 1998, 1–30.

Richards, Jonathan. "*Whale Rider:* And a Little Girl Shall Lead Them." *Santa Fe New Mexican,* July 4, 2003, 67.

Rickey, Carrie. "A Maori Girl Sure She Will Be Chief." *Philadelphia Inquirer,* June 20, 2003, W4.

Robertson, James C. *The Hidden Cinema.* London: Routledge, 1989.

Rocha, João Cezar de Castro. "Dialética da marginalidade. Caracterização da cultura contemporânea." *Folha de São Paulo* Caderno *Mais,* Feb. 29, 2004, 4–8.

Rocky Mountain Daily News. April 21, 1999. www.denver.rockymountain news.com.

Roger, Diana. *A Critical Study of the Works of Nawal el Saadawi, Egyptian Writer and Activist.* Lewiston: Mellen, 2001.

Romero, Edgar, Matilde Molina, Lidia González, Rosa T. Rodríguez, and Liliana Rodríguez. "Juventud y valores en los umbrales del siglo XXI." In *Cuba: Jóvenes en los 90.* Havana: Editoria Abril, 1999, 330–370.

Rony, Fatimah Tobing. "Robert Flaherty's *Nanook of the North:* The Politics of Taxidermy and Romantic Ethnography." In *The Birth of Whiteness: Race and the Emergence of U.S. Cinema,* ed. Daniel Bernardi. New Brunswick: Rutgers University Press, 1996, 300–327.

Ruppersburg, Hugh. "The Alien Messiah in Recent Science Fiction Films." *Journal of Popular Film and Television* (Winter 1987): 159–166.

Saliba, Terese. "Military Presences and Absences: Arab Women and the Persian Gulf War." *Seeing through the Media: The Persian Gulf War,* ed.

Susan Jeffords and Lauren Rabinovitz. New Brunswick: Rutgers University Press, 1994, 263–284.

Salmond, Anne. *Hui: A Study of Maori Ceremonial Gatherings.* Wellington: A. H. and A. W. Reed, 1975.

Sarlo, Beatriz. *Escenas de la vida posmoderna: Intelectuales, arte y videocultura en la Argentina.* Buenos Aires: Ariel, 1994.

Scheler, Max. *Ressentiment.* Milwaukee: Marquette University Press, 2003.

Schumach, Murray. *The Face of the Cutting Room Floor.* New York: William Morrow, 1964.

Schwarzbaum, Lisa. "*Whale Rider:* A Powerful Old Maori Legend Gets a Modern Feminist Twist." *Entertainment Weekly,* June 13, 2003, 73.

Schwenger, Peter. *Letter Bomb: Nuclear Holocaust and the Exploding Word.* Baltimore: Johns Hopkins University Press, 1992.

Scott, A. O. "Her Mom May Kick, but a Girl Plays to Win." *New York Times,* March 12, 2003, E5.

Sedgwick, Eve K. *Between Men: English Literature and Male Homosocial Desire.* New York: Columbia University Press, 1985.

———. *Epistemology of the Closet.* London and New York: Penguin, 1990.

———. "Queer Performativity: Henry James's *The Art of the Novel.*" *GLQ* 1, no. 2 (1993): 1–21.

Seiter, Ellen, and Vicki Mayer. "Diversifying Representation in Children's TV: Nickelodeon's Model." *Nickelodeon Nation: The History, Politics, and Economics of America's Only TV Channel for Kids,* ed. Heather Hendershot. New York: New York University Press, 2004, 120–133.

Şen, Abdurrahman. "Milli Sinemadan Beyaz Sinemaya" [From National Cinema to White Cinema]. In *Yeşilçam'la Yüzyüze* [*Face-to-face with Yeşilçam*], ed. Burçak Evren. Istanbul: Açı Yayıncılık, 1995, 152–172.

Shafik, Viola. *Der Arabische Film: Geschichte und Kulturelle Identität.* Bielefeld: Aisthesis, 1996.

Shandler, Sara. *Ophelia Speaks: Adolescent Girls Write about Their Search for Self.* New York: HarperPerennial, 1999.

Shapiro, Jerome F. *Atomic Bomb Cinema: The Apocalyptic Imagination on Film.* New York: Routledge, 2001.

Shary, Timothy. *Generation Multiplex: The Image of Youth in Contemporary American Cinema.* Austin: University of Texas Press, 2002.

———. "Teen Films: The Cinematic Image of Youth." In *Film Genre Reader III,* ed. Barry Keith Grant. Austin: University of Texas Press, 2003, 490–515.

———. *Teen Movies: American Youth on Screen.* London: Wallflower, 2005.

Sherman, Sharon R. "Bombing, Breakin', and Getting' Down: The Folk and Popular Culture of Hip-Hop." *Western Folklore* 43 (Oct. 1984): 287–293.

Sherrod, Drury. "The Bonds of Men: Problems and Possibilities in Close Male Relationships." In *The Making of Masculinities: The New Men's Studies,* ed. Harry Brod. Boston, London, Sydney, and Wellington: Allen and Unwin, 1987, 213–239.

"She's 18, Taking Hollywood by Storm, and Still Living with Her Parents. Keira Knightley: Isn't She Lovely?" *Vanity Fair,* April 2004, 157–168.

Shohat, Ella. "The Media's War." *Social Text* 28 (1991). Rpt. in *Seeing through the Media: The Persian Gulf War*, ed. Susan Jeffords and Lauren Rabinovitz. New Brunswick: Rutgers University Press, 1994, 147–154.

Silverman, Kaja. *The Acoustic Mirror*. Bloomington: Indiana University Press, 1988.

Silverstein, Ken. "Tale of the Radioactive Boy Scout." *Harper's Magazine*, Nov. 1998, 17–22.

Simmons, Jerold. "The Censoring of *Rebel Without a Cause*." *Journal of Popular Film and Television* 23 (Summer 1995): 56–63.

Simmons, Rachel. *Odd Girl Out: The Hidden Culture of Aggression in Girls*. New York: Harcourt, 2002.

Simonsen, Jorgen, ed. *Youth and Youth Culture in the Contemporary Middle East*. Aarhus, Denmark: Aarhus University Press, 2005.

Sissons, Jeffrey. "The Traditionalisation of the Maori Meeting House." *Oceania* 69, no. 1 (1998): 36–46.

Skelton, Christine. *Schooling the Boys: Masculinities and Primary Education*. Buckingham and Philadelphia: Open University Press, 2001.

Sontag, Susan. "The Imagination of Disaster." In *Hal in the Classroom: Science Fiction Films*, ed. Ralph J. Amelio. 1965; Dayton, OH: Pflaum, 1974, 54–60.

Sparks, Colin. "Media Theory after the Fall of European Communism." In *De-Westernizing Media Studies*, ed. James Curran and Myung-Jin Park. London: Routledge, 2000, 35–49.

Speed, Leslie. "Tuesday's Gone: The Nostalgic Teen Film." *Journal of Popular Film and Television* 26, no. 1, 1998: 24–36.

Sreedhar, K. Santhanam, and Sudhir Saxena Manish. *Jihadis in Jammu and Kashmir*. New Delhi: Sage, 2003.

Steakley, James. *The Homosexual Emancipation Movement*. New York: Arno Press, 1975.

Stein, Ellin. "*Wild Style*." *American Film* 9, no. 2 (Nov. 1983): 49–50.

Stewart, Susan. *Crimes of Writing: Problems in the Containment of Representation*. Oxford: Oxford University Press, 1991.

Straayer, Chris. "The Hypothetical Lesbian Heroine in Narrative Feature Film." In *Out In Culture: Gay, Lesbian, and Queer Essays on Popular Culture*, ed. Corey K. Creekmur and Alexander Doty. Durham: Duke University Press, 1995, 44–59.

Strauss, Bob. "Girls Just Want to Be Maori Tribal Leaders." *Daily News of Los Angeles*, June 6, 2003, U11.

Stuart, Jan. "An Ingénue from Down Under." *Newsday*, Feb. 29, 2004, C14.

Szalóky, Melinda. "Somewhere in Europe: Exile and Orphanage in Post–World-War-II Hungarian Cinema." In *East European Cinemas in New Perspectives*, ed. Anikó Imre. New York: Routledge (forthcoming).

Tahir, Kemal. *Notlar 11: Batılılama* [Notes 11: Westernization]. Istanbul: Balam, 1989.

Tarabay, Jamie. "Australian movie *Whale Rider* on Crest of Popularity Wave." *Associated Press*, June 6, 2003, sec. Entertainment News.

Tasker, Yvonne. "Pussy Galore: Lesbian Images and Lesbian Desire in the

Popular Cinema." In *The Good, the Bad and the Gorgeous: Popular Culture's Romance with Lesbianism*, ed. Diane Hamer and Belinda Budge. London: Pandora, 1994, 162–192.

Thomson, Patricia. "Walking the Halls of Fate." *American Cinematographer* 84, no. 10 (Oct. 2003): 60–71.

Toop, David. *Rap Attack 2: African Rap to Global Hip-Hop*. London: Pluto Press, 1984.

Tosun, Necip. *Mesut Uçakan'la Sinema Söyle/sileri* [Interviews on Cinema with Mesut Uçakan]. Istanbul: Nehir, 1992.

Toumarkine, Doris. "*Bend It Like Beckham.*" *Film Journal International* (March 2003): 100–101.

Trenzado Romero, Manuel. "La imagen de la juventud y la familia en el reciente cine español." *Revista de estudios de juventud* 39 (1997): 93–106.

Trevelyan, John. *What the Censors Saw*. London: Michael Joseph, 1973.

Triana-Toribio, Núria. "A Punk Called Pedro: La Movida in the Films of Pedro Almodóvar." In *Contemporary Spanish Cultural Studies*, ed. Barry Jordan and Rikki Morgan-Tamosunas. London and New York: Arnold, 2000, 274–282.

Trigo, Abril. "Rockeros y grafiteros: La construcción al sesgo de una antimemoria." In *Memoria colectiva y políticas del olvido: Argentina y Uruguay (1970–1990)*, ed. Adriana J. Bergero and Fernando Reati. Rosario, Argentina: Beatriz Viterbo, 1997, 299–319.

Turan, Kenneth. "Riding High—and Low: *Whale Rider*, Set in a Maori Village in New Zealand, Is a Powerful Film That Survives a Leap into the Mythical." *Los Angeles Times*, June 6, 2003, E1.

———. "A Soccer Film with Perfect Pitch: A Phenomenon in Britain, *Bend It Like Beckham* Is a Feel-Good Movie That Actually Makes You Feel Good." *Los Angeles Times*, March 12, 2003, E3.

Uçakan, Mesut. *Türk Sinemasında deoloji* [Ideology in Turkish Cinema]. Istanbul: Düünce, 1977.

Van Hoorn, Judith L., Ákos Komlósi, Elzbieta Suchar, and Doreen A. Samelson. *Adolescent Development and Rapid Social Change: Perspectives from Eastern Europe*. Albany: State University of New York Press, 2000.

Vila, Pablo. "El rock nacional: Género musical y construcción de la identidad juvenil en Argentina." In *Cultura y pospolítica: El debate sobre la modernidad en América Latina*, ed. Néstor García Canclini. Mexico City: Consejo Nacional para la Cultura y las Artes, 1991, 240–270.

Wachtel, Eleanor. "[Interview with] Bernardo Bertolucci." In *Original Minds: Conversations with CBC Radio's Eleanor Wachtel*. Toronto: HarperPerennial, 2003, 77–96.

Wagnleitner, Reinhold. *Coca-Colonization and the Cold War: The Cultural Mission of the United States in Austria after the Second World War*. Chapel Hill and London: University of North Carolina Press, 1994.

Wang, Jing. *High Culture Fever: Politics, Aesthetics, and Ideology in Deng's China*. Berkeley: University of California Press, 1996.

Ward, Vincent, et al. *Edge of the Earth: Stories and Images from the Antipodes*. Auckland: Heinemann Reed, 1990.

Warner, Marina. "The Uses of Enchantment." Lecture at the National Film Theatre, Feb. 7, 1992. In *Cinema and the Realms of Enchantment: Lectures, Seminars and Essays by Marina Warner and Others,* ed. Duncan Petrie. London: British Film Institute, 1993, 13–35.

Watkins, Craig S. *Representing: Hip-Hop Culture and the Production of Black Cinema.* Chicago: University of Chicago Press, 1998.

Watney, Simon. *Policing Desire.* Minneapolis: University of Minnesota Press, 1987.

Weart, Spencer W. *Nuclear Fear: A History of Images.* Cambridge, MA: Harvard University Press, 1988.

Weinkauf, Gregory. "The Young Girl and the Sea: In *Whale Rider* a Maori Lass Confronts Her Heritage and Destiny." *SF Weekly,* June 18, 2003, sec. Film.

Welsh, Jim. "*Beat Street.*" *Films in Review* 35 (Aug./Sept. 1984): 434–435.

Whitty, Stephen. "Beauty and the Beast Called Tradition." *Star-Ledger* (Newark, NJ), June 6, 2003, 43.

Williams, Linda. *Playing the Race Card: Melodramas of Black and White from Uncle Tom to O. J. Simpson.* Princeton: Princeton University Press, 2001.

Williams, Raymond. "Structures of Feeling." In *Marxism and Literature.* Oxford: Oxford University Press, 1977, 128–135.

Wise, Wyndham, ed. *Take One's Essential Guide to Canadian Film.* Toronto: University of Toronto Press, 2001.

Wiseman, Rosalind. *Queen Bees and Wannabes: Helping Your Daughter Survive Cliques, Gossip, Boyfriends, and Other Realities of Adolescence.* New York: Crown, 2002.

Yiming, Li. "Shifu xingwei zhihou—Dangdai dianying zhong de jiating: Queshi yu buchang" [After Father Was Beheaded—Family in Contemporary Cinema: Absence and Compensation]. *Dianying yishu* [Film Art], no. 6 (1989): 1–15.

Yunzhen, Wang. "Fang Mi Jiashan tan *Wan Zhu*" [Interviewing Mi Jiashan and Chatting about *Masters of Mischief*]. *Dianying yishu* [Film Art], no. 5 (1989): 3–8.

Zacharek, Stephanie. "*Bend It Like Beckham.*" *Salon.com,* March 12, 2003, sec. Movie Reviews.

Zixiang, Zhao, et al. "Qingnian wenhua yu shehui bianqian" [Youth Culture and Social Changes]. *Shehui kexue zhanxian* [Social Science Front], no. 4 (1988): 109–116.

CONTRIBUTORS

Savaş Arslan is an assistant professor in the Film and Television Department at Bahcesehir University, Istanbul. His work on various aspects of Turkish cinema has been presented at international conferences in the U.S. and in Italy and published in several books and magazines in Turkey. Among these are studies of the language of film criticism in Turkey, center-periphery differences in melodramas, and remakes and adaptations of Western films such as *The Exorcist*, *Superman*, and *Zorro*. He is also one of the founding editors and writers of *Geceyarisi Sinemasi [Midnight Cinema]*, a film magazine specializing in low-budget cinema. He is currently a regular contributor to *Altyazi [Subtitle]*, a mainstream film magazine.

Daniel Biltereyst is a professor in film, television, and cultural media studies in the Department of Communication Studies, Ghent University (Belgium), where he leads the Working Group Film and Television Studies. He is the promoter of several wide-scale research projects funded by the National Research Council of Belgium, including one on cinema, controversy, and censorship in the low countries (*Forbidden Images*, 2003–2006). He has been published widely in various European and international journals (including *European Journal of Communication*, *European Journal of Cultural Studies*, *Journal of Media Practice*, *Journal of International Communication*, *Media, Culture & Society*, and *Studies in French Cinema*) and readers (such as *The Media Handbook*, *Understanding Reality TV*, *Media Cultures in a Changing Europe*, *Cinema of the Low Countries*, *Big Brother International*, *Rebel Without a Cause: Approaches to a Maverick Masterwork*, and *Communication Theory and Research in Europe*). He has been chosen recently as a member of the group of academics within the European Science Foundation's program, *Changing Europe, Changing Media*.

Mick Broderick teaches Media Analysis at Murdoch University, Western Australia, and is Associate Director of the Centre for Millennial Studies at the University of Sydney. He is the author of *Nuclear Movies* (1991) and *Hibakusha Cinema: Hiroshima, Nagasaki and the Nuclear Image in Japanese Film* (1996; trans. 1999). His scholarly writing has been published in numerous international collections and peer-reviewed journals, with translations into French, Japanese, and Italian. He is currently in preproduction on an ABC-commissioned television documentary, *Sins of the Father*, and co-curating a national touring exhibition of atomic cultural artifacts entitled "Half Lives: Everyday Ephemera of the Nuclear Age."

Susan Driver is Assistant Professor of Contemporary Studies at Wilfrid Laurier University in Toronto, and has written a thesis and published articles on representations of queer maternal sexuality. She works on social constructions of gender identities and sexual desires and is currently focusing on visual cultures of "girl power" in film, television, and advertising as part of a broader attempt to integrate feminist and queer theories with interpretive work on youth cultures. Central to this project is a detailed examination of images and narratives of queer girl desires across popular media and subcultural practices.

Santiago Fouz-Hernández lectures on Spanish cinema at the University of Durham (U.K.). He earned his PhD at the University of Newcastle upon Tyne in 2002, where he wrote his dissertation on masculinity in recent films. He has published articles in *Romance Studies, Leeds Iberian Papers, Moenia,* and *The Journal of Iberian and Latin American Studies,* and has contributed to *Territories of Desire in Queer Culture* (2000). He coedited a collection of essays on the performer Madonna, *Madonna's Drowned Worlds: New Approaches to Her Cultural Transformations, 1983–2003* (2004). He is currently working on research about Pedro Almodóvar, youth in Spanish cinema, Spanish actor Javier Bardem, and British actor Ewan McGregor. Fouz-Hernández is also the review editor of *Studies in Hispanic Cinemas.*

Scott Henderson is currently a lecturer in Film Studies and Popular Culture in the Department of Communications, Popular Culture and Film at Brock University in St. Catharines, Ontario, Canada. He has taught numerous film and popular culture courses at Brock since 1991. At present, he is in the final stages of a PhD program at the University of East Anglia in Norwich, England. His thesis is titled "Youth on Film, Youth in Culture: Liminality, Identity and the Construction of Cultural Spaces." His essay "Youth Identity and the 'Musical Moment' in Contemporary Youth Cinema" will be part of a collection, *Musical Moments: Film and the Performance of Song and Dance,* edited by Ian Conrich and Estella Tincknell.

Anikó Imre earned her PhD in English from the University of Washington in 2002. She is the editor of *East European Cinemas* (2005) in the AFI's *Film Readers* series. She also has a book in progress: *Allegories of the Global: Post-Socialist Central European Films and Identities.* She has published articles in such journals as *Camera Obscura, Framework,* and *Screen,* as well as a number of chapters in books on Eastern European cinema.

Sonia Cristina Lino earned a PhD from Universidade Federal Fluminense (UFF) in 1995 with the thesis "História e cinema: Uma imagem do Brasil nos anos 30" (History and Cinema: An Image of Brazil in the '30s). She has been an adjunct professor at the Universidade Federal de Juiz de Fora (UFJF), Minas Gerais, Brazil, since 1997, and teaches contemporary and cultural history, film and media history, and cultural studies. Since 2002, she has presided over the editorial board of *Locus — Revista de História* [*Locus — History Magazine*], published by UFJF. Recently, her work has focused on the representations of history and identity in Brazilian cinema and television.

Kimberley Bercov Monteyne is completing her doctoral dissertation in the Cinema Studies Department at New York University. Her previous work has focused primarily on French New Wave cinema and issues of technology, gender, and urban space.

Laura Podalsky is Assistant Professor of Latin American film and cultural studies at Ohio State University. She is the author of *Specular City: Transforming Culture, Consumption, and Space in Buenos Aires, 1955–1973* (2004). She has published articles on prerevolutionary Cuban cinema, Brazilian director Ana Carolina, tango films, and Mexican *telenovelas* in journals such as *Archivos de la Filmoteca* (Spain), *Cinemais* (Brasil), and *Screen*, as well as in anthologies such as *Contemporary Latin American Cultural Studies* (2003), *Visible Nations* (2000), *Framing Latin American Cinema* (1997), and *Mediating Two Worlds* (1993). She is currently working on a book on Latin American film, the politics of affect, and the contemporary public sphere.

Murray Pomerance is Professor and Chair of the Department of Sociology at Ryerson University (Toronto), and the author of *An Eye for Hitchcock* (2004), as well as the editor of numerous volumes including *BAD: Infamy, Darkness, Evil, and Slime on Screen* (2002), *Enfant Terrible! Jerry Lewis in American Film* (2003), and, with Frances Gateward, *Where the Boys Are: Cinemas of Masculinity and Youth* (2004). He is editor of the "Horizons of Cinema" series at SUNY Press, and with Lester D. Friedman, coeditor of the "Screen Decades" series at Rutgers University Press.

Claudia Preckel is currently a member of the junior research group Islamic Networks in Local and Transnational Contexts (Volkswagen Foundation) at the Ruhr-University Bochum, Germany. She is presently writing her dissertation on the Islamic Princely State of Bhopal (nineteenth century). Besides her interest in Islamic movements, she is publishing on Indian and Arabic cinema.

Sarah Projansky is an Associate Professor in the Unit for Cinema Studies and the Gender and Women's Studies Program at the University of Illinois, Urbana-Champaign. She is a coeditor of *Enterprise Zones: Critical Positions on Star Trek* (1996) and author of *Watching Rape: Film, Television, and Postfeminist Culture* (2001). She has published on topics such as sports, girls, rape, whiteness, authorship, and Asian Americans in film, television, and popular culture, in journals such as *Cinema Journal* and *Signs,* and in various anthologies. She is currently writing a book on high-profile, disruptive girls in 20th/21st century popular culture.

Alexandra Seibel is a PhD candidate in Cinema Studies at New York University and is currently teaching film at the University of Vienna. Her main areas of research include representations of the city of Vienna in international filmmaking from 1920 to 1950, teen films and youth culture, and feminist film and video practice. Her publications include "A Topography of Excess: Visions of Vienna in Erich von Stroheim's *The Wedding March* (1928)," in *Reverberations: Representations of Modernity, Tradition and Cultural Value in-between Central Europe and North America* (2002), and "Carnival of Repression: German Left Wing Politics and *The Lost Honor of Katharina Blum,*" in *Film and Literature* (2004).

Timothy Shary is Associate Professor and Director of the Screen Studies Program at Clark University in Worcester, Massachusetts, where he teaches courses on film and television. He is the author of numerous articles on teen films, including two books, *Generation Multiplex: The Image of Youth in Contemporary American Cinema* (2002) and *Teen Films: American Youth on Screen* (2005). His commentary has appeared in over 30 newspapers and magazines around the world, and in 2004 he was named Outstanding Teacher of the Year at Clark University and given the Distinguished Alumni Award by Ohio University.

Stephen Tropiano is the founding director of the Ithaca College Communications Program in Los Angeles, where he teaches courses in film and television studies. He is the author of *The Prime Time Closet: A History of Gays and Lesbians on Television* (2002) and *Rebels and Chicks: A History of the Hollywood Teen Movie* (2006). Stephen contributes a bi-monthly column for the Web site PopMatters entitled, "The Prime Time Closet," which addresses issues on contemporary queer representation on television. He is currently editor of the *Journal of Film and Video,* the oldest film journal in the United States.

Mary M. Wiles published an essay on Rivette's film adaptation of Debussy's *Pelléas et Mélisande* in the anthology *Between Opera and Cinema* (2002). Other publications include "French Folie: Memory and Madness in Bunuel's *Belle de Jour,*" in *Paroles Gelées: UCLA French Studies,* and an essay on Luc Besson's *La Femme Nikita* in the journal *Post Identity.* Her future projects include a book that traces the figure of the coming-of-age girl in contemporary international cinema. She has published an essay on the construction of lesbian subjectivity and the coming-of-age girl in Dorothy Allison's *Bastard Out of Carolina* and she is currently working on an essay on Julie Dash's *Daughters of the Dust,* in which the coming-of-age narrative of girlhood overlaps with themes of race and nationalism. This piece will be included in a forthcoming anthology titled *On the Fringe and in the Center: Women and Avant-Garde Filmmaking 1920–2000.*

Xuelin Zhou is a lecturer in the Department of Film, Television and Media Studies at the University of Auckland, New Zealand. He has published research on British popular culture and Chinese-language film, and his recent research has focused on the representation of "marginalized youth" in a variety of national and semi-national cinemas in East Asia, such as those of Japan, South Korea, mainland China, Hong Kong, and Taiwan. His forthcoming book on "young rebels" in contemporary Chinese cinema will be published by Hong Kong University Press.

INDEX